QuarkXPress®
to InDesign®
Face to Face

QuarkXPress® to InDesign®
Face to Face

Galen Gruman

WILEY

Wiley Publishing, Inc.

QuarkXPress® to InDesign® Face to Face

Published by
Wiley Publishing, Inc.
111 River Street
Hoboken, NJ 07030-5774
www.wiley.com

Copyright © 2005 by Wiley Publishing, Inc.

Published simultaneously in Canada

Library of Congress Card Number: 2004117997

ISBN: 0-7645-8379-4

Manufactured in the United States of America

10 9 8 7 6 5 4 3 2 1

1O/SY/QS/QV/IN

WILEY

About the Author

Galen Gruman is principal at The Zango Group, an editorial and marketing consulting firm, and senior editorial associate at BayCreative, a creative consultancy, as well as editorial director at EmergeMedia, publisher of *IT Wireless*. Currently a frequent contributor to *SBS Digital Design*, *Macworld*, *CIO*, and *InfoWorld*, he has also been editor of *Macworld* and *M-Business*, executive editor of *Upside*, West Coast bureau chief of *Computerworld*, and vice president of content for ThirdAge.com.

He is coauthor of 16 other books on desktop publishing, covering InDesign, QuarkXPress, and PageMaker. Gruman led one of the first successful conversions of a national magazine to desktop publishing in 1986 and has covered publishing technology since then for several publications, including the trade weekly *InfoWorld*, for which he began writing in 1986, *Macworld*, whose staff he joined in 1991, and most recently the design newsletter *SBS Digital Design*. Originally a newspaper reporter in Los Angeles, Gruman got caught by the production-technology bug in 1979 and hasn't recovered.

Acknowledgments

Thanks to the development and product marketing staffs at Adobe Systems and Quark for providing early versions of the InDesign and QuarkXPress software over the years and for listening to suggestions on making them even better. And thanks to the editors and production staff at Wiley Publishing and BayCreative for their efforts in making this book possible, especially to Wiley acquisitions editor Michael Roney who came up with the concept, BayCreative development editor Barbara Assadi for ensuring a top-quality result, technical reviewer Jonathan Woolson of thinkplaydesign for his insights on production issues in a QuarkXPress-to-InDesign transition, Lissa Auciello-Brogan of Wiley Publishing for reinventing my baseline book design, and Arne Hurty of BayCreative and Jonathan Woolson for enhancing that design even further.

The www.InDesignCentral.com and www.QuarkXPressCentral.com Web sites and their contents are copyrighted by The Zango Group and are not affiliated with Adobe Systems or Quark. Original photographs were taken by Galen Gruman and Ingall W. Bull III and are copyrighted by their photographers. The *IT Wireless* contents and logos are copyrighted by EmergeMedia Inc. All materials are used by permission.

Credits

Acquisitions Editor
Michael Roney

Project Editor
Michael Roney

Development Editor
Barbara Assadi, BayCreative

Technical Editor
Jonathan Woolson, thinkplaydesign

Vice President & Executive Group Publisher
Richard Swadley

Vice President and Publisher
Barry Pruett

Production Specialist
Jonathan Woolson, thinkplaydesign

Book Designers
Lissa Auciello-Brogan
Galen Gruman
Arne Hurty, BayCreative
Jonathan Woolson, thinkplaydesign

Proofreading and Indexing
BayCreative and The Zango Group

Cover Image
Daniela Richardson

Interior Photographs
Ingall W. Bull III
Galen Gruman

To my mother, Leah Walthert,
for sparking my creative impulses at any early age and
sharing her love of design, architecture, color, and aesthetics.

toc

Table of Contents

Introduction

Part I: Interface and Program Basics

Part II: Layout Building Blocks

Part III: Working with Colors

Part IV: Working with Text Blocks

Part V: Working with Text Formatting

Part XII: What Only InDesign Can Do

Appendixes

fore words

 There are many ways to transition to InDesign from QuarkXPress. Here, you'll find two stories where two different organizations share their experiences. One is a large publishing company with more than 100 magazines that has taken a systematic, measured approach to smooth the transition. The other is a scrappy organization whose small staffs started making the switch on their own, showing the parent company it could be done..

Finally, follow the road that led to InDesign. Desktop publishing's 20-year history is now beginning its third epoch, with a significant changing of the guard.

How Meredith Made the Switch

At Meredith, we've been interested in InDesign for several years, despite our total reliance on QuarkXPress for more than a decade. Our stable of 17 general-circulation magazines, including *Better Homes and Gardens*, *Ladies Home Journal*, *More*, and *American Baby*, as well as in our custom publishing division (which produces about 170 titles) and book division (which has produced more than 300 titles), have been designed and edited in Quark-XPress since 1993.

Reasons for the Change

Our interest in InDesign is ironic in one sense, since one of us, Bob Furstenau, introduced QuarkXPress to Meredith as an Atex typesetting system replacement. But times change, and we've always been uncomfortable relying so heavily on a product that is a provider's only product. Adobe's Systems' tools such as Photoshop, Illustrator, Adobe Type Manager, and Acrobat sit alongside QuarkXPress on our publishing system, and we've watched with intense interest as Adobe has integrated these key applications into a cohesive suite that now includes InDesign. One common set of tools with one point of support mean a lot in today's application environment. Standardization is helpful to the entire organization.

So three years ago, we asked Adobe to demo InDesign to our designers, editors,0 and IT support staff. We all liked what we saw, and we were very excited about several unique InDesign capabilities such as transparency (we'll no longer have to manipulate our source graphics for use in specific layouts), nested styles (perfect for our many recipes), and its highly exact control over objects and text. As InDesign CS was introduced we watched carefully to see if Adobe would deliver on its promises of strong integration, a content management approach that addressed more than print layouts (we see publishing become more database-oriented, with components used in multiple media), and sophisticated design tools. What we saw in InDesign CS gave us the resolve to move to a new platform.

At the same time, we felt if we stayed with QuarkXPress, we'd end up delaying our goal of creating a true asset-management system by 18 months to two years. We felt that Quark was not working with our selected publishing systems partners, such as Artesia and Adobe. The continued concerns by customers over Quark's poor support, unresolved for more than a decade, also gave us pause. It says something that we still use QuarkXPress 4.1 running on Mac OS 9, even though there have been two major versions of the program in the six years since its release. While the table-editing additions in version 5 interested us, they weren't enough to make such a significant continued investment.

Another factor in our decision was Mac OS X. With the Panther (10.3) version, this operating system has reached the needed maturity to base our workflow on it. To move forward to Mac OS X meant we could no longer delay a decision on whether to continue with QuarkXPress or switch to InDesign. InDesign's support of Mac OS X since version 2 gave us confidence it would work well on the new Mac platform; QuarkXPress has supported Mac OS X only in its most recent version, raising questions about its maturity. So in mid-

2004, we gave about a dozen of our power-user designers Mac OS X systems to experiment with InDesign.

At first, the designers were split about making the switch, but after they spent some time with InDesign, it quickly became a universal consensus: Let's go to InDesign. Involving everyone in the due-diligence process, gaining consensus, and envisioning the benefits of working with Adobe as the primary component of our publishing system gave our final decision a sense of confidence that we have not felt before.

How We Managed the Change

As you read this, we'll have converted several publications to InDesign. Each department will have a 13-week transition period, with 60 days' hands-on preparation before their transition period starts. This lets us roll out InDesign and Mac OS X in a predictable, manageable pace, as well as ensure that each publication can schedule the conversion and learning efforts within their distinct publishing cycles. We start with the power users, who create new templates and re-create the magazine step by step, so the other designers have a solid basis on which to do their InDesign work. What we haven't yet resolved is how to convert our book-publishing division. Because books are in production for four or five months, we know we'll have both QuarkXPress and InDesign — on Mac OS 9 and Mac OS X, respectively — in parallel operation for some time, which raises some serious IT management and project management issues that we're still resolving but will be resolved… no doubt. These issues didn't come up for the magazines because of shorter production cycles and constant start dates.

We've decided not to convert our QuarkXPress 4.1 templates to InDesign, even though InDesign supports that. Designers are free to use that feature to create files from which they can copy some elements, but all templates in InDesign must be created from scratch. This will help our designers truly understand how InDesign works rather than simply copy our standard QuarkXPress approaches in a new tool. It also will help free us from habits we've formed to get around some of QuarkXPress's quirks and limitations, such the implementation of guides, columns, and master pages that we learned to deal with but were never exactly what was needed to enhance productivity. Likewise, we won't provide QuarkXPress keyboard shortcuts as the default in InDesign, so users instead learn how InDesign works and the transition will be as short as possible.

We know this transition will take a huge effort, but because of our upfront work and consensus building with our creative staffs and IT, we think the effort will pay off handsomely. No two publishing situations are alike, however, so we encourage you to look at the transition yourself very carefully, using the insights from this hands-on transition guide and its step-by-step translation of QuarkXPress approaches to their InDesign counterparts.

We've noted at conferences that many publishers' and designers' eyes light up when we mention we're switching to InDesign. These publishers and designers would then say, "We wish we could do that, but our situation is so unique compared to yours." Well, we are here to say that it took us four years to make this decision and it is a good decision that will have a truly positive impact to our business for many years to come. So, have a look, think about the potentials of true desktop publishing, cross-media publishing opportunities, increased productivity, reduced IT support, and go for it. You will not be sorry.

Bob Furstenau, director of publishing services
Eric Ware, senior applications development manager
Meredith Corp.

Future USA's Leap to InDesign

It was 2002. The computing magazine I art-directed at the time, *MacAddict*, had just reviewed Adobe's InDesign 2 layout software. In all my years of designing, I had used only QuarkXPress, and I hadn't heard great things about the first iterations of InDesign. However, the reviewer's strong endorsement led the editors to commission a story on how to move from QuarkXPress to InDesign. We decided to lay out the story in InDesign and to include a sidebar about the art team's experience using InDesign for the first time. I set aside a weekend to get to know InDesign better. Learning to use the application was surprisingly simple, and I was able to finish laying out the story in a relatively short time. Sure, the design was overloaded with drop shadows and transparencies, but I was excited and intrigued by the application's power.

Soon I was using InDesign to build a feature story each month, and within a few months we began producing the entire magazine using only InDesign. My colleagues and I enjoyed InDesign's powerful capabilities as well as its ease of use; the application's interface was intuitive and very similar to that of Photoshop and Illustrator, which were familiar to us. Its native support for PDF/X1a output was a perfect fit for our computer-to-plate printing process. Ironically, that PDF support was necessary for us to use InDesign, since very few service bureaus could work with native InDesign files at the time.

Then art directors at Future Network USA's five other publications saw what *MacAddict* was doing and started trying out InDesign for themselves — one by one, they switched over, too. InDesign seemed to be invading us! Our editorial director saw the individual art directors' guerrilla adoption of InDesign and, instead of approving a significant investment in QuarkXPress upgrades, he asked if we wanted to make the switch to InDesign formal. We did.

From there, our parent company in the U.K. began transitioning its 200-plus magazines to InDesign, and the U.S. branch transitioned five newly acquired magazines in 2004. When Future Network USA launched *Mobile PC* magazine in late 2003, I took the helm as art director — and of course created it in InDesign. The entire U.S. branch of Future now uses InDesign CS — the small scale of our company let us upgrade within just a few months of its release.

We did encounter a few transition issues along the way — most notably, our foreign licensees used QuarkXPress and needed to extract text and images from PDF files until they too converted to InDesign. Otherwise, the switch was very easy. And the gains were significant: We can now edit Illustrator vector images in InDesign; work with native Photoshop files; gain easy access to dingbats and other symbols through the Glyphs pane; and work with transparencies and overlays rather than use awkward clipping paths or composite complex images, such as covers, in Photoshop and Illustrator.

We also made the transition clean. After all, if you're going to make the switch, do it right. For us, that meant *not* converting QuarkXPress files to InDesign, but instead rebuilding them from scratch to avoid any odd translation glitches or Quarkisms. In a pinch, we might have converted layouts from QuarkXPress so that we could buy more time to build new templates, but we didn't want to treat InDesign as if it were QuarkXPress with a different interface. To really take advantage of the application's power, you need to start from scratch.

This book focuses primarily on how to do what you know in QuarkXPress using InDesign. That's important because it covers the bread-and-butter issues — your everyday tasks — and helps translate QuarkXPress thinking into native InDesign thinking. (Soon you won't want to go back to QuarkXPress — trust me!) For busy designers, you can quickly compare how to complete tasks in QuarkXPress with the methods in InDesign — a real timesaver. But you really should go beyond the QuarkXPress equivalents when you switch to InDesign. To help you do that, you'll see a whole section in this book on 20 of InDesign's unique capabilities to give you a taste of what else you can do.

The most important thing about making any switch is to be open to new ways of doing things. Everyone works differently and can find different ways to do the same thing in the same program, but don't use that as an excuse to work in InDesign as if it were Quark-XPress. Even though those old approaches might work, you just might be doing things for reasons that are no longer valid and missing ways to work smarter. It's really worth exploring the tools you use to support your livelihood. Try to think differently — InDesign can help.

Christopher Imlay
Art Director, Mobile PC magazine
Future Network USA

The Road to InDesign: A History

For many years, publishers and layout artists have been unhappy with the direction of QuarkXPress. It missed the Mac OS X transition and seemed to rest on its laurels for core typographic and layout functions. While exciting capabilities such as transparency and OpenType began to appear in various creative tools, QuarkXPress's changes focused on extensions to existing capabilities, such as multiple page sizes in documents. Major enhancements, such as table editing, already existed in some less-popular competing programs. But the publishing community stuck with QuarkXPress since it had become an integral part of their production process, so the prospect of replacing such a fundamental tool was simply too daunting for most. And, frankly, the competition had not been strong, so there was not a big incentive to undertake such an effort. But with the release of InDesign CS in fall 2003, that situation changed, and it's clear that an industrywide shift to InDesign is now under way. InDesign CS2 will increase that momentum, even if Quark continues to revise QuarkXPress, as it has recently shown renewed interest in doing.

For publishers, this period marks the third major transition in electronic publishing since the technology was developed in the mid-1980s. I've been fortunate to be there from the beginning, heading one of the first efforts by a national magazine to go from traditional tools to electronic ones in 1986.

Back then, the industry went through the extraordinary transition from physical layout of typeset galleys and half-toned photographs onto large pieces of paper that were then photographed and turned into negatives for printing. This transition killed the typesetting industry and created wholesale changes in the entire editorial process, not just in the tools. In the mid-1980s, the PC-based Ventura Publisher and cross-platform Aldus PageMaker were the leaders, and publishers were split between the two. After a few years, Ventura was acquired by Xerox (and later by Corel). It lost its direction, giving PageMaker the undisputed leadership in the 1987-89 period.

The second major transition was less disruptive but nonetheless widespread. Quark's first version of QuarkXPress in the mid-1980s excelled at typographic functions but was weak in layout. However, with version 2.1, QuarkXPress came into its own as a credible alternative to PageMaker. That version of QuarkXPress tended to absorb the last of the Ventura users, given the two products' similar approaches to typography and layout. QuarkXPress 3 and 4 cemented that leadership position. In the meantime, PageMaker stalled, partly because it was being digested by its new owner, Adobe Systems. By the early 1995, Page-Maker was largely abandoned by large publishers who preferred QuarkXPress's stronger typographic control and more structured layout approaches, which let them produce templated documents more quickly. PageMaker had its diehard admirers, but by 1999, Adobe itself had all but abandoned PageMaker in favor of its all-new InDesign.

Thus began the third major transition. The first two versions of InDesign (1.0 and 1.5) showed lots of promise, but they also had many gaps that compelled users to stick with QuarkXPress, even though Quark's new version (5) was significantly delayed and the company's arrogance had greatly offended many. InDesign 2, released in 2002, corrected many of the previous deficiencies, and user adoption of InDesign accordingly skyrocketed in 2002. Finally, in late 2003, Adobe released InDesign CS, the first version that pundits such as myself found credibly matched — and in many cases, overpowered — QuarkXPress, whose version 6 upgrade was merely moderate and reinforced the belief that product was losing creative steam. Although Quark followed up twice in 2004 with some upgrades through the free 6.1 and 6.5 updates, that impression of inertia has not changed. And although QuarkXPress 6 does a few things that InDesign CS does not, InDesign CS does many things that QuarkXPress 6 does not. All of these trends explain why many publishers have now begun seriously considering moving from QuarkXPress to InDesign. Several national publishers — Meredith Corp., Hearst, and Future Networks USA among them — have already made the switch.

Today, there's yet again a new version of InDesign (version CS2) that provides more evidence of its creative momentum. I predict that in a matter of a few short years, InDesign will be the standard, much as PageMaker had been in the first desktop-publishing era and as QuarkXPress was in the second era. The purpose of this book is to let you make that transition quickly and productively.

While change may be scary, I remember what happened at *Macworld* in the early 1990s when the design director decided to move from PageMaker to QuarkXPress: There was much concern over the switch among the layout staff, so much that the magazine's management decided to let them use both PageMaker and QuarkXPress in parallel to help ease the transition, rather than require a cold-turkey switch. But within the space of one issue cycle, the layout artists had all abandoned PageMaker. The superior tools of that generation's QuarkXPress were one reason, but an equal factor was that it is in fact easier to work with one program rather than go back and forth between two. I believe that most publishers considering a switch to InDesign will come to the same conclusion that we did at *Macworld*.

Galen Gruman
Principal, The Zango Group
Senior Associate Writer, BayCreative

preface

What This Book Offers

QuarkXPress to InDesign: Face to Face will do exactly what the title implies: Help you make the transition from QuarkXPress to InDesign. What's special about this book is that is shows you side by side — face to face — how to accomplish in InDesign what you already do in QuarkXPress. This face-to-face approach will also quickly show you where InDesign does better than QuarkXPress, and will help you overcome the few deficiencies that InDesign still has relative to QuarkXPress.

This book uses the techniques and screen shots from QuarkXPress 6.5 and InDesign CS2, for both Mac OS and Windows users. But because many QuarkXPress users never upgraded from version 4, it covers steps and issues in versions 4, 5, 6, and 6.1 where they differ from version 6.5. Likewise, this book shows techniques and screen shots from InDesign CS2, but also notes differences in InDesign 2 and CS, so organizations that bought an earlier version and have decided to wait a while to upgrade yet again can still benefit from this book's guidance. Finally, the book uses Mac OS screen shots, but the techniques and steps apply to Windows as well, and so you'll see both Mac and Windows shortcuts and menu sequences noted. In the very few cases where the Windows versions of these programs have significant differences, I highlight those differences.

Many good books are available that provide comprehensive details on every InDesign capability and show in-depth techniques for almost any layout need. But this book is different. It will help you make the transition quickly and effectively, so the time and learning cost of transitioning is low. Once you've made that transition, the *Adobe InDesign CS Bible* and the *Adobe InDesign CS2 Bible* will bring you to the next level of expertise.

How to Read This Book

Face to Face: QuarkXPress to InDesign is made up of 12 parts and four appendices. I've arranged the sections based on basic types of tasks, such as working with text and setting up documents. The first 11 parts cover more than 150 specific tasks in QuarkXPress and show you how to accomplish them (and often do more) in InDesign. Each technique is self-contained on a face-to-face spread, with the QuarkXPress method on the left and the InDesign method on the right, so you can quickly compare the two approaches. The 12th part highlights 20 techniques that QuarkXPress cannot do — but that InDesign can. The four appendices collect in one place the differences between the two programs, as well as present the InDesign shortcuts in one convenient location.

This book assumes you know the basics of how to use QuarkXPress and understand basic design and layout theory; pick up the *Adobe InDesign CS Bible*, *Adobe InDesign CS2 Bible*, or *Adobe InDesign CS2 For Dummies* to learn more about these issues. Both Quark-XPress and InDesign let you accomplish many tasks in multiple ways, so in such cases I've chosen what I believe to be the most popular or effective approaches.

Note that on QuarkXPress-related pages, I use QuarkXPress terms (such as *style sheet* and *item*), while on InDesign-related pages, I use InDesign terms (such as *style* and *object*) — this is meant to help you make the mental shift between the programs, which will help you when you are using their documentation and online help, and when you are visiting online support forums.

You don't need to read this book from front to back — if you're working in InDesign and are trying to figure out how to do something you already know how to do in QuarkXPress, just use the index or table of contents to find that technique in the book and go straight there. If you do decide to read it from front to back, as a primer, I've organized the techniques in increasing level of complexity, so basic issues are covered first. You'll find cross-references to related techniques as well. I've likewise organized the sections to follow the layout process, so creating pages and document standards precede specific such as working with text or printing.

Part I: Interface and Other Program Basics

This part gives you a basic introduction to InDesign itself, showing the interface and tools that you'll use every day and how they equate to QuarkXPress. InDesign and QuarkXPress have very different interface approaches, and understanding the differences is key to becoming comfortable in InDesign.

Part II: Layout Building Blocks

This part compares setting up fundamental elements — pages, sections, templates, libraries, guides, and so forth — between QuarkXPress and InDesign. Veteran QuarkXPress users will see many similarities in the basics, but there are many refinements in InDesign not available in QuarkXPress, as well as substantial differences in the operational aspects of these elements.

Part III: Working with Color

This part shows how to import, create, and apply colors, as well as gradient fills and shades (tints). InDesign's color approach can easily be misused, creating problematic output files, so it's important to understand the differences.

Part IV: Working with Text Blocks

This part shows you how to create and import text and manage the flow of text on and among pages. This is an area where QuarkXPress and InDesign have very different approaches that can easily confuse the veteran QuarkXPress user.

Part V: Working with Text Formatting

QuarkXPress has long been known for its typographic controls, but InDesign meets or beats it on almost every count. In this part, you'll learn how to achieve the fine typography you expect from QuarkXPress and augment it with InDesign's capabilities.

Part VI: Working with Tables

This part shows you how to create and format tables, a capability that QuarkXPress introduced only in version 5. InDesign's table capabilities at first glance are similar to Quark-XPress's, but include many subtle differences.

Part VII: Working with Graphics Files

This part covers how to import, place, and update graphics files. Again, subtle differences exist between the two programs, as well as some significant differences relating to modifying source files.

Part VIII: Creating and Manipulating Graphics

One of InDesign's strengths is its integration with Adobe Photoshop and Illustrator. This has many implications for veteran QuarkXPress users, as it greatly affects how a designer creates and modifies graphics in InDesign.

Part IX: Working with Objects

You can make many finishing touches to objects, such as changing the corners, skewing them, or adding drop shadows. QuarkXPress and InDesign differ strongly in such object effects, and this part explains the differences.

Part X: Working with Output

The ultimate goal of publishing is to create a printed or electronic version for distribution to the audience. This part shows you how to output your documents in InDesign, translating the techniques from QuarkXPress to their InDesign equivalents.

Part XI: Specialty Issues

This is the odds-'n'-ends part, covering the transition from a variety of QuarkXPress functions to their InDesign equivalents. Topics include managing fonts, working with multichapter documents, creating indexes and TOCs, sharing files, and working cross-platform.

Part XII: What Only InDesign Can Do

This part differs from the preceding 11 in that it doesn't compare QuarkXPress to InDesign. That's because it can't — its pages highlight 20 features unique to InDesign, providing a visual guide to using the most intriguing and powerful of them.

Part XIII: Appendixes

The appendixes in this book take you through the ins and outs of converting QuarkXPress files to InDesign's format and consolidates in one location the differences between Quark-XPress and InDesign. It also provides an appendix with all the shortcuts in one place, and another that showcases related Web sites and books for further education.

Conventions Used in This Book

Before I begin showing you the ins and outs of moving from QuarkXPress to InDesign, I need to spend a few minutes reviewing the terms and conventions used in this book.

QuarkXPress and InDesign commands

The QuarkXPress and InDesign commands, which you select by using the program menus, appear in this book in normal typeface. When you choose some menu commands, a related pull-down or pop-up menu appears. If I describe a situation in which you need to select one menu and then choose a command from a secondary menu or list box, I use an arrow symbol. For example, "Choose Layout ➪ Margins and Columns" means that you should choose the Margins and Columns command from the Layout menu. InDesign has a special menu in its tabbed panes called the *palette menu*; this is a set of commands specific to that pane, and you access it from the triangle symbol (▶) in the pane's title bar (at the upper right corner if the pane is not docked and at the upper left corner if it is docked).

Like most modern programs, QuarkXPress and InDesign have an interface feature that has proven to be quite popular called *tabbed panes*. This is a method of stuffing several dialog boxes into one dialog box or into one floating palette. You see tabs, like those in file folders, and by clicking a tab, the pane of options for that tab comes to the front of the dialog box. In InDesign's floating panes, you can even move tabs from one pane to another to create the arrangement that best suits your work style. In this book, I will tell you to go to the pane, which you do by clicking on the tab where the name of the pane is to display the pane. For example, "Go to the General pane" means click the General tab in the current dialog box or palette.

Mouse conventions

Because you use a mouse to perform many functions in QuarkXPress and InDesign, you need to be familiar with the following terms and instructions. And, yes, when I say *mouse*, I also mean other pointing devices, such as trackballs and pen tablets.

- **Pointer:** The small icon that moves on the screen as you move your mouse is a pointer (also called a cursor). The pointer takes on different shapes depending on the tool you select, the current location of the mouse, and the function you're performing.
- **Click:** Most Mac mice have only one button, but some have two or more; all PC mice have at least two buttons. If you have a multibutton mouse, quickly press and release the leftmost mouse button once when I say to click the mouse. (If your mouse has only one button — you guessed it — just press and release the button you have.)
- **Double-click:** When I say to double-click, quickly press and release the leftmost mouse button twice (if your mouse has only one button, just press and release twice the button you have). On some multibutton mice, one of the buttons can function as a double-click (you click it once, the mouse clicks twice); if your mouse has this feature, use it — it

saves strain on your hand.

- **Right-click**: A Windows feature since Windows 95, right-clicking means clicking the righthand mouse button. On a Mac's one-button mouse, hold the Control key when clicking the mouse button to achieve the right-click effect. On multibutton Mac mice, Mac OS X automatically assigns the righthand button to Control+click.

- **Drag:** Dragging is used for moving and sizing items in a QuarkXPress or InDesign document. To drag an item, position the mouse pointer on it. Press and hold down the mouse button, and then slide the mouse across a flat surface to drag the item. Release the mouse button to drop the dragged item in its new location.

Dealing with computer-platform appearance issues

InDesign CS and CS2 run on Mac OS X 10.2 (Jaguar) and Windows 2000 with Service Pack 2 or later installed, as well as later versions of these operating systems such as Mac OS X 10.3 (Panther), Mac OS X 10.4 (Tiger), and Windows XP. InDesign 2 runs on Mac OS 9 or later and on Windows 98 or later. Most desktop publishers use Apple Macintosh computers, and thus most readers of this book will likely be Mac-based. That's why I use Mac screenshots in the illustrations throughout this book. (Plus, Adobe uses Windows screen shots in its documentation.) But the minority in publishing who use Microsoft's Windows continues to grow, especially for business-oriented and personal publishing, so I do show Windows screenshots when notable differences exist. Both Quark and Adobe have done a good job of ensuring that the interfaces for their products are almost identical — within the natural differences between Mac and Windows — on the two platforms.

Keyboard conventions

This book provides both the Macintosh and Windows shortcuts throughout, with the Mac shortcut first. In most cases, the Mac and Windows shortcuts are the same, except for the names of the keys, as follows:

- The Mac's Command key (⌘) is the most-used shortcut key. Its Windows equivalent is Ctrl.

- Shift is the same on the Mac and Windows. In many Mac program menus — including InDesign — Shift is displayed by the symbol ⇧.

- The Option key on the Mac is usually the same as the Alt key in Windows. In many Mac programs' menus — including InDesign's — you'll see the symbol ⌥ used.

- The Control key on the Mac has no Windows equivalent (it is not the same as the Windows Ctrl key). Many Mac programs indicate it with the symbol ^ in their menus.

- The Tab key is used both to move within fields in panes and dialog boxes and to insert the tab character in text. InDesign and many other Mac programs indicate it in menus with the symbol ⇥.

- The Return key (Mac) or Enter key (Windows) is used to apply a dialog box's settings and close the dialog box (equivalent to clicking OK or Done), as well as to insert a hard paragraph return in text. In InDesign and many other Mac programs, it is indicated in menus by the symbol ↵. Note that there is another key labeled Enter on most key-boards, in the numeric keypad. This sometimes works like the regular Return or Enter, but in InDesign text, it inserts a column break. I refer to it as *keypad Enter* in this book.

- The Delete key (Mac) and Backspace key (Windows) deletes text, one character at a time, to the left of the text-insertion point. On the Mac, programs like InDesign use the symbol ⌫ to indicate Delete. Windows also has a separate Delete key that deletes text, one character at a time, to the right of the text-insertion point. The Mac's Clear key, although in the same position on the keyboard, does not delete text.

If you're supposed to press several keys at the same time, I indicate that by placing plus signs (+) between them. Thus, Shift+⌘+A means press and hold the Shift and ⌘ keys, then press A. After you've pressed the A key, let go of all three keys. (You don't need to hold down the last letter in the sequence.)

I also use the plus sign (+) to join keys to mouse movements. For example, Option+drag means to hold the Option key while dragging the mouse on the Mac, and Alt+drag means to hold the Alt key while dragging the mouse in Windows.

Also note that InDesign lets you change the shortcuts associated with menu and other commands (by choosing Edit ⇨ Keyboard Shortcuts). Throughout the book, I assume the shortcuts in use are the default ones and that you haven't altered them.

Icons

You'll notice special graphic symbols, or icons, used throughout this book. I use these icons to call your attention to points that are particularly important or worth noting:

 The Go Further icon indicates you to an InDesign capability that does more than QuarkXPress can do.

 The Workaround icon indicates a tip on achieving a QuarkXPress capability not sup-ported in InDesign.

 The Watch Out icon alerts you to something that could go wrong if you do it the standard QuarkXPress way when in InDesign.

 The Cross-Reference icon points you to different parts of the book that contain related information on a particular topic.

part i

Interface and Program Basics

This section gives you a basic introduction to InDesign itself, showing the interface and tools that you'll use everyday and how they equate to their counterparts in QuarkXPress. InDesign and QuarkXPress have very different interface approaches, and understanding the differences is key to becoming comfortable in InDesign.

This section makes it easy to match up differing elements by showing a visual translation between the interfaces. You'll also see what interface elements are not the same, even though they may at first appear to be, so you don't mistakenly use an inappropriate element.

✿ Translating Basic Terms   ◀ **QuarkXPress**

Major Terminology Differences

QuarkXPress	InDesign	Meaning
Anchored item	inline frame	An object placed within text that flows with the text as it is edited
Background color	Fill	Color applied to an object's background
Blend	Gradient	Gradation of one color to another
Box	Frame	Container for text or graphic
Color	Swatch	A defined color that can be separated onto its own plate (for printing)
Frame	Stroke	Outline of an object, graphic, or text character
Get or Import	Place	Bring an outside element into the layout
Item	Object	Something you can select, such as a line, picture, or text box
Link	Thread	Connection between text boxes to control text flow
Picture	Graphic	An image or drawing, usually created in another application
Runaround	Text wrap	Having text follow closely around another object's shape
Shade	Tint	A color with less than complete saturation
Style	Character format	A single text attribute, such as italics or boldface
Style sheet	Style	Collection of text attributes that are saved and can be applied all at once
XTension	Plug-in	Optional program that adds features to QuarkXPress or InDesign

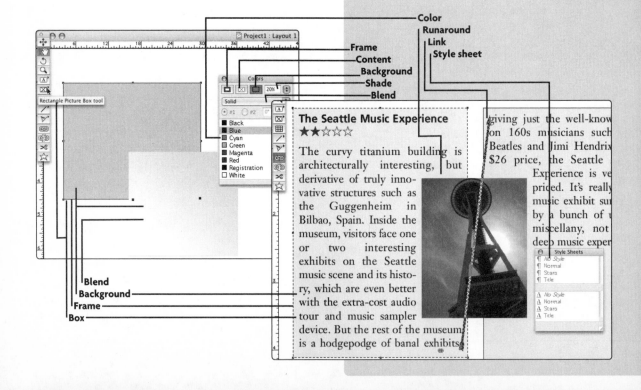

InDesign

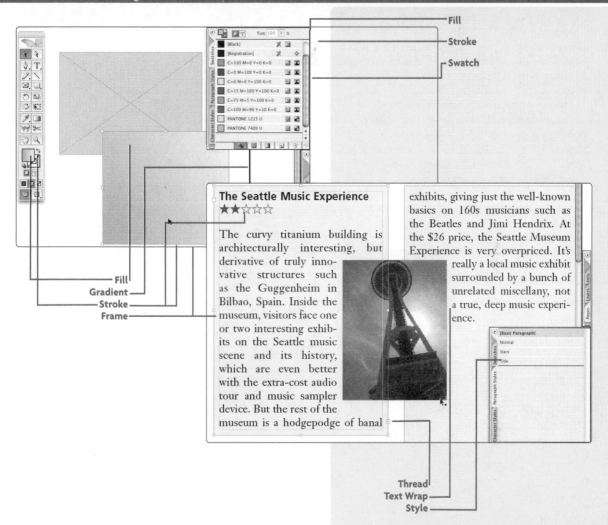

Fill
Stroke
Swatch

Fill
Gradient
Stroke
Frame

The Seattle Music Experience
★★☆☆☆

The curvy titanium building is architecturally interesting, but derivative of truly innovative structures such as the Guggenheim in Bilbao, Spain. Inside the museum, visitors face one or two interesting exhibits on the Seattle music scene and its history, which are even better with the extra-cost audio tour and music sampler device. But the rest of the museum is a hodgepodge of banal

exhibits, giving just the well-known basics on 160s musicians such as the Beatles and Jimi Hendrix. At the $26 price, the Seattle Museum Experience is very overpriced. It's really a local music exhibit surrounded by a bunch of unrelated miscellany, not a true, deep music experience.

Thread
Text Wrap
Style

Keep in Mind

QuarkXPress and InDesign use different terms for the same things, which can be confusing. This book uses QuarkXPress terms on QuarkXPress pages and InDesign terms on InDesign pages, to highlight the differences as if they were two languages. The table at left highlights the major terminology differences. The screen shots show the terms applied to actual interface elements.

■ Comparing Palettes and Panes   〈 QuarkXPress

Note These Differences

InDesign has lots of palettes, which often contain multiple panes. QuarkXPress has a fair number of self-contained palettes but not as many as InDesign, since QuarkXPress leaves many detailed actions to its dialog boxes.

Because it has so many palettes, the transition to InDesign can be bewildering. On this spread, I've indicated the InDesign panes that correspond to QuarkXPress palettes by giving them the same numerical labels. Note that, in some cases, a pane or palette may contain functions covered in more than one pane or palette in the other program.

All palettes and panes are available in the Window menu (for QuarkXPress 5 or earlier, in the View menu). Note that InDesign groups its text-oriented panes under the Type & Tables submenu. I've indicated keyboard shortcuts for those that have them. In one case, InDesign uses a dialog box where QuarkXPress has a palette (the Lists palette), so I've also shown the menu path for that dialog box.

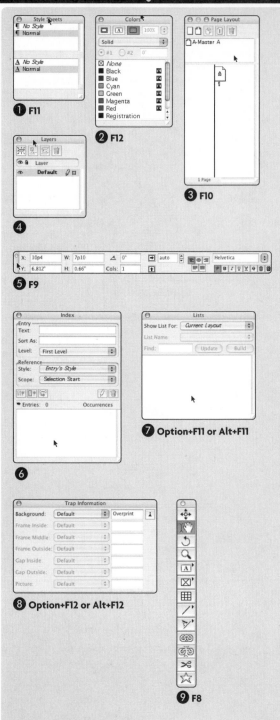

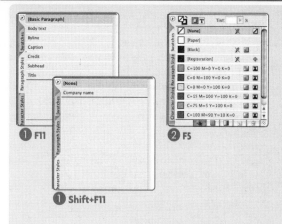

1 F11

1 Shift+F11

2 F5

3 F12

4 F7

5 Option+⌘+6 or Ctrl+Alt+6

6 Shift+F8

8

9

Keep in Mind

One key issue for QuarkXPress users making the switch is InDesign's palette menu. The triangle symbol (▶) in the upper left or upper right of each palette (depending on whether the palette is docked) is actually a pop-up menu for the currently active pane. The palette menu is how you access most InDesign functions; only a few are available only through dialog boxes. QuarkXPress, by contrast, has no equivalent to the palette menu, although a few palettes, such as Colors and Style Sheets, let you ⌘+click or Ctrl+click an entry to add, modify, or delete a setting. Otherwise, you use the various menus in QuarkXPress to access functions, such as modifying boxes, setting runarounds, defining hyphenation settings, setting line styles, and aligning items.

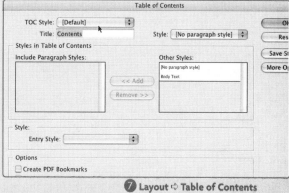

7 Layout ⇨ Table of Contents

Comparing Dialog Boxes, part one QuarkXPress

Note These Differences

Both InDesign and QuarkXPress use dialog boxes accessed from their menu bars, but the interfaces are quite different. On this and the next spread, I've indicated the InDesign dialog boxes (and sometimes panes) that correspond to QuarkXPress dialog boxes by giving them the same numerical labels. I've also shown the menu sequence and, if it exists, the keyboard shortcut.

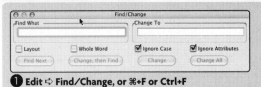

❶ Edit ➪ Find/Change, or ⌘+F or Ctrl+F

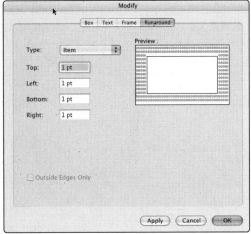

❷ Item ➪ Modify, or ⌘+B or Ctrl+B

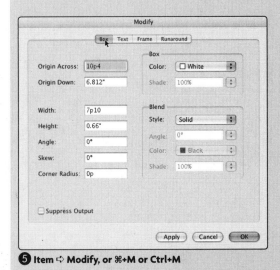

❸ Item ➪ Modify, or ⌘+T or Ctrl+T

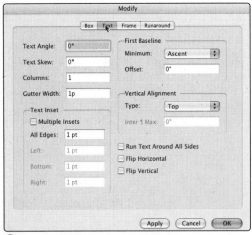

❹ Item ➪ Modify, or ⌘+M or Ctrl+M

❺ Item ➪ Modify, or ⌘+M or Ctrl+M

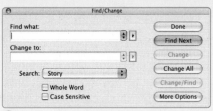

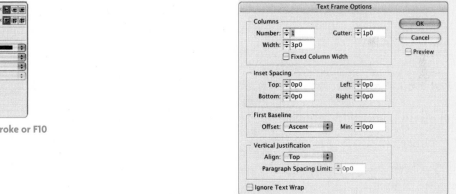

① Edit ⇨ Find/Change, or ⌘+F or Ctrl+F

② Window ⇨ Text Wrap (InDesign 2 and CS2) or Window ⇨ Type & Tables ⇨ Text Wrap (InDesign CS), or Option+⌘+W or Ctrl+Alt+W

③ Window ⇨ Swatches or F5

③ Window ⇨ Control, or Option+⌘+6 or Ctrl+Alt+6 (InDesign CS and CS2)

④ Window ⇨ Stroke or F10

Text Frame Options

Columns
Number: 1   Gutter: 1p0
Width: 3p0
☐ Fixed Column Width

Inset Spacing
Top: 0p0   Left: 0p0
Bottom: 0p0   Right: 0p0

First Baseline
Offset: Ascent   Min: 0p0

Vertical Justification
Align: Top
Paragraph Spacing Limit: 0p0

☐ Ignore Text Wrap

OK
Cancel
☐ Preview

⑤ Object ⇨ Text Frame Options, or ⌘+B or Ctrl+B

Comparing Dialog Boxes, part two ◀ **QuarkXPress**

⑥ Edit ➪ H&Js, or Option+⌘+J and Ctrl+Alt+J (QuarkXPress 6), or Option+⌘+H or Ctrl+Shift+F11 (QuarkXPress 4 and 5)

Step and Repeat

Repeat Count:	1
Horizontal Offset:	1p6
Vertical Offset:	0.25"

Cancel OK

⑧ Item ➪ Step and Repeat, or Option+⌘+D or Ctrl+Alt+D

Super Step & Repeat

Repeat Count:	1	End Frame/Line Width:	0 pt
Horizontal Offset:	0p	End Box Shade:	100%
Vertical Offset:	0"	End Box Shade 2:	100%
Angle:	0°	End Item Scale:	100%
☐ Scale Contents		End Item Skew:	0°
Rotate & Scale Relative To:	Center		

Cancel OK

⑧ Item ➪ Super Step and Repeat (QuarkXPress 5 and 6)

Section

☐ Section Start
☐ Book Chapter Start

Page Numbering

Prefix:	
Number:	
Format:	1, 2, 3, 4

Cancel OK

⑩ Page ➪ Section

Dashes & Stripes for Project2

Show: All Dashes & Stripes

••••••••	All Dots
▬ - ▬ -	Dash Dot
▬ ▬ ▬ ▬	Dotted
▬ ▬ ▬ ▬	Dotted 2
▬▬▬▬▬	Solid
▬▬▬▬▬	Double

Dash; Number of Segments: 2; Miter Style: Miter; Endcap Style: Projecting Round; Pattern Length: 2; Segments: 0%, 100%; Stretch To Corners

New ▾   Edit   Duplicate   Delete
Append...   Cancel   Save

⑦ Edit ➪ Dashes & Stripes

Underline Styles for Project2:Layout 1

Underline Styles:

Default

Color: Black; Shade: 100%; Width: 1 pt; Offset: 0 pt;

New   Edit   Duplicate   Delete
Import...   Export...   Cancel   Save

⑨ Edit ➪ Underline Styles

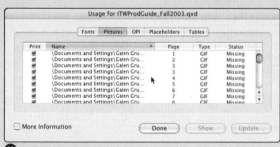

Usage for ITWProdGuide_Fall2003.qxd

Fonts   Pictures   OPI   Placeholders   Tables

Print	Name	Page	Type	Status
☑	\Documents and Settings\Galen Gru...	1	GIF	Missing
☑	\Documents and Settings\Galen Gru...	2	GIF	Missing
☑	\Documents and Settings\Galen Gru...	3	GIF	Missing
☑	\Documents and Settings\Galen Gru...	3	GIF	Missing
☑	\Documents and Settings\Galen Gru...	4	GIF	Missing
☑	\Documents and Settings\Galen Gru...	5	GIF	Missing
☑	\Documents and Settings\Galen Gru...	6	GIF	Missing
☑	\Documents and Settings\Galen Gru...	7	GIF	Missing
☑	\Documents and Settings\Galen Gru...	6	GIF	Missing

☐ More Information   Done   Show   Update...

⑪ Utilities ➪ Usage

Usage for ITWProdGuide_Fall2003.qxd

Fonts   Pictures   OPI   Placeholders   Tables

Name
Amasis MT «Plain»
Concorde BE Regular «Plain»
Helvetica «Plain»
Helvetica Condensed «Bold»
Helvetica CondensedBlack «Plain»
HelveticaNeue BlackCond «Plain»
HelveticaNeue BlackCond «Italic»
HelveticaNeue Condensed «Plain»

☐ More Information   Done   Show First   Replace...

⑫ Utilities ➪ Usage

InDesign

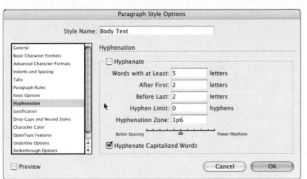

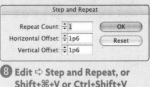

⑧ Edit ⇨ Step and Repeat, or Shift+⌘+V or Ctrl+Shift+V (InDesign 2 and CS), or Shift+⌘+U or Ctrl+Shift+U (InDesign CS2)

⑦ Window ⇨ Stroke or F10

⑥ Handled through paragraph style sheet: Window ⇨ Type & Tables ⇨ Paragraph Styles (InDesign CS and CS2) and Window ⇨ Type ⇨ Paragraph Styles (InDesign 2), or F11

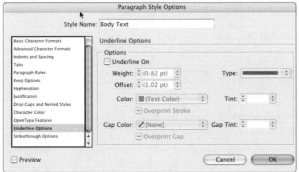

⑩ Layout ⇨ Numbering & Section Options

⑨ Handled through paragraph style sheet: Window ⇨ Type & Tables ⇨ Paragraph Styles (InDesign CS and CS2) or Window ⇨ Type ⇨ Paragraph Styles (InDesign 2), or F11

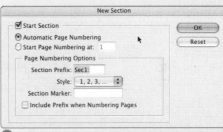

⑪ Window ⇨ Links, or Shift+⌘+D or Ctrl+Shift+D

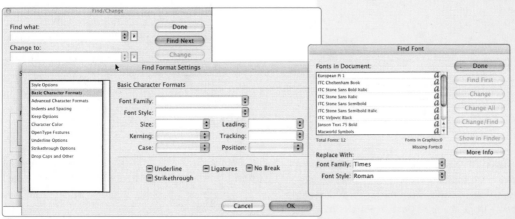

⑫ Missing fonts are highlighted onscreen; replace those in use via Find/Change: (Edit ⇨ Find/Change, or ⌘+F or Ctrl+F) or more globally via Type ⇨ Find Font

✳ Comparing the Measurements and Control Palettes
◀ QuarkXPress

Note These Differences

The QuarkXPress Measurements palette was a breakthrough innovation in its time, and put many commonly used capabilities within quick reach. Even better, the palette changed its options based on what was selected, minimizing space on the screen and presenting only relevant options.

InDesign CS finally introduced an equivalent feature, called the Control palette, that offers more controls, both in the palette itself and through its palette menu.

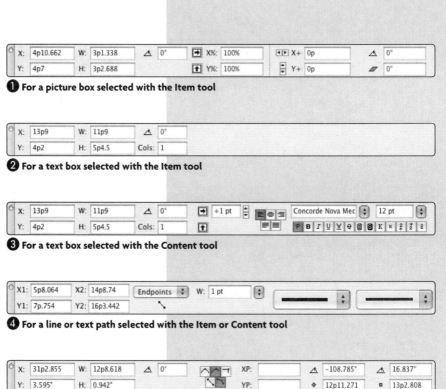

❶ For a picture box selected with the Item tool

❷ For a text box selected with the Item tool

❸ For a text box selected with the Content tool

❹ For a line or text path selected with the Item or Content tool

❺ For a Bézier line's node selected with the Content tool

Go Further: The InDesign Control palette can be docked to the top or bottom of the screen, so it is always visible but away from the layout you're working on. Just choose Dock at Top or Dock at Bottom from the Control palette's palette menu. To have the Control palette float à la QuarkXPress's Measurements palette, choose Float from the palette menu.

InDesign

① For a graphic frame selected with the Selection or Direct Selection tool

② For a text frame selected with the Text tool, with Paragraph (¶) button clicked

③ For a text frame selected with the Text tool, with Character (A) button clicked

④ For a line selected with the Selection or Direct Selection tool

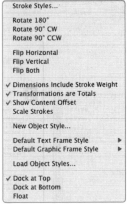

⑤ Tools to edit Bézier lines' nodes (there is no Control palette or other dialog box with controls more equivalent to those in QuarkXPress)

Palette menu ①

Stroke Styles...

Rotate 180°
Rotate 90° CW
Rotate 90° CCW

Flip Horizontal
Flip Vertical
Flip Both

✓ Dimensions Include Stroke Weight
✓ Transformations are Totals
✓ Show Content Offset
Scale Strokes

New Object Style...

Default Text Frame Style ▶
Default Graphic Frame Style ▶

Load Object Styles...

✓ Dock at Top
Dock at Bottom
Float

① **Palette menu**

Palette menu ②

Only Align First Line To Grid
Balance Ragged Lines

Justification...   ⌥⇧⌘J
Keep Options...   ⌥⌘K
Hyphenation...
Drop Caps and Nested Styles...   ⌥⌘R
Paragraph Rules...   ⌥⌘J
Bullets and Numbering...

New Paragraph Style...
Duplicate Style...
Delete Style

Style Options...

Load Paragraph Styles...
Load All Styles...

✓ Dock at Top
Dock at Bottom
Float

② **Palette menu**

Palette menu ③

Stroke Styles...

Rotate 180°
Rotate 90° CW
Rotate 90° CCW

Flip Horizontal
Flip Vertical
Flip Both

✓ Dimensions Include Stroke
✓ Transformations are Total
✓ Show Content Offset
Scale Strokes

New Object Style...

③ **Palette menu**

Stroke Styles...

Rotate 180°
Rotate 90° CW
Rotate 90° CCW

Flip Horizontal
Flip Vertical
Flip Both

✓ Dimensions Include Stroke Weight
✓ Transformations are Totals
✓ Show Content Offset
Scale Strokes

New Object Style...

Redefine Object Style
Clear Overrides

Default Text Frame Style ▶
Default Graphic Frame Style ▶

Load Object Styles...

✓ Dock at Top
Dock at Bottom
Float

④ **Palette menu**

Watch Out: When you resize a frame or its content by entering a specific percentage in InDesign, such as in the Control palette or Transform pane, the percentage will change back to 100% in the pane or palette after the frame or content is resized — if you use the Selection tool. To see the actual percentage in InDesign, you must use the Direct Selection tool to select the object. (In QuarkXPress, the percentage value is displayed accurately in the Measurements palette whether you use the Item or Content tool.)

✳ Comparing Tools

Note These Differences

At the heart of the interface of both QuarkXPress and InDesign is the Tools palette. This floating palette contains the tools that you use to work with objects.

Both programs' palettes have tools that are invisible by default. In both cases, look for the tiny triangle on the right side of a tool's icon; that triangle means more related tools are available by clicking and holding the mouse button. If you choose an alternative tool, it then becomes visible in the Tools palette.

As is the case with the Control palette versus Measurements palette, the InDesign Tools palette offers more functions than the QuarkXPress Tools palette. Furthermore, you can more easily customize tool settings in the InDesign Tools palette by double-clicking some of the tools, as shown on this spread. (QuarkXPress lets you customize a few tools, also as shown here.)

Note that the InDesign Selection and Direct Selection tools are not always equivalent to the QuarkXPress Item and Content tools, as the "Comparing Selection Tools" section on page 16 explains.

Another common tool that can confuse QuarkXPress veterans is the InDesign Type tool. It's best to think of the Type tool as a combination of the QuarkXPress Rectangle Text Box tool and the Content tool for text. In InDesign, you use the Type tool to create text frames and then use it to edit and format the text. But you can't move or resize text frames with the Type tool as you can with the QuarkXPress Content tool.

For some QuarkXPress tools, InDesign lacks equivalent tools:

- Link and Unlink: InDesign handles these functions by having you click on thread handles in text frames.

- Table (QuarkXPress 5 and later): InDesign handles tables through the Table pane (Windows ⇨ Type & Tables ⇨ Table, or Shift+F9.

- Starburst (QuarkXPress 5 and later): InDesign handles this capability through the Polygon and Polygon Frame tools

- Web-publishing tools (QuarkXPress 5 and later): InDesign has no equivalents to the Web-publishing tools — except for the button tool used for interactive documents exported as PDF files — since InDesign CS and C2 do not offer the Web-page creation capabilities that were part of InDesign 2.

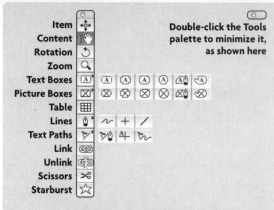

Item
Content
Rotation
Zoom
Text Boxes
Picture Boxes
Table
Lines
Text Paths
Link
Unlink
Scissors
Starburst

Double-click the Tools palette to minimize it, as shown here

Double-click the Starburst tool to set the default star's shape

Starburst Preferences

Number of Spikes: 5
Spike Depth: 50%
Random Spikes: 0

Cancel   OK

Preferences

Double-click a tool to open the General Preferences dialog box, which has a pane that lets you change the default settings for each of the tools. You can also access this dialog box as follows:

- **Version 6 on Mac: QuarkXPress ⇨ Preferences, or Option+Shift+⌘+Y**
- **Version 6 in Windows: Edit ⇨ Preferences, or Ctrl+Alt+Shift+Y**
- **Version 5: Edit ⇨ Preferences ⇨ Preferences, or Option+Shift+⌘+Y or Ctrl+Alt+Shift+Y**
- **Version 4: Edit ⇨ Preferences ⇨ Document, or ⌘+Y or Ctrl+Y**

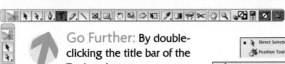

Go Further: By double-clicking the title bar of the Tools palette, you can change its shape to single-column. Double-clicking it again makes the palette horizontal. And double-clicking the title bar a third time returns the palette to its normal two-column, vertical shape.

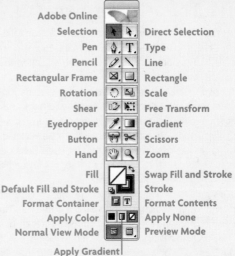

Adobe Online	
Selection	Direct Selection
Pen	Type
Pencil	Line
Rectangular Frame	Rectangle
Rotation	Scale
Shear	Free Transform
Eyedropper	Gradient
Button	Scissors
Hand	Zoom
Fill	Swap Fill and Stroke
Default Fill and Stroke	Stroke
Format Container	Format Contents
Apply Color	Apply None
Normal View Mode	Preview Mode
Apply Gradient	

Note: The Button tool was introduced in InDesign CS and the Position tool was introduced in InDesign CS2.

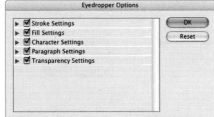

Eyedropper Options

▶ ☑ Stroke Settings
▶ ☑ Fill Settings
▶ ☑ Character Settings
▶ ☑ Paragraph Settings
▶ ☑ Transparency Settings

OK
Reset

Double-click the Eyedropper tool

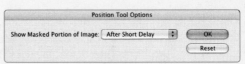

Position Tool Options

Show Masked Portion of Image: After Short Delay ⇕   OK   Reset

Double-click the Position tool

Type on a Path Options

Effect: Rainbow ⇕   ☐ Flip   OK
Align: Baseline ⇕   To Path: Center ⇕   Cancel
Spacing: ⇕ 0 ⇕   Delete
☑ Preview

Double-click the Type on a Path tool

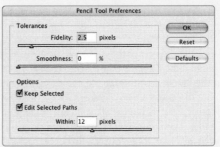

Pencil Tool Preferences

Tolerances
Fidelity: 2.5 pixels
Smoothness: 0 %

Options
☑ Keep Selected
☑ Edit Selected Paths
Within: 12 pixels

OK   Reset   Defaults

Double-click the Pencil tool

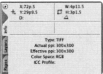

X:72p.5   W:4p11.5
Y:29p9.5   H:3p1.5
D:

Type: TIFF
Actual ppi: 300x300
Effective ppi: 300x300
Color Space: RGB
ICC Profile:

Double-click the Measure tool

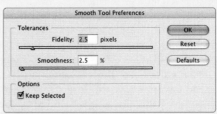

Smooth Tool Preferences

Tolerances
Fidelity: 2.5 pixels
Smoothness: 2.5 %

Options
☑ Keep Selected

OK   Reset   Defaults

Double-click the Smooth tool

Weight: 1 pt   Cap:
Miter Limit: 4   x   Join:
Align Stroke:
Type:
Start: None
End: None
Gap Color: [None]
Gap Tint: 100%

Double-click the Stroke tool

Type:
Location: % Angle: 0
Reverse

Double-click the Gradient tool

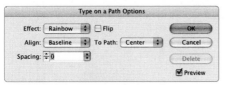

✳ Comparing the Selection Tools ◀ **QuarkXPress**

Note These Differences

One of the most confusing changes for a veteran QuarkXPress user switching to InDesign is the set of InDesign selection tools. Although both programs have two selection tools, they are not the same.

The two QuarkXPress tools have a clear separation: The Item tool works on items such as boxes and lines and their attributes, while the Content tool works on item contents such as text or pictures. The distinction used to be ironclad, but as QuarkXPress has evolved, Quark has let users select either tool when an action, such as reshaping a line, doesn't differentiate between the content and the container.

InDesign's two tools have strict but muddy distinctions: The Selection tool by and large works on the container. The Direct Selection tool by and large works on the contents, but not always. So QuarkXPress veterans need to forget about the QuarkXPress way of working entirely. And the truth is that the difference between the InDesign Selection tool and Direct Selection tool takes some getting used to.

In InDesign, you'll be switching tools constantly. When you create an object, its tool remains selected so you can't move or resize the objects immediately after you create them — unlike in QuarkXPress. The Selection tool only lets you move and resize objects, while the Direct Selection tool lets you reshape objects and work with graphics.

In terms of working with content, the Direct Selection tool is much like the QuarkXPress Content tool, but it also lets you edit the frame as if it were a Bézier object. For example, if the Direct Selection tool is selected and you drag a point on the frame, you'll move that point and thus change the shape of the object — a rectangle is converted into a polygon, since the lines immediately adjacent to the moved point will move with the point, while the rest of the frame will not be affected. In QuarkXPress, if the Content tool is selected and you drag a point on the frame, you'll resize the frame (perhaps nonproportionally) but the entire side(s) adjacent to the point will move with the point, so a rectangle will still be a rectangle. To change a frame in the way that QuarkXPress does with both the Content and Item tools, use the Selection tool in InDesign.

Some functions in the QuarkXPress Item and Content tools cannot be achieved through the InDesign Selection and Direct Selection tools. For example, to edit text in InDesign, you use the Type tool, not the Direct Selection tool. (You can quickly switch to the Type tool by double-clicking in a text frame.)

At right, I show the QuarkXPress Item and Content tools used for various actions, then the InDesign Selection and Direct Selection tools that are equivalent. To help you match actions across the two programs, like actions have like numbers.

❶ Dragging a corner or side handle with the Item tool resizes the box.

❶ Dragging a corner or side handle with the Content tool also resizes the box.

❷ You could also edit or format the text

❸ Dragging anywhere inside with the Item tool moves the box.

❹ After selecting a picture with the Content tool, you can change the X% or Y% field in the Measurements palette to resize a picture but not its box (not shown).

❺ Dragging anywhere inside the box with the Content tool moves the picture within the box.

❻ To edit a box's shape, first change the box shape to a Bézier box by choosing Item ⇨ Shape ⇨ *Bézier shape icon.* You can then reshape the box by dragging the handles with the Content tool.

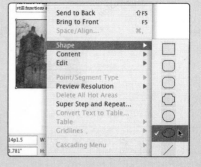

InDesign

Keep in Mind

InDesign CS2 introduces the Position tool, a renamed version of PageMaker's Crop tool. You access it from the pop-out menu in the Direct Selection tool. The Position tool combines some aspects of the Selection tool with some aspects of the Direct Selection tool:

- As with the Selection tool, you can resize an object's frame by dragging its handles.
- As with the Direct Selection tool, you can click on a graphic and reposition it (crop it) within the frame by dragging.

1 Dragging a corner or side handle with the Selection tool resizes the frame.

2 Use the Type tool to edit or format the text.

3 Dragging anywhere inside with the Selection tool moves the frame.

4 Click an image with the Direct Selection tool, then click-and-drag to move the graphic within its frame.

In InDesign CS2, you can also choose Object ➪ Convert Shape.

5 Click an image with the Direct Selection tool, then click-and-drag any of the graphic's handles to resize the graphic.

6 Dragging a handle with the Direct Selection tool reshapes the frame.

Using the Contextual Menus

Keep in Mind

Contextual menus are a great way to avoid interface clutter, and can ease your need to remember how to find needed panes and dialog boxes. This is especially true for InDesign, which has an unwieldy number of panes that are a challenge to keep track of and for which it is difficult to remember their functionality. Contextual menus are also a great way to learn what you can do with an object, even understanding that additional obscure or specialized functions may be available that don't show up in a contextual menu.

In each new version, QuarkXPress has added more and more contextual-menu options, though InDesign still offers far more. Veteran QuarkXPress users are not in the habit of using contextual menus, so many InDesign converts ignore this very convenient way to work with objects. Note that the options displayed in each program's contextual menus will vary based on which version you are using; the screenshots here are for QuarkXPress 6 and InDesign CS2.

Because contextual menus are, well, contextual, it's impossible to show every possible contextual menu available. I've highlighted the contextual menus from the objects you'll use the most.

A final note: QuarkXPress 6 brought contextual menus to many palettes (Colors, Style Sheets, Layers, Page Layout, Synchronized Text, Index, and Lists). InDesign offers contextual menus in two panes (Paragraph Styles and Character Styles), but it offers the palette menu, which opens a pane-specific set of options in every pane. It's best to think of the palette menu as a hard-wired contextual menu for each pane.

Contextual menu for a box via the Item tool

Contextual menu for a picture via the Content tool

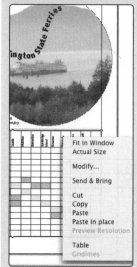

Contextual menu for a table box via the Item tool

Contextual menu for table text via the Content tool

Contextual menu for the Colors palette

Contextual menu with nothing selected

Contextual menu for the rulers and origins

Contextual menu the for a graphic frame via the Selection or Direct Selection tool

Contextual menu for a text frame via the Selection or Direct Selection tool

Contextual menu with nothing selected

Contextual menu for the rulers

Lock Zero Point

Contextual menu for the origin points

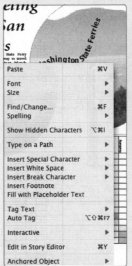

Contextual menu for a text path via the Type tool

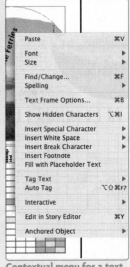

Contextual menu for a text path via the Type tool

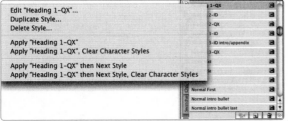

Contextual menu for the Paragraph Styles pane; the Character Styles and Object Styles panes have similar contextual menus

✻ Controlling What You See Onscreen ⟨ QuarkXPress

Keep in Mind

InDesign has many panes — 28 in Indesign 2, 35 in Indesign CS, and 39 in InDesign CS2 — so it's very easy to get overwhelmed. QuarkXPress has seven to 14 panes, depending on what version you use, and relies more on dialog boxes, particularly the Modify dialog box, to handle key layout settings in one place.

In both programs, you can choose which panes and palettes to display via the Window menu (the View menu in Quark-XPress 5 or earlier). And you can double-click a palette's title bar to minimize it. But InDesign offers several more options to manage what you see onscreen:

- A pane can be combined with other panes into palettes, simply by dragging the pane by the title bar into another pane's palette. This lets you logically group panes.

- In InDesign CS and later, palettes can be docked to either side of the screen, so they are visible but not in the way. (InDesign 2 does not support palette docking.) Double-click the palette title to open it. (Palettes that are not docked will appear as floating palettes when you open them from the Window menu; they will appear at their last location.)

- Some palettes can be expanded to display additional controls; keep them in their basic view to minimize screen usage until you need those additional features.

- You can dock the Control palette — which consolidates several features into one place — at the top or bottom of the screen. This keeps the palette conveniently available without it getting in the way of your document.

- You can save your interface settings as workspaces (in the Window menu) so you can easily change from, for example, a designer's set of palettes to a copy editor's set.

Both QuarkXPress and InDesign have similar View menu controls, managing how guides and rulers are displayed. And both let you customize such elements in their Preferences dialog boxes. InDesign can also highlight onscreen any text that violates various hyphenation and justification rules, as well as text using an unavailable font.

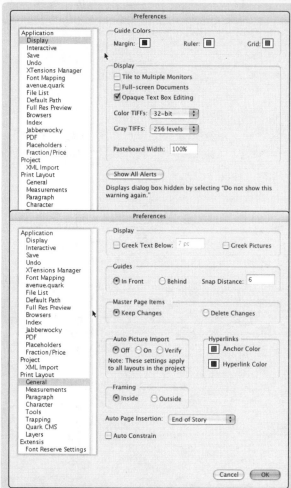

The Display and General panes (above), as well as the Interactive pane (not shown) of the Preferences dialog box control view preferences.

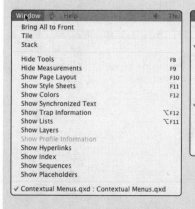

Double-click a palette title bar to minimize it

The Window menu in QuarkXPress 6 controls placement of document windows and palettes. (The View menu does this in earlier versions.)

In all versions, the View menu also manages magnification and display of rulers and guides, as well of preview settings.

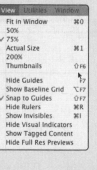

InDesign

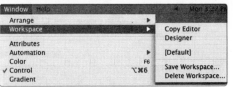

The Workspace function saves interface settings.

The Tools palette includes a button for choosing preview modes.

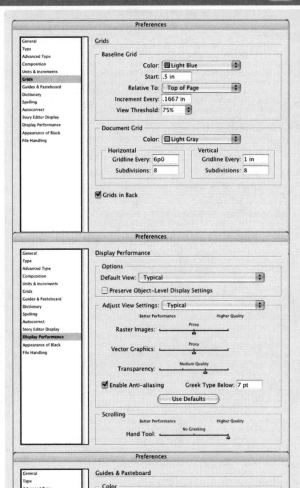

Docked palettes (at right) can be expanded (above) by double-clicking their title bars.

Double-clicking the title bar minimizes a pane (left), while double-clicking a double-arrow icon (right) expands or contracts panes with additional functions.

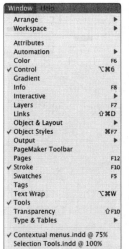 

The Window menu controls placement of document windows and palettes. The View menu manages magnification and display of rulers and guides, as well of preview settings.

The Display Performance, Grids, and Guides & Pasteboard panes (above) of the Preferences dialog box control view preferences, as does the Units & Increments pane (not shown).

part ii

Layout Building Blocks

This section shows you how to set up pages, templates, sections, and other fundamental components. You'll also learn about layers, page numbering, libraries, and guides. These building blocks are not terribly dissimilar in the two programs, but you'll quickly see that InDesign provides more controls in most cases than does QuarkXPress. One area in particular stands out: InDesign's much stronger support for moving elements around, from layout to layout as well as within documents.

As is true in most areas, InDesign's superior control comes with the price of having more options and therefore, in many cases, more interface elements to deal with.

Setting Up Pages and Margins

QuarkXPress

The page is the most basic element of a publication, and both QuarkXPress and InDesign provide similar capabilities in defining them, though InDesign offers several ways to reuse custom page sizes that QuarkXPress does not.

Follow These Steps

In QuarkXPress, set up the page specification as follows:

1. Choose File ▷ New ▷ Layout to open the New Project dialog box (QuarkXPress 6) or File ▷ New ▷ Document to open the New Document dialog box (QuarkXPress 5 or earlier). Either way, the shortcut is ⌘+N or Ctrl+N.

2. Set the Page, Margin Guides, and Column Guides as desired. You can use any measurement system you want, not just the default inches. For page sizes, QuarkXPress offers several standard sizes in the pop-up menu. To create a custom size, enter the desired dimensions in the Width and Height fields. (In QuarkXPress 6, be sure to specify whether you want to create a print or Web document.)

3. For the document to have facing pages (two-sided printing), check the Facing Pages checkbox. The Right and Left margins will change to Outside and Inside if you do so.

4. To have an automatic text box that fits within the specified margins (and has the column settings set in the Column Guides area) placed on the document's master pages, check the Automatic Text Box checkbox.

5. Click OK when done. QuarkXPress will display a new document with a blank page based on those settings.

6. To set up document bleed settings, choose File ▷ Page Setup, or press Option+⌘+P or Ctrl+Alt+P, then select the Bleed pane. Set the bleed amount and click Capture Settings.

7. To create additional pages, choose Page ▷ Insert.

8. To later change the page dimensions, choose Layout ▷ Layout Properties (QuarkXPress 6) or File ▷ Document Setup (QuarkXPress 5 or earlier). Change bleed settings by repeating step 6. Note that you cannot convert a document from facing pages to single pages, or vice versa.

Keep in Mind

QuarkXPress 6 lets you create multiple documents (called *layouts*) in one project file. The process is the same as described above, except you choose Layout ▷ New to create the subsequent layouts within the project file. QuarkXPress 6 lets you convert layouts between Web and print; QuarkXPress 5 lets you create both print and Web documents but not convert one to the other.

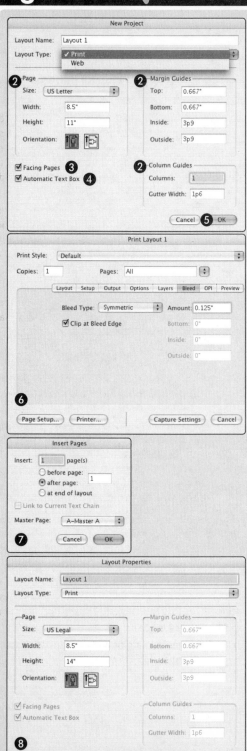

InDesign

Follow These Steps

In InDesign, you also set specifications when you create a new document:

① Choose File ➪ New ➪ Document, or press ⌘+N or Ctrl+N, to open the New Document dialog box.

② Set the Page Size, Columns, and Margins as desired. You can use any measurement system you want, not just the default inches. For page sizes, InDesign offers several standard page sizes in the pop-up menu; to create a custom size, enter the desired dimensions in the Width and Height fields.

③ If you want the document to have facing pages (two-sided printing), be sure to check the Facing Pages checkbox. Note that the Right and Left margins will change to Outside and Inside if you do so, reflecting the two-sided nature of the page.

④ To have an automatic text frame that fits within the specified margins (and has the column settings set in the Columns area) placed on the document's master pages, check the Master Text Frame checkbox.

⑤ To set up document bleed settings in InDesign CS and CS2, set the bleed amount in the Bleed and Slug section; if this section is not visible, click More Options. (In InDesign 2, you set the bleed amount in the Bleed pane when you print by choosing File ➪ Print or pressing ⌘+P or Ctrl+P.)

⑥ You can create a document with as many pages as you like by entering a value in the Number of Pages field. You can also add pages later by choosing Insert Pages from the Pages pane's palette menu. And you can change the number of pages in the Document Setup dialog box (see step 8).

⑦ Click OK when done. InDesign will display a new document with the specified number of blank pages based on those settings.

⑧ To later change the page dimensions, choose File ➪ Document Setup or press Option+⌘+P or Ctrl+Alt+P. Note that through this dialog box, you *can* convert a document from facing pages to single pages, or vice versa, after you've created it — unlike in QuarkXPress.

⑨ To later change the margins and columns settings, choose Layout ➪ Margins and Columns.

 Cross-Reference: InDesign lets you set up custom page sizes for easy reuse, as described on page 343.

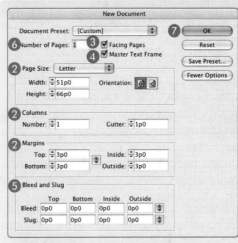

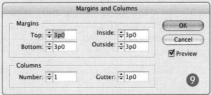

✸Setting Up Master Pages

One of the most powerful layout tools is the master page, which is a collection of page settings that you can apply to new and existing pages rather than create all those settings of each page.

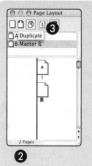

Follow These Steps

1 When you create a new document (or layout in Quark-XPress 6), QuarkXPress automatically creates a new master page, called A-Master A, based on those settings.

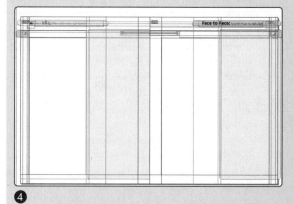

2 To apply and manage master pages, open the Page Layout palette in QuarkXPress 6 by choosing Window ⇨ Show Page Layout or pressing F10. In QuarkXPress 5 or earlier, open the Document Layout palette by choosing View ⇨ Show Document Layout or pressing F10. Master pages appear at the top of the palette. (You can rename master pages by clicking the name and then entering a new one.)

3 To create a new master page, select an existing one and click the Duplicate icon. (In QuarkXPress 6, you can also Control+click or right-click the master-page icon and choose New Facing Pages Master or New Single Page Master, as preferred.) A new master page will appear.

4 To edit an existing master page, double-click its icon in the Page Layout or Document Layout palette to open that page. (You can also choose Page ⇨ Display ⇨ *master page name* or select a master page from the Page pop-up menu at the bottom of the window.) Now add, delete, move and otherwise create the page's objects and settings you want to have on all layout pages based on this master page.

Note that you cannot link text boxes across master pages. But the automatic text box, if you select one when you create the document, automatically links across pages.

Cross-Reference: See pages 28-31 for details in applying master pages and moving elements among them.

Follow These Steps

InDesign has a similar approach to master pages.

1 When you create a new document, InDesign automatically creates a new master page based on those settings, called A-Master.

2 To apply and manage master pages, open the Pages pane by choosing Window ⇨ Pages or pressing F12. Master pages appear at the top of the palette. (You can rename master pages by selecting the master-page icon and choosing Master Options in the Pages pane's palette menu.)

3 To create a new master page, choose New Master in the Pages pane's palette menu. The New Master dialog box will appear, letting you set the name, number of pages, and whether it is based on an existing master page. (If you create a master page and later want to base it on another master page, just drag the icon of the parent master page in the Pages pane onto the target master page's icon to make that target master based on the other master.) You can also create a master page from an existing document page by choosing Save as Master from the Pages pane's palette menu.

4 To edit an existing master page, double-click its icon in the Pages pane to open that page or select a master page from the Page pop-up menu at the bottom of the window. Now add, delete, move and otherwise create the page's objects and settings you want to have on all layout pages based on this master page.

 Go Further: Note that you can link text boxes across master pages, unlike in QuarkXPress. (The automatic text frame, if you select one when you create the document, also automatically links across pages.)

 Go Further: The ability to base master pages on other master pages provides significant flexibility in InDesign. It lets you easily create several variations of your pages that share common features. If you change those common features in the parent master page, they are also automatically changed in the child master pages. In QuarkXPress, master pages are unrelated so similar master pages must be changed individually. See page 344 for more information.

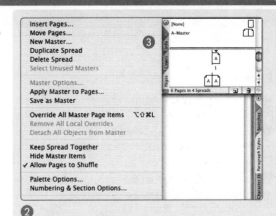

2

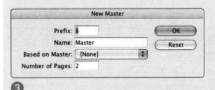

3

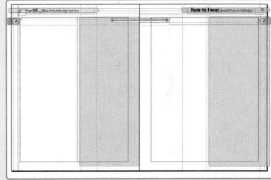

4

Applying Master Pages

WIth master pages defined, you apply them to pages to automate the repetitive formatting.

Follow These Steps

QuarkXPress lets you apply master pages to both existing and new document pages.

1. To apply a master page, drag the master-page icon onto an existing document page in the bottom section of the palette.

2. Drag a master-page icon between, above, or below pages to insert new pages based on those master-page settings. Or choose Page ➪ Insert to insert pages, choosing a master page from the pop-up menu.

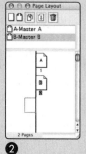

3. If you apply a master page to an existing page, Quark-XPress will retain any changes made to that document page unless you change the Master Page Items pop-up menu (QuarkXPress 6) or radio button (QuarkXPress 5 or earlier) to Delete Changes. Do so in the General pane of the Preferences dialog box, which you access as follows:

   • Version 6 on Mac: QuarkXPress ➪ Preferences, or Option+Shift+⌘+Y

   • Version 6 in Windows: Edit ➪ Preferences, or Ctrl+Alt+Shift+Y

   • Version 5: Edit ➪ Preferences ➪ Preferences, or Option+Shift+⌘+Y or Ctrl+Alt+Shift+Y

   • Version 4: Edit ➪ Preferences ➪ Document, or ⌘+Y or Ctrl+Y

Cross-Reference: See pages 26-27 for details in applying master pages and pages 30-31 for details on moving elements among them.

Follow These Steps

InDesign also lets you apply master pages to both existing and new document pages, as well as to other master pages.

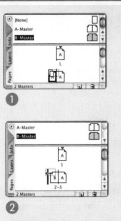

❶ To apply a master page, drag the master-page icon onto an existing document page in the bottom section of the palette. You can also choose Layout ➪ Page ➪ Apply Master Page, which opens a dialog box of available master pages and lets you apply them to a specified range of pages. (QuarkXPress requires you to apply master pages to document pages one page at a time.)

❷ Drag a master-page icon between, above, or below pages to insert new pages based on those master-page settings. Or choose Insert Pages from the Pages pane's palette menu, choosing a master page from the dialog box. In InDesign CS2, you can also choose Layout ➪ Pages ➪ Insert Pages to insert pages, again choosing a master page from the dialog box.

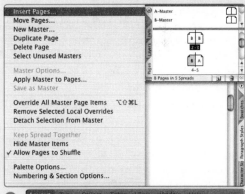

❸ You can selectively "detach" objects on document pages from their master pages, so they are not changed if the master page is changed. To do so, select the object(s) by Shift+⌘+clicking or Ctrl+Shift+clicking it or them and choose Detach Selected Object from Master from the Pages pane's palette menu. If no objects are selected, the menu option is Detach All Objects from Master. You can also detach all overridden objects by choosing Detach All Objects from Master (see step ❹).

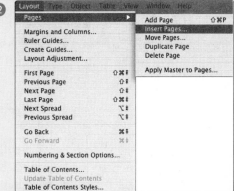

❹ Similarly, you can "override" objects, which makes them selectable on the document page like any other object but still able to be updated when their master-page equivalent is changed. To do so, select the object(s) by Shift+⌘+clicking or Ctrl+Shift+clicking it or them. To override all objects in InDesign CS and later, choose Override All Master Page Items from the Pages pane's palette menu or pressing Option+Shift+⌘+L or Ctrl+Alt+Shift+L.

Go Further: The selective detachment of objects from the master pages permits more flexibility in the use of master pages than the QuarkXPress all-or-nothing approach in the General pane of its Preferences dialog box.

Go Further: Note that you can apply or add individual pages or the entire spread, based on whether you select one or both pages before dragging them into the Pages pane. QuarkXPress requires that you add each page one at a time.

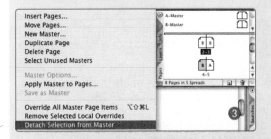

Moving Elements among Master Pages

When you create master pages, you may find that you later realize that an element (or a variation of it) in one master page would be appropriate for another master page, either in the current document or in another document.

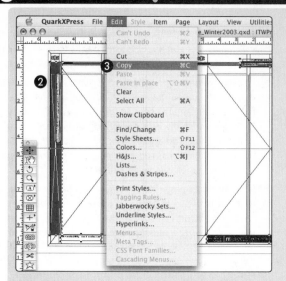

Follow These Steps

The techniques in QuarkXPress differ based on your goal.

Moving Elements among Master Pages

1 Open the source master page in QuarkXPress 6 by double-clicking its icon in the Page Layout palette by choosing Window ➪ Show Page Layout (F10). In earlier versions, click its icon in the Document Layout palette (View ➪ Show Document Layout or F10). In all versions, you can also choose Page ➪ Display ➪ *master page name* or select a master page from the Page pop-up menu at the bottom of the window.

2 Select the element(s) you want to move or copy to the other master page.

3 Cut or copy the element(s) by choosing Edit ➪ Cut (⌘+X or Ctrl+X) or Edit ➪ Copy (⌘+C or Ctrl+C).

4 Switch to the other master page by using the techniques in step 1. (If the other master page is in a different document or layout in a QuarkXPress 6 project file, open that other document or layout before choosing the new master page.)

5 Paste the element(s) in the new master page by choosing Edit ➪ Paste (⌘+V or Ctrl+V), then adjusting the position and other attributes as desired. In QuarkXPress 6, you can paste the element(s) in the same location as the source master page by choosing Edit ➪ Paste in Place (Option+Shift+⌘+V or Ctrl+Alt+Shift+V).

Note that style sheets, H&J sets, dashes and stripes, underline styles (QuarkXPress 5 and later), and color definitions are available to all master pages in a QuarkXPress document or project.

Moving Master Pages among Documents

To move entire master pages among documents (or layouts):

1 Open the source master page.

2 Using the Item tool, choose Edit ➪ Select All (⌘+A or Ctrl+A).

3 Then follow steps 3 through 5 in the section above.

Any style sheets, H&J sets, dashes and stripes, underline styles (QuarkXPress 5 and later), and color definitions will also transfer to the new document. You can also drag the selected master page elements to a library, creating a pseudo master page that can be dragged from the library to multiple other documents' master pages or document pages.

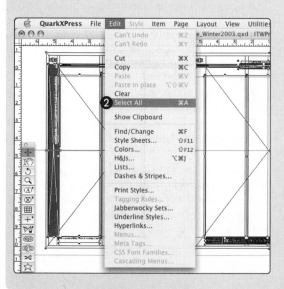

Follow These Steps

Likewise, the techniques in InDesign are based on your goal.

Moving Elements among Master Pages

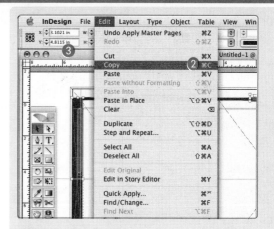

① Open the source master page by double-clicking its icon in the Pages pane by choosing Window ⇨ Pages (F12) or by selecting a master page from the Page pop-up menu at the bottom of the window.

② Select the object(s) you want to move or copy to the other master page.

③ Cut or copy the object(s) by choosing Edit ⇨ Cut (⌘+X or Ctrl+X) or Edit ⇨ Copy (⌘+C or Ctrl+C).

④ Switch to the other master page as described in step 1. (If the other master page is in a different document, open that other document or layout before choosing the new master page.)

⑤ Paste the object(s) in the new master page by choosing Edit ⇨ Paste (⌘+V or Ctrl+V), then adjusting the position and other attributes as desired. You can paste the object(s) in the same location as the source master page by choosing Edit ⇨ Paste in Place (Option+Shift+⌘+V or Ctrl+Alt+Shift+V).

Note that any style sheets, object styles (InDesign CS2), stroke styles (InDesign CS and later), and color and gradient swatches will also transfer to the new document.

Moving Master Pages among Documents

To move entire master pages from one document to another:

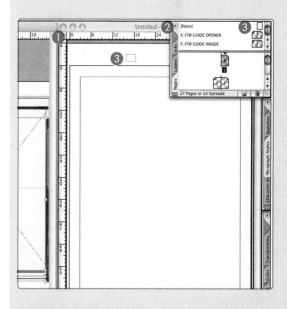

① Open the two documents and make sure that at least portions of both are visible onscreen. (Consider choosing Window ⇨ Arrange ⇨ Tile in InDesign CS and CS2 or Window ⇨ Tile in InDesign 2 to do so.)

② Open the Pages pane by choosing Window ⇨ Pages (F12).

③ Select the master page(s) to copy and drag the page(s) into the window of the other document. InDesign will copy the master pages into the target document, and will make them visible in its Pages pane.

Note that any style sheets, object styles (InDesign CS2), stroke styles (InDesign CS and later), and color and gradient swatches will also transfer to the new document.

✳ Setting Up Templates

A template is fundamentally a document like any other, containing the same kinds of page settings, master pages, style sheets, document preferences, dashes and stripes, colors, and other elements. The only difference is that a template, when opened, opens a copy of the template and requires you to give that copy a name. Thus you don't have to worry about inadvertently changing your master template file as you would if you used a regular document for the same purpose.

Follow These Steps

1 Create a document with the desired standards (style sheets, colors, master pages, folios, placeholder picture and text boxes, etc.).

2 Save the document as a template by choosing File ➪ Save As (Option+⌘+S or Ctrl+Alt+S). In QuarkXPress 6, select Project Template from the Type pop-up menu. In Quark-XPress 5 or earlier, choose Template from the Type pop-up menu.

3 I recommend using the filename extension (.qpt for Quark-XPress 6 and .qxt for QuarkXPress 5 or earlier) as part of the filename to help reinforce the fact that the file is a template.

To later modify a template, open and modify it as you would any document, and then choose File ➪ Save (⌘+S or Ctrl+S), being sure to choose Project Template or Template from the Type pop-up menu. Changes to a template will *not* alter any documents previously created from it.

Keep in Mind

QuarkXPress uses different icons to represent documents and templates. At right are the icons for (from top to bottom) QuarkXPress 6, QuarkXPress 5, and QuarkXPress 4. The left icons are the document icons and the right icons are the template icons.

Follow These Steps

① Create a document with the desired standards (style, swatches, master pages, folios, placeholder picture and text frames, etc.).

② Save the document as a template by choosing File ⇨ Save As (Shift+⌘+S or Ctrl+Shift+S). In InDesign CS and later, select InDesign CS Template from the Format pop-up menu. In InDesign 2, choose InDesign 2.0 Template from the Format pop-up menu.

③ Use the filename extension (.indt) as part of the filename to reinforce the awareness that the file is a template. (InDesign CS or later changes the filename extension for you automatically.)

To later modify a template, open it as you would any document, modify it as you would any document, and then choose File ⇨ Save As (Shift+⌘+S or Ctrl+Shift+S), being sure to choose InDesign CS Template or InDesign 2.0 Template from the Format pop-up menu. Also, note that changes to a template will not alter any documents previously created from it.

⚜ Setting Up Sections

Sections let you create page-numbering divisions within a document so you can change page numbers within a layout, or reset them at each chapter for a book project.

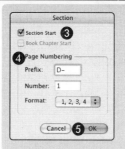

Follow These Steps

1 Go to the page that you want to begin a new section by choosing the page from the Page pop-up menu at the bottom of the screen, by choosing Page ➪ Go To (⌘+J or Ctrl+J) by double-clicking the target page in the Page Layout palette in QuarkXPress 6 (Window ➪ Show Page Layout or F10) or Document Layout palette in QuarkXPress 5 or earlier (View ➪ Show Document Layout or F10).

2 Choose Page ➪ Section to open the Section dialog box.

3 Check the Section Start checkbox to enable a section start. (To undo a section, just uncheck the Section Start checkbox.)

4 Enter the Prefix (if you want one) for the page numbers (such as *D-* for D-1), the starting page number (typically this is 1, but to start on an even (lefthand) page, choose an even number), and the numbering style from the Format pop-up menu.

5 Click OK when done.

6 The Page Layout or Document Layout palette will indicate sections by adding an asterisk next to the page number, as shown at right.

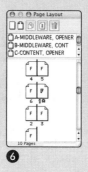

 Cross-Reference: For more on books and multichapter projects, see pages 310-315.

Keep in Mind

If the document is part of a book, checking Section Start via the Section dialog box while working on the first page will override the Book Chapter Start checkbox, in essence preventing the page numbers from being consistent between the previous and the current chapter. In most book-type projects, you want the page numbers to flow consecutively across the chapters, but in some cases, such as manuals or for the first chapter after the roman-numeraled front matter, you may want to reset the page numbering.

Follow These Steps

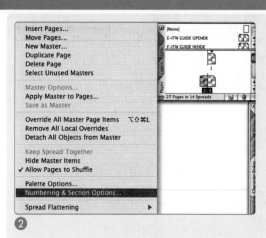

① Go to the page that you want to begin a new section by choosing the page from the Page pop-up menu at the bottom of the screen or by double-clicking the target page in the Pages pane (Window ➪ Pages or F12).

② Choose Numbering & Section Options from the Pages pane's palette menu to open the New Section dialog box.

③ Check the Start Section checkbox to enable a section start. (To undo a section, just uncheck the Section Start checkbox.)

④ Select the Start Page Numbering At radio button and enter a starting page number in the field to its right to reset the page numbering (to start on an even, or lefthand, page, enter an even number). Or leave it set at the default Automatic Page Numbering to continue the previous numbering sequence.

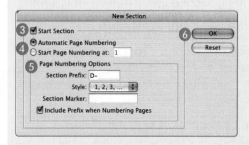

⑤ Choose the numbering style from the Style pop-up menu. Enter a prefix (if you want one) (such as *D-* for D-1) for the page numbering in the Section Prefix field, and a separate prefix (again, only if desired) for display in InDesign's dialog boxes. (You'll also need to check the Include Prefix When Numbering pages checkbox to enable this onscreen numbering for the Pages pop-up menu.)

⑥ Click OK when done.

⑦ The Pages pane will indicate sections by adding a downward triangle above the page icon, as shown at right.

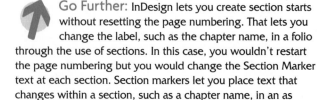 **Go Further:** InDesign lets you create section starts without resetting the page numbering. That lets you change the label, such as the chapter name, in a folio through the use of sections. In this case, you wouldn't restart the page numbering but you would change the Section Marker text at each section. Section markers let you place text that changes within a section, such as a chapter name, in an as many places you want, such as in every folio.

Keep in Mind

If the document is part of a book, you control the numbering options for the chapter from the book pane (Open ➪ Book), choosing Book Page Numbering Options from the palette menu. You then enter the page-numbering specifications in the Book Page Numbering Options dialog box, shown at right. This provides more control than QuarkXPress which, for example, requires that you add any required initial blank pages in each chapter, while inDesign lets you also add them through the book pane.

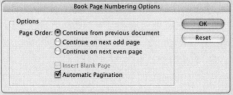

❋ Creating Automatic Page Numbers ◂ QuarkXPress

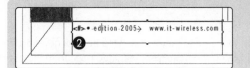

In most documents, stories and other forms of text flow as text changes, pages are added and removed, and so forth. So entering page numbers for current pages or for cross-references would be a nightmare if you had to change all these numbers manually each time something changed. Fortunately, you don't have to — both Quark-XPress and InDesign provide automated page numbering tools that work similarly to each other.

Follow These Steps

QuarkXPress provides keyboard shortcuts for current-page, next-page, and previous-page automatic numbering.

Page Numbers for Folios

For current page numbers, such as for use in folios:

❶ Using the Content tool, place the text-insertion cursor wherever you want the current page number to be displayed.

❷ Type ⌘+3 or Ctrl+3. On a master page, you will see <#> as the text; in a document page, you will see the actual page number.

Page Numbers in Continued Lines

For continued-on lines, such as *continued on page x* and *continued from page y*, the process is a little more involved:

❶ Create separate text boxes for the *continued on* and *continued from* text.

❷ Link them with the Link tool.

❸ Switch to the Content tool, then enter your text, such as **continued on**, and format as desired.

❹ Enter ⌘+2 or Ctrl+2 to have QuarkXPress insert the previous text frame's page number and ⌘+4 or Ctrl+4 to insert the next text frame's page number. (This is why the frames must be linked, so QuarkXPress knows what page numbers to insert.)

Note that there is no way to insert cross-references to specific text on other pages, such as for *see page x for more details* text.

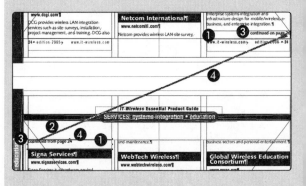

Follow These Steps

InDesign provides a keyboard shortcut only for current-page references. For next-page and previous-page automatic numbers, you must use menu commands.

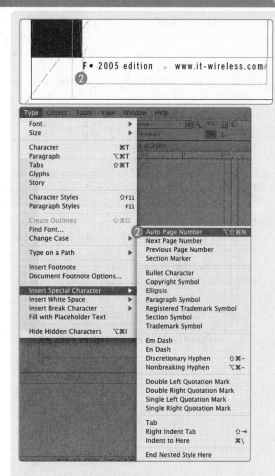

Page Numbers for Folios

For current page numbers:

1. Using the Type tool, place the text-insertion cursor wherever you want the current page number to be displayed.

2. Choose Type ⇨ Insert Special Character ⇨ Auto Page Number or press Option+Shift+⌘+N or Ctrl+Alt+Shift+N. On a master page, you will see a letter corresponding to the master page's label as the text (*F* in the screenshot at right); in a document page, you will see the actual page number.

 Go Further: InDesign also lets you insert the section marker (choose Type ⇨ Insert Special Character ⇨ Section Marker) into text, which places whatever section-marker text you defined in the current section (see page 34). This is a handy way to insert chapter titles and so forth in folios.

Page Numbers in Continued Lines

For continued-on lines, such as *continued on page x* and *continued from page y*, the process is a little more involved:

1. Create separate text frames for the *continued on* and *continued from* text.

2. Link them by clicking on the first frame's out port and then clicking the resulting paragraph-icon text-flow tool within the second frame.

3. Enter your text, such as **continued on**, and format as desired.

4. Choose Type ⇨ Insert Special Character ⇨ Previous Page Number to have InDesign insert the previous text frame's page number, and choose Type ⇨ Insert Special Character ⇨ Next Page Number to insert the next text frame's page number. (This is why the frames must be linked, so InDesign knows what page numbers to insert.) Sorry, there are no keyboard shortcuts for these special characters, but you can define your own by choosing Edit ⇨ Keyboard Shortcuts.

Note that there is no way to insert cross-references to specific text on other pages, such as for *see page x for more details* text.

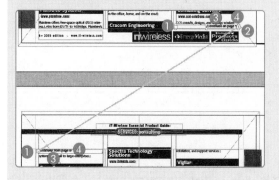

✸Creating Gatefold Spreads

Some documents, such as typical brochures and foldouts, use wider paper for certain pages that are then folded into the document. One use would be to deliver a fold-out poster or map in a travel magazine, for example. This type of spread is called a gatefold, a foldout, or an island, depending who you talk to.

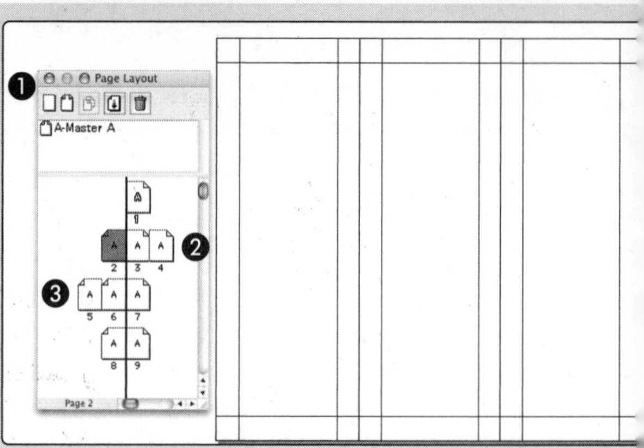

Follow These Steps

To create gatefolds in QuarkXPress:

❶ Open the Page Layout palette in QuarkXPress 6 (Window ➪ Page Layout or F10) or the Document Layout in Quark-XPress 5 or earlier (View ➪ Show Document Layout or F10).

❷ Choose the appropriate master page to use as the basis for the gatefold pages. Then drag the master page to the bottom part of the pane, creating document pages based on it. For the pages that fold out, drag an additional master page next to an existing page to create the folded-out portion.

❸ If your document is two-sided, be sure to have the same number of pages on the opposite side of the next spread.

Keep in Mind

QuarkXPress 6 offers the ability have layouts of multiple page sizes in one file, called a *project*. But you cannot really use this feature to create foldouts. That's because the separate layouts in a QuarkXPress 6 project cannot have text flow among them, so you can't insert, for example, a foldout-sized page from Layout 2 between smaller pages in Layout 1.

InDesign

Follow These Steps

InDesign's process is similar to QuarkXPress, except you must tell InDesign not to shuffle pages for it to work.

① Open the Pages pane (Window ⇨ Pages or F12).

② Choose the appropriate master page to use as the basis for the gatefold pages. Then drag the master page to the bottom part of the pane, creating document pages based on it.

③ Select the document spreads (or single document pages if you're working in a single-sided document) that will have the foldouts, and then choose Keep Spread Together from the Pages pane's palette menu. Brackets will appear around the page numbers for the selected pages in the Pages pane.

④ For the pages that fold out, you can now drag one or more additional master pages next to an existing page to create the folded-out portion. (If you do not do step 3, a step not required by QuarkXPress, InDesign will not let the gatefold pages attach next to existing pages.)

⑤ If your document is two-sided, be sure to have the same number of pages on the opposite side of the next spread.

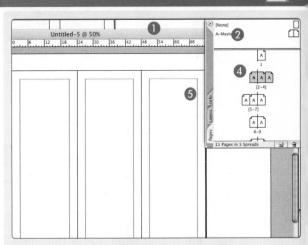

Keep in Mind

The very first version of InDesign introduced the term *island spread* to indicate a gatefold page (so what is now Keep Spreads Together used to be called Create Island Spread). Although the software's interface dropped the term after version 1.5, the terminology has stuck among parts of the InDesign community.

Shuffling Pages

As your layout changes, you may need to move pages around. QuarkXPress and InDesign both provide multiple ways to do this.

Follow These Steps

QuarkXPress offers several ways to rearrange pages in your document. Use any of the following three approaches:

❶ Open the Page Layout palette in QuarkXPress 6 (Window ➪ Page Layout or F10) or the Document Layout palette (View ➪ Show Document Layout or F10). Then drag the page icon for the page you want to move to a new location.

❷ Change the view to Thumbnails (View ➪ Thumbnails, or enter **T** in the View percentage field at the bottom the screen). Then drag the actual page to a new location.

❸ Choose Page ➪ Move to open the Move Pages dialog box. Enter the number(s) of the page(s) you want to move and then specify where you want to move them.

Whichever approach you use, the other pages will reshuffle themselves accordingly. Note that moving pages around could affect their layout, as master-page items are reapplied from, for example, lefthand pages converted to righthand pages. Be sure to review all pages affected by reshuffling.

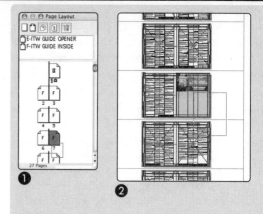

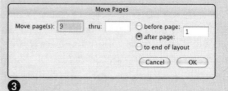

Cross-Reference: For more on applying master pages, see page 28.

Follow These Steps

InDesign offers fewer ways than QuarkXPress to rearrange pages in your document. Use the first option in InDesign 2 or CS; use either option in InDesign CS2.

① Open the Pages pane (Window ⇨ Pages or F12). Then drag the page icon for the page you want to move to a new location.

② In InDesign CS2, choose Layout ⇨ Pages ⇨ Move Pages to open the Move Pages dialog box. Enter the number(s) of the page(s) you want to move and then specify where you want to move them.

Go Further: The other pages will reshuffle themselves accordingly — except for pages that you've previously selected and for which you have chosen Keep Spread Together in the Pages pane's palette menu. If applied to a spread, this command assures that the spread is kept intact if other pages are moved.

Watch Out: However, the use of Keep Spreads Together could result in a situation where, to keep a spread together, InDesign will have to skip a page in another spread. Be sure to review the page arrangements in the Pages pane to make sure all spreads have pages, moving additional pages as necessary. Also note that moving pages around could affect their layout, as master-page items are reapplied from, for example, lefthand pages converted to righthand pages. Be sure to review all pages affected by reshuffling.

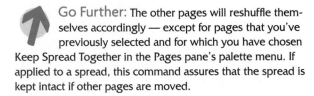

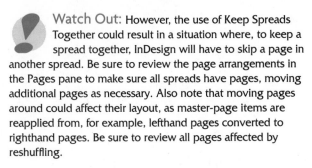

①

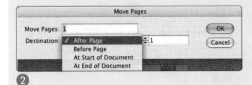

②

Working with Layers

Layers let you separate items into distinct groups. They're often used to hold nonprinting items, such as layout specifications, so they can be viewed and hidden as needed while not affecting output. They're also handy for multiple-language documents, where there is a separate layer for each language's text boxes. Finally, layers are useful in complex layouts that have many overlapping elements, letting you hide groups of elements until you need to work on them.

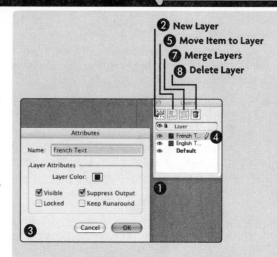

2 New Layer
5 Move Item to Layer
7 Merge Layers
8 Delete Layer

Follow These Steps

Note that layers are not available in QuarkXPress 4 or earlier.

1 Open the Layers palette by choosing Window ➪ Show Layers in QuarkXPress 6 or by choosing View ➪ Show Layers in QuarkXPress 5.

2 Click the New Layer button to create a new layer.

3 Double-click a layer's name to open the Attributes dialog box. Here, you control whether a layer prints (the Suppress Output checkbox) and whether text on other layers will still wrap around items in this layer when this layer is hidden (the Keep Runaround checkbox). Both options have significant effects on your actual output. You can also change the layer name and color in this dialog box, as well as make a layer visible or locked. But you don't have to open this dialog box to show/hide a layer or lock/unlock it: Just click the eye and lock icons in the Layers palette to toggle these two settings.

4 Items are automatically placed on the active layer, which is indicated by the pencil icon in the Layers palette. You can change active layers by simply clicking the desired layer.

5 To move an item to a different layer, select that item with the Item tool, then select the desired layer in the Layers palette. (You can select multiple items to move them all at once.) Now click the Move Item to Layer button. (Selected objects will display a layer icon in their upper right corners that shows the color of the layer they are on.)

6 To change the order of layers (which changes the stacking order of objects in the document but retains the relative stacking order within each layer), drag a layer above or below another in the Layers palette.

7 To merge several layers, select them all in the Layers palette (Shift+click the first and last to select a range; ⌘+click or Ctrl+click to select noncontiguous layers) and the click the Merge Layers button.

8 Delete layers by selecting them in the Layers palette and clicking the Delete Layers button.

Keep in Mind

In QuarkXPress 6, you can determine which layers print, no matter their setting in the Layout palette's Attributes dialog box, by using the Layers pane of the Print dialog box (File ➪ Print, or ⌘+P or Ctrl+P).

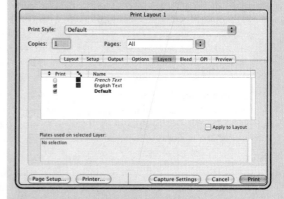

InDesign

Follow These Steps

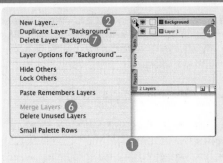

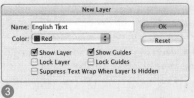

Layers in InDesign work almost the same way as layers in QuarkXPress, although InDesign offers less control over printing hidden layers.

1. Open the Layers pane by choosing Window ➪ Layers (F7).

2. Choose New Layer in the Layers pane's palette menu to create a new layer.

3. In the New Layer dialog box (or later in the identical Layers Options dialog box accessed by selecting a layer in the Layers pane and then choosing Layer Options in the palette menu), you control whether a layer displays (the Show Layer checkbox) and whether text on other layers will still wrap around items in this layer when this layer is hidden (the Suppress Text Wrap When Layer Is Hidden checkbox, not available in InDesign 2). You can also change the layer name and color in this dialog box, as well as make a layer locked. But you don't have to open this dialog box to show/hide or lock/unlock a layer: Just click the eye and crossed-out pencil icons in the Layers pane to toggle these two settings.

4. Items are automatically placed on the active layer, which is indicated by the pen icon in the Layers pane. You can change active layers by simply clicking the desired layer.

5. To change the order of layers (which changes the stacking order of objects in the document but retains the relative stacking order within each layer), drag a layer above or below another in the Layers pane.

6. To merge several layers, select them all in the Layers pane (Shift+click the first and last to select a range; ⌘+click or Ctrl+click to select noncontiguous layers) and the choose Merge Layers in the palette menu.

7. Delete layers by selecting them in the Layers pane and choosing the Delete Layer in the palette menu.

8. To move objects from one layer to another, first select the objects. Notice how a small square appears to the right of objects' layer name in the Layers pane. (All selected objects must be on the same layer for this to work. The frames of selected objects will display in the color of their layer.) Now just drag that square to another layer in the pane. That moves the selected objects to that other layer.

    To move objects from multiple layers to a new layer, select them with the Selection tool, then cut them. Now select the desired layer in the Layers pane, and paste-in-place (Edit ➪ Paste in Place, or Option+Shift+⌘+V or Ctrl+Alt+Shift+V) the objects into the new layer.

9. To prevent objects from being moved to other layers when you paste them, select Paste Remembers Layers in the Layers pane's palette menu.

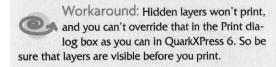

Workaround: Hidden layers won't print, and you can't override that in the Print dialog box as you can in QuarkXPress 6. So be sure that layers are visible before you print.

Setting Up Libraries

Using libraries is a great way to keep commonly accessible items available, so they don't clog up your pasteboard and so they are available for use in multiple documents, even by multiple users.

Follow These Steps

1 Create a library by choosing File ⇨ New ⇨ Library (Option+⌘+N or Ctrl+Alt+N). You'll get the New Library dialog box, where you give the library a name and decide what folder to save it in. Then click Create, and an empty library palette will appear. (By default, the library is one column wide, but you can resize it as desired to make it as wide and as deep as you prefer; the wider the library palette, the more columns it will display.)

2 Drag items to the library palette to add them to the library. Items will be placed wherever you drag them — QuarkXPress does not alphabetize or otherwise automatically sort them for you.

3 To replace an item, you must first delete it from the library and add back the revised item.

4 To delete a library item, click it in the library and press Delete or Backspace. You will be asked to confirm the deletion.

5 To save a library, close it (or quit QuarkXPress). You can make QuarkXPress automatically save a library as items are added by checking Auto Library Save in the General pane of the QuarkXPress 6 Preferences dialog box (QuarkXPress ⇨ Preferences on the Mac, Edit ⇨ Preferences in Windows), in the Save pane of the QuarkXPress 5 dialog box (Edit ⇨ Preferences ⇨ Preferences), or in the Save pane of the QuarkXPress 4 Application Preferences dialog box (Edit ⇨ Preferences ⇨ Application). All three versions use the same shortcut: Option+Shift+⌘+Y or Ctrl+Alt+Shift+Y.

6 To open a library, simply select it in the Open dialog box (File ⇨ Open, or ⌘+O or Ctrl+O). You can have multiple libraries open. And if a library happens to be open when you close a document, that library will reopen automatically when you next open that document. Note that although libraries can be opened by multiple users, only one user can open a specific library at a time. Finally, Windows users cannot open Macintosh libraries, nor can Macintosh users open Windows libraries.

7 To use a library item, just drag it into your layout; QuarkXPress will place a copy wherever you release the mouse.

 Cross-Reference: See pages 46-47 for details on searching within libraries.

Follow These Steps

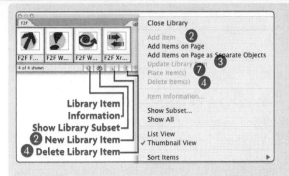

**Library Item
Information**
Show Library Subset
2 New Library Item
4 Delete Library Item

❶ Create a library by choosing File ➪ New ➪ Library. You'll get the New Library dialog box, where you give the library a name and decide what folder to save it in. (Libraries have the filename extension .indl, which InDesign CS or later automatically adds to the library name.) Then click Save, and an empty library palette will appear. (By default, the library is one row deep, but you can resize it as desired to make it as wide and as deep as you prefer; the deeper the library palette, the more rows it will display.)

❷ Drag objects to the library palette to add them to the library. (You can also select objects and place them in the library by clicking the New Library item button in the library palette or by choosing Add Item in the library's palette menu.) Objects will be placed wherever you drag them and have a default name of Untitled.

❸ To replace an item in InDesign CS or earlier, you must first delete it from the library and add back the revised item. In InDesign CS2, you can also replace an existing library item by clicking it in the library palette, then clicking the new object in your document, and choosing Update Library Item in the library's palette menu.

❹ To delete a library item, click it in the library and choose Delete Item(s) from the palette menu.

❺ InDesign automatically saves libraries as you add and change items.

❻ To open a library, simply select it in the Open a File dialog box (File ➪ Open, or ⌘+O or Ctrl+O). You can have multiple libraries open. And if a library happens to be open when you close a document, that library will reopen automatically when you next open that document.

❼ To use a library item, just drag it into your layout; InDesign will place a copy wherever you release the mouse. Or click the item in the library and choose Place Item(s) from the palette menu; InDesign will copy the item to the current page.

Go Further: When libraries are opened by multiple users, only one user at a time can open a specific library unless you lock the file in the General Information dialog box (⌘+I) on the Mac or in the Properties dialog box in Windows (right-click the file and choose Properties from the contextual menu). Then anyone can use the objects but no one can add new objects until the library is unlocked.

Go Further: InDesign libraries can be opened by both Macintosh and Windows users.

Go Further: In InDesign 2 and CS, you can add all items on a page to a library by choosing Add All Items on Page from the library's palette menu. In InDesign CS2, you can choose Add All Items on Page to make the entire page a library item, or you can choose Add All Items on Page as Separate Objects to make each a separate library item.

⁂ Searching Library Contents

Large libraries can be difficult to navigate, so both Quark-XPress and InDesign provide some facility for narrowing down your choices. InDesign offers a more capable approach to this than does QuarkXPress.

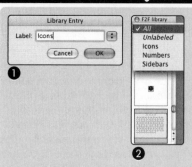

Follow These Steps

If you have many items in a library, it can be unwieldy to scroll through all of them when searching for one item.

❶ If you want to label items so you can later display just those with specific labels, double-click the library item and enter the label in the Library Entry dialog box. You can also choose from previously defined labels using the pop-up menu. Click OK when done.

❷ To display just items with a specific label, use the library palette's pop-up menu to select items with a specific label, those with no labels, or all items.

Cross-Reference: See pages **44-45** for details on creating and using libraries.

InDesign

Follow These Steps

InDesign provides more options for searching library contents than does QuarkXPress.

① If you want to label items so you can later search based on those labels, double-click the library item and enter the label (and, if you prefer, a description) in the Item Information dialog box. Click OK when done. You can also click an object in the library and click the Library Item Information button or choose Item Information from the palette menu.

② To display just items with a specific label, description text, creation date, or object type, use the Subset dialog box (choose Show Subset from the library pane's pop-up menu or click the Show Library Subset button).

③ You can also sort library items (by name, type, and creation date) by choosing Sort Items from the palette menu.

④ InDesign also lets you choose between the default Thumbnail view and the List view through options in the library's palette menu.

Go Further: InDesign's ability to search labels and descriptions, as well as its multiple library palette views and ability to sort items, provides more sophisticated library-item management than does QuarkXPress.

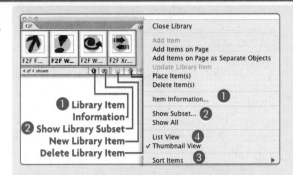

① Library Item Information
② Show Library Subset
New Library Item
Delete Library Item

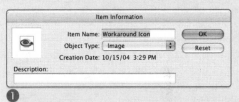

①

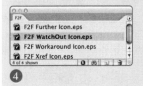

②

F2F Further Icon.eps
F2F WatchOut Icon.eps
F2F Workaround Icon.eps
F2F Xref Icon.eps
4 of 4 shown

④

☼ Copying Objects among Documents ‹ QuarkXPress

Copying objects within documents is easy — you use the standard copy and paste functions — but copying objects among documents raises issues of their associated attributes. Both QuarkXPress and InDesign keep those associated attributes and provide several methods for copying the objects themselves.

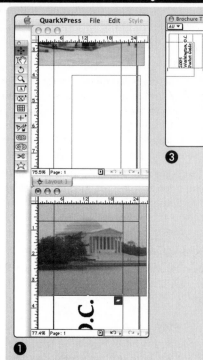

③

①

Follow These Steps

It's easy to move items among documents. QuarkXPress gives you several options.

① The simplest way is to open the source and target documents, and arrange them onscreen so the items you want to move are visible in the source document and so at least some of the target document(s) are visible. Then just drag the items from the source to the target document(s). Note that items must be unlocked before you can drag them to another document.

② Alternatively, open the source and target documents, copy the items from the source document, and paste them to the target document(s). (This can be easier than dragging the items because it makes the screen less cluttered.) In Quark-XPress 6, you can paste them to the same location by choosing Edit ⇨ Paste in Place (Option+Shift+⌘+V or Ctrl+Alt+Shift+V).

③ Move items to a library and then drag them from the library to the target document. This is most effective when someone else is working on the target document.

No matter which method you use, any associated colors, style sheets, H&J sets, etc. are also transferred to the target document. Items can be copied to document pages or master pages.

Also, no matter which method you choose, the item remains in the source document. If you want to move the item rather than copy it, you'll have to delete the original item after copying it to the target document — or just use cut-and-paste instead of copy-and-paste.

Cross-Reference: See pages 26-29 for more on master pages and pages 44-47 for more on libraries.

Follow These Steps

InDesign also gives you several options.

① The simplest way is to open the source and target documents, and arrange them onscreen so the objects you want to move are visible in the source document and so at least some of the target document(s) is visible. Then just drag the objects from the source to the target document(s). Note that objects must be unlocked before you can drag them to another document.

② Alternatively, open the source and target documents, copy the objects from the source document, and paste them into the target document(s). (This can be easier than dragging the objects because it makes the screen less cluttered.) You can paste them to the same location by choosing Edit ⇨ Paste in Place (Option+Shift+⌘+V or Ctrl+Alt+Shift+V).

③ Move objects to a library and then drag them from the library to the target document. This method is most effective when someone else is working on the target document.

④ In InDesign CS2, you can drag objects to the desktop, which creates XML snippets that you can then drag into other InDesign CS2 documents. This has the same advantages as a library in that it lets another user access the object(s).

No matter which method you use, any associated swatches, styles, and so on are also transferred to the target document. Objects can be copied to document pages or master pages.

Also, no matter which method you choose, the object remains in the source document. If you want to move the object rather than copy it, you'll have to delete the original object after copying it to the target document — or just use cut-and-paste instead of copy-and-paste.

 Go Further: InDesign CS2's support for XML snippets is a handy way to share individual elements with users of InDesign CS2 and other XML-compatible programs.

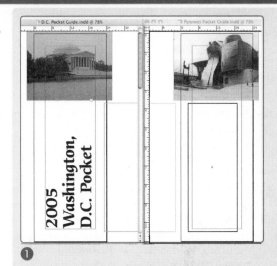
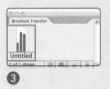

✸ Working with Individual Guides   ◀ QuarkXPress

Guides are a handy way to ensure item alignment in your document.

Follow These Steps

In QuarkXPress:

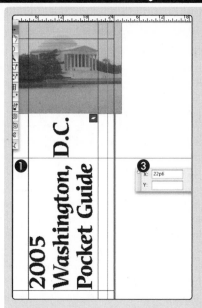

① Create individual ruler guides by dragging them from one of the rulers onto the document or master page.

② The default color is green, although you can change this ruler guide color using the Guide Colors options in the Display pane of the QuarkXPress 5 and 6 Preferences dialog box and in the QuarkXPress 4 Applications Preferences dialog box. You also can choose to have ruler guides appear in front of or behind layout objects in the General pane. (In QuarkXPress 6, choose QuarkXPress ⇨ Preferences on the Mac or Edit ⇨ Preferences in Windows; in QuarkXPress 5, choose Edit ⇨ Preferences ⇨ Preferences; and in QuarkXPress 4, choose Edit ⇨ Preferences ⇨ Application. All three versions use the same shortcut: Option+Shift+⌘+Y or Ctrl+Alt+Shift+Y.)

③ Reposition guides by dragging them. Watch the Measurements palette to see what the X and Y positions are, to help ensure they are placed precisely where you want if you are using the guides to align objects. You can't enter coordinates for guides in the Measurements palette, but you can see the coordinates change as you drag them. Be sure to zoom in if you need to drag the guide in finer increments. Note that you cannot undo the repositioning of a ruler guide, so be careful not to move guides accidentally when trying to select other objects.

④ Delete guides by dragging them past the rulers.

⑤ Show and hide guides by choosing View ⇨ Hide Guides or View ⇨ Show Guides or pressing F7.

⑥ To have items snap to guides, choose View ⇨ Snap to Guides or press Shift+F7. Set the snap threshold — how far an object needs to be from a guide before it snaps to that guide — using the Snap Distance field in the General pane of the Preferences dialog box. See step 1 for the menu sequences and shortcuts.

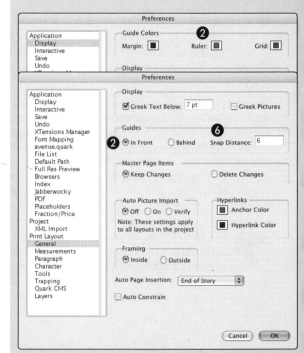

Cross-Reference: You can also create automatic guides, as covered on pages 52-51.

Follow These Steps

In InDesign:

❶ Create individual ruler guides by dragging them from one of the rulers onto the document or master page.

❷ The ruler guide color is cyan, which you cannot change in InDesign. But you can choose to have ruler guides appear in front of or behind layout objects in the Guides & Pasteboard pane of the Preferences dialog box (InDesign ➪ Preferences or ⌘+K on the Mac, or Edit ➪ Preferences or Ctrl+K in Windows).

❸ Reposition guides by dragging them. Watch the Transform pane, or the Control palette in InDesign CS and later, to see what the X and Y positions are, to help ensure they are placed precisely where you want if you are using the guides to align objects. (Or you can just enter coordinates for guides in the Control palette or Transform pane.) The selected guide will be a light version of the layer color (light blue for the default layer) to distinguish it from other ruler guides.

❹ Delete guides by dragging them past the rulers.

❺ To prevent accidental repositioning of guides, you can lock them. Choose View ➪ Grids & Guides ➪ Lock in InDesign CS2 and View ➪ Lock Guides in InDesign CS or earlier, or press Option+⌘+; or Alt+;. Be sure the menu option is checked to have the guides locked.

❻ Show and hide guides by choosing View ➪ Grids & Guides ➪ Show/Hide Guides in InDesign CS2 and View ➪ Show/Hide Guides in earlier versions, or by pressing ⌘+; or Ctrl+;.

❼ To have items snap to guides, choose View ➪ Grids & Guides ➪ Snap to Guides in InDesign CS2 and View ➪ Snap to Guides in InDesign CS or earlier, or press Shift+⌘+; or Ctrl+Shift+;. Be sure the menu option is checked to have objects snap to the guides. Set the snap threshold — how far an object needs to be from a guide before it snaps to that guide — using the Snap to Zone field in the Guides & Pasteboard pane of the Preferences dialog box (InDesign ➪ Preferences or ⌘+K on the Mac, or Edit ➪ Preferences or Ctrl+K in Windows).

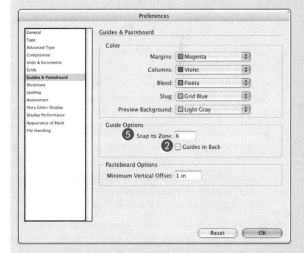

Go Further: InDesign lets you lock guides so they can't be moved accidentally. You can also precisely position them with the Control palette or Transform pane. InDesign CS2 also lets you lock column guides separately from other ruler guides (View ➪ Grids & Guides ➪ Lock Column Guides).

✺ Creating Automatic Guides

QuarkXPress

Many layouts use a grid — a series of gridlines that objects must fit within and align to. Automatic guides — baseline and custom — are a good way to create that grid.

Follow These Steps

In QuarkXPress, first decide what type(s) of guides you want.

Baseline Grids

Baseline grids are meant to ensure proper text alignment; in the Format pane of a style sheet (Edit ➪ Style Sheets or Shift+F11), you can specify that a specific style's text aligns to the baseline grid, overriding any other leading, a technique often used on headlines to ensure they don't cause the rest of the column to have different depth than surrounding columns.

❶ Set the start position and the grid increment in the Paragraph pane of the Preferences dialog box. (In QuarkXPress 6, choose QuarkXPress ➪ Preferences on the Mac or Edit ➪ Preferences in Windows; in QuarkXPress 5, choose Edit ➪ Preferences ➪ Preferences; and in QuarkXPress 4, choose Edit ➪ Preferences ➪ Document. QuarkXPress 5 and 6 use the same shortcut, Option+Shift+⌘+Y or Ctrl+Alt+Shift+Y, while QuarkXPress 4 uses ⌘+Y or Ctrl+Y.) You can also change the baseline grid's color, as explained in step 1 on page 50.

❷ Turn on the baseline grid by choosing View ➪ Show Baseline Grid (Option+F7 or Alt+F7). Turn it off by choosing View ➪ Hide Baseline Grid (Option+F7 or Alt+F7).

Custom Grids

You can also create your own grids using the Guide Manager:

❶ Open the Guide Manager dialog box by choosing Utilities ➪ Guide Manager.

❷ In the Add Guides pane, select the guide direction(s), location, spacing, number of guides (if unchecked, QuarkXPress will fill out the page or spread), and origin and boundaries. Check the Locked Guides checkbox to lock the guides so they cannot be accidentally moved. Click the Add Guides button and then click OK to add the guides.

❸ To remove custom guides after clicking Add Guides, go to the Remove or Lock Guides pane. Choose which guides to remove based on location, direction, and lock status, then click the Remove Guides. Click OK to exit the dialog box.

❹ Similarly, use the Remove or Lock Guides pane to lock or unlock custom guides. Choose which location and direction of guides you want to lock or unlock, then click Lock Guides or Unlock Guides, as appropriate. Click OK to exit the dialog box.

❺ You can also change the custom grid's color, as explained in step 2 on page 50.

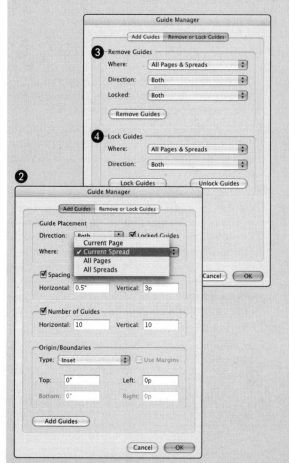

Follow These Steps

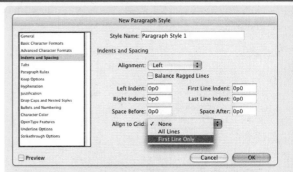

InDesign also provides two kinds of automatic guides: baseline grids and document grids, the latter of which take a different approach from the custom grids of QuarkXPress.

Baseline Grids

Baseline grids are meant to ensure proper text alignment; in the Indent and Spacing pane of a paragraph style sheet (Window ⇨ Type & Tables ⇨ Paragraph Styles in InDesign CS and later, Window ⇨ Type ⇨ Paragraph Styles in InDesign 2, or F11), you can specify that a specific style's text (or, unlike QuarkXPress, just the first line) aligns to the baseline grid, overriding any other leading, a technique often used on headlines to ensure they don't cause the rest of the column to have different depth than surrounding columns.

❶ Set the start position and the grid increment in the Grids pane of the Preferences dialog box (InDesign ⇨ Preferences or ⌘+K on the Mac or Edit ⇨ Preferences or Ctrl+K in Windows). You can also change the baseline grid's color in this pane.

❷ Turn on the baseline grid by choosing View ⇨ Grids & Guides ⇨ Show Baseline Grid in InDesign CS2 and View ⇨ Show Baseline Grid in earlier versions, or by pressing Option+⌘+' or Ctrl+Alt+'). To hide the baseline grids, use the same menu commands (the word *Show* will have changed to *Hide*) or the same shortcut.

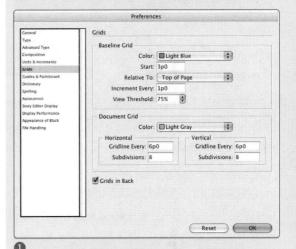

Go Further: InDesign CS2 lets you set separate baseline grids for your text frames, as shown in the bottom screenshot at right.

Document Grids

You can also set documentwide grids:

❶ Set the start position and the grid increment in the Grids pane of the Preferences dialog box (InDesign ⇨ Preferences or ⌘+K on the Mac or Edit ⇨ Preferences or Ctrl+K in Windows). You can also change the baseline grid's color in this pane.

❷ Turn on the document grid by choosing View ⇨ Grids & Guides ⇨ Show Document Grid in InDesign CS2 and View ⇨ Show Document Grid in earlier versions, or by pressing ⌘+' or Ctrl+'). To hide the grid, use the same menu commands (the word *Show* will have changed to *Hide*) or the same shortcut.

Workaround: To simulate the custom grids of QuarkXPress, select a ruler guide (see page 51) and duplicate it by choosing Edit ⇨ Step and Repeat (Option+⌘+U or Ctrl+Alt+U in InDesign CS2 and Option+⌘+V or Ctrl+Alt+V in earlier versions).

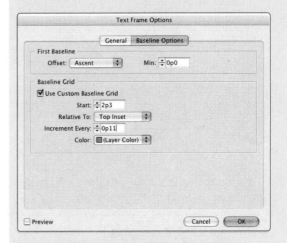

part iii

Working with Colors

This section shows how to import, create, and apply colors, as well as gradient fills and shades (tints). While the underlying techniques are similar in some respects — you define colors that you can then apply again and again, like style sheets — InDesign takes that approach and extends it to gradients and shades, while QuarkXPress requires you to apply those settings manually each time you use them.

But InDesign also lets you apply colors in a way that can result in problematic output files, so it's important to understand the differences between the approaches of the two programs.

☀Creating Colors

To use colors, you must first define them. QuarkXPress and InDesign both let you create color swatches that ensure consistent colors across all objects to which they are applied, while InDesign also provides a more freeform approach — similar to Photoshop's and Illustrator's — that poses issues when printing.

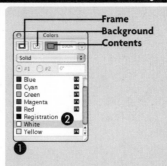

Follow These Steps

To create colors in QuarkXPress:

❶ Open the Colors palette (Window ➪ Show Colors in Quark-XPress 6 and View ➪ Show Colors in earlier versions, or F12.)

❷ In the Colors palette, ⌘+click or Ctrl+click an existing color.

❸ In the resulting Colors dialog box, click the New button.

❹ In the Edit Color dialog box, select the color model (CMYK is shown here) and use either the color wheel or list of swatches, depending on the selected color model, to define the desired color. If you want the color to print on its own plate, check the Spot Color checkbox.

❺ When done, click OK to complete the color definition.

You can continue to add colors; when done, click Save to save all new and changed colors. The Colors dialog box will close and the new colors will then appear in the Colors palette.

When applying colors, be sure to first click the Frame, Content, or Background buttons in the Colors palette so Quark-XPress knows what part of the object you want colored. Then click the object and the desired color.

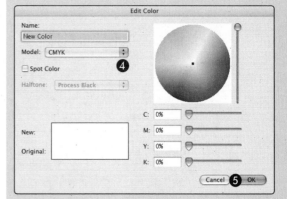

InDesign

Follow These Steps

To create colors in InDesign:

① Open the Swatches pane by choosing Window ➪ Swatches or pressing F5.

② Select New Color Swatch from the palette menu.

③ In the New Color Swatch dialog box, select the color model from the Color Model pop-up menu (CMYK is shown here) and use either the color sliders or list of swatches, depending on the selected color model, to define the desired color. If you want the color to print on its own plate, choose Spot from the Color Type pop-up menu.

④ When done, click OK to complete the color definition and close the dialog box, or click Add to add another color.

When applying colors, first click the object, and then click the Fill or Stroke button on the Tools palette, depending on what you want to color. Then click the desired color in the Swatches pane.

Watch Out: Never use the InDesign Color pane to define colors. (It works like Photoshop's Color pane.) Colors created this way are not named, so they are not seen by InDesign when you output color separations. In InDesign CS and later, the Color pane's palette menu does have an Add to Swatches menu item, but it's easy to forget to use it.

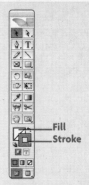

— Fill
— Stroke

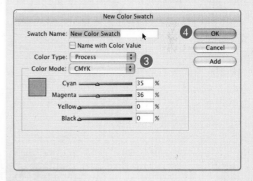

Creating Gradients

Gradients, called *blends* in QuarkXPress, provide gradual transitions between colors. QuarkXPress lets you create blends composed of two colors, while InDesign lets you use an unlimited number of colors in its gradients. InDesign also lets you save gradients as color swatches, while in QuarkXPress each blend is applied individually.

Follow These Steps

To create blends in QuarkXPress:

① Open the Colors palette (Window ➪ Show Colors in Quark-XPress 6 and View ➪ Show Colors in earlier versions, or F12).

② After selecting the object to which you will apply the blend and then and clicking the Frame, Content, or Background button, choose one of the six types of blends in the Gradient menu.

③ Click the #1 radio button and then select a start color from the Colors palette.

④ Click the #2 radio button and the select an end color from the Colors palette.

⑤ If you want the blend to be tilted (for a linear blend), enter a rotation angle to the right of the #2 radio button. For circular blends, entering an angle alters the blend's radius, with a larger number making the start color take more of the blend's radius.

①

②

> **InDesign**

Follow These Steps

To create gradients in InDesign:

① Open the Swatches pane by choosing Window ➪ Swatches, or pressing F5.

② Select New Gradient Swatch from the palette menu.

③ In the Gradient Options dialog box, select gradient type from the Type pop-up menu.

④ In the Gradient Ramp, double-click on the ramp to create a stop point — where colors change. (Unlike in QuarkXPress, you can have multiple stop points.) Click the color square for the stop point.

⑤ Choose the color model in the Stop Color pop-up menu, then select the desired color from the swatches or color wheel, as appropriate for the selected color model.

⑥ Repeat steps 4 and 5 for each stop point.

⑦ Slide the diamond icons to change the relative proportion of each color gradient. You can also enter a value in the Location field.

⑧ Click OK when done. The gradient will appear as a swatch in the Swatches pane.

You apply gradients just like you do color swatches.

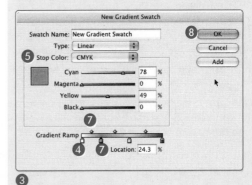

Keep in Mind

InDesign's Fill button corresponds to the QuarkXPress Background and Content buttons, depending on what type of object is selected; the Stroke button corresponds to the QuarkXPress Frame button, though it also affects text outlines as well as box outlines. Choosing a fill gradient with the Direct Selection tool for a black-and-white or grayscale graphic using the regular Selection tool will color the box's background. You cannot apply a gradient to a color graphic.

✳ Importing Colors from Graphics ◀ QuarkXPress

Creating colors in your layout program is necessary but insufficient. Imported vector graphics may have their own colors defined within them; both QuarkXPress and InDesign let you import and modify these colors.

Follow These Steps

QuarkXPress will automatically import color plates (spot colors) defined in EPS files. (In other formats, colors are converted to their RGB or CMYK equivalents.) The colors are automatically imported when you import a graphic, as follows:

1️⃣ Select or create the picture box to contain the graphic.

2️⃣ Choose File ➪ Get Picture, or press ⌘+E or Ctrl+E, to open the Get Picture dialog box. Navigate to the appropriate folder and file, click it, then click OK.

3️⃣ QuarkXPress will place the graphic in the selected picture box, and will automatically add any spot colors to the Colors palette. You can now use those colors on any object.

Converting Spot Colors to Process Colors

You can convert imported spot colors to process (CMYK) colors by editing them in the Colors palette as follows:

1️⃣ ⌘+click or Ctrl+click the color in the Colors palette (Window ➪ Show Colors in QuarkXPress 6 and View ➪ Show Colors in QuarkXPress 5 and earlier, or F12).

2️⃣ When the Colors dialog box appears, click the Edit button. (To work on a duplicate color swatch, click Duplicate instead. This is handy if you want both a process-color and a spot-color swatch of the same color in your document.)

3️⃣ In the Edit Color dialog box, uncheck the Spot Color checkbox, then click OK.

4️⃣ Click Save in the Colors dialog box. In the Colors palette, the icon to the right of the color name will have changed from the spot-color icon to the process-color icon.

Imported spot-color swatch
Spot-color icon
Process-color icon

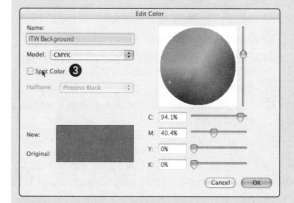

 Cross-Reference: See page 56 for more information on creating and editing colors.

InDesign

Follow These Steps

Like QuarkXPress, InDesign will automatically import color plates (spot colors) defined in EPS files, plus those from Illustrator and PDF files. (In other formats, colors are converted to their RGB or CMYK equivalents.) The colors are automatically imported when you import a graphic, as follows:

① Choose File ⇨ Place, or press ⌘+D or Ctrl+D, to open the Place dialog box. Navigate to the appropriate folder and file, click it, then click OK.

② InDesign will place the graphic wherever you click (or in the selected frame, if you have selected one), and it will automatically add any spot colors to the Swatches pane. You can now use those colors on any object.

Converting Spot Colors to Process Colors

You can convert imported spot colors to process (CMYK) colors by editing them in the Swatches pane as follows:

① Select the color in the Swatches pane (Window ⇨ Swatches or F5).

② Select Swatch Options in the pane's palette menu. (To work on a duplicate color swatch, click Duplicate Swatch instead. This is handy if you want both a process-color and a spot-color swatch of the same color in your document.)

③ In the Swatch Options dialog box, change the Color Type pop-up menu's setting to Process. Click OK.

④ The icon to the right of the color name in the Swatches pane will have changed from the spot-color icon to the process-color icon.

Creating Swatches from Bitmapped Images

① Select the Eyedropper tool.

② Click the tool on the object whose color you want to sample (for a multicolor image such as a photo, be sure to click on the specific area that has the desired color). At right, I'm sampling the color of a roof in this French village.

③ In the Swatches pane, select New Color Swatch from the palette menu. InDesign will automatically create a new swatch based on the sampled color. You can adjust the color, as shown above.

Go Further: InDesign gives you another way to import color from images, no matter what format they are in. You can use the Eyedropper tool to determine the color of any object at any location and then create a new color swatch from that sampling.

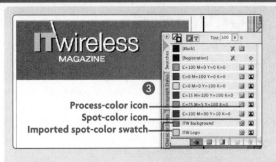

Process-color icon
Spot-color icon
Imported spot-color swatch

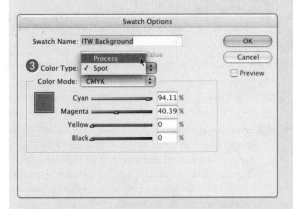

Importing Colors from Other Documents

Chances are that you already have documents that use colors you need — especially if you have developed as palette of approved colors. Both QuarkXPress and InDesign let you transfer those colors from other documents into your current document or template, though InDesign's approach was less sophisticated until version CS2 arrived.

Follow These Steps

QuarkXPress offers two related ways to import colors from other QuarkXPress documents. The processes are almost the same, depending on where you start.

1 From the Colors palette (Windows ➪ Show Colors in Quark-XPress 6 and View ➪ Show Colors in QuarkXPress 5 or earlier, or F12).

2 In the Colors palette, ⌘+click or Ctrl+click an existing color.

3 In the resulting Colors dialog box, click the Append button. When the Append Colors dialog box appears, navigate to the appropriate folder and file, click it, then click OK.

4 In the Appendix dialog box, select the colors you want to import from the list at left, then click the ➧ button to transfer them to the current document. (You can undo a transfer by clicking a color name in the list at right and clicking the ◄ button. You can also include all colors by clicking the Include All button; you will be asked whether to overwrite any same-named colors in the target document.

5 When done, click OK to complete the color transfer.

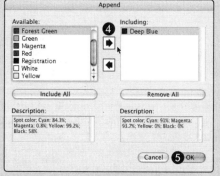

You can also start from the File menu (choose File ➪ Append, or press Option+⌘+A or Ctrl+Alt+A), which opens the Append dialog box. In the Append dialog box, you can import multiple items, not just colors.

The Append dialog box is very similar to the Append Colors dialog box, except that it has an added column from which to choose the various types of items to import (at far left of its dialog box)

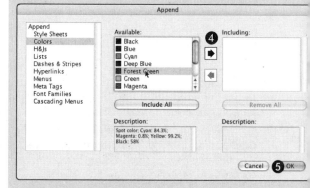

Keep in Mind

QuarkXPress will also import the colors from any objects transferred from a library or copied from another document.

InDesign

Follow These Steps

Compared with QuarkXPress, InDesign is more limited in its ability to flexibly import colors from other documents. Here's what you can do:

① In the Swatches pane (Window ➪ Swatches or F5), choose Load Swatches from the palette menu.

② In the resulting Open a File dialog box, navigate to the appropriate folder and InDesign document file, click it, then click OK.

③ InDesign will now import all colors from that document into the current document, and it will automatically add them to the Swatches pane.

 Workaround: To import specific colors from one InDesign document to another, you can do any of the following:

• Copy an item with the desired color from one document to another.

• Drag an item with the desired color from one document to another.

• Copy an item with the desired color from a library to the document.

In all three cases, the color definition will be transferred to the target document. Apply the color to another object, then delete the copied item. (If you delete the copied item before using its color elsewhere, that imported color will also be deleted.)

If you are using InDesign CS2, you have a fourth method available, as described next.

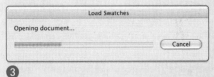

Sharing Colors in InDesign CS2

InDesign CS2 lets you save selected swatches to an Adobe Swatch Exchange file, which any Adobe Creative Suite 2 application can import. (Adobe Swatch Exchange files have the filename extension .ase.) Here's how this feature works:

① Select the colors to save in the Swatches pane (Window ➪ Swatches or F5); use Shift+click to select a range or ⌘+click or Ctrl+click to select noncontiguous color swatches.

② Choose Save Swatches from the palette menu.

③ In the resulting Save dialog box, navigate to the appropriate folder, give the Adobe Swatch Exchange file a name, then click Save.

Other InDesign CS2 and Creative Suite 2 users can import these specific swatches by choosing Load Swatches from the Swatches pane, navigating to the Adobe Swatch Exchange file in the resulting Open dialog box, clicking the filename, and then clicking OK.

✳ **Creating Tints**

Tints, called *shades* in QuarkXPress, are essentially a lightening of a color. As with gradients, both QuarkXPress and InDesign let you apply a tint percentage manually, but InDesign also lets you create tint swatches for consistent application.

Follow These Steps

QuarkXPress lets you apply shades to text, lines, and grayscale and black-and-white bitmapped graphics, but you cannot save specific shades for reuse. Here's how to apply shades:

1. Select the object to which you want to apply the shade.

2. Open the Colors palette (Window ⇨ Show Colors in Quark-XPress 6 and View ⇨ Show Colors in QuarkXPress 5 and earlier, or F12). In the Colors palette, be sure to select the appropriate item component (frame, content, or background) so the shade is applied to the correct part.

3. In the Shade menu, select the desired shade amount. Or designate a specific percentage by entering the value in the Shade field; the percentage can be very exact, such as 35.8%. (To apply a colored shade, also apply a color to the item as described on page 56.)

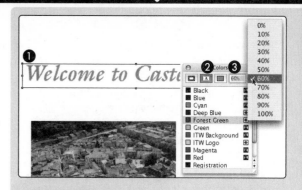

InDesign

Follow These Steps

InDesign lets you apply tints to text, strokes, and lines, plus you can save specific tints for reuse.

Creating Tint Swatches

❶ In the Swatches palette, select a color.

❷ Choose New Tint Swatch from the palette menu.

❸ In the New Tint Swatch dialog box, adjust the tint by using the Tint slider or by entering a tint percentage value in the Tint field.

❹ Click OK when done. (Click Add if you want to create more tints from the current color. Then click OK when done.)

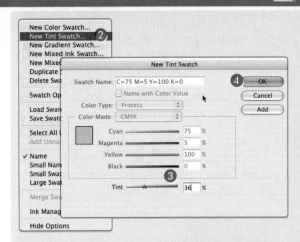

Applying Tints to Text

❶ Select the text to which you want to apply the tint.

❷ In the Swatches pane (Window ➪ Swatches or F5) or in the Tools palette, select the appropriate item component (frame or stroke) so the tint is applied to the correct part.

❸ In the Tint menu, select the desired tint amount. Or enter a specific percentage in the Tint field; the percentage can be very exact, such as 43.2%.

Applying Tints to Objects

Follow the steps above for applying tints to text, but instead select an object, such as a line or shape.

Applying Transparency to Bitmapped Graphics

You can apply a tint swatch to images to achieve a QuarkXPress-like tint. Or you can use InDesign's transparency options. The difference is that a tint doesn't make the white components any less white, while transparency actually makes the white areas fade away, so objects underneath become visible.

❶ Select the bitmapped graphic to which you want to apply the transparency that simulates a tint. In InDesign, the image can be a color, grayscale, or black-and-white graphic. (If you want a color tint applied, first apply a color to the image as described on page 57.)

❷ Open the Transparency pane (Window ➪ Transparency or Shift+F10). In the Opacity pop-up menu, select the desired transparency amount, or enter a percentage in the field.

Go Further: The Transparency pane lets you do more than change an image's opacity; it also lets you apply special lighting effects, called *blending modes*, to that image, as shown in the bottom right image.

Applying Color Profiles

In some production workflows, color management is used to calibrate color output so that the output better matches the original source. This is done by associating color profiles to each image (which specifies color range) and by selecting the rendering intent (which affects color saturation). Be sure to discuss the use of color management with your service bureau.

Follow These Steps

QuarkXPress lets you apply profiles either before or after importing a graphic, as you prefer.

Applying Profiles during Import

1 Create the picture box in which to place the image. Choose File ➪ Get Picture, or press ⌘+E or Ctrl+E, to open the Get Picture dialog box. Navigate through folders and files to the image you want to import.

2 In the Get Picture dialog box, choose the profile and rendering intent in the Color Management pane. Note that you can apply color profiles only to color bitmapped files.

3 Click Open to import the image.

Applying Profiles after Import

1 Select the image with either the Content or Item tool. Open the Profile Information palette (Window ➪ Show Profile Information in QuarkXPress 6 and View ➪ Show Profile Information in QuarkXPress 5 or earlier).

2 Choose the color profile and rendering intent.

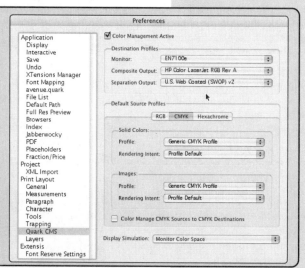

Keep in Mind

To use color management in QuarkXPress, you must have QuarkCMS turned on, via the Preferences dialog box's QuarkCMS section, shown at left. You also set the default source and destination profiles here, so QuarkXPress knows what calibration is required.

InDesign

Follow These Steps

Remember to discuss the use of color management with your service bureau; many prefer to handle such calibration themselves and can have trouble when the layout files are already calibrated.

Applying Profiles during Import

① Choose File ➪ Place, or press ⌘+D or Ctrl+D, to open the Place dialog box. Navigate through folders and files to the image you want to import.

② Be sure to check the Show Import Options checkbox.

③ Click Open.

④ In the Image Import Options dialog box, choose the profile and rendering intent in the Color pane. (Note that you can apply color profiles only to color bitmapped files.)

⑤ Click OK to import the image.

Applying Profiles after Import

① Select the image with either the Selection or Direct Selection tool. Control+click or right-click the image and choose Graphics ➪ Image Color Settings, or choose Object ➪ Graphics ➪ Image Color Settings.

② In the resulting Image Color Settings dialog box, choose the color profile and rendering intent.

③ Click OK.

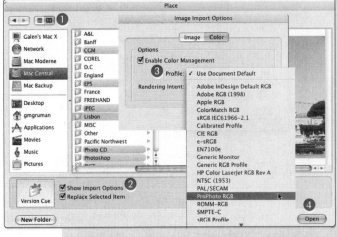

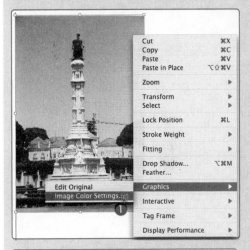

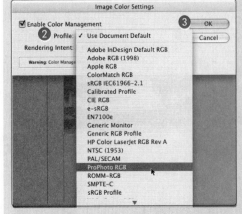

Keep in Mind

InDesign's color management does not need to be enabled for you to apply profiles to images. But it does need to be turned on to affect the final output. To turn on and set default profiles and rendering intents, choose Edit ➪ Color Settings. The resulting dialog box is similar to the QuarkXPress dialog box on the opposite page.

part iv

Working with Text Blocks

This section shows you how to create and import text and manage the flow of text on and among pages. This is an area where QuarkXPress and InDesign have very different approaches that can easily confuse the veteran QuarkXPress user.

InDesign is more oriented to manual text flow, so its automatic flow approaches are not so obvious. But InDesign provides richer control over imported text's formatting, especially in its most recent version.

Creating Text Frames

Text frames (called *text boxes* in QuarkXPress) contain text and let you control its shape on the page as well as the flow of text among frames. QuarkXPress requires you to set up text frames before importing text, while InDesign will create a frame as you import text. Both programs require you to create a frame or select an existing one before entering new text.

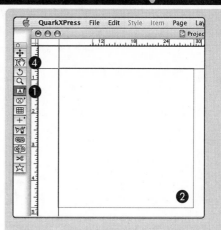

Follow These Steps

To create a text box in QuarkXPress:

1. Select one of the text-box tools.

2. Draw the text box in the desired location at the desired size.

3. With the text box selected with either the Item tool or Content tool, modify the size and settings using the Measurements palette and/or by choosing Item ➪ Modify (⌘+M or Ctrl+M).

4. Click in the text box with the Content tool to enter text or import it (File ➪ Get Text, or ⌘+E or Ctrl+E).

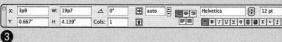

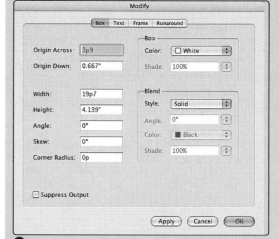

Cross-Reference: Specific text-box and text-frame settings are covered throughout Part IV.

InDesign

Follow These Steps

To create a text frame in InDesign, there are two methods if you import text and one if you are entering it.

Creating a Frame to Import Text or Type in Text

❶ Select the Type tool.

❷ Draw the text frame in the desired location at the desired size.

❸ To enter text, click in the text frame with the Type tool to enter text. If you want to import text, choose File ➪ Place, or ⌘+D or Ctrl+D).

❹ With the text frame selected with the Selection tool or Direct Selection tool, modify the size and settings using the Control palette (InDesign CS and later), the Transform pane (Window ➪ Object & Layout ➪ Transform in InDesign CS2 and Window ➪ Transform in InDesign CS or earlier, or F9), and/or by choosing Object ➪ Text Frame Settings (⌘+B or Ctrl+B).

Note that you can reverse the order of steps 3 and 4.

Importing Text with No Frame Created

❶ Select the Type tool.

❷ Choose File ➪ Place (⌘+D or Ctrl+D), select a text file, and click Open.

❸ The mouse pointer will change to a paragraph icon. When you click on the page, InDesign will create a new text frame that fits within the page margins.

❹ Do step 4 above.

 Workaround: Because InDesign does not have the equivalent of the QuarkXPress text-box tools, you may wonder how to create nonrectangular text frames. That's easy: Use one of the frame tools (the ones with an *X* through them) or shape tools (those without the *X*) to create a frame, then place text into it. Then switch to the Type tool to enter text, or import text by choosing File ➪ Place, or by pressing ⌘+D or Ctrl+D, and then click on the frame or shape. InDesign will convert it to a text frame.

 Go Further: To change a frame or shape to hold text or graphics, QuarkXPress requires that you choose Item ➪ Content ➪ Text or Item ➪ Content ➪ Picture. In InDesign, just import or paste whatever type of object you want the frame or shape to contain and it will convert automatically. But if you want to work the QuarkXPress way, InDesign lets you also choose Object ➪ Content ➪ Text or Object ➪ Content ➪ Graphic.

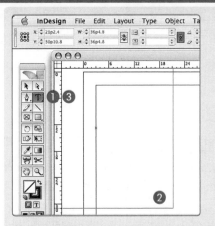

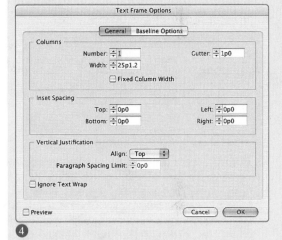

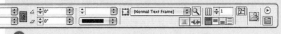

Setting Up Text Position in Frames QuarkXPress

Text boxes with frames and/or backgrounds should have an inset of at least 3 points, and in most cases at least 6 points, for sufficient visual separation. Generally, there needs to be no inset for text boxes that have no frames around them or backgrounds behind them.

Follow These Steps

When you create a text box, QuarkXPress automatically indents the text 1 point from the box's edge. You can change that setting after the fact or by changing the preferences for each text-box shape. Whether you modify existing or default text boxes, QuarkXPress 5 and later let you set the inset separately for each side of a rectangular text frame; just be sure to check the Multiple Insets checkbox in the Modify dialog box.

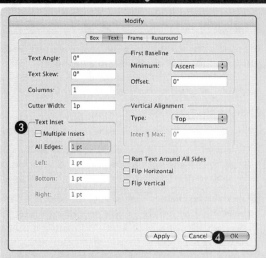

Changing Existing Text Boxes

❶ Select the text box with either the Item tool or Content tool.

❷ Choose Item ➪ Modify (⌘+M or Ctrl+M), and then go to the Text pane.

❸ Change the Text Inset value(s) to match your needs.

❹ Click OK.

Changing Default Text Boxes

❶ Double-click any of the box tools in the Tools palette. This opens up the Tools pane of the Preferences dialog box in QuarkXPress 5 and 6 and the Tools pane of the Document Preferences dialog box in QuarkXPress 4. (Or do it the long way: In QuarkXPress 6, choose QuarkXPress ➪ Preferences on the Mac or Edit ➪ Preferences in Windows; in Quark-XPress 5, choose Edit ➪ Preferences ➪ Preferences; and in QuarkXPress 4, choose Edit ➪ Preferences ➪ Document. QuarkXPress 5 and 6 use the same shortcut, Option+Shift+⌘+Y or Ctrl+Alt+Shift+Y, while QuarkXPress 4 uses ⌘+Y or Ctrl+Y.)

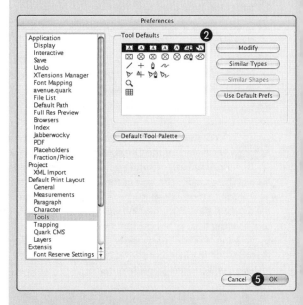

❷ Select the text box shape(s) to which you want to apply the new text insets. You can select multiple shapes by Shift+click-ing a range or ⌘+clicking or Ctrl+clicking noncontiguous shapes. Or select any shape and then click the Similar Types button to select all text-box shapes. Click the Modify button to open the Modify dialog box, then go to the Text pane.

❸ Change the Text Inset value(s) to match your needs.

❹ Click OK to close the Modify dialog box

❺ Click OK to close the Preferences dialog box.

For default text boxes, note that if no document is open when you change settings, all future documents will use the new defaults. Otherwise, defaults apply just to the open document.

Follow These Steps

When you create a text frame, InDesign does not automatically indent the text from the frame's edge. You can change that default setting of 0 points after the fact or by changing the preferences for new documents.

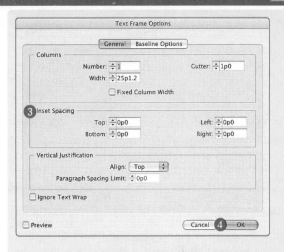

Changing Existing Text Frames

① Select the text frame with either the Selection tool, Direct Selection tool, or Type tool.

② Choose Object ⇨ Text Frame Options (⌘+B or Ctrl+B) and, in InDesign CS2, make sure you are in the General pane.

③ Change the Inset Spacing value(s) to match your needs.

④ Click OK.

Changing Default Text Frames

① Make sure that no document is open if you want the new inset settings to apply to all future documents. Or make sure that no other text frames are selected if you want to make sure that the new inset settings apply to all new text frames in the current document.

② Choose Object ⇨ Text Frame Options (⌘+B or Ctrl+B). In InDesign CS2, make sure you are in the General pane.

③ Change the Inset Spacing value(s) to match your needs.

④ Click OK.

InDesign does not let you set separate default insets for different-shaped text frames, as QuarkXPress does. If you convert a shape — such as a circle or a polygon — to a text frame, and your text-frame inset defaults use different settings for different sides, InDesign will use the Top inset's value as the inset amount for nonrectangular frames.

Setting Up Columns

Although page-layout software for years has let users set up multicolumn text boxes, it's amazing how many designers still create separate boxes for each frame, inviting inconsistent alignment and requiring more work.

Follow These Steps

QuarkXPress offers basic column-creation controls and also lets you force column breaks.

Creating Columns

❶ Select a text box with the Item tool or Contents tool.

❷ Change the number of columns in the Measurements palette's Cols text field or in the Columns text field in the Text pane of the Modify dialog box (Item ➪ Modify, or ⌘+M or Ctrl+M). You can also set the gutter width in the Modify dialog box's Text pane (the default is 1p).

Forcing Column Breaks

❶ Press keypad Enter to force a column break, which moves the text insertion point to the top of the next column in the current text box or in the next linked text box.

❷ You can also search and replace text to include a forced column break as part of the searched or replaced text. In Find/Replace dialog box, enter the code **\c** in the Find What and Change To fields.

Breaking Text across Columns

One frustration in the use of columns is how to handle items such as headlines that you want to extend across multiple columns.

❶ Create a text box for the text that must run across several columns.

❷ Link that text box to the multicolumn text box.

❸ Enter the text, using a paragraph return or column-break character (keypad Enter) to ensure that the rest of the text is in the multicolumn text box.

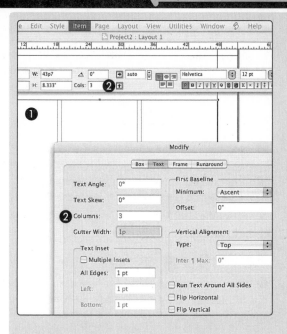

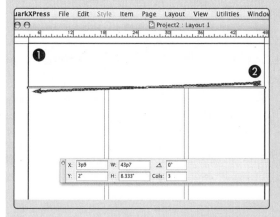

Follow These Steps

InDesign offers comparable column-creation controls, although there are some differences.

Creating Columns

① Select a text frame with the Selection tool, Direct Selection tool, or Type tool.

② Change the number of columns in the Control palette's Columns field or in the Number field in the Text Frame Options dialog box (Object ⇨ Text Frame Options, or ⌘+B or Ctrl+B). You can also set the gutter width in the Text Frame Options dialog box (the default is 1p).

Go Further: If you check the Fixed Column Width checkbox, InDesign will resize the text frame to fit the specified column widths and number of columns rather than resize the columns to fit the text frame.

Forcing Column Breaks

① Press keypad Enter to force a column break, which moves the text insertion point to the top of the next column in the current text frame or in the next linked text frame.

Workaround: InDesign provides no code for use in the Find/Change dialog box to search for or replace a column break, frame break, or page break. You'll have to add or change these breaks manually.

Breaking Text across Columns

One frustration in the use of columns is how to handle items such as headlines that you want to extend across multiple columns.

① Create a text frame for the text that must run across several columns.

② Link that text frame to the multicolumn text frame.

③ Enter the text, using a paragraph return or column-break character to ensure that the rest of the text is in the multi-column text frame.

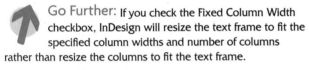
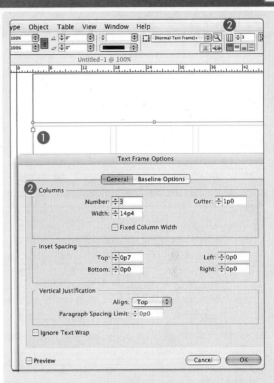
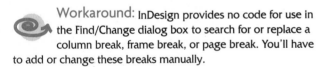
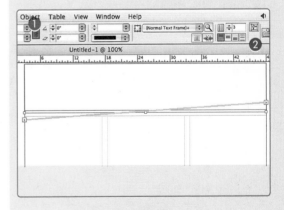

Comparing Automatic Text Boxes to Master Text Frames

While they seem to be the same, QuarkXPress's automatic text box is not quite the same as InDesign's master text frame, although their fundamental purpose is the same: to provide a default container for text.

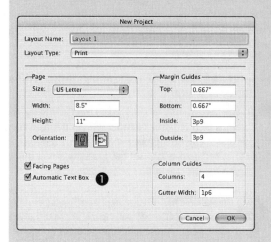

Follow These Steps

QuarkXPress lets you create an automatic text box on your initial master page that lets text flow automatically from page to page, as well as have the program add pages automatically as needed when you import text in this automatic text box.

1 When creating a new document (File ➪ New ➪ Project in QuarkXPress 6 and File ➪ New ➪ Document in QuarkXPress 5 or earlier, or ⌘+N or Ctrl+N), be sure to check Automatic Text Box in the New Document dialog box (the New Project dialog box in QuarkXPress 6). In QuarkXPress 6, you can also check Automatic Text Box when creating a new layout (Layout ➪ New) in your project.

Note that only the initial master page (A-Master A) will have this automatic text box.

You cannot link text boxes across pages within a master-page spread.

Cross-Reference: See pages 78-79 for managing text flow with automatic text boxes and master text frames. See pages 26-31 for details on creating master pages and pages 24-25 for details on creating a new document.

InDesign

Follow These Steps

InDesign lets you link text frames on master pages, so you can have new pages created automatically when you import large text files.

① When creating or editing master pages, simply link text frames within and across pages in a master spread. (You cannot link frames across different master spreads.)

② Or you can check Master Text Frame in the New Document dialog box (File ➪ New ➪ Document, or ⌘+N or Ctrl+N). The text frames in a spread are automatically linked.

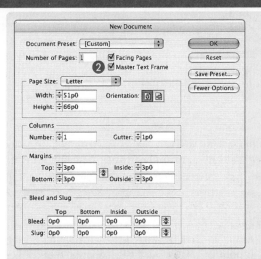

Automatically Flowing Text

QuarkXPress

In books, magazines, and other long-form documents, text rarely fits on one page, so layout programs let you link text from one page to another. QuarkXPress and InDesign offer different ways to automatically flow text from one page to another.

Follow These Steps

With the automatic text box set up (see page 76), you can now flow text automatically in your QuarkXPress document.

1 When importing text (File ➪ Get Text, or ⌘+E or Ctrl+E) into the automatic text frame, QuarkXPress will use this automatic text box to flow the story into all subsequent pages.

2 QuarkXPress will also add new pages as needed to hold the text. You can turn off this automatic page insertion by choosing Off in the Auto Page Insertion pop-up menu in the General pane of the QuarkXPress 5 and 6 Preferences dialog box, or in the General pane of the QuarkXPress 4 Document Preferences dialog box. (In QuarkXPress 6, choose QuarkXPress ➪ Preferences on the Mac or Edit ➪ Preferences in Windows; in QuarkXPress 5, choose Edit ➪ Preferences ➪ Preferences; and in QuarkXPress 4, choose Edit ➪ Preferences ➪ Document. QuarkXPress 5 and 6 use the same shortcut, Option+Shift+⌘+Y or Ctrl+Alt+Shift+Y, while QuarkXPress 4 uses ⌘+Y or Ctrl+Y.)

3 When inserting pages, you can tell QuarkXPress to flow text to the automatic text box if the pages you're inserting are to be based on the master page that has the automatic text box. Check the Link to Current Text Chain checkbox in the Insert Pages dialog box (Pages ➪ Insert). This option is grayed out unless, in the Master Page pop-up menu, you choose the master page that has the automatic text box.

4 Another way to automatically flow text is to create a document with no text in it — a template (see page 32) — and have the text boxes already linked. Then import or type your text.

InDesign

Follow These Steps

Whether or not a master text frame is set up (see page 77), you can now flow text automatically in your InDesign document.

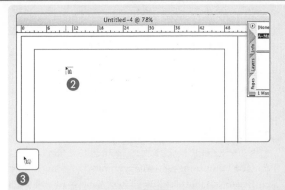

① When importing text (File ⇨ Place, or ⌘+D or Ctrl+D), InDesign automatically flows the text just in the currently selected frame. To have automatic text flow among pages, creating new pages as needed, you must *not* select a text frame first.

② After importing the text file, hold the Shift key to display the automatic text-flow icon. Now click into a text frame. The text will flow into that text frame and then into the master text frame on subsequent pages, with new pages added as needed. If there is no master text frame, InDesign will create text frames that fit within the page's margins.

③ If you don't want pages added automatically, hold the Option key instead to display the semiautomatic text-flow icon. This requires that you click on each page where you want the text to flow. That's less work than with the normal text-flow icon, which flows text only into the currently selected text frame, requiring you to click the frame's out port before selecting the next frame to flow the text to.

Linking Text Frames

In addition to automatic linking, you can link text frames and/or text paths manually (called *threading* in InDesign). This is handy when linking text frames or text paths within a page or when linking multiple stories in one document (such as a newsletter or magazine), where the single flow of an automatic text frame is inappropriate.

Follow These Steps

❶ WIth the Link tool, click the source text frame or text path. (The text box or path does not need to contain text.) Note that when you click the Link tool, all existing links are displayed.

❷ Now click the destination text box or path. If that box or path already contains text, QuarkXPress will not let you link to it. (If the text box or text path is on a different page, just switch to that page first. Note that in QuarkXPress 6 you cannot link from one layout to another, just across pages within a layout.)

❸ Repeat steps 1 and 2 to continue to link to other text boxes and/or text paths.

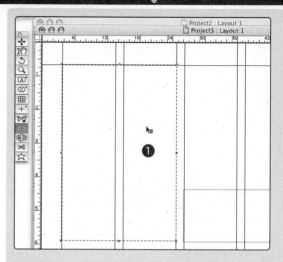

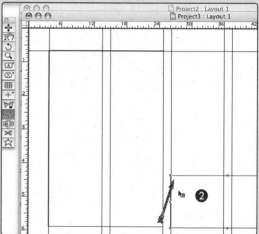

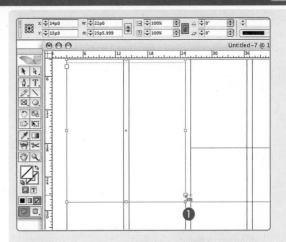

InDesign

Follow These Steps

You can link text frames and/or text paths automatically or manually in InDesign.

1. With the Selection or Direct Selection tool, click the out port (the red plus sign at lower right) of the source text frame or text path. (The text frame or path does not need to contain text.) The pointer will change to a paragraph icon.

2. As you hover the pointer over a text frame or path, its icon changes to a chain icon. Now click the destination text frame or path. If that box or path already contains text, InDesign will not let you link to it. (If the text frame or text path is on a different page, just switch to that page first.)

3. To see what text frames and paths are linked, choose View ➪ Show Text Threads (Option+⌘+Y or Ctrl+Alt+Y).

4. Repeat steps 1 and 2 to continue to link to other text frames and/or text paths.

Go Further: To speed up the linking of text frames and paths, hold the Option or Alt key. This changes the pointer to the semiautomatic text-flow icon, which lets you simply click in turn each text frame and/or text path to link. That saves you the effort of first clicking the out port of the previous text frame or path to link to the next frame or path.

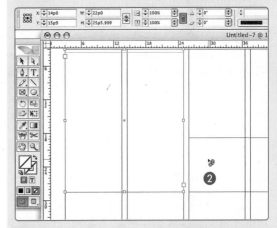

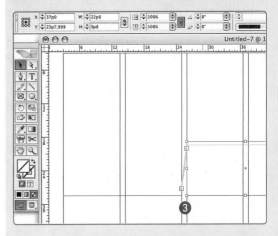

❇Redirecting Text Flow

Often, you'll discover that you need to rearrange pages or text frames. That will mess up your text flow, but both QuarkXPress and InDesign let you redirect text flow, changing the order of which frames the text flows into as well as severing links between frames.

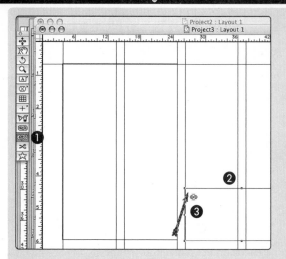

Follow These Steps

If you change your layout, perhaps by adding new text boxes or deleting some, you'll likely need to redirect your text flow.

Breaking Text Flow

❶ Click the Unlink tool.

❷ Click the text box (or path) that you want to remove from the text chain.

❸ Click the arrowhead that indicates the link. The link between the two text boxes (and/or text paths) is now removed.

Any links to other frames (or paths) later in the chain are unaffected, although the two sets of text chains are no longer related. That means text will not skip over the unlinked box or path and continue on to subsequent ones. Instead, the chain will end where the link was broken and a new link will start there.

Rerouting Text Flow to Other Boxes

❶ Delete any text boxes and/or text paths that are no longer needed in the layout. The text flow will simply reroute itself automatically to the other boxes and paths in the chain.

❷ For text boxes and paths that you want to keep in your layout but no longer have linked to the other text boxes, break any links to text boxes and text paths as described above. (Note that the unlinked text boxes and/or paths will no longer contain any text.) Link to a new target text box or path as described on page 80.

❸ If you simply want to change the order of text flow, link between text boxes and/or paths as described on page 80 — the text flow will follow your new links.

Follow These Steps

InDesign also lets you redirect text flow.

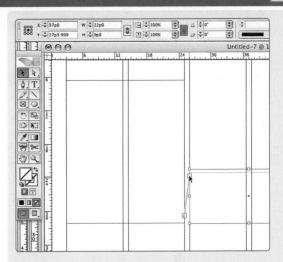

Breaking Text Flow

❶ Move to the page that has the text frame (or path) that you want to remove from the text chain and be sure the frame (or path) is visible.

❸ With the Selection tool or Direct Selection tool, double-click the in port or the out port to break the link. The link between the two text frames (and/or text paths) is now removed.

Any links to other frames (or paths) later in the chain are unaffected, although the two sets of text chains are no longer related. That means text will not skip over the unlinked frame or path and continue on to subsequent ones. Instead, the chain will end where the link was broken and a new link will start there.

Rerouting Text Flow to Other Frames

❶ Delete any text frames and/or text paths that are no longer needed in the layout. The text flow will simply reroute itself automatically to the other frames and paths in the chain.

❷ For text frames and paths that you want to keep in your layout but no longer have linked to the other text frames, break any links to text frames and text paths as described above. (Note that the unlinked text frames and/or paths will no longer contain any text.) Link to a new target text frame or path as described on page 81.

❸ If you simply want to change the order of text flow, link between text frames and/or paths as described on page 81 — the text flow will follow your new links.

❋ Preparing Word Files

Microsoft Word is by far the most-used word processor, and most text files will use its format.

Follow These Steps

If text is destined for QuarkXPress, its formatting in Microsoft Word should be minimal:

1. Use paragraph style sheets that have the same names as the style sheets used in the QuarkXPress layout. This will save you, or the designer, from having to manually apply style sheets to all the text.

2. Use only meaning-oriented local formatting, such as boldface and italics.

3. Only use Word's automated bullets and numbering feature if you use tabs between the bullets or numerals and the text that follows (which is how Word formats it) in QuarkXPress. Otherwise, you'll have to strip out those tabs.

4. Be sure to use either two hyphens or real em dashes in Word to indicate a dash. In several versions of the program — all versions but Word 98 for Mac and Word 2002/XP for Windows — you'll need to uncheck the Symbol Characters checkbox in the AutoCorrect setting (Tools ➪ AutoCorrect ➪ Autoformat as You Type) that convert two hyphens as you type. Instead, use the AutoCorrect pane to have Word replace two hyphens with an em dash. That's because these versions' autoformat function converts the two hyphens to an en dash (–) rather than an em dash (—). (To enter an em dash in Word's AutoCorrect, enter Option+Shift+– on the Mac or hold the Alt key and enter **0151** from the keypad in Windows.)

5. Do not use Word's table feature. Instead, convert your Word tables to text, so that there's a tab between "cells." If you forget, QuarkXPress will try to figure out the cell boundaries and will substitute tabs during import.

6. Be sure that Fast Save is turned off in Word's Options dialog box (Tools ➪ Options); otherwise fragments of previously deleted text may appear in your QuarkXPress document.

7. Don't use double spaces after sentences or use tabs or spaces to line up text; you'll handle any alignment when the text is imported into QuarkXPress.

8. Don't use footnotes, page numbers, text boxes, or other such layout features. They either don't import into Quark-XPress or don't import fully (see page 86).

InDesign

Follow These Steps

If text is destined for InDesign, its formatting in Microsoft Word should be minimal, although InDesign CS2 supports more of Word's formatting.

❶ Use paragraph style sheets that have the same names as the style sheets used in the InDesign layout. This will avoid the need of having to manually apply style sheets to all the text.

❷ Use only meaning-oriented local formatting such as bold-face and italics.

❸ Only use Word's automated bullets and numbering feature if you use tabs between the bullets or numerals and the text that follows (which is how Word formats it) in InDesign. Otherwise, you'll have to strip out those tabs in InDesign.

❹ Be sure to use real em dashes in Word to indicate a dash. In all versions but Word 98 for Mac and Word 2002/XP for Windows, you'll need to uncheck the Symbol Characters checkbox in the AutoCorrect setting (Tools ➪ AutoCorrect ➪ Autoformat as You Type) that convert two hyphens as you type. Instead, use the AutoCorrect pane to have Word replace two hyphens with an em dash. That's because these versions' autoformat function converts the two hyphens to an en dash (–) rather than an em dash (—). (To enter an em dash in Word's AutoCorrect, enter Option+Shift+– on the Mac or hold the Alt key and enter **0151** from the keypad in Windows.)

❺ InDesign can import Word tables.

❻ Be sure that Fast Save is turned off in Word's Options dialog box (Tools ➪ Options); otherwise fragments of previously deleted text may appear in your InDesign document.

❼ Don't use double spaces after sentences or use tabs or spaces to line up text; you'll handle any alignment in InDesign.

❽ Don't use footnotes, page numbers, text boxes, or other such layout features. They either don't import at all or don't import fully into most versions of InDesign.

 Go Further: Although InDesign CS2 converts Word's automated bullets and numbers to static bullets and numbers, it has similar controls to create and work with automated bullets and numbers within InDesign.

Go Further: InDesign CS2 imports footnotes, end-notes, inline graphics, and text boxes from Word files.

 Warning: InDesign does not convert two consecutive hyphens to em dashes when you import Word files. (Use the Find/Change dialog box to search and replace them, as covered on page 143.)

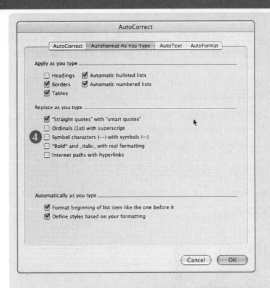

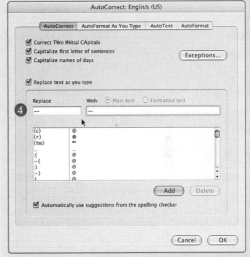

Comparing Supported Formatting ‹ QuarkXPress

Microsoft Word is very capable, approaching the level of layout programs in some of its formatting. However, layout programs don't fully use that Word formatting.

Keep in Mind

QuarkXPress supports most character-level formatting but is weaker on layout-oriented formatting. Here's what it imports from Microsoft Word and how it treats that text.

Supported As Is

- Italics
- Boldface
- Superscript
- Subscript
- Underline
- Strikethrough
- Shadow
- Outline
- Small caps
- All caps
- Baseline shift
- Font and size change
- Paragraph style sheets

Converted to Normal

- Highlighted
- Tables

Converted Otherwise

- Double strikethrough: converted to single strikethrough
- Word underline: converted to underline
- Embossed text: converted to white with gray shadow
- Engraved text: converted to white
- Bulleted lists: bullets removed
- Numbered lists: numbers removed
- Condensed/expanded: converted to normal spacing
- Footnotes: converted to endnotes
- Text boxes: merged into the text
- Character style sheets: converted to local formatting

Removed

- Hidden characters

Word

QuarkXPress

InDesign

Keep in Mind

Likewise, InDesign supports most Word formatting, although with some differences from QuarkXPress.

Supported As Is

- Italics
- Boldface
- Superscript
- Subscript
- Underline
- Double strikethrough
- Strikethrough
- Small caps
- All caps
- Baseline shift
- Condensed/expanded
- Font and size change
- Paragraph style sheets
- Tables

Converted to Normal

- Shadow
- Outline
- Highlighted

Converted Otherwise

- Word underline: converted to underline
- Embossed text: converted to white
- Engraved text: converted to white
- Bulleted lists: bullets retained but no longer automatic
- Numbered lists: numbers retained but no longer automatic
- Footnotes: converted to endnotes (footnotes are supported in InDesign CS2)
- Text boxes: merged into the main text (anchored text boxes and the links to them are supported in InDesign CS2)
- Character style sheets: converted to local formatting (character styles are supported in InDesign CS2)

Removed

- Hidden characters

Word

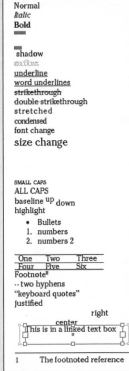

InDesign CS2

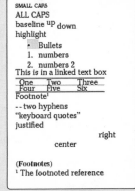

InDesign 2 and CS (where they differ from CS2)

Go Further: InDesign CS2 supports several types of formatting not supported by the previous versions: character styles, footnotes, and anchored text boxes.

Importing Word Files

When you import Word files into QuarkXPress or InDesign, you have the chance to control how some Word features are handled to better work in your layout.

Follow These Steps

QuarkXPress has straightforward options for importing Word files:

❶ Using the Content tool, select the text box in which to import the Word file. If the box already contains text, the Word file will be imported at the text-insertion point and any highlighted text will be replaced.

❷ Choose File ➪ Get Text (⌘+E or Ctrl+E) to open the Get Text dialog box.

❸ If you want QuarkXPress to convert keyboard quotes to typographic (curly) quotes and two consecutive hyphens to em dashes, check the Convert Quotes checkbox,

❹ If you want QuarkXPress to import all style sheets in the Word file into QuarkXPress, check the Import Style Sheets checkbox.

❺ Click Open to import the file.

QuarkXPress uses the same process for importing RTF, Word-Perfect, XTags, and ASCII text files, although — because ASCII files have no style sheets — the Import Style Sheets checkbox is grayed out.

Cross-Reference: Style-sheet import options are covered on pages 90-91, while issues related to importing Word tables are covered on pages 94-95.

InDesign

Follow These Steps

InDesign offers more options than QuarkXPress for importing Word files:

1. If the target text frame already exists, select it using the Selection tool, Direct Selection tool, or Type tool. If the frame already contains text, the Word file will be imported at the text-insertion point and any highlighted text will be replaced.

2. Choose File ➪ Place (⌘+D or Ctrl+D) to open the Place dialog box.

3. If you want InDesign to replace all text in the target text frame, even if that text is not highlighted, check the Replace Selected Item checkbox.

4. If you want to control how InDesign handles various types of formatting, check the Show Import Options checkbox.

5. In the Import Options dialog box, you'll usually want to check the Use Typographer's Quotes checkbox (in InDesign 2, check Convert Quotes in the Place dialog box instead). You also decide about layout-oriented text formatting (table of contents, index entries, footnotes, and endnotes) by checking the appropriate checkboxes in the Include section. Unchecked items are deleted during import. Note that in many cases, especially index entries and table-of-contents text, there's little value to importing the text because the InDesign layout will likely result in very different page numbering. Click OK when done.

6. Click Open to import the file.

InDesign uses the same process for importing RTF, Tagged Text, and ASCII text files. (InDesign does not import WordPerfect files.)

Go Further: InDesign's Import Options dialog box gives you much more flexibility over Word-file import. Also, InDesign CS2 lets you save Import Options settings as preset files, so you can reuse them consistently even among multiple users.

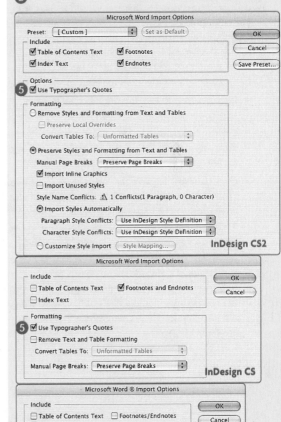

✳️Importing Word Style Sheets QuarkXPress

Because Microsoft Word is the format most likely to be used for importing text, handling Word's style sheets is also a fact of life for many files. That's why QuarkXPress and InDesign give you control over that import, so you can decide how to handle conflicts between Word and layout-program style sheets.

Follow These Steps

QuarkXPress provides basic control over Word style sheets during text-file import.

❶ When you import a text file, be sure that Import Style Sheets is checked in the Get Text dialog box (File ➪ Get Text, or ⌘+E or Ctrl+E).

❷ QuarkXPress will import all style sheets in the Word file, including the several that are predefined in Word, even if you haven't used them on any text.

❸ If QuarkXPress detects that the Word file uses style sheets with the same names as the style sheets already defined in QuarkXPress, it will ask you how to handle the conflicts (check the Repeat For All Conflicts checkbox to apply the same solution to all conflicts; leave unchecked if you want to make a separate decision for each conflict):

- Click Rename to rename the Word style sheet, so it no longer conflicts with the QuarkXPress style sheet.

- Click Auto Rename to have QuarkXPress rename the Word style sheet for you (it will add *1* to the end of the name).

- Click Use New to have the Word style sheet override the QuarkXPress style sheet. That will change the formatting of any text in the QuarkXPress file using the style sheet to match that of the Word style sheet.

- Click Use Existing to preserve the QuarkXPress style sheet, applying it to any Word text that uses the Word style sheet of the same name. This is usually the best option, since it lets your editors tag text in Word with the correct style name while not having to worry about the formatting, which QuarkXPress will define and handle during import.

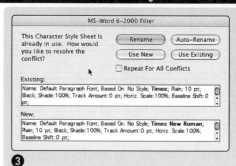

❸

Cross-Reference: Basic import options are covered on pages 88-89, while issues related to importing Word tables are covered on pages 94-95.

InDesign

Follow These Steps

InDesign CS2 supports richer control over importing Word style sheets during text-file import than QuarkXPress does, while InDesign CS or earlier offers fewer options.

InDesign CS2

1 When you import a text file, be sure to check the Show Import Options checkbox in the Place dialog box (File ⇨ Place, or ⌘+D or Ctrl+D) to get the Import Options dialog box.

2 InDesign CS2 will import only the style sheets in the Word file that you have actually applied to text in that file, unless you check the Import Unused Styles checkbox.

3 You control how InDesign CS2 handles style sheets that have the same name in InDesign and Word. Do this by selecting the Import Styles Automatically radio button and choosing whether InDesign uses the existing InDesign styles (Use InDesign Style Definition), or the Word styles instead (Redefine InDesign Style), or if it renames the Word styles automatically (Auto Rename). You can also decide how to handle each style individually by selecting the Customize Style Import radio button and then clicking the Style Mapping button.

4 Click OK when done. (You can save these settings by first clicking Save Preset.)

InDesign 2 and CS

InDesign 2 and CS provide no option for handling style-sheet conflicts. InDesign's styles will override any Word style sheets of the same name, while any Word style sheets that don't conflict with InDesign styles will be imported into InDesign.

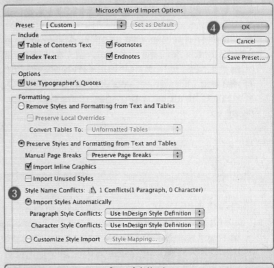

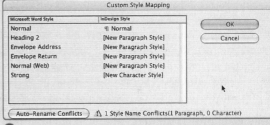

Importing Style Sheets from Other Documents

You'll often discover that another document has a style sheet already defined that you want to use, whether as is or as the basis for your ultimate style sheet. Both Quark-XPress and InDesign let you do that, although Quark-XPress has historically provided more flexibility when doing so.

Follow These Steps

QuarkXPress lets you import style sheets from another document into your current one.

1 Choose Edit ⇨ Style Sheets (Shift+F11) to open the Style Sheets dialog box. (Or you can open the Style Sheets dialog box by ⌘+clicking or Ctrl+clicking an existing style sheet in the Style Sheets palette [Window ⇨ Show Style Sheets in QuarkXPress 6 and View ⇨ Show Style Sheets in Quark-XPress 5 or earlier, or F11].)

2 Click the Append button to open the Append dialog box.

3 Choose the style sheets to copy into the current document by selecting them in the Available pane and clicking the ▶ button. (To copy them all, click Include All.) If you change your mind and decide not to copy certain style sheets, select them in the Including pane and click the ◀ button. (To remove them all, click Remove All.)

4 Click OK when done.

You can also import style sheets by choosing File ⇨ Append (Option+⌘+A or Ctrl+Alt+A). Doing so opens the Append dialog box at bottom right, and lets you import colors, H&J sets, and many other style-like attributes.

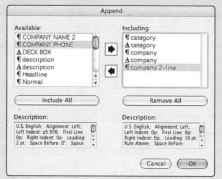

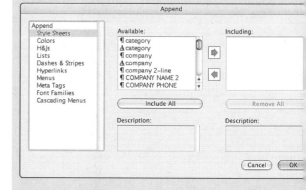

InDesign

Follow These Steps

InDesign also lets you import style sheets from another document.

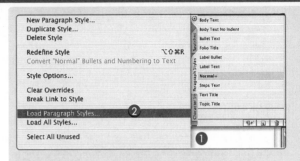

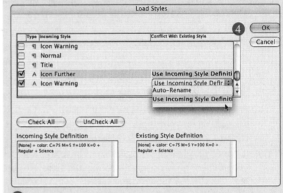

1. Open either the Paragraph Styles pane (Window ➪ Type & Tables ➪ Paragraph Styles in InDesign CS or later and Window ➪ Type ➪ Paragraph Styles in InDesign 2, or F11) or the Character Styles pane (Window ➪ Type & Tables ➪ Character Styles in InDesign CS and later or Window ➪ Type ➪ Character Styles in InDesign 2, or Shift+F11).

2. Choose Load All Styles from the palette menu to load both character and paragraph styles (and object styles in InDesign CS2). If you are using the Character pane, you can also choose Load Character Styles. If you are using the Paragraph pane, you can also choose Load Paragraph Styles.

3. InDesign 2 and InDesign CS will import all the style sheets, ignoring any that already exist in the current document. InDesign CS2 will open the Load Styles dialog box to let you choose which styles to import. If it detects conflicts, the program will also let you choose whether to rename the incoming style (Auto-Rename) or have it override the current document's style (Use Incoming Style Definition).

4. Click OK when done.

Importing Word and Excel Tables ‹ **QuarkXPress**

For years, layout programs generally offered poor table support, even as Microsoft Word and Excel got more and more sophisticated. An early InDesign advantage was its table support, which QuarkXPress lags on even today; this is particularly true for imported tables.

Follow These Steps

Here's how QuarkXPress handles imported tables:

1 During import (File ⇨ Get, or ⌘+E or Ctrl+E), any tables formatted in Word import with all formatting removed and with cells converted to text separated by tabs.

2 Excel tables are barely supported as well: In QuarkXPress 6.0 or earlier, you can only copy an Excel selection and paste it as a graphic into a QuarkXPress picture frame.

3 QuarkXPress 6.1 or later gives you two ways to import tables from an Excel spreadsheet. One way is to import embedded charts into picture frames (File ⇨ Get, or ⌘+E or Ctrl+E). When you import charts in QuarkXPress 6.1 and later, QuarkXPress lets you select the desired chart and then it opens Excel and copies the chart in to the selected picture frame. The other way is to use the Link to External Data checkbox in the Table Properties dialog box when you create a table (see page 178). If checked, Link to External Data opens the Table Link dialog box from which you can import a Microsoft Excel spreadsheet as a table and control which formatting is retained.

4 Realistically, QuarkXPress users need to convert Word tables to tab-delimited text in Word by choosing Table ⇨ Convert ⇨ Table to Text, as well as convert Excel tables to tab-delimited text by saving them as tab-delimited text files. Then, in QuarkXPress, you would format the tabbed text or, in QuarkXPress 5 and later, convert the tabbed text to a table by selecting the tabbed text and then choosing Item ⇨ Text to Table.

3

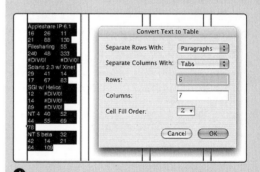

4

InDesign

Follow These Steps

InDesign has long had superior support for tables imported from both Word and Excel:

1️⃣ Tables in Word are imported with both text and table formatting (such as fills and lines) intact when you place them (File ⇨ Place, or ⌘+D or Ctrl+D).

2️⃣ InDesign CS and later lets you remove table formatting from Word tables in the Import Options dialog box. Select the Remove Styles and Formatting from Text and Tables radio button. (in InDesign CS2, check the Preserve Local Overrides checkbox to keep local formatting such as italics, and then choose Unformatted Tables or Unformatted Tabbed Text in the Convert Tables To pop-up menu.) With these options, you can remove all formatting and convert it to tabbed text, or simply remove the local formatting such as fonts and lines but retain it as a table. If you do not check Show Import Options in the Place dialog box, InDesign will retain the table's formatting and import it as a table.

3️⃣ When you import Excel spreadsheets (File ⇨ Place, or ⌘+D or Ctrl+D), InDesign will automatically open the Import Options dialog box so you can choose which worksheet and cells to import. You can also choose whether to retain the spreadsheet's complete formatting, delete the formatting and import the spreadsheet as a table, or delete the formatting and import the spreadsheet as tabbed text.

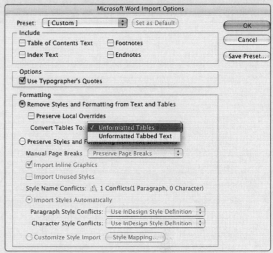

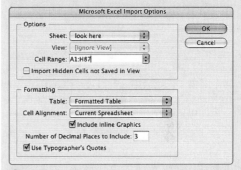

✳ Exporting Text

Although a layout program is typically the final destination for text, you may need to export the text back for use in a word processor, such as when you made significant changes in your layout or for text that you wrote in the layout program in the first place. Both QuarkXPress and InDesign let you export text, though InDesign supports fewer word-processor formats.

Follow These Steps

QuarkXPress gives you several file-format options for text export:

1 Using the Content tool, select a block of text to export, or click anywhere in a text frame if you want to export all text in the text frame and all text frames linked to it (a story).

2 Choose File ⇨ Save Text (Option+⌘+E or Ctrl+Alt+E) to open the Save Text dialog box.

3 Select the Entire Story or Selected Text radio buttons as desired.

4 In the Format pop-up menu, choose the format into which you want to export the text. Your choices are Microsoft Word, WordPerfect, Rich Text Format (RTF), ASCII (text-only), HTML, and XTags (QuarkXPress's own format that specifies all text attributes so it can be imported into another QuarkXPress document and have those attributes re-created). QuarkXPress 4 also supports MacWrite and Microsoft Works formats.

5 Give the file a name and navigate to the desired disk and folder.

6 Click Save to save the file.

For formats that support style sheets, such as Word, RTF, and WordPerfect, QuarkXPress will also export style sheets, so the text files will be formatted using the QuarkXPress style settings. (Any formatting in QuarkXPress not supported by the word-processor format is removed during export.)

Follow These Steps

InDesign offers fewer text-file export options than Quark-XPress:

1. Using the Type tool, select a block of text to export, or click anywhere in a text frame if you want to export all text in the text frame and all text frames linked to it (a story). It's critical you make the right choice, because you can't modify this choice later in the Export dialog box.

2. Choose File ➪ Export (⌘+E or Ctrl+E) to open the Export dialog box.

3. In the Format pop-up menu, choose the format into which you want to export the text. Your choices are Rich Text Format (RTF), ASCII (text-only), and InDesign Tagged Text (InDesign's own format that specifies all text attributes so that the text can be imported into another InDesign document and have those attributes re-created). Note that you could also export to one of the graphics formats listed as well. Also, InDesign 2 supports the HTML format for export.

4. Give the file a name and navigate to the desired disk and folder.

5. Click Save to save the file.

When exporting to RTF, InDesign will also export styles, so the text files will be formatted using the InDesign style settings. (Any formatting in InDesign not supported by the RTF format is removed during export.)

Workaround: Most people edit in Microsoft Word, a format to which InDesign cannot export. Fortunately, Word opens the RTF format without difficulty and also preserves its style sheets.

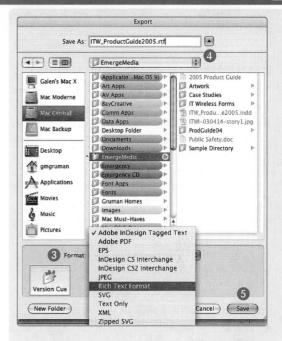

❊ Selecting Text

Selecting text is straightforward and works as it does in most Macintosh and Windows programs.

Follow These Steps

No matter what method you use, you must have first selected the Content tool.

① Click and hold in the text and drag to a different location, then release the mouse, to select the text between that start point and end point.

② You can also click in the text, hold the Shift key, and then use the up, down, left, and right arrows to make your selection. Release the Shift key when done.

③ Use the following mouse-click combinations to select the specified text, based on the current text-cursor position:

- Double-click: Select the current word.
- Triple-click: Select the current line.
- Quadruple-click: Select the current paragraph.
- Quintuple-click: Select the current story.

④ Choose Edit ➪ Select All (⌘+A or Ctrl+A) to select all text in the current story. Note that the text-insertion cursor must be active or text must be selected first.

Kayaking the San Juans

Dotted with islands and prtected by Washington State's Olympic Peninsula and British Columbia's Vancouver Island, the San Juan de Fuca Strait is a calm environment even though it's technically the ocean. That makes it a great place for kayaking. The waters are not rough, so you get to explore th emany islands in a pleas urable way. The natural beauty of the area — forested islands with small coves and the occasional sand beach, dark sapphire waters, and sunny skies in the late summer — make it a striking, soul-pleasing locale.

InDesign

Follow These Steps

Selecting text is also straightforward in InDesign. No matter what method you use, you must have first selected the Type tool.

1 Click and hold in the text and drag to a different location, then release the mouse, to select the text between that start point and end point.

2 You can also click in the text, hold the Shift key, and then use the up, down, left, and right arrows to create your selection. Release the Shift key when done.

3 Use the following mouse-click combinations to select the specified text, based on the current text-cursor position:

- Double-click: Select the current word.
- Triple-click: Select the current line.
- Quadruple-click: Select the current paragraph.
- Quintuple-click: Select the current story.

Note that if you uncheck the Triple Click to Select a Line checkbox in the Type pane of InDesign CS2's Preferences dialog box, or in the Text pane of earlier versions' Preferences dialog box (InDesign ⇨ Preferences or ⌘+K on the Mac or Edit ⇨ Preferences in Windows or Ctrl+K), triple-clicking will select the current paragraph and quadruple-clicking will select the current story. The Triple Click to Select a Line option is checked by default.

4 Choose Edit ⇨ Select All (⌘+A or Ctrl+A) to select all text in the current story. Note that the text-insertion cursor must be active or text must be selected first.

Kayaking the San Juans

Dotted with islands and prtected by Washington State's Olympic Peninsula and British Columbia's Vancouver Island, the San Juan de Fuca Strait is a calm environment even though it's technically the ocean. That makes it a great place for kayaking. The waters are not rough, so you get to explore th emany islands in a pleasurable way. The natural beauty   of the area — forested islands with small coves and the occasional   sand beach, dark sapphire waters, and sunny skies in the late summer — make it a striking, soul-pleasing locale.

✳Copying Text

Copying text works as it does in most other Macintosh and Windows programs, although there are some issues to note when copying among applications rather than solely within either of these two programs.

Follow These Steps

To begin, first select the text to be copied.

Copying within QuarkXPress

① Choose Edit ⇨ Copy (⌘+C or Ctrl+C) to copy the text into the Macintosh or Windows Clipboard, where it remains to be pasted until you copy or cut something else.

② Go to the location you want to copy the text to, whether in the current document or in another document. With the Content tool selected, click in the target text box at the desired location.

③ Choose Edit ⇨ Paste (⌘+V or Ctrl+V) to paste the copied text.

④ If drag-and-drop text is enabled, you can select text and then drag it to a new location. This moves the text rather than copies it. You enable drag-and-drop text by checking the Drag and Drop checkbox in the Interactive pane of the Preferences dialog box. (In QuarkXPress 6, choose Quark-XPress ⇨ Preferences on the Mac or Edit ⇨ Preferences in Windows; in QuarkXPress 5, choose Edit ⇨ Preferences ⇨ Preferences; and in QuarkXPress 4, choose Edit ⇨ Prefer-ences ⇨ Application. All three versions use the same short-cut: Option+Shift+⌘+Y or Ctrl+Alt+Shift+Y.)

Note that formatting is retained in the copied text.

Copying from Elsewhere into QuarkXPress

Copying text into QuarkXPress works like copying within QuarkXPress with this major exception: The copied text takes on the formatting of the QuarkXPress text around it. If pasted into an empty text box, text takes on the document's default text formatting.

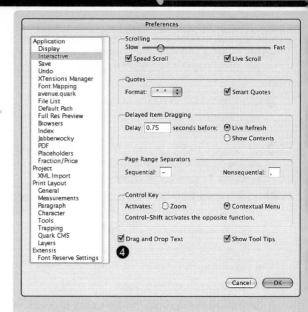

InDesign

Follow These Steps

Note that InDesign CS or later offers some controls over whether formatting is retained when you copy text, so you may want to set your preferences before copying. When you're ready to copy text, first select the text to be copied.

Copying within InDesign

❶ Choose Edit ➪ Copy (⌘+C or Ctrl+C) to copy the text into the Mac or Windows Clipboard, where it remains to be pasted until you copy or cut something else.

❷ Go to the location where you want to copy the text, whether in the current document or in another document. With the Type tool selected, click in the target text frame at the desired location.

❸ Choose Edit ➪ Paste (⌘+V or Ctrl+V) to paste the copied text. In InDesign CS2, you can instead choose Edit ➪ Paste without Formatting (Shift+⌘+V or Ctrl+Shift+V) to strip out formatting from the copied text, so it takes on the style (if any) of where it is pasted (or the default style if no style is applied). InDesign CS doesn't let you choose whether to strip out formatting on a case-by-case basis, but it does let you set this behavior universally by unchecking the Preserve Text Attributes When Pasting checkbox in the General pane of the Preferences dialog box (InDesign ➪ Preferences or ⌘+K on the Mac or Edit ➪ Preferences in Windows or Ctrl+K). InDesign 2 offers no controls over copied formatting.

❹ In InDesign CS2, if drag-and-drop text is enabled, you can select text and then drag it to a new location. This moves rather than copies the text, unless you click and hold Option or Alt just before you release the mouse character. (You can't hold Option or Alt to copy text while dragging, as you can with objects, as this will cause InDesign to scroll through the current window.) You enable drag-and-drop text by checking the Enable in Layout View and Enable in Story Editor check-boxes in the Type pane of the Preferences dialog box.

Copying from Elsewhere into InDesign

Copying text into InDesign from elsewhere works like copying within InDesign, except that different versions of InDesign handle the formatting of that copied text differently:

- InDesign CS2 does *not* retain the original formatting unless All Information is selected in the Preferences dialog box's Type pane.
- InDesign CS does *not* retain the original formatting unless Preserve Text Attributes is checked in the Preferences dialog box's General pane.
- InDesign 2 *always* preserves the formatting of the original text.

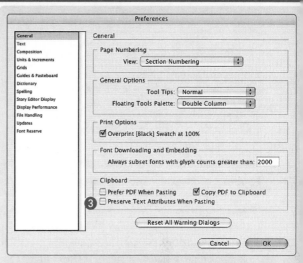

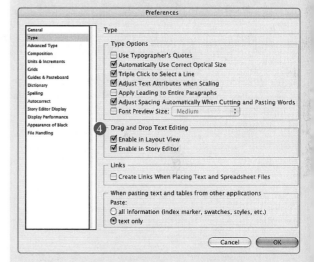

Go Further: InDesign CS and later lets you control whether copied text's format-ting is retain when pasted in your docu-ment, unlike QuarkXPress, which always retains the original formatting.

Editing Text in the Document

Most editing in your layout is for touch-up work: fixing typos that weren't caught in the source text, trimming text to make it fit the layout, and so on. Both Quark-XPress and InDesign provide basic text-editing capabilities, and InDesign's recent versions let you perform that editing in a separate window if desired.

②

Follow These Steps

QuarkXPress provides basic text-editing capabilities — but no more. Note that the Content tool must be selected to edit text.

① You can edit text by retyping selected text, or backspacing to delete text to the left of the text cursor by pressing Backspace or Delete. (In Windows, you can also delete text to the right of the text cursor by pressing Delete.)

② You can search and replace text using the Find/Change dialog box (Edit ➪ Find/Change, or ⌘+F or Ctrl+F). Quark-XPress searches from the current text-insertion point forward, so it's critical to start a find/replace operation at the beginning of the document. Use the Layout (Quark-XPress 6) or Document (QuarkXPress 5 or earlier) checkbox to search the entire layout or document; otherwise the current story is searched. Use the Whole Word and Ignore Case checkboxes to control what is found and replaced.

InDesign

Follow These Steps

InDesign also provides basic text-editing capabilities. Note that the Type tool must be selected to edit text.

① You can edit text by retyping selected text, or backspacing to delete text to the left of the text cursor by pressing Back-space or Delete. (In Windows, you can also delete text to the right of the text cursor by pressing Delete.)

② You can search and replace text using the Find/Change dia-log box (Edit ⇨ Find/Change, or ⌘+F or Ctrl+F). Use the Search pop-up menu to determine the search's scope (Selection, Story, To End of Story, Document, and All Docu-ments), and the Whole Word and Case Sensitive check-boxes to control what is found and replaced.

③ InDesign CS or later lets you edit text in a special window, where you can see all the text in a consistent, readable size and font, saving you the effort of having to constantly change your position in the layout and your zoom level. Open the Story Editor by choosing Edit ⇨ Edit in Story Editor (⌘+Y or Ctrl+Y). The editing itself is done the same way as in layout view, by replacing, deleting, and adding text, and by using the Find/Change dialog box. You control the Story Editor display settings in the Story Editor Display pane of the Preferences dialog box (InDesign ⇨ Preferences or ⌘+K on the Mac or Edit ⇨ Preferences in Windows or Ctrl+K).

 Go Further: The Story Editor appeals to many users who do extensive editing of text in their documents. QuarkXPress has no equivalent capability.

 Go Further: InDesign CS2 adds a depth ruler to the Story Editor and also marks overset text (text that doesn't fit in any of the story's text frames) so you can try to make it fit while editing in the Story Editor.

①

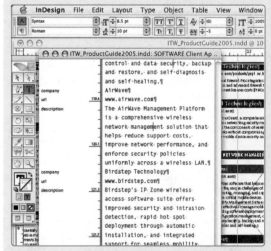

③

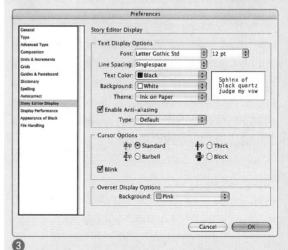

Setting Up Spelling Dictionaries   QuarkXPress

Often, the built-in spelling dictionaries don't include many words that you use, such as those for specific industries. Both QuarkXPress and InDesign let you supplement their dictionaries with your own words.

Follow These Steps

No spelling dictionary is complete, so you will want to add your own words to supplement the dictionary that came with QuarkXPress. Here's how to create and edit an auxiliary dictionary:

① If someone else has already created the auxiliary dictionary, attach it to your current document by choosing Utilities ⇨ Auxiliary Dictionary and then locating that dictionary and clicking Open. (Note that only QuarkXPress 6 can share auxiliary dictionaries between Mac and Windows users.) QuarkXPress will consult this dictionary whenever you check spelling, and will add any new words to it that you specify. Note that in QuarkXPress 6, the auxiliary dictionary selected is used only in the current layout in a project file, not for all layouts. Each time you add a new layout, you'll need to choose an auxiliary dictionary for it if you want to use such a dictionary.

② If no auxiliary dictionary is available, create a new one by clicking the New button in the Auxiliary Dictionary dialog box.

③ You can edit the auxiliary dictionary by choosing Utilities ⇨ Edit Auxiliary. Select an existing word if you want to delete or change it. Type in a new word and click Add to add it. You can also add words by clicking the Add button for suspect words when spell-checking. Note that you cannot indicate capitalization, only the sequence of letters in the word.

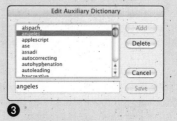

 Cross-Reference: See pages 106-107 for details on how to check spelling. See pages 108-109 for details on how to customize hyphenation dictionaries.

InDesign

Follow These Steps

InDesign offers similar spelling-checker dictionary capabilities as QuarkXPress but with a different interface. Here's how create and edit the supplemental user dictionaries:

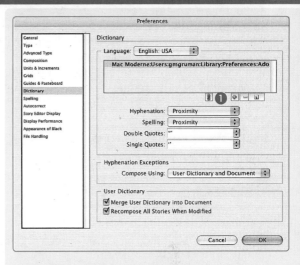

1 In InDesign CS or earlier, the program automatically creates a user dictionary in your preferences folder (*user name*\Library\Preferences\Adobe InDesign\ Version *x*.0\Dictionaries\Proximity on the Mac and Document and Settings*user name*\ Application Data\Adobe\InDesign\Version *x*.0\Dictionaries\Proximity in Windows). The user dictionary has the same name as the main dictionary for the selected language but the filename extension .udc, such as ENG.UDC. In InDesign CS2, you create your own user dictionaries by clicking the New button (the plus sign) in the Dictionary pane of the Preferences dialog box (InDesign ➪ Preferences or ⌘+K on the Mac or Edit ➪ Preferences or Ctrl+K in Windows). In all versions of InDesign, you choose the spell-checking language in this pane.

2 You can edit the user dictionary by choosing Edit ➪ Dictionary in InDesign CS or earlier, and by choosing Edit ➪ Spelling ➪ Dictionary in InDesign CS2. Type in a new word and click Add to add it. In InDesign CS2, you can also indicate capitalization by clicking the Case Sensitive checkbox. In all versions, choose whether to add the word to the user dictionary or to just add it to the document's spelling list through the Target pop-up menu.

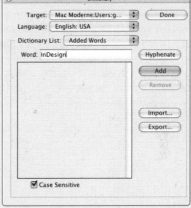

Keep in Mind

InDesign lets you merge the user dictionary into your document, which is a good thing to do if you are sharing documents with other users, since it keeps everyone's spelling checks in synch. You enable this by checking Merge User Dictionary into Document option in the Dictionary pane of the Preferences dialog box. A drawback to this approach is that different documents could have different versions of the user dictionaries in each document. In a workgroup environment, it's best to ensure that everyone's user dictionaries are kept up-to-date and consistent, perhaps by copying a master user dictionary to each user's computer.

✳ Checking Spelling

Although imported text should have been spell-checked in a word processor, it's a good idea to check spelling in your documents before printing them, to catch editing errors. QuarkXPress and InDesign provide basic spelling checkers, but InDesign CS2 has added dynamic spelling checks so you can see possible errors in your layout.

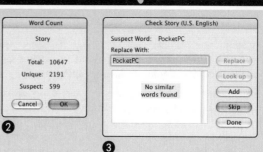

Follow These Steps

Here's how to spell-check a document:

❶ Choose the appropriate option from the Utilities ⇨ Check Spelling submenu: Word (⌘+L or Ctrl+W), Story (Option+⌘+L or Ctrl+Alt+W), or Document (Option+Shift+⌘+L or Ctrl+Alt+Shift+W).

❷ QuarkXPress will identify how many words it suspects are misspelled. Click OK to continue.

❸ In the next dialog box, you will be presented suspect words in alphabetical order. If QuarkXPress has suggested alternatives, they will display in the pane at bottom. Click Skip to leave the word unchanged throughout the document. Click Add to add the word to the auxiliary dictionary (the button is grayed out if there is no auxiliary dictionary attached to the document). Select a suggested word or enter your own and click Replace to correct the word. Click Look Up to spell-check a suggested replacement word. Click Done to end the spell-check.

Cross-Reference: See pages 104-105 for details on how to set up supplemental spelling dictionaries.

Follow These Steps

Here's how to spell-check a document:

1 Choose Edit ⇨ Check Spelling in InDesign CS or earlier, or Edit ⇨ Spelling ⇨ Check Spelling in InDesign CS2, or press ⌘+I or Ctrl+I, to open the Check Spelling dialog box.

2 Choose the spell-check scope (Story, To End of Story, Document, and All Documents) in the Search pop-up menu and then click Start.

3 You will be presented each suspect word as it occurs. If InDesign has suggested alternatives, they will display in the pane at bottom. Click Ignore to skip the current occurrence and Ignore All to leave the word unchanged throughout the document. Click Skip to move on to the next word, leaving the current word still noted as misspelled. Click Add to add the word to the user dictionary and Dictionary to open the Dictionary pane to change the spell-check language. Select a suggested word or enter your own and click Change to correct the word. Click Done when done.

 Go Further: InDesign CS2 also lets you see spelling errors in your layout by choosing Edit ⇨ Spelling ⇨ Dynamic Spelling. Suspect words will have a red squiggle under them so you can quickly identify them.

2

3

❋ Setting Up Hyphenation Dictionaries ◄ **QuarkXPress**

The hyphenation dictionaries that come with Quark-XPress and InDesign do a good job for most words. But there are times you either want to override their hyphenation settings (such as having the word *project* hyphenate as the noun *proj–ect* rather than as the verb *pro–ject*) or add specialty words they don't know about.

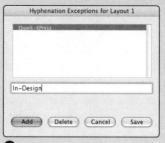

②

Follow These Steps

Setting up hyphenation-exception dictionaries, which lets you override QuarkXPress's own hyphenation rules, is similar to working with spelling-exception dictionaries.

❶ Choose Utilities ➪ Hyphenation Exceptions to open the Hyphenation Exceptions dialog box.

❷ Enter the word for which you want to specify the hyphenation, placing hyphens where you want QuarkXPress to hyphenate the word. Enter a word with no hyphens to prevent hyphenation. Click Add. (Select any exceptions you no longer want and click Delete to get rid of them.) Repeat until you are done, then click Save. (Click Cancel to leave the dialog box without saving any of the exceptions you entered.)

QuarkXPress makes all hyphenation exceptions local to the current document, so you could end up with different hyphenation-exception settings across documents. Ideally, you would create hyphenation exceptions in a template file so future documents use the same exceptions, but if someone makes a change in one document, it will affect only that document. If you add hyphenation exceptions when no document is open, these exceptions are applied to all new documents created by that copy of QuarkXPress. You cannot import or otherwise share hyphenation exceptions among users or documents unless you buy an XTension from a company, such as Vision's Edge, that provides this ability.

 Cross-Reference: See pages 104-105 for details on how to set up supplemental spelling dictionaries.

Follow These Steps

InDesign's hyphenation-exception approach is almost identical to how it handles spelling exceptions, and in fact the user dictionaries contain both spelling and hyphenation exceptions.

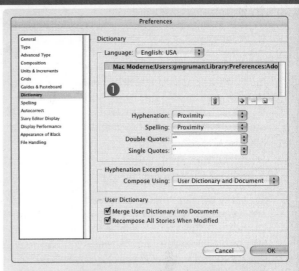

1 In InDesign CS or earlier, the program automatically creates a user dictionary in your preferences folder (`user name\Library\Preferences\Adobe InDesign\ Version x.0\Dictionaries\Proximity` on the Mac and `Document and Settings\user name\ Application Data\Adobe\InDesign\Version x.0\Dictionaries\Proximity` in Windows). The user dictionary has the same name as the main dictionary for the selected language but the filename extension .udc, such as ENG.UDC. In InDesign CS2, you create your own user dictionaries by clicking the New button (the plus sign) in the Dictionary pane of the Preferences dialog box (InDesign ➪ Preferences or ⌘+K on the Mac or Edit ➪ Preferences or Ctrl+K in Windows). In all versions of InDesign, you choose the hyphenation language in this pane.

2 You can edit the user dictionary by choosing Edit ➪ Dictionary in InDesign CS or earlier and by choosing Edit ➪ Spelling ➪ Dictionary in InDesign CS2. Type in a new word, indicate hyphens with the tilde (~) character (Shift+`), and click Add to add the word. You can specify hyphenation priorities by using multiple tildes; the more tildes, the lower the priority InDesign will give to using that hyphenation point. To inhibit hyphenation, put a tilde at the beginning of the word. Choose whether to add the word to the user dictionary or to just the document's spelling list through the Target pop-up menu.

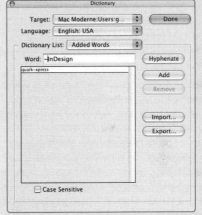

You can also indicate hyphenation preferences when using the spelling checker (see page 105). Enter the hyphenation points, as described above, to the words you add.

Specifying Language

Multilingual publishers face a more complicated challenge when it comes to spelling and hyphenation, since they must be able to support multiple languages' rules. A special version of QuarkXPress is required to support multilingual publishing, while the standard version of InDesign can handle this need. Both use the approach of letting you specify the language of your text, so the appropriate spelling and hyphenation dictionaries can be applied.

Follow These Steps

To specify different languages for spell-checking and hyphenation, you must use QuarkXPress Passport rather than standard QuarkXPress. The Passport edition is a multilingual version that supports multiple simultaneous languages. Two settings in this version control text's language characteristics:

❶ You determine a paragraph's language either locally through the Formats pane of the Paragraph Attributes dialog box (Style ⇨ Formats, or Shift+⌘+F or Ctrl+Shift+F), or as part of a style sheet through the Formats pane of a style sheet (Edit ⇨ Style Sheets or Shift+F11). Choose the language in the Language pop-up menu.

❷ You set the hyphenation preferences for each language in the Paragraph pane of the Preferences dialog box, using the pop-up menu for each language in the Hyphenation section. (In QuarkXPress 6, choose QuarkXPress ⇨ Preferences on the Mac or Edit ⇨ Preferences in Windows; in QuarkXPress 5, choose Edit ⇨ Preferences ⇨ Preferences; and in QuarkXPress 4, choose Edit ⇨ Preferences ⇨ Document. QuarkXPress 5 and 6 use the same shortcut, Option+Shift+⌘+Y or Ctrl+Alt+Shift+Y, while QuarkXPress 4 uses ⌘+Y or Ctrl+Y.)

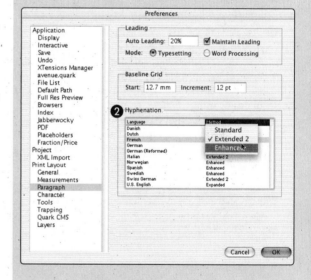

Cross-Reference: See pages 104-105 for details on how to set up supplemental spelling dictionaries. See pages 108-109 for details on setting hyphenation exceptions.

InDesign

Follow These Steps

InDesign supports multiple Western European languages in its standard version, so you don't need to buy a different version to support multiple languages.

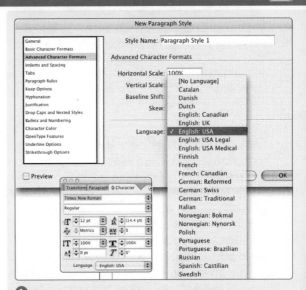

1 In the Advanced Character Formats pane of the Paragraph Styles pane (Window ⇨ Type & Tables ⇨ Paragraph Styles in InDesign CS and later or Window ⇨ Type ⇨ Paragraph Styles in InDesign 2, or F11) or the Character Styles pane (Window ⇨ Type & Tables ⇨ Character Styles in InDesign CS and later or Window ⇨ Type ⇨ Character Styles in InDesign 2, or Shift+F11), or in the Character pane (Type ⇨ Character, Window ⇨ Type ⇨ Character Styles in InDesign 2, or ⌘+T or Ctrl+T), using the Language pop-up menu. Use the Paragraph Styles pane to apply text to entire paragraphs and the Character Styles and Character panes to apply a language to specific text.

2 To control the hyphenation rules for a language, choose a new provider in the Hyphenation pop-up menu of the Dictionary pane of the Preferences dialog box (InDesign ⇨ Preferences or ⌘+K on the Mac or Edit ⇨ Preferences or Ctrl+K in Windows). Note that you'll need to buy a third-party dictionary, if you can find one, to replace the default Proximity dictionary.

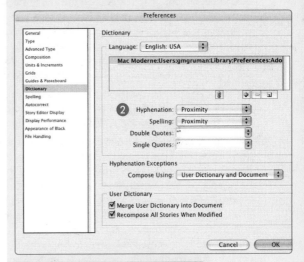

3 You can edit the user dictionary by choosing Edit ⇨ Dictionary in InDesign CS or earlier and by choosing Edit ⇨ Spelling ⇨ Dictionary in InDesign CS2. (User dictionaries contain both spelling and hyphenation exceptions.) Type in a new word, indicate hyphenation points by typing the tilde (~) character (Shift+`), and click Add to add it. Choose whether to add the word to the user dictionary or to just the document's hyphenation list through the Target pop-up menu.

 Go Further: In InDesign, you can apply language settings to highlighted characters, not just to paragraphs as in QuarkXPress Passport.

 Go Further: In InDesign CS2's Dictionary pane you can link to multiple user dictionaries, which include user-specified hyphenation exceptions, by adding dictionaries using the window and buttons under the Language pop-up menu.

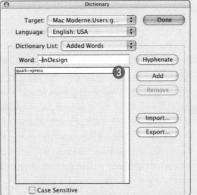

Wrapping Text around Other Objects ⟨ QuarkXPress

Text wrap is one of those techniques popularized by the desktop publishing revolution in the 1980s. With traditional layout tools, it was a painstaking manual process. Today, text wrap is almost a no-brainer to implement. While QuarkXPress and InDesign provide similar text-wrapping features, there are differences to note.

Follow These Steps

In QuarkXPress, text wrap is an automatic function for most boxes. But you can change those settings to meet your layout's specific needs, even turning off text wrap when appropriate.

❶ To set text wrap around an object, select that item with the Item tool and then choose Item ➪ Modify (⌘+T or Ctrl+T) and go to the Runaround pane.

❷ Choose the type of wrap in the Type pop-up menu. In most cases, you'll choose Item (the default setting for boxes), which wraps any text in other boxes around that selected box. Other options wrap text around the image's contours or, if available, clipping path or alpha channel. Choose None to prevent text wrapping, something you'll do when placing headlines over images or creating drop shadows by overlaying text boxes with slight differences in positions. You can see the effects of each option in the Preview window.

❸ Set the wrap distance — how far the text is kept from the selected box — using the Top, Left, Right, and Bottom fields. The default is 1 point, which is usually too little.

❹ For pictures that have a clipping path or alpha channel, or for which a contour is created with the Auto Image, Picture Bounds (for images larger or smaller than the box that contains them), or Non-White Areas options — you can also choose from three checkboxes to control the wrap further: Invert, which puts the text inside the contour, Outside Edges Only, which doesn't let text intrude inside a complex shape's interior spaces, and Restrict to Box, which ignores any part of the contour that falls outside the box (such as when the picture is bigger than the box).

❺ Click Apply to see the text-wrap effects in your layout; click OK when you are satisfied and want to implement those settings. (Click Cancel if you decide not to apply the settings.)

❻ You can change the default wrap settings for various picture and text boxes by double-clicking a tool in the Tools palette, which opens the Tools pane of the Preferences dialog box, and then selecting the tools for which you want to change settings. Then click Modify and go to the Runaround pane, which works as described above. These changes affect all new boxes created in the current document or, if no document is open, all future documents.

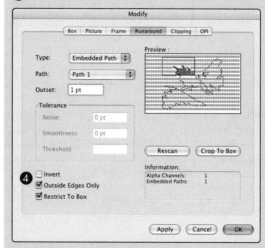

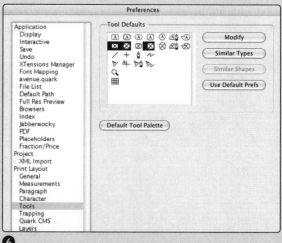

InDesign

Follow These Steps

In InDesign, text wrap is by default disabled for frames. But you can easily turn on text wrap when desired.

1️⃣ To set text wrap around an object, open the Text Wrap pane (Window ➪ Text Wrap in InDesign 2 and CS2 or Window ➪ Type & Tables ➪ Text Wrap in InDesign CS, or Option+⌘+W or Ctrl+Alt+W). Then select that object with the Selection or Direct Selection tool.

2️⃣ Choose the type of wrap using the five buttons at the top of the pane (from left to right: No Text Wrap, Wrap around Bounding Box, Wrap around Object Shape, Jump Object, and Jump to Next Column). In most cases, you'll choose Wrap around Bounding Box. Other options wrap text around the image's contours or, if available, clipping path or alpha channel. Click No Text Wrap to prevent text wrap, something you'll do when placing headlines over images.

3️⃣ Set the wrap distance — how far the text is kept from the selected box — using the Top, Left, Right, and Bottom fields. The default is 0 points, which is usually too little.

4️⃣ For graphics that have a clipping path or alpha channel, choose the appropriate contour option in the Type pop-up menu. The program also will try to create a contour if you choose Detect Images, or it will use the object's contour (as opposed to the frame's) if you choose Graphic Frame. By default, InDesign does not let text intrude inside a complex shape's interior spaces, but you can override that by checking the Include Inside Edges checkbox.

5️⃣ To wrap text inside an object, check the Invert checkbox. Unlike QuarkXPress, InDesign provides this option for any type of text wrap.

6️⃣ You can change the default wrap settings for graphics and text frames by ensuring that no objects are selected and then adjusting the settings in the Text Wrap pane. These changes affect all new frames created in the current document or, if no document is open, all future documents.

Workaround: Unlike QuarkXPress, InDesign cannot set different default text-wrap settings for different kinds of frames. One workaround is to create various text frames with the desired wrap settings and then store them in a library for reuse (see page 45). Also, there is no way to preview settings in the Text Wrap pane; they're immediately applied. Of course, you can undo the action if you don't like the result.

Go Further: InDesign lets text frames ignore the text-wrap settings of other frames: Check the Ignore Text Wrap checkbox in the Text Frame Options dialog box (Object ➪ Text Frame Options, or ⌘+B or Ctrl+B).

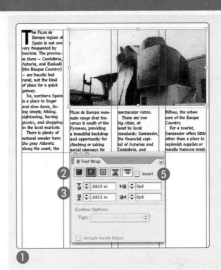

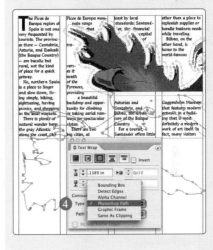

✳ Creating Text Paths

Text that follows a curve or other shape can create a very powerful effect, especially in advertising and other pro-motional copy. QuarkXPress and InDesign both provide similar text-on-a-path capabilities, although InDesign offers a tad more.

Follow These Steps

Text doesn't have to reside in a box; it can also follow a path:

1. Choose one of the four Text Path tools (Line, Orthogonal Line, Bézier, and Freehand) from the Tools palette.

2. Draw the path as desired. For Bézier and freehand paths, edit them as needed to refine their shapes (you can do this before or after you add the text). To convert a closed shape — such as a rectangle or ellipse — so text can run around its outline, select it with the Item or Content tool and then choose Item ⇨ Shape ⇨ Freehand (the bottommost icon). You now have a closed text path. (If the original frame was not a text box, choose Item ⇨ Content ⇨ Text to let it hold text.) Note that such closed paths cannot contain pictures or text inside them.

3. Select the path with the Content tool. You can now enter text, and style it using all the regular formatting options in QuarkXPress, including style sheets.

Cross-Reference: For more on editing paths and lines, see Part VIII

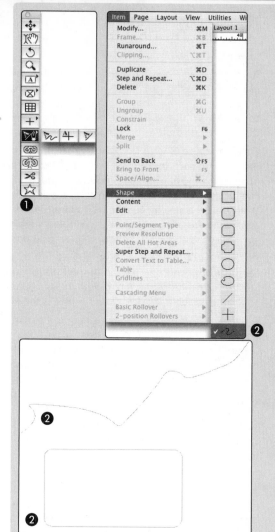

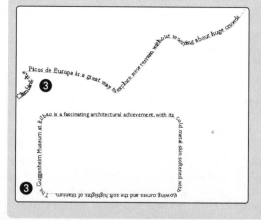

Follow These Steps

In InDesign, text also doesn't have to reside in a box; it can also follow a path:

1. Choose one of the drawing tools (Pen, Pencil, or Line) or one of the frame or shape tools (Rectangle, Ellipse, or Polygon) from the Tools palette.

2. Draw the path or shape as desired. For Bézier and freehand paths created with the Pen and Pencil tools, edit them as needed to refine their shape.

3. Select the path or frame with the Type on a Path tool (hold the Type tool until the pop-up menu appears, then choose the Type on a Path tool from it). Unlike QuarkXPress, you don't have to convert a frame to a path for it to hold text in its outline. You can now enter text, and style it using all the regular formatting options in InDesign, including styles.

Go Further: For closed paths in QuarkXPress, the text will start at the origin point for the original shape (the starting corner when you drew it). But InDesign will start the text where you first click with the Type on a Path tool, giving you more control over its placement.

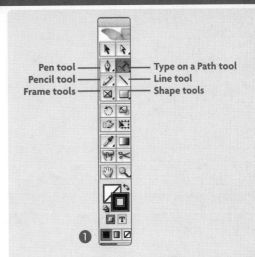

Pen tool — Type on a Path tool
Pencil tool — Line tool
Frame tools — Shape tools

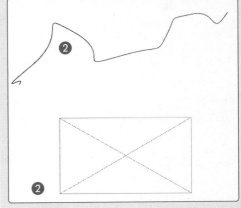

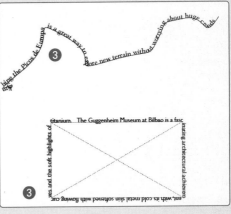

part V

Working with Text Formatting

QuarkXPress has long been known for its typographic controls, but InDesign meets or beats it on almost every count. In this part, you'll learn how to achieve the fine typography you expect from QuarkXPress and how to augment it with InDesign's capabilities.

Also, while many fundamental capabilities are the same in Quark-XPress and InDesign, InDesign has several unique ways of expressing or delivering them, which can confuse veteran QuarkXPress users. This part highlights those issues as well.

Working with Font Attributes

Fonts are the building blocks of text formatting. Both QuarkXPress and InDesign provide significant controls, although InDesign offers more.

Follow These Steps

QuarkXPress provides several tools that apply font attributes (called *styles* and sometimes *type styles* in QuarkXPress): the Measurements palette, the Character dialog box (Style ➪ Character, or Shift+⌘+D or Ctrl+Shift+D), the Style menu's Font and Type Style options, and style sheets. These many tools work with fonts pretty much the same way:

① You can choose a font from a menu or pop-up menu and then separately apply a type style — such as boldface — through a button, keyboard shortcut, checkbox, or menu.

② You can choose a font and its style from a menu or pop-up menu, using submenus to select the specific style. To change to boldface, italic, or boldface italic, you do not select the style in QuarkXPress but instead use the Font menu to choose the boldface or italic variant of your font. When dealing with faces such as light, semibold, and black, QuarkXPress typically treats these as separate fonts using the plain type style for the roman variant and the italic type style for the italic or oblique variant. In some cases, all styles of a font are listed in the main font menu, while in others you will get a submenu for each font — your font manager (such as Adobe Type Manager, Extensis Suitcase, or Extensis FontReserve) controls how these styles display.

③ For many styles — underlines, strikethrough, shadow, outline, subscript, superscript, superior, small caps, and all caps — you use the Type Style option in the Style menu or in the equivalent checkboxes in the Character and Style Sheets dialog box, in the equivalent buttons in the Measurements palette, and via the equivalent keyboard shortcuts. That's because these attributes don't involve the font file but are simply changes to font elements, such as size, outline and fill, and overprinting lines.

Most savvy designers and practically all service bureaus beg their colleagues and clients not to use the method in option 1 above, since applying a style such as boldface or italics on top of a font can lead to output errors. In some cases, QuarkXPress doesn't choose the correct font for that style, and in other cases the chosen font has no bold or italic variant even though QuarkXPress lets you apply that style anyhow. While the problem is due to how PostScript fonts are managed (each face and style is a separate font file, so programs have to know which ones are related to each other so they can choose the correct boldface or italic variant), QuarkXPress makes it easier for such problems to surface. That's why you should always use option 2.

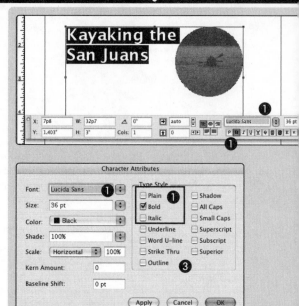

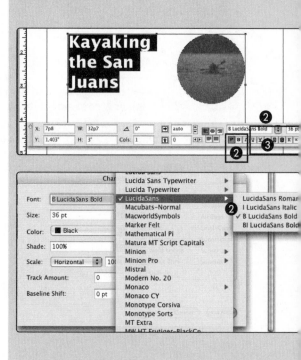

InDesign

Follow These Steps

InDesign also provides several tools to apply font attributes (called *font styles* in InDesign): the Control palette, the Character dialog box (Type ⇨ Character, or ⌘+T or Ctrl+T), the Type menu's Font option, and through type styles:

❶ You choose a font and its font style from a menu or pop-up menu, using submenus to select the specific font style such as boldface, italics, compressed, black, or book. In some cases, all font styles are listed in the main font menu, while in others you will get a submenu for each font — the font manager in use (such as Adobe Type Manager, Extensis Suitcase, or Extensis Font Reserve) controls how these font styles display in menus. In many dialog boxes and panes, InDesign offers two pop-up menus: one for the main font and one for the font style.

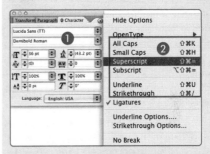

❷ For font-style attributes that don't actually involve the font file — including underline, strikethrough, small caps, all caps, superscript, and subscript — you use the buttons in the Control palette, palette menu options in the Character pane's palette menu, or in the Basic Character Attributes of the Character Styles and Paragraph Styles panes.

The reason InDesign doesn't use buttons, checkboxes, or keyboard shortcuts for font styles such as boldface and italics is due to how PostScript fonts are managed (each face and type style is a separate font file, so programs have to know which ones are related to each other to choose the correct boldface or italic variant). Rather than making an incorrect choice, InDesign forces you to select the specific font style. That will annoy some QuarkXPress users, but since most service bureaus have long recommended selecting the specific font style instead of using the boldface and italics options, it should be fairly easy to adjust to InDesign's approach.

Go Further: A major difference between QuarkXPress and InDesign is their handling of OpenType fonts, which contain multiple variants within them. QuarkXPress sees just the regular characters and styles in such fonts, while InDesign provides access to them, as described on page 360.

Creating Paragraph Styles

Style sheets (simply called *styles* in InDesign) are essential tools in a layout program, as they let you easily apply consistent formatting to text throughout your document. Paragraph style sheets format the paragraph as a whole — spacing, indents, hyphenation, tabs, and ruling lines — rather than the characters the paragraph contains.

Follow These Steps

Here is how you create paragraph style sheets in QuarkXPress:

1 To create a style sheet, you have two options. One is to choose Edit ⇨ Style Sheets (Shift+F11) to open the Style Sheets dialog box. The other is to ⌘+click or Ctrl+click an existing style in the Style Sheets palette (Window ⇨ Show Style Sheets in QuarkXPress 6 or View ⇨ Show Style Sheets in QuarkXPress 5 and earlier, or F11), which also opens the Style Sheets dialog box.

2 Click the New button and select ¶ Paragraph from its pop-up menu. (If no document is open, the new style sheet[s] will be available in all future documents.) You can also import style sheets from other documents by clicking Append.)

3 In the resulting Edit Paragraph Style Sheet dialog box, use the General, Formats, Tabs, and Rules panes to set your style sheet's specifications. (If text was selected when you clicked New, its settings will be used in the various panes.) Note that in the General pane you can base one paragraph style on another, so any changes to the parent style sheet also alter the child style sheet. (If an attribute in the child paragraph style sheet differs from that in the parent paragraph style sheet, that attribute will not be updated when the paragraph style sheet is changed.)

4 The Formats pane contains the style attributes you'll use most often, those controlling indents, leading, spacing, drop caps, keep options, hyphenation, and alignment.

5 In QuarkXPress, you can either have the paragraph style sheet use a character style sheet for the character attributes, or you can click Edit and modify the default character settings for this paragraph style sheet (see page 124). But you can't use a character style sheet and then decide to override some of its attributes; any overrides change the character style sheet for all paragraph styles that use it.

6 Click OK when done with this paragraph style sheet.

7 Click Save in the Style Sheets pane to save the style sheet(s).

Cross-Reference: See pages 128-129 for how to set hyphenation specifications used in paragraph style sheets. For information on drop caps, see pages 132-133. For information on ruling lines, see pages 150-151. For information on tabs, see pages 174-175.

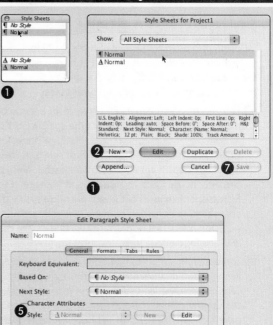

Follow These Steps

Paragraph styles in InDesign format the paragraph as a whole — spacing, indents, hyphenation, tabs, and ruling lines — as well as the characters the paragraph contains.

1 To create a style, you choose New Paragraph Style in the Paragraph Styles pane's palette menu (Window ➪ Type & Tables ➪ Paragraph Styles in InDesign CS and later or Window ➪ Type ➪ Paragraph Styles in InDesign 2, or F11) to open the New Paragraph Style dialog box. (If no document is open, the new style[s] will be available in all future documents.) You can also import style sheets from other documents by choosing Load Styles from the palette menu.

2 Use the various panes to set your style's specifications. (If text was selected when you chose New Paragraph Style, its settings will be used in the various panes.) Note that in the General pane you can base one paragraph style on another, so any changes to the parent style also alter the child style sheet. (If an attribute in the child style differs from that in the parent style, that attribute will not be updated when the paragraph style is changed.) Check the Preview checkbox to see the effects of the settings; you must have a paragraph activated (clicked) with the Type tool and visible to see the preview.

3 The Indents and Spacing pane contains many of the style attributes that you'll use most often, those controlling indents, leading, spacing, and alignment. Use the Keep Options pane (not shown) to set whether and how paragraphs "stick" with subsequent paragraphs, and use the Drop Caps and Nested Styles pane (called the Drop Caps pane in InDesign 2), shown on page 133, to set up drop caps.

4 Use the Basic Character Formats and Advanced Character Formats panes for character attributes (see page 124).

5 Click OK when done.

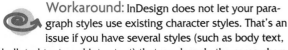

Workaround: InDesign does not let your paragraph styles use existing character styles. That's an issue if you have several styles (such as body text, bulleted text, and intro text) that use largely the same character attributes. In QuarkXPress, changing the one character style would update all paragraph styles using it. In InDesign, you'll need to change the character settings for each.

You can minimize such effort by using the Based On pop-up menu in the General pane of the New Paragraph Style dialog box; that way, if the initial paragraph style's character attributes are changed, all paragraph styles based on it will also have their character attributes change accordingly.

When you have multiple styles that have the same character formatting but are not based on one another (as QuarkXPress allows), you'll have to change them in each paragraph style.

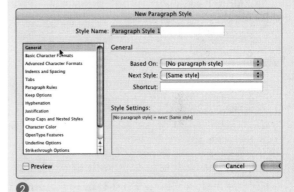

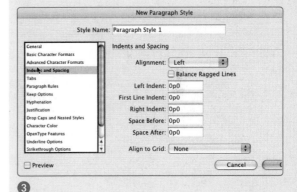

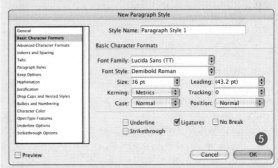

❋Overriding Paragraph Styles

From time to time you will need to override a paragraph's style sheet, either to apply local formatting or to apply a different paragraph style.

Follow These Steps

Applying Local Formatting

Overriding paragraph formatting for specific layout needs is easy:

❶ With the Content tool, activate (click) the paragraph to modify.

❷ Use the Measurements palette or the various relevant Style menu options, or the appropriate keyboard shortcuts, to override paragraph styles sheet. For example, you could change the alignment or the space above for just the active paragraph. Note that a plus sign (+) will appear in the Style Sheets palette next to the paragraph style sheet's name to remind you that this paragraph has been modified. (This reminder appears only if your text cursor is in the modified paragraph.)

Applying a Different Style Sheet

Applying a different paragraph style sheet to a paragraph is a bit trickier:

❶ With the Content tool, activate (click) the paragraph to which you will apply a different paragraph style sheet.

❷ Click the replacement paragraph style sheet in the Style Sheets palette. QuarkXPress will apply that paragraph style sheet's settings but will not override any character style sheets or local formatting applied to the paragraph or its text. To override all local and character-style formatting, hold the Option or Alt key when you click the replacement paragraph style sheet's name.

❸ To keep the style sheet but lose any overrides, do step 2 but select the current paragraph style sheet's name.

Removing Style Sheets

You can also remove a style sheet from a paragraph so it is no longer updated when the style sheet is changed:

❶ Follow steps 1 and 2 in the "Applying a Different Style Sheet" section above but click No Style in the paragraph style sheets section of the Style Sheets palette. The paragraph will retain its formatting (unless you hold Option or Alt), but it will all be converted to local formatting.

❷ You can also delete a style sheet by clicking its name in the Style Sheets dialog box (see page 120) and clicking Delete. QuarkXPress will then ask you to select what style sheet to apply in its place from a list that includes No Style.

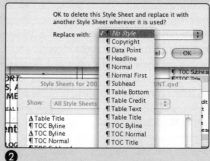

Follow These Steps

Applying Local Formatting

Here is how you override paragraph formatting for specific layouts in InDesign:

1. With the Type tool, activate (click) the paragraph to modify.

2. Use the Control palette or the various relevant Type menu options, or the appropriate keyboard shortcuts, to override paragraph styles. For example, you could change the alignment or the space above for just the active paragraph. Note that a plus sign (+) will appear in the Paragraph Styles pane after the paragraph style's name to remind you that this paragraph has been modified. (This reminder appears only if your text cursor is in the modified paragraph.)

Applying a Different Style

Applying a different paragraph style to a paragraph takes a bit more work:

1. With the Type tool, activate (click) the text to which you want to apply a different paragraph style.

2. Click the replacement character style in the Paragraph Styles pane. InDesign will apply that paragraph style's settings but will not override any character styles or local formatting applied to the paragraph or its text. To override just local formatting, hold Option or Alt when you click the replacement paragraph style's name. To override both local and character-style formatting, hold Option+Shift or Alt+Shift.

3. To keep the style but lose any overrides, choose Clear Overrides from the Paragraph Styles pane's palette menu or do step 2 and select the current paragraph style's name.

InDesign 2 and CS

Removing Styles

You can also remove a style from a paragraph so it is no longer updated when the style is changed:

1. Follow steps 1 and 2 in the "Applying a Different Style" section above but, in InDesign CS2, choose Break Link to Style in the Paragraph Styles pane's palette menu. In InDesign 2 or CS, click [No Paragraph Style] in the Paragraph Styles pane. Either way, the paragraph will retain its formatting but that formatting will all be converted to local formatting, unless you use the override options as described in step 2 above.

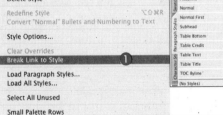

InDesign CS2

2. You can also delete a style by clicking its name in the Paragraph Styles pane (see page 120) and clicking Delete. (You can also choose Delete Style from the Paragraph Styles pane's palette menu.) InDesign CS2 will then ask you what style to apply in its place, and will provide a list of styles that includes [No Paragraph Style]. In previous versions, [No Paragraph Style] is applied automatically.

■Creating Character Styles

Styles (called *style sheets* in QuarkXPress) are essential tools in a layout program, as they let you easily apply consistent formatting to text throughout your document.

Follow These Steps

Character style sheets format text, whether as entire paragraphs or as text selections.

① To create a style sheet, you have two options. One is to choose Edit ➪ Style Sheets (Shift+F11) to open the Style Sheets dialog box. The other is to ⌘+click or Ctrl+click an existing style in the Style Sheets palette (Window ➪ Show Style Sheets in QuarkXPress 6 or View ➪ Show Style Sheets in QuarkXPress 5 and earlier, or F11), which also opens the Style Sheets dialog box.

② Click the New button and select A Character from its pop-up menu. (If no document is open, the new style sheet[s] will be available in all future documents.) You can also import style sheets from other documents by clicking the Append button.

③ In the resulting Edit Character Style Sheet dialog box, set your style sheet's specifications. (If text was selected when you clicked New, its settings will be used in the dialog box.) Note that you can base one character style on another, so any changes to the parent style sheet also alter the child style sheet. (If an attribute in the child style sheet differs from that in the parent style sheet, that attribute will not be updated when the character style sheet is changed.)

④ Click OK when done with this character style sheet.

⑤ Then click Save in the Style Sheets pane to save the new style sheet(s).

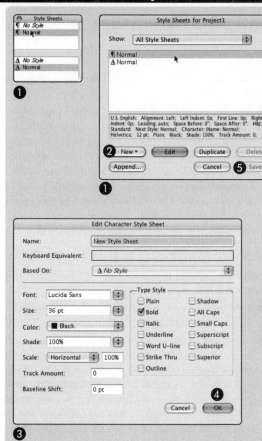

InDesign

Follow These Steps

Character styles in InDesign format the selections of text that you want to be consistently formatted with other text.

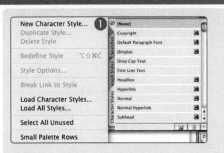

1 To create a style, you choose New Character Style in the Character Styles pane's palette menu (Window ➪ Type & Tables ➪ Character Styles in InDesign CS and later or Window ➪ Type ➪ Character Styles in InDesign 2, or Shift+F11) to open the New Character Style dialog box. (If no document is open, the new style[s] will be available in all future documents.) You can also import styles from other documents by choosing Load Styles in the palette menu.

2 Use the various panes to set your style's specifications. (If text was selected when you chose New Character Style, its settings will be used in the various panes.) Note that in the General pane you can base one character style on another, so any changes to the parent style also alter the child style. (If an attribute in the child style differs from that in the parent style, that attribute will not be updated when the character style is changed.) Check the Preview checkbox to see the effects of the settings; you must have text visible and selected with the Type tool to see the preview.

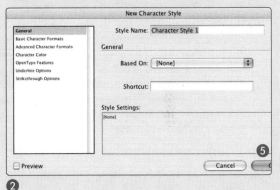

3 The Basic Character Formats pane is where you set most attributes, as the common ones are all here. Note that for attributes such as underline, you have three options: on (checked), off (empty) and "leave the text however it is" (dash); InDesign cycles through these options as you click the checkboxes. (QuarkXPress has just the checked and unchecked options, but the unchecked option leaves alone any local formatting unless you explicitly override that formatting as described on page 125.)

4 The Advanced Character Formats pane offers more specialized options. Multilingual publishers will often use the Language pop-up menu so that spelling and hyphenation dictionaries don't flag foreign words and phrases. (See page 111 for details on multiple-language publishing.)

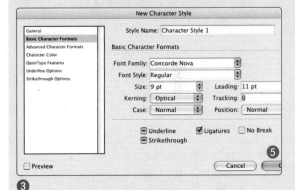

5 Click OK when done.

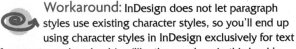 **Workaround:** InDesign does not let paragraph styles use existing character styles, so you'll end up using character styles in InDesign exclusively for text fragments, such as lead-ins (like the numbers in this book's steps and the word "Workaround" in this paragraph) or other repeatedly used local formatting. See page 121 for more details.

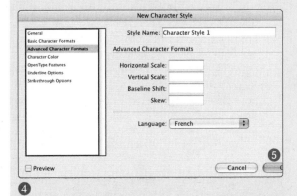

Overriding Character Styles

You will from time to time need to override text's character style sheet, either to specify local formatting or to apply a different character style to it.

Follow These Steps

Applying Local Formatting

Overriding character formatting for specific layout needs is easy:

1 With the Content tool, select the text to modify.

2 Use the Measurements palette or the various relevant Style menu options, or the appropriate keyboard shortcuts, to override style sheets. For example, you could change the font, kerning, or underlining. Note that a plus sign (+) will appear in the Style Sheets palette next to the character (and paragraph) style sheet's name to remind you that this text has been modified. (This reminder appears only if your text cursor is in the modified text.)

Applying a Different Style Sheet

Applying a different character style sheet to text is a bit trickier:

1 With the Content tool, select the text to which you want to apply a different character style sheet.

2 Click the replacement character style sheet in the Style Sheets palette. QuarkXPress will apply that character style sheet's settings but will not override any local formatting applied to the text. To override both local and character-style formatting, hold the Option or Alt key when you click the replacement character style sheet's name.

3 To keep the style sheet but lose any overrides, do step 2 but select the current character style sheet's name.

Removing Style Sheets

You can also remove a style sheet from text, so it is no longer updated when the style sheet is changed:

1 Follow steps 1 and 2 in the "Applying a Different Style Sheet" section above but click No Style in the character style sheets section of the Style Sheets palette. The text selection will retain its formatting (unless you hold Option or Alt), but it will all be converted to local formatting.

2 You can also delete a style sheet by clicking its name in the Style Sheets dialog box (see page 124) and clicking Delete. QuarkXPress will then ask you what style sheet to apply in its place, providing a list of styles that includes No Style.

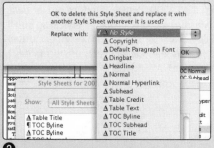

InDesign

Follow These Steps

InDesign's methods for overriding text formatting differ from those in QuarkXPress:

Applying Local Formatting

To override text formatting:

1 With the Type tool, select the text to modify.

2 Use the Control palette or the various relevant Type menu options, or the appropriate keyboard shortcuts, to override styles. For example, you could change the font, kerning, or underlining. Note that a plus sign (+) will appear in the Character Styles pane after the character style's name to remind you that this text has been modified. (This reminder appears only if your text cursor is in the modified text.)

Applying a Different Style

Here's how you apply a different character style to text:

1 With the Type tool, select the text to which you want to apply a different style.

2 Click the replacement character style in the Character Styles pane. InDesign will apply that character style's settings but will not override local formatting applied to the text. To override local formatting, hold Option or Alt when you click the replacement character style's name.

3 To keep the style but lose any local overrides, choose Clear Overrides from the Character Styles pane's palette menu or do step 2 and select the current character style's name.

Removing Styles

You can also remove a character style from text, so it is no longer updated when the style is changed:

1 Follow steps 1 and 2 in the "Applying a Different Style" section above but click [None] (in InDesign CS2) or [No Character Style] (in earlier versions of InDesign) in the Character Styles pane. The text will retain its formatting, but it will all be converted to local formatting. Note that you have the same override options as described in step 2 above. In InDesign CS2, you can also choose Break Link to Style in the Character Styles pane's palette menu to apply [None].

2 You can also delete a style by clicking its name in the Character Styles pane (see page 125) and clicking Delete. (You can also choose Delete Style from the Character Styles pane's palette menu.) InDesign will then ask you what style to apply in its place, providing a list of character styles that includes [None] (InDesign CS2) or {No Character Style} (InDesign CS or earlier).

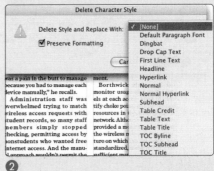

Specifying Hyphenation and Justification

Hyphenation and justification are two key tools to control paragraph appearance and spacing. Although their functions are distinct, layout programs have historically used a single dialog box or pane for both.

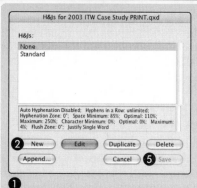

Follow These Steps

Hyphenation is a key part of paragraph spacing, so you might think that its settings would be part of paragraph style sheets, but QuarkXPress treats hyphenation as a separate function that paragraph style sheets access. The logic is that you can set a few hyphenation specifications and then have them used by a variety of style sheets. Typically, you'd have two hyphenation and justification sets (H&J sets): one with hyphenation turned on and one with hyphenation turned out. You might have additional hyphenation sets to set different character and word spacing values, such as for headlines versus body text.

Creating H&J Sets

To create an H&J set:

1. Choose Edit ➪ H&Js (Option+⌘+J or Ctrl+Shift+F11 in QuarkXPress 6 or Option+⌘+H or Ctrl+Shift+F11 in earlier versions).

2. In the H&Js dialog box, click the New button. (If no document is open, the new H&J set(s) will be available in all future documents. You can also import H&J sets from other documents by clicking the Append button.)

3. Set the hyphenation and justification settings.

4. Click OK when done.

5. When done creating H&J sets, click Save in the H&Js dialog box to save them.

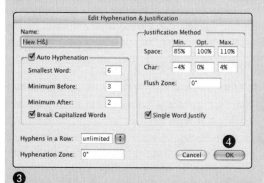

Applying H&J Sets

After H&J sets are defined, you can have your paragraph style sheets use them:

1. In the Formats pane of the Edit Paragraph Style Sheet dialog box (see page 120), choose the H&J set to be used for the style sheet in the H&J pop-up menu.

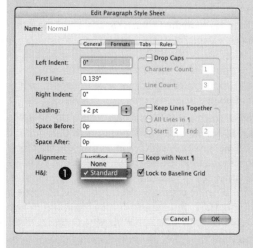

InDesign

Follow These Steps

InDesign treats hyphenation as part of the paragraph styles, not as separate settings as QuarkXPress does. This means that you will set hyphenation and justification settings directly in paragraph styles. (See page 121 for details on creating paragraph styles.) Here's how:

❶ In the Hyphenation page, set the hyphenation settings.

❷ In the Justification pane, set the justification settings.

 Workaround: The fact that InDesign defines hyphenation and justification settings as part of paragraph styles can be an issue if you have several styles (such as body text, bulleted text, and intro text) that use largely the same hyphenation and justification attributes. In QuarkXPress, changing the one H&J set would update all paragraph styles using that set. In InDesign, you'll need to change the hyphenation and justification settings for each paragraph style.

You can minimize such effort by using the Based On pop-up menu in the General pane of the New Paragraph Style dialog box; that way, if the initial paragraph style's hyphenation and justification attributes are changed, all paragraph styles based on it will also have their hyphenation and justification attributes changed accordingly.

In those cases where you have multiple styles with the same hyphenation and justification formatting but that are not based on each other (as QuarkXPress allows), you'll have to change them in each paragraph style.

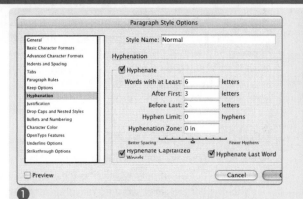

❶

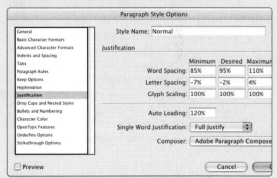

❷

✸ Preventing Hyphenation

There are times when you don't want text to hyphenate, even if that hyphenation is permitted by the style sheet's hyphenation settings. For example, it just may look awkward if a short word on a long line hyphenates and so appears to be hanging in space because the lines above and below happen to be short.

Follow These Steps

Here's how to prevent hyphenation in QuarkXPress:

① Type ⌘+– or Ctrl+– immediately before the word's first letter to prevent the entire word from hyphenating. (This same character, called a discretionary hyphen, also overrides the hyphenation point if placed within a word.)

② To turn off hyphenation globally, use paragraph style sheets. First, create an H&J set that has hyphenation turned off (see page 128). Then have your paragraph style sheets use that H&J set. Typically, you'd have such a nonhyphenating H&J set used by paragraph style sheets for elements such as headlines that are not usually hyphenated. Because H&J sets operate through paragraph style sheets, you can have some types of text be consistently hyphenated and other types of text not be hyphenated at all.

Cross-Reference: See pages 128-129 for details on setting hyphenation and pages 120-121 for details on creating paragraph style sheets.

InDesign

Follow These Steps

InDesign also lets you prevent hyphenation:

① Type Shift+⌘+− or Ctrl+Shift+− (or choose Type ⇨ Special Characters ⇨ Discretionary Hyphen) immediately before the word's first letter to prevent the entire word from hyphenating. (The discretionary hyphen also overrides the hyphenation point if placed within a word.)

② Select the word and choose No Break from the Control palette's palette menu.

③ Select the word and uncheck the Hyphenate checkbox in the Paragraph pane (Type ⇨ Paragraph, or Option+⌘+T or Ctrl+Alt+T).

④ Turn off hyphenation in the paragraph style that is applied to the text.

✳Setting Up Drop Caps

A drop cap is a popular, effective way to set an introductory or concluding paragraph or section apart from the rest of the story.

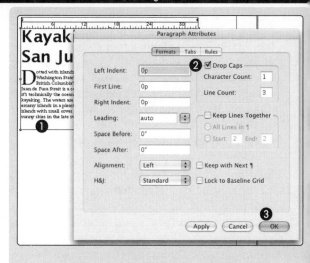

Follow These Steps

In QuarkXPress, a drop cap is part of a paragraph's formatting, so it can be set in a paragraph style sheet or through local formatting:

① Select the paragraph to which you want to apply the drop cap and open either the Paragraph Formats dialog box for local formatting (Style ⇨ Formatting, or Shift+⌘+F or Ctrl+Shift+F) or the Edit Paragraph Style Sheets dialog box for style-sheet formatting (choose Edit ⇨ Style Sheets or press Shift+F11 to open the Style Sheets dialog box and then click Edit to edit the selected style sheet; see page 120 for more details). Either way, go to the Formats pane.

② Check the Drop Caps checkbox to enable drop caps, then enter a value for the number of lines the drop cap should fit into and the number of characters that should comprise the drop cap (1 is typical). If you're applying local formatting, you can click the Apply button to preview the formatting; the paragraph must also be visible onscreen.

③ Click OK to close the dialog box. (If editing or creating a style sheet, be sure to also click Save in the Style Sheets dialog box to save the style sheet.) Your paragraph will now have the specified drop cap.

④ QuarkXPress's drop-cap controls don't let you specify character attributes for the drop cap itself, and it's very common to change the font for a drop cap. So select the drop cap character and either apply local formatting via the Measurements palette or Style menu, or apply a character style sheet to it. You'll have to do this for every drop cap in your document, even those that use paragraph style sheets.

⑤ To use a graphic as a drop cap, put it in a box, then delete it with the Item tool. Set a text wrap for the box. Now cut the box and switch to the Content tool. Place the text-insertion cursor at the beginning of the paragraph and paste the box. You may need to apply a baseline shift to the anchored box to move it down into the text.

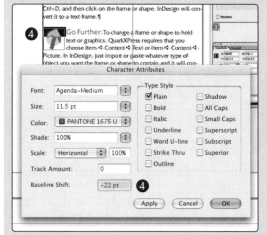

Cross-Reference: See pages 250-251 and 354-355 for more on anchoring items into text.

Follow These Steps

In InDesign, a drop cap is part of a paragraph's formatting, so it can be set as part of a paragraph style sheet or through local formatting. Because InDesign paragraph formatting also includes character formatting, you can set its character attributes in the style, unlike in QuarkXPress.

1 To set a drop cap locally, select the paragraph to which you want to apply the drop cap and use the Control palette's paragraph (the ¶ button) pane or the Paragraph pane for local formatting (Type ➪ Paragraph, or Option+⌘+T or Ctrl+Option+T). Set the drop cap depth and number of characters using the two fields that appear near the bottom of the pane. To apply different formatting to the drop cap itself, such as changing the font, switch to the character pane (the A button) of the Control palette or to the Character pane and apply the desired formatting to the drop cap character(s). Your paragraph will now have the specified drop cap.

2 To set a drop cap as part of a paragraph, create a new paragraph style or edit an existing one, as appropriate, to apply the drop-cap attributes. Choose Window ➪ Type & Tables ➪ Paragraph Styles (in InDesign CS and later) or Window ➪ Type ➪ Paragraph Styles (in InDesign 2), or press F11, to open the Paragraph Styles pane and choose either New Paragraph Style or Style Options from the palette menu. (See page 121 for more details on paragraph styles.) Either way, go to the Drop Caps & Nested Styles pane (in InDesign CS and later) or the Drop Caps pane (in InDesign 2). Set the depth and number of characters in the pane and, optionally, select a character style to apply to the drop cap's text. (You must define the character style for a drop cap before setting up the paragraph style that uses it.) Click OK to close the dialog box. Any paragraphs with this style applied will get the specified drop cap.

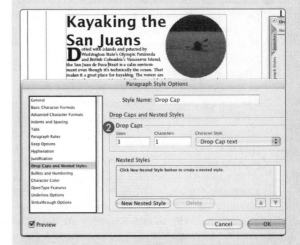

3 To use a graphic as a drop cap, you have two choices. You can cut an existing frame with the Selection tool and then switch to the Type tool and place the text-insertion cursor at the beginning of the paragraph and paste the frame. Or you can place the text-insertion cursor at the beginning of the paragraph and choose File ➪ Place (⌘+D or Ctrl+D) to import it as a graphic at that location. Either way, you will likely need to apply a baseline shift to the anchored graphic to move it down into the text.

✻ Creating Bulleted and Numbered Lists   QuarkXPress

Bulleted lists are a great device for listing a series of items, calling attention to each. Likewise, numbered lists are great to call attention to steps, priorities, or other lists whose order of presentation is meaningful. Quark-XPress and earlier versions of InDesign give you basic capabilities for such lists, while the newest version of InDesign goes much further.

Follow These Steps

QuarkXPress does not really support numbered or bulleted lists in the automatic fashion that word processors offer.

1 You manually enter bullets and numbers in your text. For numbered lists, you'll have to renumber the paragraphs if you insert or delete paragraphs. The normal bullet character (·) is accessed by pressing Option+8 on the Mac and by holding Alt and entering **0149** on the numeric keypad in Windows, and the thin bullet (·) is accessed via Option+Shift+9 on the Mac and by holding Alt and entering **0183** on the numeric keypad in Windows. You can use other characters in symbol fonts as well, accessing them through a program such as PopChar X, the Mac's Character Palette or older Key Caps utility, and the Windows Character Map utility. You'll typically want a fixed space, such as an en space (Option+ space or Ctrl+Alt+6) or punctuation space, (Shift+space or Ctrl+6) after a bullet or number so the text after the bullet starts at the same location in all paragraphs. For numbered lists, you might use a right tab to align the number against (so the periods of single– and double-digit numbers align properly) and then a second (left) tab to indicate the start position for the following text.

2 You can use hanging indents (set in paragraph style sheets or locally by choosing Style ➪ Format or pressing Shift+⌘+F or Ctrl+Shift+F) or use the indent-to-here character (⌘+\ or Ctrl+\) to have QuarkXPress have subsequent lines of a paragraph hang off the bullet or number.

The best coffeehouses in San Francisco:¶
· **Martha & Bros.**, 3868 24th St., (415) 641-4433. Family-owned and –managed, Martha's is the neighborhood coffee joint, with big crowds on weekends. The staff knows its customers, serving regulars their favorites before they even reach the counter. And the coffee is excellent.¶
  Other locations:¶
  ··1551 Church St., (415) 648-1166¶
  ··745 Cortland St., (415) 642-7585¶
  ··2800 California St., (415) 931-2281¶
· **Farley's Coffeehouse**, 1315 18th St., (415) 648-1545. Farley's is a wonderful place to go for a traditional East Coast coffeehouse. You go there for the coffee, the magazines, and the conversation. No nonfat milk, and the only flavoring is vanilla—just real coffee and real milk.¶
· **Diamond Corner Café**, 751 Diamond St., (415) 282-9551. Away from the bustle up 24th Street is this friendly corner café frequented by

The most popular destinations in San Francisco:¶
→ 1.→Fisherman's Wharf, Pier 39, and Ghirardelli Square, covering about half a dozen blocks along San Francisco's waterfront, constitute much of the stereotypical San Francisco image and together are perhaps the most popular things to do. Tourists walking here are entertained by street performers and tempted by souvenir shops and restaurants.¶
→ 2.→Union Square, one of the city's three original parks, is now a public space atop a multilevel underground parking garage and ringed with elegant shops and hotels. The Powell cable car line begins about a block away, and the theatre district is nearby.¶
→ 3.→The Golden Gate Bridge is an engineering marvel. Not only is it one of the city's most enjoyable things to do, but it's also one of the most-photographed sights in the world.¶
→ 4.→Cable cars are often called San Francisco's moving landmark.¶

1

 Cross-Reference: For more on how bulleted and numbered lists import, see pages 86-87. For more on setting up style sheets, see pages 120-121.

Go Further: InDesign CS2 offers true automatic bullets and numbered lists, as explained on the opposite page.

InDesign

Follow These Steps

Until InDesign CS2, InDesign's handling of bullets and numbering was as limited as QuarkXPress's.

InDesign CS2

❶ Open the Bullets and Numbering dialog box by choosing Bullets and Numbering in the palette menu of the Paragraph pane (Type ⇨ Paragraph, or Option+⌘+T or Ctrl+Alt+T) or by going to the Bullets and Numbering pane for a new or existing style in the Paragraph Styles pane (Window ⇨ Type & Tables ⇨ Paragraph Styles in inDesign CS and later or Window ⇨ Type ⇨ Paragraph Styles, or F11).

❷ Choose Bullets or Numbers in the List Type pop-up menu.

❸ Choose the bullet or numbering styles in the top section of the dialog box.

❹ Choose the spacing attributes in the Bullet or Number Position section of the dialog box.

❺ Click OK when done. (You can preview your settings by checking the Preview checkbox before clicking OK to apply them.) You now have automated bullets or numbers.

InDesign 2 and CS

❶ You manually enter bullets and numbers in your text. For numbered lists, you'll have to renumber the paragraphs if you insert or delete paragraphs. The normal bullet character (·) is accessed by pressing Option+8 on the Mac and by holding Alt and entering **0149** on the numeric keypad in Windows, and the thin bullet (·) is accessed via Option+ Shift+9 on the Mac and by holding Alt and entering **0183** on the numeric keypad in Windows. You can use other characters in symbol fonts as well, accessing them through the Glyphs pane (Type ⇨ Glyphs) or through a program such as PopChar X, the Mac's Character Palette or older Key Caps utility, and the Windows Character Map utility. You'll typically want a fixed space, such as an en space (Shift+⌘+N or Ctrl+ Shift+N) or thin space (Option+Shift+⌘+M or Ctrl+Alt+ Shift+M), after a bullet or number so the text after the bullet starts at the same location in all paragraphs. For numbered lists, you'll be inclined to use a right tab to align the number against (so the periods of single– and double-digit numbers align properly) and then a second (left) tab to indicate the start position for the following text.

❷ You can use hanging indents (set in paragraph styles or locally by choosing Type ⇨ Paragraph or pressing Option+⌘+T or Ctrl+Alt+T) or use the indent-to-here character (⌘+\ or Ctrl+\) to have InDesign have subsequent lines of a paragraph hang off the bullet or number.

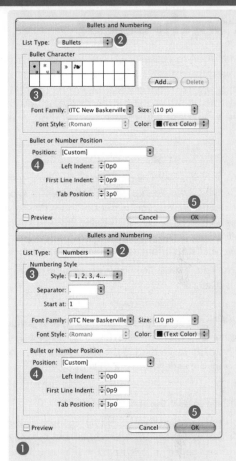

Creating Underlines and Strikethroughs

More common to typewritten documents, underlines and strikethroughs can sometimes be effective for emphasis. QuarkXPress and InDesign let you create your own custom underlines and strikethroughs; you can be creative in how you apply them.

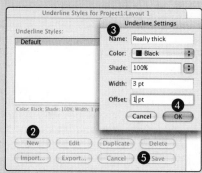

Follow These Steps

QuarkXPress comes with its own standard underlines and strikethroughs, available through the Style menu's Type Style submenu or the Measurements palette, and via the keyboard shortcuts Shift+⌘+U or Ctrl+Shift+U and Shift+⌘+/ or Ctrl+Shift+/, respectively. But you can also create your own underlines and strikethroughs in QuarkXPress 5 and later:

❶ Choose Edit ⇨ Underline Styles to open the Underline Styles dialog box.

❷ Click the New button to create a new style.

❸ Set the underline thickness, color, shade, and position (negative numbers move the line down). By using a positive number of at least a third of the text's point size, you essentially turn the underline into a strikethrough.

❹ Click OK.

❺ Click Save to save the underline style.

❻ Apply the underline style to text by highlighting the text and choosing Style ⇨ Underline Styles and then selecting the desired underline style from the submenu. Note that you cannot apply underline styles through character style sheets, but you can simulate them using ruling lines in paragraph style sheets (see page 150).

Follow These Steps

InDesign also comes with a set of standard underlines and strikethroughs, available through the palette menu of the Character pane (Type ⇨ Character, or ⌘+T or Ctrl+T) or the Control palette, and via the keyboard shortcuts Shift+⌘+U or Ctrl+Shift+U and Shift+⌘+/ or Ctrl+Shift+/, respectively. But you can also create your own underlines and strikethroughs in InDesign CS or later:

❶ Open the Character pane (Type ⇨ Character, or ⌘+T or Ctrl+T) to apply local underlines or strikethroughs, or the Character Styles pane and edit or create a style (Window ⇨ Type & Tables ⇨ Character Styles in InDesign CS and later or Window ⇨ Type ⇨ Character Styles in InDesign 2, or Shift+F11).

❷ In the Character pane, choose Underline Options or Strikethrough Options, as desired, from the palette menu. In the Character Styles pane's New Character Styles or Character Style Options dialog box, go to the Underline Options or Strikethrough Options pane. The options are the same for both underlines and strikethroughs in both the Character pane and Character Styles pane.

❸ Set the underline's or strikethrough's thickness, color, tint, type, and position (negative numbers move the line down). Note that for both underlines and strikethroughs, an offset of 0 points places the line at the text's baseline, even though you might think a strikethrough with an offset of 0 points would be placed in the middle of the text.

❹ Click OK.

Go Further: InDesign lets you apply both underlines and strikethroughs to text, while QuarkXPress lets you apply only one at a time. Also, InDesign lets you choose the line type (solid, dashed, dotted, or striped), while underlines in QuarkXPress can be only solid lines.

Workaround: Note that the only way to reuse an underline or strikethrough in InDesign is to set it through a character style. QuarkXPress's underline styles can be applied to any text, but they cannot be incorporated into character style sheets — which means they must be applied manually every time. In both programs, it would be better if you could define underline and strikethrough styles and then use those in character style sheets.

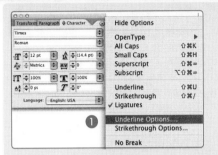

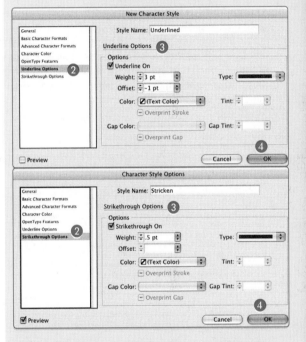

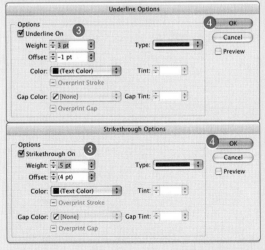

✿ Using Special Characters

There is a large variety of special characters commonly used in documents. QuarkXPress relies on the operating system's shortcuts, or a third-party utility, to make many of these characters accessible. InDesign provides those conduits as well, but it also has a very handy menu and an even handier pane for quick access to special characters that doesn't require remembering arcane codes.

Keep in Mind

QuarkXPress has no easy way to insert special characters into your text. You either need to know the Mac or Windows keyboard shortcuts for accented characters and special symbols or the QuarkXPress shortcuts for symbols, spaces, and dashes. Another option is to use software such as the shareware PopChar on either platform, the built-in Character Palette or older Key Caps on the Mac, or the built-in Character Map in Windows.

QuarkXPress vs. InDesign Shortcuts

	QuarkXPress	
Special character	Macintosh	Windows
Bullet (•)	Option+8	Alt+Shift+8
Ellipsis (…)	Option+;	*not available*
Copyright (©)	Option+G	Alt+Shift+C
Registered trademark (®)	Option+R	Alt+Shift+R
Trademark (™)	Option+2	Alt+Shift+T
Paragraph (¶)	Option+7	Alt+Shift+7
Section (§)	Option+6	Alt+Shift+6
Switch between keyboard and typographic quotes	*no shortcut*	*no shortcut*
Em dash (—)	Option+Shift+–	Ctrl+Shift+=
En dash (–)	Option+–	Ctrl+Alt+Shift+–
Nonbreaking hyphen (-)	⌘+=	Ctrl+=
Discretionary hyphen (-)	⌘=–	Ctrl+–
Em space ( )	*no shortcut*	*no shortcut*
En space ( )	Option+space	Ctrl+Shift+6
Thin space ( )	*not available*	*not available*
Punctuation space ( )	Shift+space	Shift+space
Nonbreaking space	⌘+5	Ctrl+5
Soft return (new line)	Shift+Enter	Shift+Return
Column break	keypad Enter	keypad Enter
Frame break	Shift+keypad Enter	Shift+keypad Enter
Page break	*not available*	*not available*
Indent to here	⌘+\	Ctrl+\
Right-indent tab	Shift+Tab	Shift+Tab
Current page number	⌘+3	Ctrl+3
Next frame's page number	⌘+4	Ctrl+4
Previous frame's page number	⌘+2	Ctrl+2

InDesign

Follow These Steps

To insert special characters, you can use the Mac or Windows keyboard shortcuts or you can use software such as the shareware PopChar, the included Character Palette or older Key Caps on the Mac, or the included Character Map in Windows. Or you can use InDesign's tools:

① Choose Type ➪ Insert Special Character and then the desired character from the symbol menu.

② Use the Glyphs pane to select from the current font's available characters (Type ➪ Glyphs). With OpenType fonts, you can choose subsets of the symbols to make it easier to find them.

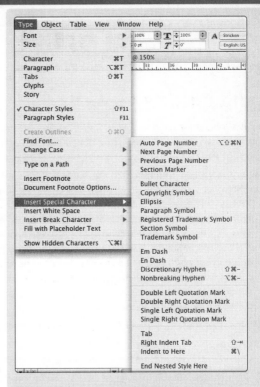

InDesign		
Macintosh	**Windows**	**Special character**
Option+8	Alt+8	Bullet (•)
Option+;	Alt+;	Ellipsis (…)
Option+G	Alt+G	Copyright (©)
Option+R	*no shortcut*	Registered trademark (®)
Option+2	Alt+2	Trademark (™)
Option+7	Alt+7	Paragraph (¶)
Option+6	Alt+6	Section (§)
Option+Shift+⌘+"	Ctrl+Alt+Shift+"	Switch between keyboard and typographic quotes
Option+Shift+–	Alt+Shift+–	Em dash (—)
Option+–	Alt+–	En dash (–)
Option+⌘+–	Ctrl+Alt+–	Nonbreaking hyphen (-)
Shift+⌘+–	Ctrl+Shift+–	Discretionary hyphen (-)
Shift+⌘+M	Ctrl+Shift+M	Em space ( )
Shift+⌘+N	Ctrl+Shift+N	En space ( )
Option+Shift+⌘+M	Ctrl+Alt+Shift+M	Thin space ( )
Option+Shift+⌘+I	Ctrl+Alt+Shift+I	Hair space ()
Option+⌘+X	Ctrl+Alt+X	Nonbreaking space
Shift+Enter	Shift+Return	Soft return (new line)
keypad Enter	keypad Enter	Column break
Shift+keypad Enter	Shift+keypad Enter	Frame break
⌘+keypad Enter	Ctrl+keypad Enter	Page break
⌘+\	Ctrl+\	Indent to here
Shift+Tab	Shift+Tab	Right-indent tab
Option+Shift+⌘+N	Ctrl+Alt+Shift+N	Current page number
Option+Shift+⌘+]	Ctrl+Alt+Shift+]	Next frame's page number*
Option+Shift+⌘+]	Ctrl+Alt+Shift+]	Previous frame's page number*

*no shortcut available in InDesign CS2

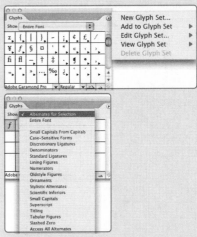

Go Further: InDesign's Glyphs pane and Insert Special Character menu make it easy to insert special characters without the use of extra software as QuarkXPress requires. InDesign also provides full access to OpenType fonts' characters, again unlike QuarkXPress.

✦ Creating Fractions

Fractions are very common in certain kinds of content, such as recipes, instruction manuals, math books, and engineering articles. QuarkXPress provides a simple tool to create fractions as needed, while InDesign does not.

Follow These Steps

QuarkXPress comes with a built-in fraction editor (included with QuarkXPress 5 and later, a free download for QuarkXPress 4 and earlier from www.quark.com):

1️⃣ Set the fraction preferences in the Fraction/Price pane of the Preferences dialog box. In QuarkXPress 6, choose Quark-XPress ➪ Preferences or Option+Shift+⌘+Y on the Mac and Edit ➪ Preferences or Ctrl+Alt+Shift+Y in Windows. In QuarkXPress 5 and earlier, choose Edit ➪ Preferences ➪ Fraction/Price. Set the size and position of the denominator and numerator. Note that on the Mac, you can have Quark-XPress use the virgule character (/, or Option+Shift+1) for the slash (/); the virgule is a tad shorter and thinner so it works better with the fraction's denominator.

2️⃣ Type your fraction, such as **7/8**, and then highlight it.

3️⃣ Choose Style ➪ Type Styles ➪ Make Fraction to have QuarkXPress convert the highlighted text into a fraction.

4️⃣ You may want to manually kern the fraction in some cases, depending on the font and size, to optimize the appearance of the fraction's numerator and/or denominator.

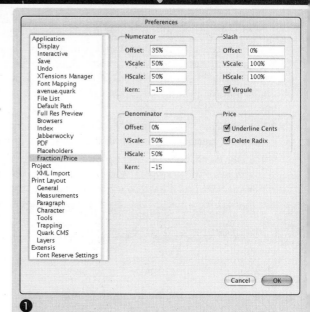

1️⃣

InDesign

Follow These Steps

InDesign has no equivalent to the QuarkXPress fraction builder. That means you'll have to use one of four options to create fractions:

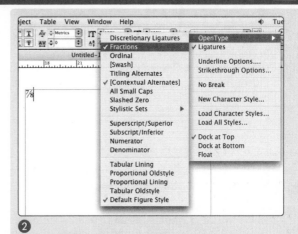

1. Manually build fractions by highlighting numerators and denominators and changing their size and baseline position. Adjust the kerning between the numerator and slash (/) or virgule (/, or Option+Shift+1), as well as between the denominator and virgule or slash. (The virgule character is not available in most Windows fonts, and for those that have it, you'll need to use the Glyphs pane as described on page 137).

2. Use OpenType or expert-collection fractions. Expert-collection fonts are essentially an additional version of a font that includes true small caps, several preformatted fractions, and Eastern European characters. If you are using OpenType fonts, they will likely contain those same characters without requiring you to switch to a separate font to get them. Be sure to select Fractions from the OpenType submenu in the Control palette or in the Character pane (Type ➪ Character, or ⌘+T or Ctrl+T), or in the Advanced Character pane of a paragraph or character style, as covered on pages 121 and 125. The OpenType font will automatically build fractions for you.

3. You can also select fractions from the Glyphs pane (Type ➪ Glyphs), assuming that the font has the fraction you need.

4. Write a script to create fractions and then apply it to highlighted text as needed.

Workaround: All four techniques above are workarounds with drawbacks. The first is labor-intensive, the second requires additional investment in fonts, the third depends on the fonts having the needed fractions, and the fourth requires programming skills.

Searching and Replacing Special Characters

Searching and replacing special characters can be difficult, since you often can't enter them in dialog boxes. In QuarkXPress and InDesign, you'll use a mixture of special codes and cut-and-paste of symbol characters into the Find/Change dialog box.

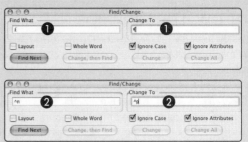

Follow These Steps

When using the Find/Change dialog box (Edit ➪ Find/Change, or ⌘+F or Ctrl+F) to find or replace text, it can be difficult to find special characters. Here's how to do it:

1 In some cases, you can use the operating system's keyboard shortcuts (see page 138 for common ones) to enter the character into the Find What or Change To fields.

2 You can use codes that indicate spaces and other nonprinting characters, as shown in the table.

3 You can copy and paste the character from your text into the Find What or Change To fields of the Find/Change dialog box.

QuarkXPress vs. InDesign Find/Replace Code

Special character	QuarkXPress
Tab	\t
Right-indent tab	*paste into Find/Change*
Indent to here	*paste into Find/Change*
Paragraph return	\p
Soft return (new line)	\n
New column	\c
New box	\b
Current page number	\3
Em space ( )	*paste into Find/Change*
En space ( )	*paste into Find/Change*
Nonbreaking space	*paste into Find/Change*
Punctuation space ( )	\.
Hair space ( )	*not supported in QuarkXPress*
Flex space	\f
Flush space	*not supported in QuarkXPress*
Discretionary hyphen	*paste into Find/Change*
Nonbreaking hyphen	*paste into Find/Change*
Em dash (—)	*use OS shortcut*
En dash (–)	*use OS shortcut*
Wild card	\?
Bullet (•)	*use OS shortcut*
Paragraph symbol (¶)	*use OS shortcut*
Section symbol (§)	*use OS shortcut*
Registered trademark (®)	*use OS shortcut*
Copyright (©)	*use OS shortcut*
Caret (^)	^
Backslash (\)	\\

InDesign

Follow These Steps

InDesign's Find/Change dialog box (Edit ⇨ Find/Change, or ⌘+F or Ctrl+F) provides several ways to find special characters:

❶ In some cases, you can use the operating system's keyboard shortcuts (see page 139 for common ones) to enter the character into the Find What or Change To fields.

❷ You can use codes that indicate spaces and other nonprinting characters, as shown in the table.

❸ You can copy and paste the character from your text into the Find What or Change To fields of the Find/Change dialog box.

❹ You can use the pop-up menus in the Find What and Change To fields of the Find/Change dialog box.

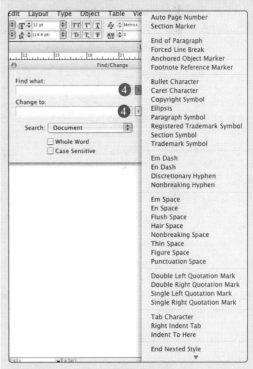

InDesign	Special character
^t	Tab
^y	Right-indent tab
^i	Indent to here
^p	Paragraph return
^n	Soft return (new line)
paste into Find/Change	New column
paste into Find/Change	New frame
^#	Current page number
^m	Em space ( )
^.	En space ( )
^s	Nonbreaking space
^,	Thin space ( )
^|	Hair space ( )
not supported in InDesign	Flex space
^f	Flush space
^_	Discretionary hyphen
^~	Nonbreaking hyphen
^_	Em dash (—)
^=	En dash (–)
^? (character), ^9 (digit), ^$ (letter)	Wild card
^8	Bullet (•)
^7	Paragraph symbol (¶)
^6	Section symbol (§)
^r	Registered trademark (®)
^c	Copyright (©)
^^	Caret (^)
\	Backslash (\)

Go Further: You can quickly put highlighted text into the Find What field of the Find/Change dialog box by typing ⌘+F2 or Ctrl+F2 and in the Change To field by typing ⌘+F3 or Ctrl+F3.

✤ Searching and Replacing Formatting ◀ QuarkXPress

You often will want to search and replace formatting, either to replace that formatting wherever it is applied or just for specific text that uses (or should use) it. Both QuarkXPress and InDesign let you do so.

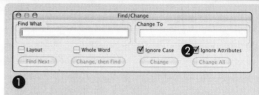

Follow These Steps

Often, you want specific formatting in your search and replace, either to search text that has specific formatting or replace it with specific formatting, or to search and replace formatting no matter what text it is applied to. The Find/Change dialog box lets you do that as well. Here's how:

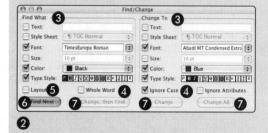

① Open the Find/Change dialog box by choosing Edit ➪ Find (⌘+F or Ctrl+F).

② Uncheck the Ignore Attributes checkbox to get the expanded dialog box.

③ In the Find What and Change To areas, check the various attributes you want to find or replace, then select the appropriate options for each. Note that in the Type Style section, the various attributes have three modes indicated by the background color of each icon: White means that the text should not have this formatting, shaded means leave that attribute alone no matter how it is set in the text, and black means that the text should have this formatting.

④ Check or uncheck the Whole Word and Ignore Case check-boxes as appropriate for your search.

⑤ Check the Document checkbox (QuarkXPress 5 and earlier) or Layout checkbox (QuarkXPress 6) if you want to search the entire document or layout. Otherwise, only the current story will be searched, from the current text-cursor location to the end of the story.

⑥ Click Find Next for the first instance of a search and replace, or for any instance of a find.

⑦ If you are replacing found text, choose Change Then Find, Change, or Change All as desired. The Change button changes just one instance and then stops, while Change Then Find changes the one instance and finds the next.

InDesign

Follow These Steps

InDesign also lets you search text that has specific formatting or replace it with specific formatting, or to search and replace formatting no matter what text it is applied to. But its Find/Change dialog box lets you search and replace more types of formatting than does QuarkXPress:

1 Open the Find/Change dialog box by choosing Edit ➪ Find (⌘+F or Ctrl+F).

2 Click More Options to expand the dialog box.

3 Next to the Find Format Settings and the Change Format Settings windows are Format buttons. Click the Format button for either one (you can do both by clicking one, performing steps 4 and 5, then click the second one and performing steps 4 and 5 for it).

4 Go through each pane and set the desired attributes. Note that several panes have checkboxes that can have three settings: Empty means that the text should not have this formatting, a minus sign (–) means leave that attribute alone no matter how it is set in the text, and a checkmark means that the text should have this formatting.

5 Click OK when done entering attributes.

6 Your settings will appear in the Find Format Settings and/or Change Format Settings windows.

7 In the Search pop-up menu, choose a search scope (Document, All Documents, Story, and To End of Story).

8 Check the Whole Word and Case Sensitive checkboxes as appropriate to your search.

9 Click Find Next for the first instance of a search and replace, or for any instance of a find.

10 If you are replacing found text, choose Change/Find, Change, or Change All as desired. The Change button changes just one instance and then stops, while Change/Find changes the one instance and finds the next.

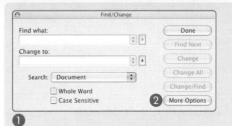

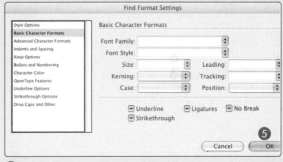

Working with Capitals

Capital letters help call attention to text by indicating sentence starts, proper names, and highlighted text when all caps or small caps are applied. QuarkXPress and InDesign let you easily apply capital letters, and InDesign extends that through its support of OpenType fonts.

Follow These Steps

QuarkXPress offers several types of capital letters, as well as controls over their appearance:

❶ In the Measurements palette, use the Small Caps and All Caps buttons to turn these formats on or off.

❷ Choose Style ➪ Type Style ➪ Small Caps (Shift+⌘+H or Ctrl+Shift+H) or Style ➪ Type Style ➪ All Caps (Shift+⌘+K or Ctrl+Shift+K) to turn these formats on or off.

❸ Set all caps or small caps in character style sheets (see page 124).

❹ No matter how you apply small caps and all caps, you can set their size in the Character pane of the Preferences dialog box. (In QuarkXPress 6, choose QuarkXPress ➪ Preferences or Option+Shift+⌘+Y on the Mac or Edit ➪ Preferences or Ctrl+Alt+Shift+Y in Windows. In QuarkXPress 5, choose Edit ➪ Preferences ➪ Preferences, or Option+Shift+⌘+Y or Ctrl+Alt+Shift+Y. In QuarkXPress 4, Edit ➪ Preferences ➪ Document, or ⌘+Y or Ctrl+Y.)

❺ Set the size of small caps in the Small Caps section. You can set separate horizontal and vertical scales, although you'll rarely do so.

❻ Set whether accents are retained for capitalized letters by checking or unchecking the Accents for All Caps checkbox.

Follow These Steps

InDesign also offers several types of capital letters and controls over their appearance:

① In the Control palette, use the Small Caps and All Caps buttons to turn these formats on or off.

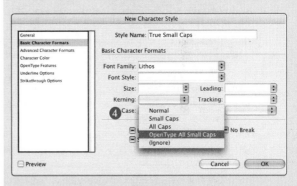

② Choose Small Caps (Shift+⌘+H or Ctrl+Shift+H) or Style ⇨ Type Style ⇨ All Caps (Shift+⌘+K or Ctrl+Shift+K) from the palette menu of the Character pane (Type ⇨ Character, or ⌘+T or Ctrl+T) to turn these formats on or off.

③ You can also choose OpenType ⇨ All Small Caps from the Character pane's palette menu for OpenType fonts. This makes all letters in the text selection use true small caps.

④ Set all caps or small caps in the Basic Character Formats panes for paragraph and character styles (see pages 121 and 125).

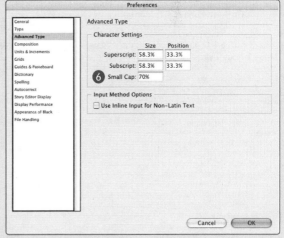

⑤ No matter how you apply small caps, you can set their size in the Advanced Type pane (InDesign CS2) or Text pane (InDesign CS or earlier) of the Preferences dialog box (choose InDesign ⇨ Preferences or ⌘+K on the Mac or Edit ⇨ Preferences or Ctrl+K in Windows).

⑥ Set the size of small caps in the Small Cap field.

Workaround: InDesign does not let you set whether accents are retained for capitalized letters. You'll need to manually remove or add them based on your house style.

Working with Leading

Leading, the space between lines of text, plays a huge role in text readability. QuarkXPress applies leading the traditional way, as a paragraph attribute, while InDesign uses a more questionable method, as a character attribute.

Follow These Steps

Leading is a paragraph format that you typically specify in a paragraph style sheet (see page 120) and then modify locally occasionally as needed:

1. Adjust the leading for the current paragraph by changing the leading settings in the Measurements palette.

2. Change the leading in the Formats pane of the Paragraph Attributes dialog box (Style ⇨ Formats, or Shift+⌘+F or Ctrl+Shift+F). You can enter a specific value, such as **11**, an incremental value, such as **+2**, or choose Auto (or enter **Auto**) from the pop-up menu, which uses whatever is set in the Preferences dialog box (see step 4).

3. You can also force text to align to the baseline grid, overriding its leading, by checking Lock to Baseline Grid in the Formats pane of the Paragraph Attributes dialog box.

4. You can choose the default leading for text without style sheets, as well as for new style sheets, in the Preferences dialog box's Paragraph pane. Set either a specific value such as **11** or an incremental value such as **+2**. (In QuarkXPress 6, choose QuarkXPress ⇨ Preferences or Option+Shift+⌘+Y on the Mac or Edit ⇨ Preferences or Ctrl+Alt+Shift+Y in Windows. In QuarkXPress 5, choose Edit ⇨ Preferences ⇨ Preferences, or Option+Shift+⌘+Y or Ctrl+Alt+Shift+Y. In QuarkXPress 4, Edit ⇨ Preferences ⇨ Document, or ⌘+Y or Ctrl+Y.)

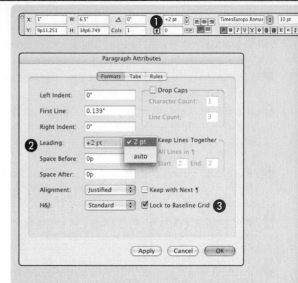

InDesign

Follow These Steps

Unlike the rest of the publishing industry, InDesign treats lead-ing as a character format rather than as a paragraph format. This can lead to different leading amounts within a paragraph. Here's how to apply leading:

① You can set leading in paragraph or character styles, as cov-ered on pages 121 and 125.

② You can override leading locally by using the Control palette or the Character pane (Type ➪ Character, or ⌘+T or Ctrl+T) for selected text (to affect just the lines containing that text) or the entire paragraph (by clicking the paragraph but not selecting text).

③ You can also override leading for entire paragraphs by click-ing the Align to Baseline Grid button in the Paragraph pane (Type ➪ Paragraph, or Option+⌘+T or Ctrl+Alt+T), or just override the first line (such as for headlines to reset them to the baseline) by also choosing Only Align First Line to Grid. You set the baseline grid in the Grids pane of the Prefer-ences dialog box (InDesign ➪ Preferences or ⌘+K on the Mac or Edit ➪ Preferences or Ctrl+K in Windows).

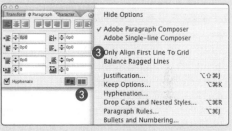

Workaround: To have InDesign apply leading to entire paragraphs, rather than to text selections, check the Apply Leading to Entire Paragraphs box in the Type pane (in InDesign CS2) or Text pane (in InDesign CS and earlier) of the Preferences dialog box. You'll still have to set up leading in the Character pane and through character styles.

Warning: InDesign does not support incremental leading, so you cannot specify a value such as **+2** to add two points to the current point size, as you can in QuarkXPress. That means that you must enter a specific leading value in all character styles and for unstyled text, or live with InDesign's default leading of 120%, which leads to odd values such as 10.8 points leading for 9-point type. These fractional values make it difficult to keep text aligned across columns. (InDesign also does not let you set your own default leading percentage.)

Go Further: InDesign CS2 lets you set a separate baseline grid in any text frame using the Text Frame Options dialog box's Baseline Options pane (Object ➪ Text Frame Options, or ⌘+B or Ctrl+B). The options are the same as in the Preference dialog box's Grids pane.

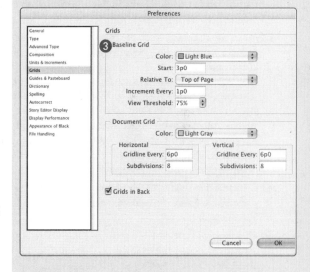

☀ Creating Ruling Lines

Ruling lines are an effective way to highlight, separate, or simply embellish text.

Follow These Steps

In QuarkXPress, you can set ruling lines with paragraphs, either as local formatting or as part of a paragraph style sheet:

❶ For local ruling lines, choose Style ➪ Rules (Shift+⌘+N or Ctrl+Shift+N). For paragraph style sheets, go to the Rules pane of the Edit Style Sheets dialog box (covered on page 120). Either way, the options are the same.

❷ Use the Rule Above and/or Rule Below checkboxes to enable the desired rule(s).

❸ Set the length as either Indents (keeps the ruling line within the paragraph's left and right indents) or Text (keeps the ruling line only as wide as the text) in the Length pop-up menu. Note that if you choose Text, a rule above will be the width of the first line's text in the paragraph, while a rule below will be the width of the last line's text in the paragraph. You can also narrow the rule's width by setting From Left and From Right values.

❹ Move the rule away from the text by setting an Offset value of more than 0%; use a negative number to move the rule in the other direction. The percentage is of the text's point size; you can also enter a specific value such as **4 pt**. Note that the Offset value can be no more than –25% of the text size for negative values and no more than 100% for positive values. You may need to calculate these values and enter them in points, picas, or inches rather than using the percentage — QuarkXPress sometimes allows different limits based on the numbering system you specify.

❺ Choose a line style with the Style pop-up menu, then set its thickness, color, and shade with the Width, Color, and Shade options.

❻ Click Apply to preview the settings. Click OK to apply the settings and close the dialog box. If you are editing a style sheet, also be sure to click Save in the Style Sheets dialog box.

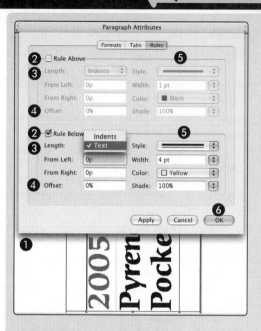

Cross-Reference: You can create your own lines, not just use the predefined styles. See pages 256-257 for more information.

Follow These Steps

InDesign's ruling lines work very much like QuarkXPress's:

❶ For local ruling lines, choose Paragraph Rules (Shift+⌘+J or Ctrl+Shift+J) from the palette menu of the Paragraph pane (Type ➪ Paragraph, or Option+⌘+T or Ctrl+Alt+T). For paragraph styles go to the Paragraph Rules pane when editing or creating the style (covered on page 121). Either way, the options are the same.

❷ Choose the Rule Above or Rule Below from the pop-up menu at top and then check Rule On to enable the desired rule. If you want both rules above and below, repeat this step through step 5 for each.

❸ Set the length as either Column (keeps the ruling line within the paragraph's left and right indents) or Text (keeps the ruling line only as wide as the text) in the Width pop-up menu. Note that if you choose Text, a rule above will be the width of the first line's text in the paragraph, while a rule below will be the width of the last line's text in the paragraph. You can also narrow the rule's width by setting Left Indent and Right Indent values.

❹ Move the rule down by entering a positive value in the Offset field; move it up by entering a negative value.

❺ Choose a line style with the Type pop-up menu, then set its thickness, color, and shade with the Width, Color, and Tint options. You can also choose the gap color for multiline stripes and dashed and dotted lines using the Gap Color and Gap Tint options. You can also have the ruling line's color overprint its stroke by checking the Overprint Stroke checkbox; otherwise the stroke will overprint the color. The gap has a similar option. (Which option to choose depends on the trapping for your document; consult your service bureau.)

❻ Check the Preview checkbox to preview the settings. Click OK to apply them and close the dialog box. If you are editing a style sheet, also be sure to click OK in the New Style Sheets or Paragraph Style Options dialog box.

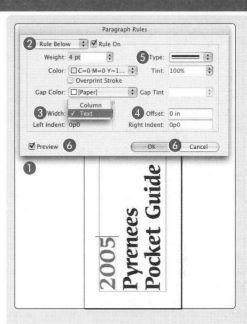

Go Further: InDesign lets you move rules both up and down, not just down as in QuarkXPress. InDesign also lets you set the gap color for multiline stripes and dashed and dotted lines; QuarkXPress leaves the gap transparent, so whatever is beneath the gap shows through.

✳ Creating Reversed-Out Text   ◀ QuarkXPress

Reversed-out, or inverted, text is a great technique for highlighting text.

Follow These Steps

There is no direct way to reverse out text in QuarkXPress, although you can simulate it for paragraphs (not text selections) by following these steps:

1️⃣ Highlight the text and apply a light color to it, such as white, using the Colors palette.

2️⃣ Create a ruling line above the text either as local style or as part of a paragraph style sheet, as covered on page 150. (Theoretically, you could use a ruling line below, but you typically can't adjust its position enough to move it completely behind the text.) Note that if you choose Text for the rule's width, QuarkXPress will ignore any spaces you place after the text, which you might do to give the background more width; one possible workaround is to type a character after the text and have it be the same color as the rule, although that requires manual work on every such paragraph.

3️⃣ Make sure the line's thickness is more than the text's point size, so there is space above and below the characters that will be in the rule color.

4️⃣ Position the the rule so it overlaps the entire text. Typically, this value is the about same as the space you want above the text. So if you have 30-point type in a 36-point rule, you would move the rule down 3 or 4 points to achieve about 3 points of rule above and below the text. (If your text is in all caps, you'll want to move the rule a bit more, since there are no descenders to cover.) Click the Apply button to see if your position is correct and adjust as needed.

5️⃣ Click OK when done. If you are creating or editing a paragraph style sheet, be sure to click Save in the Style Sheets dialog box.

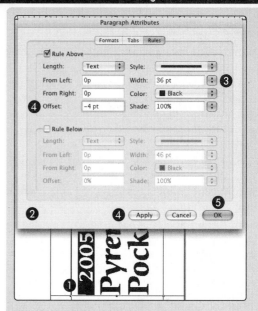

InDesign

Follow These Steps

InDesign uses a nearly identical process to reversing out text as QuarkXPress, though there's a way to apply the reversed-out effect to both paragraphs and text selections:

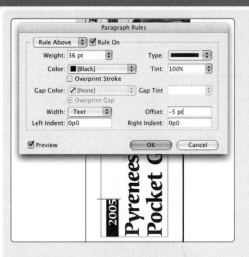

1 Highlight the text and apply a light color to it, such as white or [Paper], using the Swatches pane.

2 Create a ruling line above the text either as local style or as part of a paragraph style, as covered on page 151. (You could use a ruling line below.) Note that if you choose Text for the rule's width, InDesign will ignore any spaces you place after the text, which you might do to give the background more width; one possible workaround is to type a character after the text and have it be the same color as the rule, although that requires manual work on every such paragraph.

3 Make sure the line's thickness is more than the text's point size, so there is space above and below the characters that will be in the rule color.

4 Position the the rule so it overlaps the entire text. Typically, this value is the about same as the space you want above the text. So if you have 30-point type in a 36-point rule, you would move the rule down 3 or 4 points to achieve about 3 points of rule above and below the text. (If your text is in all caps, you'll want to move the rule a bit more, since there are no descenders to cover.) Make sure that the Preview checkbox is checked so you can see if your position is correct and adjust as needed.

5 Click OK when done.

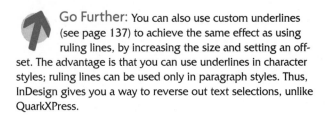

Go Further: You can also use custom underlines (see page 137) to achieve the same effect as using ruling lines, by increasing the size and setting an offset. The advantage is that you can use underlines in character styles; ruling lines can be used only in paragraph styles. Thus, InDesign gives you a way to reverse out text selections, unlike QuarkXPress.

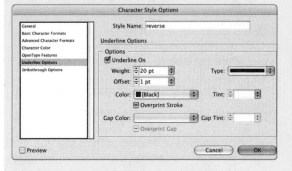

✦Applying Other Attributes

Both QuarkXPress and InDesign let you apply a variety of other text effects to text.

Follow These Steps

QuarkXPress offers several other text attributes:

1 You can have just the outlines of text appear by applying the Outline style to text, either locally via the Measurements palette or by choosing Style ➪ Type Style ➪ Outline (Shift+⌘+O or Ctrl+Shift+O) or in character style sheets.

2 You can apply a drop shadow to text by applying the Shadow style to text, either locally via the Measurements palette or by choosing Style ➪ Type Style ➪ Shadow (Shift+⌘+S or Ctrl+Shift+S) or in character style sheets.

3 You can apply superscripts and subscripts — as well as a form of superscripts called *superiors* that are ideal for footnotes — to text, either locally via the Measurements palette or by choosing Style ➪ Type Style ➪ Subscript (Shift+⌘+– or Ctrl+Shift+–), Style ➪ Type Style ➪ Superscript (Shift+⌘+= or Ctrl+Shift+=), or Style ➪ Type Style ➪ Superior (Shift+⌘+V or Ctrl+Shift+V). These options are also available in character style sheets. You set subscript and superscript size and position, as well as superior size, in the Character pane of the Preferences dialog box. (In QuarkXPress 6, choose Quark-XPress ➪ Preferences on the Mac or Edit ➪ Preferences in Windows. In QuarkXPress 5, choose Edit ➪ Preferences ➪ Preferences. The shortcuts in QuarkXPress 5 and 6 are Option+Shift+⌘+Y and Ctrl+Alt+Shift+Y. In QuarkXPress 4, choose Edit ➪ Preferences ➪ Document, or ⌘+Y or Ctrl+Y.)

4 You can move text up or down within its line by applying a baseline shift; to do so, choose Style ➪ Baseline Shift, or set this shift in a character style sheet.

5 You can condense or expand text vertically and horizontally by choosing Horizontal/Vertical Scale, or set this scale in a character style sheet.

6 You can turn ligatures on or off for your document using the Character pane of the Preferences dialog box.

7 You can turn on typographic quotes when typing in the document by checking the Smart Quotes checkbox in the Interactive pane of the Preferences dialog box. (In Quark-XPress 6, choose QuarkXPress ➪ Preferences on the Mac or Edit ➪ Preferences in Windows. In QuarkXPress 5, choose Edit ➪ Preferences ➪ Preferences. In QuarkXPress 4, choose Edit ➪ Preferences ➪ Application. For all three, the shortcut is Option+Shift+⌘+Y or Ctrl+Alt+Shift+Y.)

You can also set all of the attributes in steps 1 through 5 locally in the Character Attributes dialog box (Style ➪ Character, or Shift+⌘+D or Ctrl+Shift+D).

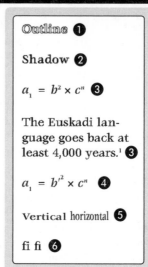

Outline **1**

Shadow **2**

$a_1 = b^2 \times c^n$ **3**

The Euskadi language goes back at least 4,000 years.[1] **3**

$a_1 = b'^2 \times c^n$ **4**

Vertical horizontal **5**

fi fi **6**

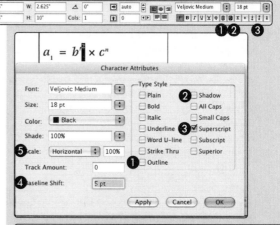

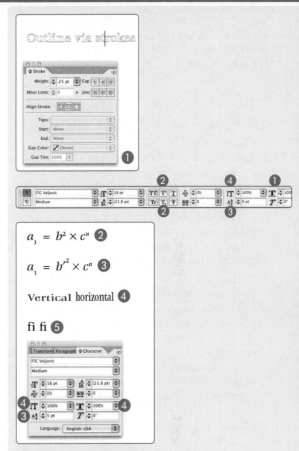

InDesign

Follow These Steps

Several of InDesign's capabilities differ from QuarkXPress's:

① You can have just the outlines of text appear by applying a stroke to the text (using the Stroke pane, accessed by choosing Window ⇨ Stroke or pressing F10) and applying the desired color to the stroke and the [Paper] color to the text using the Swatches pane (Window ⇨ Swatches or F5). You can also set these in the Paragraph Styles and Character Styles panes, as covered on pages 121 and 125.

② You can apply superscripts and subscripts either locally via the Control palette, through the Character pane (Type ⇨ Character, or ⌘+T or Ctrl+T), or by pressing respectively Option+Shift+⌘+= or Ctrl+Alt+Shift+= and Shift+⌘+= or Ctrl+Shift+=. These options are also available in character and paragraph styles. You set subscript and superscript size and position in the Advanced Type pane (in InDesign CS2) or Text pane (in InDesign CS and earlier) of the Preferences dialog box. (Choose InDesign ⇨ Preferences or ⌘+K on the Mac or Edit ⇨ Preferences or Ctrl+K in Windows.)

③ You can move text up or down within its line by applying a baseline shift; to do so, use the Character pane for local formatting or globally in the Advanced Character Formats pane when creating or editing a character or paragraph style.

④ You can condense or expand text vertically and horizontally; to do so, use the Character pane for local formatting or globally in the Advanced Character Formats pane when creating or editing a character or paragraph style.

⑤ You can turn ligatures on or off for text selections or whole paragraphs; choose Ligatures in the Character pane's palette menu or check the Ligatures checkbox in the Basic Character Formats pane for a character or paragraph style.

⑥ You can enable typographic quotes when typing in the document by checking the Use Typographer's Quotes checkbox in the Type pane (in InDesign CS2) or Text pane (in InDesign CS and earlier) of the Preferences dialog box.

Workaround: You can apply a drop shadow to entire text frames but not to text selections, as page 358 explains. But you could create a text frame with one character to which you apply a drop shadow and then insert it as an inline graphic (see pages 354-355) to create a drop cap.

Go Further: InDesign lets you set ligatures for text selections and whole paragraphs, not just for the document as in QuarkXPress. InDesign's Windows version also supports ligatures, while QuarkXPress's does not. But there is no way to globally turn ligatures on or off as in QuarkXPress.

$$a_1 = b^2 \times c^n \quad ②$$

$$a_1 = b'^2 \times c^n \quad ③$$

Vertical horizontal ④

fi fi ⑤

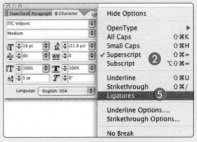

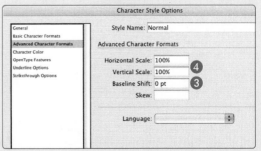

☀Applying Strokes

Strokes are the outlines of things. QuarkXPress doesn't use the stroke concept, while InDesign uses it extensively to let you work on the outlines of text as well as the edges (what QuarkXPress calls *frames*) of shapes.

Follow These Steps

QuarkXPress has two limited ways to apply strokes (outlines) to text:

❶ Apply the outline type style to text, either locally via the Measurements palette or by choosing Style ➪ Type Style ➪ Outline (Shift+⌘+O or Ctrl+Shift+O) or in character styles (see page 124). This essentially displays and prints the text's strokes. But you have no other control over text strokes, such as their thickness. While you can change the stroke color by changing the text's color, you cannot color the part of the text inside the outlines.

❷ You can convert text to a graphic by highlighting the text (with a maximum depth of one line) and choosing Style ➪ Text to Box. This creates a picture box in the shape of the text, which you can place separately or anchor into text. But this box is no longer editable as text. You can now set the stroke size and color by setting the frame specifications in the Frame pane of the Modify dialog box (Item ➪ Modify, or ⌘+B or Ctrl+B). You can also fill the box with its color, using the Box frame of the Modify dialog box (Item ➪ Modify, or ⌘+M or Ctrl+M) or by using the Colors palette. Part VIII covers graphics features in more detail.

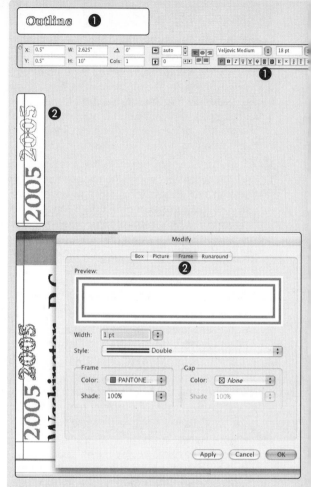

Follow These Steps

InDesign gives you direct control over text strokes:

1 Apply a stroke to the text (using the Stroke pane, accessed by choosing Window ➪ Stroke or pressing F10).

2 Apply the desired color to the stroke and the [Paper] or other desired color to the text using the Swatches pane (Window ➪ Swatches or F5).

3 You can also convert text — multiple lines, unlike Quark-XPress — to a frame by selecting the text and choosing Type ➪ Create Outlines (Shift+⌘+O or Ctrl+Shift+O). Note that you can place each line into its own graphics frame and that InDesign will replace the text with the converted text rather than leave it alone, as QuarkXPress does. You can retain the original text by holding Option or Alt when you choose Type ➪ Create Outlines or by pressing Option+Shift+⌘+O or Ctrl+Alt Shift+O.

You can also set stroke settings in the Paragraph Styles and Character Styles panes, as covered on pages 121 and 125.

 Go Further: The ability to control the display of strokes and the fill of text is available only in InDesign.

 1

 2

 3

Applying Colors and Gradients   **QuarkXPress**

The use of color and, less frequently, gradients, in text can help highlight text in body copy or make display copy more appealing.

Follow These Steps

QuarkXPress offers several ways to apply colors to text:

1 Highlight the text, be sure the Content button is selected in the Colors palette, and click a color from the palette. You can also apply a shade using the pop-up menu and field in the palette.

2 Highlight the text and choose Style ➪ Color and then select a color from the submenu.

3 Highlight the text and open the Character Attributes dialog box (Style ➪ Character, or Shift+⌘+D or Ctrl+Shift+D). Choose a color from the Color pop-up menu.

4 Edit or create a character style sheet (see page 124) and choose a color from the Color pop-up menu.

Note that QuarkXPress does not let you apply blends (gradients) to text unless you first convert the text to a graphic as explained on page 154. At that point, the text is no longer editable.

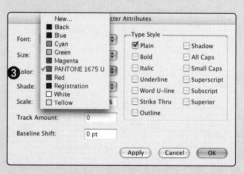

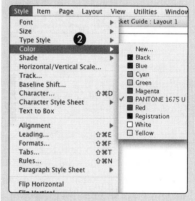

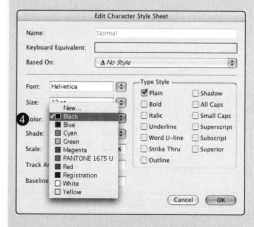

Follow These Steps

InDesign offers two ways to apply both colors and gradients to text:

① Highlight the text, be sure that the Text Fill button is selected in the Tools palette, and click a color or gradient swatch from the Swatches pane. (You can also select the Fill button there.) You can apply a tint using the pop-up menu and field in the pane.

② Edit or create a paragraph or character style (see page 125) and choose a color, gradient, and tint from the Character Color pane.

Go Further: You can apply colors, gradients, and tints to the fill and/or stroke of a text by choosing the fill or stroke button in either the Tools palette or the Swatches pane (or in the Character Colors pane when editing or creating styles).

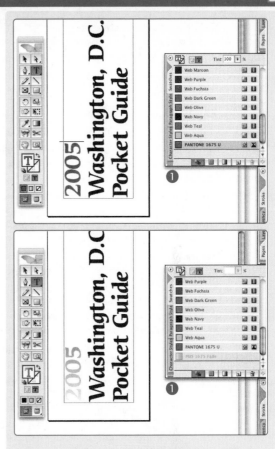

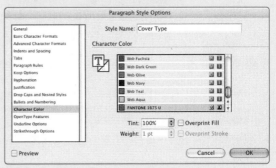

✳ Controlling Character Spacing ◀ **QuarkXPress**

Kerning, tracking, and other character spacing options help make text more readable, keeping related letters together in words — and keeping words distinct — without causing unsightly clumps or overlapping.

Follow These Steps

Here's how character-spacing options work in QuarkXPress:

① You adjust paragraph-wide spacing in paragraph style sheets through the use of H&J sets (Edit ⇨ H&Js, or Option+⌘+J or Ctrl+Shift+F11 in QuarkXPress 6 and Option+⌘+H or Ctrl+Shift+F11 in earlier versions). The Space and Char. rows in the Justification Method set the minimum, optimum, and maximum target spacing between words (the Space row) and between characters (the Char. row).

② You adjust tracking — the spacing between characters — in character style sheets. Note that the tracking setting will apply before H&J spacing settings: A 100% setting in the H&J Char. row will apply the tracking amount specified, while greater values will apply proportionally wider tracking and lower values will apply proportionally tighter tracking.

③ You can override both tracking and kerning (intercharacter adjustments to help awkward spacing in certain letter pairs such as *AV*) by using the Character Attributes dialog box (Style ⇨ Character, Style ⇨ Kern, or Style ⇨ Track, or Shift+⌘+D or Ctrl+Shift+D) or the Measurements palette. Note that if you have selected multiple characters, Quark-XPress will track the text (and the Character Attributes dialog box and Style menu will provide Track options), while if you have the text-insertion cursor placed between two characters, QuarkXPress will kern that pair (and the Character Attributes dialog box and Style menu will provide Kern options).

④ QuarkXPress lets you override a font's built-in kerning and tracking settings by choosing Utilities ⇨ Kerning Table Edit and Utilities ⇨ Tracking Edit, respectively. These changes affect only QuarkXPress, not other programs. Also, any kerning changes you make in step 3 are automatically made to the font's kerning table.

Cross-Reference: See pages 149-150 and 162-163 for information on paragraph spacing.

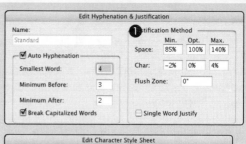

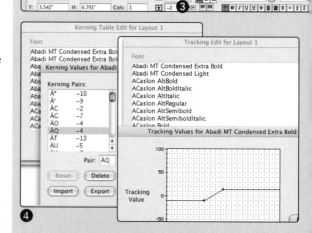

Follow These Steps

InDesign offers similar controls — although found in different places — as QuarkXPress for tracking and kerning, with one major exception: InDesign can't create kerning or tracking tables.

① You adjust paragraph-wide spacing in paragraph styles, using the Justification pane. The Word Spacing and Letter Spacing rows set the minimum, optimum, and maximum target spacing between words (the Word Spacing row) and between characters (the Letter Spacing row). You can also adjust the width of characters using the Glyph Scaling row, although that can result in awkward shifts in character appearance. Note that InDesign's spacing algorithms tend to result in more and wider spacing than QuarkXPress's, so you'll likely want to set InDesign settings to lower values to approximate your QuarkXPress spacing.

② You adjust tracking, the spacing between characters, in the Basic Character Formats pane for character and paragraph styles. Unlike in QuarkXPress, you can set tracking and kerning (intercharacter adjustments to help awkward spacing in certain letter pairs such as *AV*) independently, although because kerning is really about adjusting space between specific pairs, it really makes no sense to enter a value. You might, however, want to choose between Metrics, which uses the font designer's ideal settings, and Optical, which takes into account the character shapes.

③ You can override both tracking and kerning by using the Character pane (Type ➪ Character, or ⌘+T or Ctrl+T) or the Control palette.

④ Through both paragraph styles and the Paragraph pane, InDesign lets you choose between two types of composition, which affects alignment as well as spacing: Adobe Paragraph Composer adjusts text spacing and paragraph rag based on the overall paragraph's look, while Adobe Single-Line Composer looks at each line without regard to other lines in the paragraph (the same method QuarkXPress uses).

Workaround: QuarkXPress lets you override a font's built-in kerning and tracking settings. InDesign has no such capability (not surprising since Adobe designs fonts), leaving users to accept the basic assumptions of the font designers or override them at a local or style level.

Go Further: The ability to control spacing and rag across the entire paragraph is a strong InDesign advantage, although it does make it harder to track and edit text to make a paragraph lose a widow to better fit the available space, since inDesign may override your tracking to rebalance the paragraph.

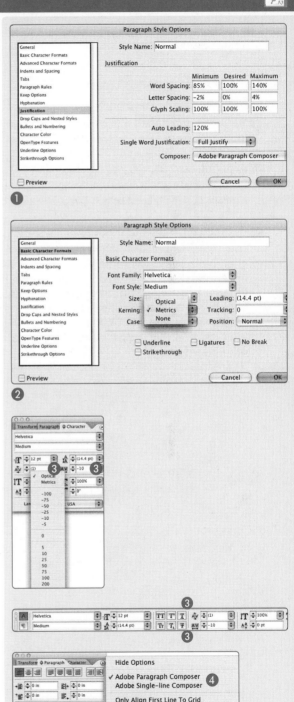

Controlling Paragraph Spacing

Like character spacing, paragraph spacing is also a key factor in text readability.

Follow These Steps

QuarkXPress offers several controls over character spacing:

1 You set paragraph leading (the space between lines), as well as any space above and/or below paragraphs, in paragraph style sheets.

2 You set the default leading for your document in the Paragraph pane of the Preferences dialog box. Be sure that Maintain Leading is checked and that the Typesetting radio button is selected.

3 You can also set spacing locally or override a paragraph style sheet's settings using the Formats pane of the Paragraph Attributes dialog box (Style ⇨ Formats, or Shift+⌘+F or Ctrl+Shift+F; you can go directly to the Leading field in this pane by choosing Style ⇨ Leading or pressing Shift+⌘+E or Ctrl+Shift+E). This pane is the same as for a paragraph style sheet. The Measurements pane also lets you override leading, but not change the space above or below paragraphs.

Cross-Reference: See pages 160-161 for information on character spacing.

Follow These Steps

InDesign offers several controls over paragraph spacing, with one key control handled in a manner counter to industry norms:

1 You set paragraph leading (the space between lines), as well as any space above and/or below paragraphs in paragraph styles. Contrary to industry practice, leading is set as a character attribute in the Basic Character Formats pane when you edit or create a paragraph style. Space above and below is set in the Indents and Spacing pane.

2 You set the default leading for your document in the Type pane (in InDesign CS2) or Text pane (in InDesign CS and earlier) of the Preferences dialog box. Be sure to check the Apply Leading to Entire Paragraphs checkbox.

3 You can also set spacing locally or override a paragraph style's settings using the Character pane (Type ➪ Character, or ⌘+T or Ctrl+T) for leading and using the Paragraph pane (Type ➪ Paragraph, or Option+⌘+T or Ctrl+Alt+T) for space above and below. You can also use the Character (A) and Paragraph (¶) forms, respectively, of the Control palette.

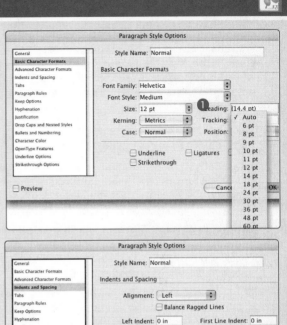

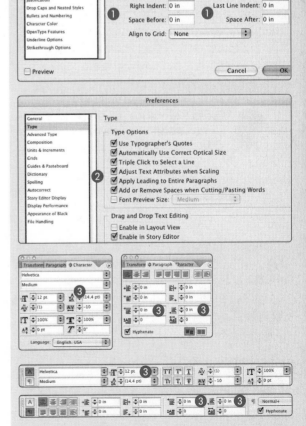

Controlling Indents

Indents are used to set paragraphs apart from others. A first-line indent is usually used to indicate a new paragraph (rather than the typewriter era's blank line above), while a block indent is used to indicate an extended quotation, and a hanging indent is used with bulleted or numbered lists.

Follow These Steps

In QuarkXPress, no matter which indents you use, you set them in the Formats pane, either when editing or creating the paragraph style or locally via the Paragraph Attributes dialog box (Style ⇨ Formats, or Shift+⌘+F or Ctrl+Shift+F):

1 Use the Left Indent, First Line, and Right Indent fields to set the indentation amount. For a hanging indent, the First Line field should be set to a negative number and the Left Indent field to the same, but positive, number.

2 You can also set your own hanging indent by inserting the indent-to-here character (⌘+\ or Ctrl+\). Text will align to that character until the next paragraph begins.

Cross-Reference: When setting up bulleted or numbered lists, follow the instructions on pages 134-135.

InDesign

Follow These Steps

InDesign provides similar methods for setting indents, and offers an extra option. No matter which indents you use, you set them in the Indents and Spacing pane when editing or creating the paragraph style or locally via the Paragraph pane (Type ➪ Paragraph, or Option+⌘+T or Ctrl+Alt+T):

1 Use the Left Indent, First Line, and Right Indent fields to set the indentation amount. For a hanging indent, the First Line field should be set to a negative number and the Left Indent field to the same, but positive, number.

2 You can also set your own hanging indent by inserting the indent-to-here character (Type ➪ Insert Special Character ➪ Indent to Here, or ⌘+| or Ctrl+\). Text will align to that character until the next paragraph begins.

 Go Further: InDesign CS2 offers a fourth option, Last Line Indent, which indents the last line of a paragraph from the right side.

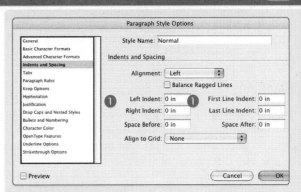

☀ Controlling Alignment

Text alignment is a key part of presentation, giving the eye resting spots when ragged edges are used and providing a streamlined look when justification is used.

Follow These Steps

Here's how QuarkXPress lets you handle alignment:

❶ You set horizontal alignment in the Formats pane, either when editing or creating the paragraph style or locally via the Paragraph Attributes dialog box (Style ➪ Formats, or Shift+⌘+F or Ctrl+Shift+F). You can also use the Measurements palette's buttons. The five settings are Left, Right, Centered, Justified, and Forced.

❷ In H&J sets (see page 160), you can control two justification aspects. First, you set the flush zone, the area from the text's margin in which lines should break. The larger the zone, the more ragged the look. Second, you can control whether single words that comprise a full line of a justified paragraph should be justified or be aligned to the left. Justifying them can result in awkward spacing, but that's usually a better result than having a different line length in the middle of a paragraph.

❸ You set vertical alignment for entire text boxes, not for selected text or specified paragraphs. To set vertical alignment, select the text box and choose Item ➪ Modify (⌘+M or Ctrl+M) and go to the Text pane. Choose the type of Alignment (Top, Centered, Bottom, and Justified) in the Type pop-up menu. If you choose Justified, set a value in the Inter ¶ Max field that specifies the maximum space permitted between paragraphs (meant to ensure that paragraphs are not so separated that they don't seem to be related).

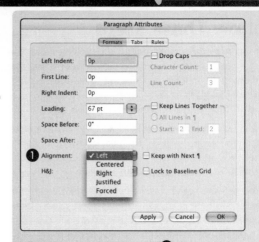

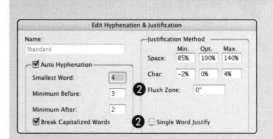

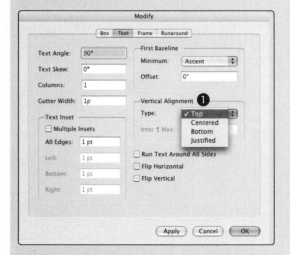

InDesign

Follow These Steps

Here's how InDesign lets you handle alignment:

① You set horizontal alignment in the Indents and Spacing pane when editing or creating the paragraph style or locally via the Paragraph pane (Type ➪ Paragraph, or Option+⌘+T or Ctrl+Alt+T). You can also use the Control palette's buttons. There are seven settings in InDesign CS and earlier: Left, Right, Center, Left Justify, Center Justify, Right Justify, and Full Justify (the same as QuarkXPress's Forced). InDesign CS2 adds two more: Away from Spine and Towards Spine, which will flip the alignment automatically as text moves between lefthand (verso) pages and right-hand (recto) pages.

② In paragraph styles, you can control whether single words that comprise a full line of a justified paragraph should be justified or be aligned to the left. Justifying them can result in awkward spacing, but that's usually a better result than having a different line length in the middle of a paragraph.

③ Through both paragraph styles and the Paragraph pane, InDesign lets you choose between two types of composition, which affects alignment as well as spacing: Adobe Paragraph Composer adjusts text spacing and paragraph rag based on the overall paragraph's look, while Adobe Single-Line Composer looks at each line without regard to other lines in the paragraph (the same method QuarkXPress uses). Note that InDesign does not offer the equivalent of QuarkXPress's flush zone since it prefers to handle the rag.

④ You set vertical alignment for entire text frames, not for selected text or specified paragraphs. To set vertical alignment, select the text frame and choose Object ➪ Text Frame Options (⌘+B or Ctrl+B) and, in InDesign CS2, go to the General pane. Choose the type of Alignment (Top, Center, Bottom, and Justify) in the Align pop-up menu. If you choose one of the justified options, set a value in the Paragraph Spacing Limit field that specifies the maximum space permitted between paragraphs (meant to ensure that paragraphs are not so separated that they don't seem to be related).

Go Further: The ability to control spacing and rag across the entire paragraph is a strong InDesign advantage, although it does make it harder to track and edit text to make a paragraph lose a widow to better fit the available space, since inDesign may override your tracking to rebalance the paragraph.

InDesign CS2's Away from Spine and Towards Spine alignment options are very handy for facing-pages documents, making it much easier to have alternative alignments for folios, captions, and other elements.

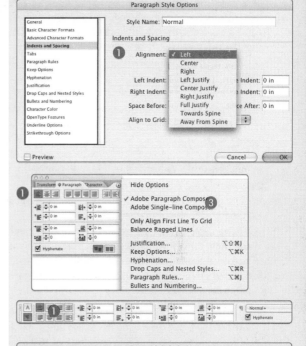

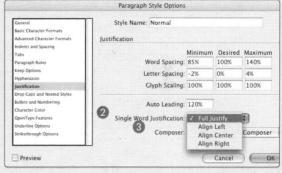

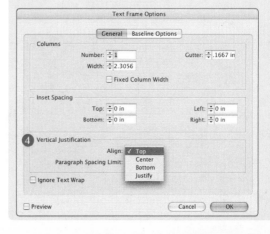

❋ Using Special Spaces

There are times when you want to set specific amounts of space in your text, such as for alignment. Several such fixed-size spaces are available, although QuarkXPress and InDesign offer different sets of them.

Follow These Steps

QuarkXPress provides several special spaces, plus you can customize your own and set the preferred value fo an em space.

Entering Special Spaces in Text

QuarkXPress provides just one option to use special spaces:

❶ Access using the shortcuts in the table below.

Customizing Special Spaces

QuarkXPress also offers the flex space, which you can customize. Most people set it to be an em space, which lets you use keyboard shortcuts to enter em spaces (otherwise, you'll need to enter two en spaces since QuarkXPress oddly has no em space character).

❶ Customize the flex space in the Character pane of the Preferences dialog box. To have the flex space equal an em space, set Flex Space Width to 200%. (A setting of 100% sets the flex space to be equal to an en space.) To open the Preferences dialog box in QuarkXPress 6, choose QuarkXPress ⇨ Preferences or press Option+Shift+⌘+Y on the Mac or Edit ⇨ Preferences or Ctrl+Alt+Shift+Y in Windows. In QuarkXPress 5, choose Edit ⇨ Preferences ⇨ Preferences, or press Option+Shift+⌘+Y or Ctrl+Alt+Shift+Y. In QuarkXPress 4, Edit ⇨ Preferences ⇨ Document, or press ⌘+Y or Ctrl+Y.

❷ You should also check Standard Em Space in this pane; it sets the value for an em space as used by QuarkXPress's tracking settings.

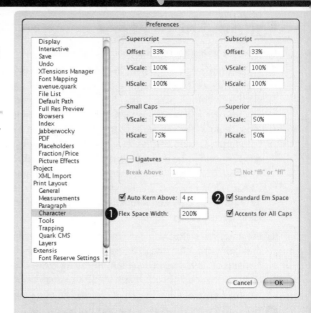

Keep in Mind

Here's what each space's size is:

- An em space is the width of the capital *M*, which is usually the same width as the current point size.
- An en space is the width of the capital *N*, which is usually the same width as half the current point size.
- A punctuation space is the width of a comma, and is used to line up numbers in tables.
- A flex space is a user-defined space.

QuarkXPress offers breaking and nonbreaking versions of the em, en, and punctuation spaces.

QuarkXPress vs. InDesign Shortcuts

Special space	QuarkXPress	
	Macintosh	Windows
Nonbreaking em space ( )	*not available*	*not available*
En space ( )	Option+space	Ctrl+Shift+6
Nonbreaking en space ( )	Option+⌘+space	Ctrl+Alt+Shift+6
Figure space	*not available*	*not available*
Thin space ()	*not available*	*not available*
Punctuation space ( )	Shift+space	Shift+space
Nonbreaking punctuation space ( )	Shift+⌘+space	Ctrl+Shift+space
Nonbreaking space	⌘+space	Ctrl+5
Flex space	Option+Shift+space	Ctrl+Shift+5
Nonbreaking flex space	Option+Shift+⌘+space	Ctrl+Alt+Shift+5
Flush space	*not available*	*not available*
Indent to here	⌘+\	Ctrl+\
Right-indent tab	Shift+Tab	Shift+Tab

InDesign

Follow These Steps

InDesign provides two ways to access special spaces:

① Use the keyboard shortcuts (see the table below).

② Choose Type ➪ Insert White Space and choose an option.

InDesign provides no equivalent to QuarkXPress's user-defined flex space, and it uses the standard definition of an em space, so there is no Preferences dialog box in InDesign to set an em space's value.

Workaround: InDesign does not offer nonbreaking spaces of anything but the regular space. That's because all of InDesign's fixed-size spaces are non-breaking, which can lead to some awkward justification.

InDesign		
Macintosh	Windows	**Special space**
Shift+⌘+M	Ctrl+Shift+M	Nonbreaking em space ( )
not available	*not available*	En space ( )
Shift+⌘+N	Ctrl+Shift+N	Nonbreaking en space ( )
no shortcut	*no shortcut*	Figure space
Option+Shift+⌘+M	Ctrl+Alt+Shift+M	Nonbreaking thin space ( )
no shortcut	*no shortcut*	Hair space ( )
Option+Shift+⌘+I	Ctrl+Alt+Shift+I	Nonbreaking hair space ( )
Option+⌘+X	Ctrl+Alt+X	Nonbreaking space
not available	*not available*	Flex space
not available	*not available*	Nonbreaking flex space
no shortcut	*no shortcut*	Flush space
⌘+\	Ctrl+\	Indent to here
Shift+Tab	Shift+Tab	Right-indent tab

Keep in Mind

Here's what each space's size is:

• An em space is the width of the capital *M*, which is usually the same width as the current point size.

• An en space is the width of the capital *N*, which is usually the same width as half the current point size.

• A figure space is the width of a numeral, and is used to line up numbers in tables.

• A thin space is the width of an exclamation mark (!), which is usually the same width as a quarter the current point size.

• A hair space is the width of a comma, and is used to line up numbers in tables.

• A flush space changes the appearance of the last line of text in a justified paragraph. InDesign normally would stretch out the words as much as permitted in the paragraph style's Justification pane. Entering a flush space prevents that, which can result in nicer-looking, but short, final lines. In nonjustified text, a flush space acts like a regular space.

※ Using Hyphens and Dashes

At times you may want to use real dashes or special types of hyphens.

Keep in Mind

Here's what dashes and hyphens that QuarkXPress makes available. You access these dashes and hyphens using the shortcuts in the table below.

- An em dash — the most commonly used dash — is the width of the capital *M*, which is usually the same width as the current point size.

- An en dash — used mainly as a minus sign and as a hyphen for multiple-word modifiers such as in *Civil War–era*) is the width of the capital *N*, which is usually the same width as half the current point size.

- A nonbreaking hyphen prevents the hyphen from being at the end of a line.

- A discretionary hyphen lets you specify preferred hyphenation points, but it only displays and prints as a hyphen if its location on a line fits within the paragraph's hyphenation settings.

QuarkXPress vs. InDesign Shortcuts

Special dash	QuarkXPress	
	Macintosh	Windows
Em dash (—)	Option+Shift+–	Ctrl+Shift+=
Nonbreaking em dash (—)	Option+⌘+=	Ctrl+Alt+Shift+=
En dash (–)	Option+–	Ctrl+Alt+Shift+–
Nonbreaking hyphen (-)	⌘+=	Ctrl+=
Discretionary hyphen (-)	⌘+–	Ctrl+–

InDesign

Keep in Mind

InDesign provides both shortcuts (see the table below) and menu options for access to special hyphens and dashes:

① Choose Type ➪ Insert Special Character and choose an option.

Here's what each dash or hyphen is:

- An em dash — the most commonly used dash — is the width of the capital *M*, which is usually the same width as the current point size.

- An en dash — used mainly as a minus sign and as a hyphen for multiple-word modifiers such as in *Civil War–era*) is the width of the capital *N*, which is usually the same width as half the current point size.

- A nonbreaking hyphen prevents the hyphen from being at the end of a line.

- A discretionary hyphen lets you specify preferred hyphenation points, but it only displays and prints as a hyphen if its location on a line fits within the paragraph's hyphenation settings.

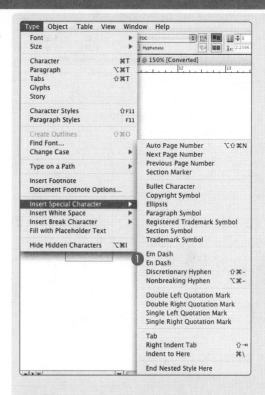

InDesign		
Macintosh	Windows	**Special dash**
Option+Shift+–	Alt+Shift+–	Em dash (—)
not available	*not available*	Nonbreaking em dash (—)
Option+–	Alt+–	En dash (–)
Option+⌘+–	Ctrl+Alt+–	Nonbreaking hyphen (-)
Shift+⌘+–	Ctrl+Shift+–	Discretionary hyphen (-)

part vi

Working with Tables

This part shows you how to create and format tables, a capability that QuarkXPress introduced only in version 5. InDesign's table capabilities at first glance are similar to QuarkXPress's, but there are many subtle differences. InDesign offers more control over formatting, especially in its unique support of tables that straddle multiple pages or frames.

✳ Working with Tabs

Tabs let you easily align text. QuarkXPress and InDesign offer similar tab capabilities.

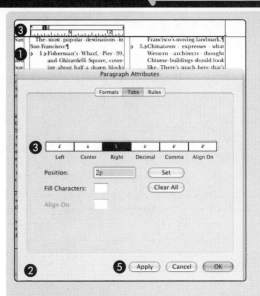

Follow These Steps

Tabs have three basic uses in QuarkXPress: to align text in tabular material, to properly position text in a numbered or bulleted list, and to align a dingbat character at the end of a story. The process is the same for all three.

Setting Tabs

❶ Enter the tab character(s) before the text you want aligned. (For example, this numbered list has a tab before the number and a tab before the first word.)

❷ Choose Style ➪ Tabs (Shift+⌘+T or Ctrl+Shift+T) to open the Tabs pane of the Paragraph Attributes dialog box. Note that QuarkXPress displays a tab ruler above the text (you may need to move the Paragraph Attributes dialog box out of the way). When defining a paragraph style sheet, the Tabs pane provides the same options, except you won't get the tab ruler over actual text. You may want to first experiment locally and then enter the final settings into your paragraph style sheet, or create a new style sheet from the formatted paragraph and let QuarkXPress automatically pick up its settings. (See page 120 for more on paragraph style sheets.)

❸ You'll see tab stops for each tab you typed. You can drag the tab stops to new positions, or click them and enter a specific location value in the dialog box's Position field and then click Set. To change the tab type to right, center, decimal, comma, or align-on, click the tab in the ruler then click the appropriate icon in the dialog box. (For align-on tabs, enter the align-on character in the Align On field.) You can also set the fill character(s) by entering that text in the Fill Characters field.

❹ Add new tab stops by clicking on the ruler. Delete tab stops by dragging them up and out of the ruler. Or click Clear All.

❺ Click Apply to preview your changes and OK to accept them.

Using Tabs for Tables

The process for creating tables using tabs is the same as described above, except that you will have multiple tab stops, and often multiple kinds of alignments, in the same paragraph. The Table tool, available in QuarkXPress 5 and later, is better suited to creating tables and is covered in the rest of this part.

Because each row is its own paragraph, it's best to create a paragraph style sheet with the final tab settings and then apply the style sheet to all paragraphs in the table. You'll also likely have several other paragraph style sheets based on this basic tabular paragraph style to, for example, put a ruling line below the final line in the table or to boldface the header row.

Follow These Steps

Tabs have two basic uses in InDesign: to position text in a numbered or bulleted list, and to align a dingbat character at the end of a story. The process is the same for both. You can also use tabs to produce simple tables, although since InDesign 2 and later have a built-in table editor, it's better to use that tool.

Setting Tabs

① Enter the tab character(s) before the text you want aligned. (For example, this numbered list has a tab before the number and a tab before the first word.)

② Choose Type ⇨ Tabs (Shift+⌘+T or Ctrl+Shift+T) to open the Tabs pane. (When defining a paragraph style, the Tabs pane provides the same options. You may want to first experiment locally and then enter the final settings into your paragraph style, or create a new style from the formatted paragraph and let InDesign automatically pick up its settings. See page 121 for more on paragraph styles.)

③ You'll see tab stops for each tab you typed. You can drag them to new positions, or click them and enter a specific location value in the Tab pane's X field. To change the tab type to right, center, decimal, comma, or align-on, click the tab in the ruler and then click the appropriate icon above the ruler. (For align-on tabs, enter the align-on character in the Align On field.) You can also set the fill character(s) by entering that text in the Leader field.

④ You can lock the Tabs pane to the top of the text frame containing the selected text by clicking the Magnet icon; this also makes the pane as wide as the text column. The Tabs pane has to be near the text frame for the Magnet icon to work.

⑤ Add new tab stops by clicking on the ruler. Delete tab stops by dragging them up and out of the ruler. Or click Clear All in the Tabs pane's palette menu to delete all the tab stops.

⑥ Your changes are applied immediately; to cancel a change, choose Edit ⇨ Undo (⌘+Z or Ctrl+Z).

Using Tabs for Tables

If don't want to use the Table tool (see the rest of this part), the process for creating tables using tabs is the same as described above, except that you will have multiple tab stops, and often multiple kinds of alignments, in the same paragraph.

Because each row is its own paragraph, it's best to create a paragraph style sheet with the final tab settings and then apply it to all paragraphs in the table. You'll also likely have several other paragraph style sheets based on this basic tabular paragraph style to, for example, put a ruling line below the final line in the table or to boldface the header row.

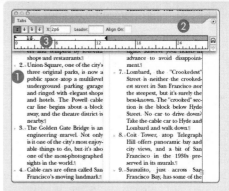

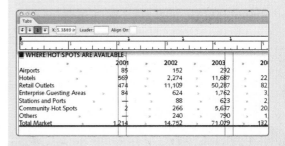

Converting Tabs to Tables

Tables are complex, and formatting them with tabs can be difficult to do. That's why it's better to use a table tool wherever possible. But because you'll likely have tables created via tabs (whether from word-processor files or layout files), you need a way to convert those tabbed tables into the real thing. Both QuarkXPress and InDesign let you do this, with some differences.

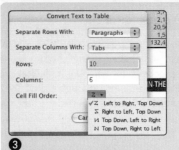

3

Follow These Steps

Chances are that you'll have many documents that use tabbed text for tables, whether because an imported Microsoft Word file's tables were converted to tabs or because the table was created in QuarkXPress 4 or earlier. But in version 5 and later, QuarkXPress offers a table tool that provides Word-like table-creation and –editing capabilities. Here's how to convert these tabbed tables to a proper QuarkXPress table:

1 Highlight the text you want to convert to a table.

2 Choose Item ⇨ Convert Text to Table.

3 In the resulting Convert Text to Table dialog box, you specify the separator characters that QuarkXPress should look for to determine cell and row boundaries. Typically, you'd set Separate Rows With to Paragraphs and Separate Columns With to Tabs. (Your other options for both pop-up menus are Commas and Spaces.) You can also set a different number of rows and/or columns than QuarkXPress detects. Finally, you can choose the import order using the Cell Fill Order pop-up menu, which lets you pivot tables by having QuarkXPress create a table in a different orientation than the source material.

4 Click OK when the settings are to your liking.

5 QuarkXPress will then generate a table in a separate text frame, leaving your tabbed text untouched. You can then edit the table as needed (see the rest of this part) and then copy the text from the new text box into your original text box, replacing that original table, or leaving it as a separate text box, based on the best approach for your layout.

5

Cross-Reference: For information on importing tables and tabular text from word processors, see pages 94-95.

InDesign

Follow These Steps

You can convert Microsoft Word tables that were converted to tabs to a proper InDesign table:

1 Highlight the text you want to convert to a table.

2 Choose Table ➪ Convert Text to Table.

3 In the resulting Convert Text to Table dialog box, you specify the separator characters that InDesign should look for to determine cell and row boundaries. Typically, you'd set Row Separator to Paragraph and Column Separator to Tab. (Your other options for both pop-up menus are Comma and Other, which display if you enter a separator character in the Row Separator or Column Separator field.)

4 Click OK when the settings are to your liking.

5 InDesign will then generate a table in the same text frame, replacing your tabbed text. You can then edit the table as needed (see the rest of this part).

 Watch Out: InDesign is less flexible than QuarkXPress when it comes to converting tabbed text to tables. You can't change the number of columns or rows (despite there being a grayed-out Number of Columns field in the Convert Text to Table dialog box) and you can't control the import order for cells. These shortcomings are merely annoying.

But a potentially dangerous difference is that InDesign replaces your original text with the converted table, which could be a problem if the conversion isn't done right (such as if the wrong separator characters were chosen). You can, of course, undo a conversion by choosing Edit ➪ Undo (⌘+Z or Ctrl+Z).

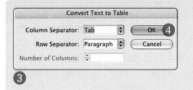

Convert Text to Table

Column Separator: Tab
Row Separator: Paragraph
Number of Columns:

OK 4
Cancel

3

■	2001	2002	2003
Airports	85	152	292
Hotels	569	2,274	11,687
Retail Outlets	474	11,109	50,287
Enterprise Guesting Areas	84	624	1,762
Stations and Ports	—	88	623
Community Hot Spots	2	266	5,637
Others	—	240	790
Total Market	1,214	14,752	71,079

5

Creating Tables

A table tool gives you strong control over text and cell appearance, as well as how to handle issues such as lines used between rows and tables. QuarkXPress 5 and InDesign 2 were the first versions, respectively, that provided true tables. InDesign's capabilities are notably superior.

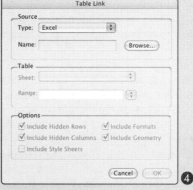

Follow These Steps

QuarkXPress 5 or later lets you create tables as follows:

① Select the Table tool.

② Draw a frame to contain the table.

③ When you release the mouse button, QuarkXPress will open the Table Properties dialog box, where you set the number of rows and columns and whether the cells will contain text or pictures (you can change that later for individual cells). In QuarkXPress 6, you can also set the tab order (which determines how the text cursor moves from cell to cell when you press Tab). Also in QuarkXPress 6, if you select the Link Cells checkbox to link the cells to each other for text flow, you can also set the link order, which controls how text will flow from cell to cell.

④ QuarkXPress 6.1 or later also provides a Link to External Data checkbox that, if checked, opens the Table Link dialog box from which you can import a Microsoft Excel spreadsheet as a table and control which formatting is retained.

⑤ After you click OK, QuarkXPress creates an empty table using equal spacing and the default rule settings (unless you are importing an Excel spreadsheet).

⑥ You can change the table defaults by double-clicking the Table tool, which opens the Tools pane of the Preferences dialog box. Click the table icon and then click Modify to open the Modify dialog box, which has several panes for which you can set default table settings. These settings affect all future tables in the current document, or all future documents if no document is open when you make the changes.

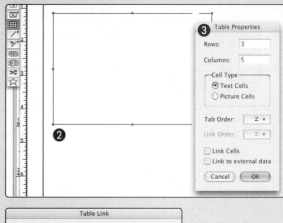

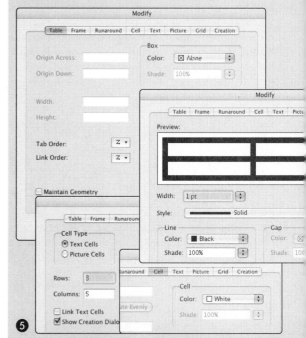

Cross-Reference: For information on importing tables and tabular text from word processors (and Excel, in inDesign), see pages 94-95.

InDesign

Follow These Steps

InDesign also lets you create tables, although its process differs:

1. Create a new text frame using the Type tool or click in an existing frame, as you prefer. Place the text-insertion cursor where you want to insert the table.

2. Choose Table ➪ Insert Table (Option+Shift+⌘+T or Ctrl+Alt+Shift+T).

3. InDesign will open the Insert Table dialog box where you set the number of rows and columns. In InDesign CS and later, you set body cells and header and footer rows separately. (There is no option as in QuarkXPress to specify that a table will contain text or graphics, since an InDesign table cell can contain either, with graphics handled as anchored objects.)

4. After you click OK, InDesign creates an empty table using equal spacing and the default rule settings.

6. You can change the table settings using the Table menu options, with most available by choosing Table ➪ Table Options ➪ Table Setup (Option+Shift+⌘+B or Ctrl+Alt+Shift+B).

Go Further: InDesign lets you set separate header and footer rows, which repeat for tables that flow across multiple text frames or pages. In QuarkXPress, you'd have to manually copy and paste any rows used as headers or footers into each text box.

InDesign also lets you place tables in text frames that hold other text. While it's often best to have tables in their own frames so their position is unaffected by text flow (just as is true for graphics), having the option to place small tables in text is a useful option that InDesign offers but QuarkXPress does not.

InDesign has two other advantages over QuarkXPress: First, table cells can contain tables, letting you create nested tables. Second, the fact that tables are inserted in text frames means they can move with their text (if you don't want that, just put the tables in their own frames).

Workaround: You cannot set up table defaults in InDesign as you can in QuarkXPress. If you have a table format that you use repeatedly, consider copying it into an empty text frame, removing its text and graphics, and then transferring it to a library for future reuse (see page 45). Or consider buying a plug-in such as WoodWing Software's Smart Styles.

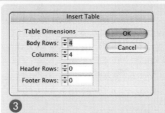

3

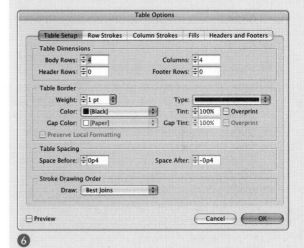

6

Applying Table Attributes

Almost every table benefits from extensive formatting of the cells, ruling lines, and the text within them to help ensure a proper fit and an effective visual presentation. QuarkXPress and InDesign let you apply such formatting, although InDesign is more flexible in its options to do so.

Follow These Steps

With a table either imported or newly created, you can set up its basic formatting:

1. Select the table with the Item tool.

2. Choose Item ➪ Modify (⌘+M or Ctrl+M).

3. In the Modify dialog box, go to the Tables pane to change the size and position and, in QuarkXPress 6, the tab order, link order, and box color. Check Maintain Geometry to resize a table's width and height proportionally even if you resize just the width or height. In both QuarkXPress 5 and 6, you can choose to suppress printing of the table by checking Suppress Output.

4. In the Grid pane, you can set the grid style, thickness, and color. You can also decide where gridlines should display by clicking one of the three buttons at right to choose all gridlines, just vertical gridlines, and just horizontal gridlines. After choosing the gridlines, use the other settings in the dialog box to change them.

5. The Runaround pane (available in QuarkXPress 5 and later) and the Frame pane (available in QuarkXPress 6) work the same as they do for picture and text boxes.

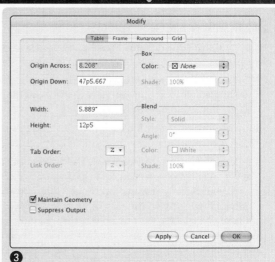

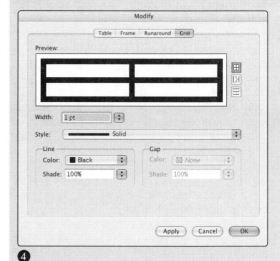

InDesign

Follow These Steps

With a table either imported or newly created, you can set up its basic formatting, with more options than QuarkXPress provides:

1. Select the table with the Type tool.

2. Choose Table ➪ Table Setup (Option+Shift+⌘+B or Ctrl+Alt+Shift+B).

3. Go to the Table Setup pane to change the number of columns and rows, as well as the table border and spacing before and after the table.

4. In the Headers and Footers pane, you can decide whether and how to repeat header and footer rows in subsequent text frames.

5. In the Row Stokes and Column Strokes panes, you can set the grid pattern, style, thickness, and color.

6. In the Fills pane, you set the pattern and colors for row background fills.

Go Further: InDesign offers much more control over the visual formatting of tables than does Quark-XPress, including greater control over gridline position and appearance and, in InDesign CS and later, the ability to manage the display of header and footer rows in multiframe tables.

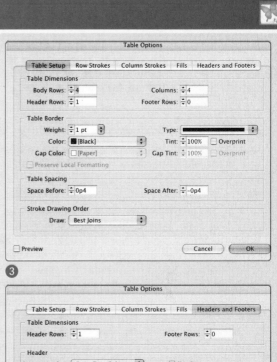

③

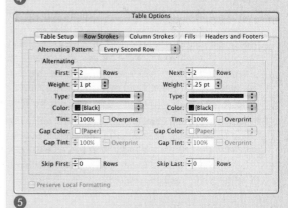

④

⑤

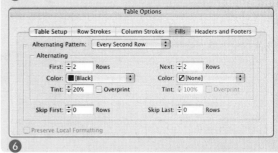

⑥

☀ Formatting Rows and Columns ◀ QuarkXPress

When you format tables, you'll spend a lot of time work-ing on the rows and columns to ensure proper separation and highlighting of table elements. InDesign offers more options than QuarkXPress for rows and columns.

Follow These Steps

QuarkXPress offers basic control over row and column size, and limited formatting control over gridlines and color back-grounds:

1 To resize rows and columns, click and drag cell boundaries with the Content tool; changing vertical boundaries changes column width, while moving horizontal boundaries changes row depth. You can also select several cells with the Con-tent tool and then choose Item ⇨ Modify (⌘+M or Ctrl+M). The Cell pane lets you set cell width (for rows) or height (for columns) or choose to distribute them evenly. Selections affect the entire row or column, not just the selected cells.

2 To set gridlines, select the table with the Item tool and choose Item ⇨ Modify (⌘+M or Ctrl+M). In the Grid pane, you set the grid style, thickness, and color. You can also decide where gridlines should display by clicking one of the three buttons at right to choose all gridlines, just vertical gridlines, and just horizontal gridlines. After choosing them, use the other settings in the dialog box to change them.

3 To give rows or columns a background color, select the row's or column's cells with the Content tool. (A quick way to select an entire row or column is to position the content tool right next to a row or column. The pointer will turn to an arrow, and if you click the mouse, the row or column will be selected.) In the Colors pane, make sure that the back-ground icon is selected and then choose a color. Use the Shade field or pop-up menu to select a tint for the color.

4 You format text in rows and columns just like any other text. (A quick way to select an entire row or column is to position the content tool right next to a row or column. The pointer will turn to an arrow, and if you click the mouse, the row or column will be selected.)

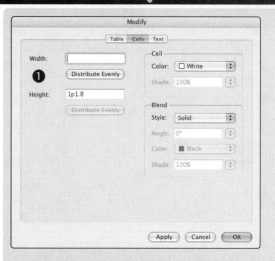

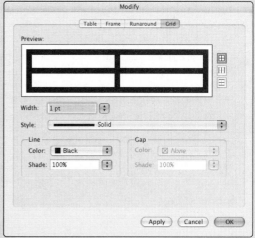

InDesign

Follow These Steps

InDesign offers basic control over row and column size, as well as more sophisticated formatting control over gridlines and color backgrounds than QuarkXPress does:

① To resize rows and columns, click and drag cell boundaries with the Type tool; changing vertical boundaries changes column width, while moving horizontal boundaries changes row depth.

② To set gridlines, select the table with the Type tool and choose Table ⇨ Table Setup (Option+Shift+⌘+B or Ctrl+Alt+Shift+B). Use the Row Stokes and Column Strokes panes to set the grid pattern, style, thickness, and color.

③ In the Fills pane, you set the pattern and colors for row background fills.

④ In the Headers and Footers pane, you can decide whether and how to repeat header and footer rows in subsequent text frames.

⑤ You format text in rows and columns just like any other text. (A quick way to select an entire row or column is to position the content tool right next to a row or column. The pointer will turn to an arrow, and if you click the mouse, the row or column will be selected.)

 Go Further: InDesign offers much more control over the visual formatting of tables than does Quark-XPress, including greater control over gridline position and appearance and, in InDesign CS and later, the ability to manage the display of header and footer rows in multiframe tables.

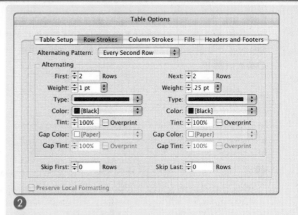

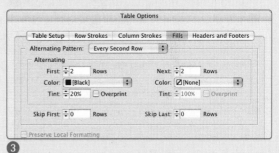

Applying Cell Attributes

Cells are the table's containers, and you often want to provide distinct formatting to cells and their contents beyond the attributes applied to rows, columns, and the overall table.

Follow These Steps

In QuarkXPress, cells are basically boxes, so you have all the formatting capabilities of a box available to cells. But you can also apply additional attributes:

1. You can set cell color by selecting cells with the Content tool and choosing Item ⇨ Modify (⌘+M or Ctrl+M). In the Cells pane, set the color or blend. You could also use the Colors pane to apply a color or blend to selected cells.

2. You can set cell text attributes by selecting cells with the Content tool and choosing Item ⇨ Modify (⌘+M or Ctrl+M). In the Text pane, set the text angle, skew, baseline position, inset, and vertical alignment. You can also use the Measurements palette, Colors palette, Style Sheets palette, and Style menu options to format text.

3. To combine cells, select them with the Content tool and choose Item ⇨ Table ⇨ Combine Cells. To split a previously combined cell, click within it with the Content tool and choose Item ⇨ Table ⇨ Split Cells.

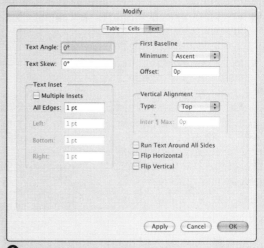

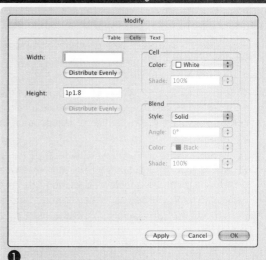

InDesign

Follow These Steps

InDesign lets you work with cells pretty much as you would in Microsoft Word:

① You can set cell fill or border color by selecting cells with the Type tool and choosing Table ⇨ Cell Options ⇨ Strokes and Fills. In the Strokes and Fills pane, set the color or gradient. For borders, select the borders in the Cell Stroke window. You could also use the Swatches pane to apply a color or gradient to the fills or strokes of selected cells.

② You can set cell text attributes by selecting cells with the Type tool and choosing Table ⇨ Cell Options ⇨ Text. In the Text pane, set the text rotation, baseline position, inset, and vertical alignment. You can also use the Control palette and the Swatches, Paragraph Styles, Character Styles, Paragraph, and Character panes to format text.

③ You can have InDesign place diagonal strokes in tables by selecting cells with the Type tool and choosing Table ⇨ Cell Options ⇨ Diagonal Lines.

④ To combine cells, select them with the Type tool and choose Table ⇨ Merge Cells. To split a cell, click within it with the Type tool and choose Table ⇨ Split Cell Horizontally or Table ⇨ Split Cell Vertically.

Go Further: InDesign offers much more control over the visual formatting of cells than does Quark-XPress, including greater control over border appearance and the ability to set diagonal strokes.

InDesign also lets you split any cells, while QuarkXPress can split only cells that were previously combined.

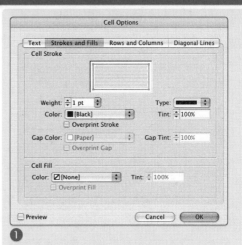

part vii

Working with Graphics Files

This part covers how to import, place, and update graphics files, which provide much of the visual impact of your documents. Both QuarkXPress and InDesign give you wide support in terms of supported file formats, but the two programs have both subtle and significant differences in how they do this.

InDesign provides tighter integration with Adobe Photoshop and Illustrator files, as well as more powerful support of the Acrobat PDF format. InDesign also makes it easier, in most cases, to manage the links to your source graphics.

Comparing Supported Formats

A key issue in any layout program is the support it offers for different kinds of source graphics. From a user's point of view, the more file formats supported the better. Supporting a long list of formats makes it difficult for the software developers to keep up, so most layout programs try to limit themselves to supporting just the most popular file formats. This tension has kept QuarkXPress and InDesign fairly equal in terms of supported graphics formats — with one key exception: Adobe formats.

Keep in Mind

Over the years, QuarkXPress has dropped support for a variety of little-used formats, such as CGM and MacPaint, but has resisted adding support for the native formats of Adobe Photoshop and Illustrator.

In December 2004, Quark finally added Photoshop support through a free XTension for version 6.5 (essentially a "lite" version of A Lowly Apprentice Production's ImagePort XTension). Native Illustrator support is somewhat moot because current versions of Illustrator now use the EPS and PDF formats as their native format.

QuarkXPress 5 or later imports PDF files and lets you select which page of a multipage PDF file to import, but it cannot import multiple pages. In QuarkXPress 4.1, you can also import PDF files and select which page if you download Quark's free PDF Filter 1.6 XTension from www.quark.com.

QuarkXPress vs. InDesign: Graphics Files

Format	QuarkXPress Version	Notes
Acrobat PDF	4.1–6.5	User can select any page in a PDF file
EPS	3.0–6.5	—
EPS DCS	3.0–6.5	—
GIF	4.0–6.5 Win, 5.0–6.5 Mac	—
Illustrator AI	*not supported*	—
JPEG	3.3–6.5	—
PCX	3.3–5.0	—
Photo CD	3.3–6.5	—
Photoshop PSD	6.5 with free XTension	Layers selectable
PICT	3.0–6.5	—
PNG	5.0–6.5	—
Scitex CT	3.0–6.5	—
TIFF	3.0–6.5	Multiple clipping paths supported in v5–6.5
Windows BMP	3.0–6.5	—
Windows EMF	*not supported*	—
Windows WMF	3.0–6.5 Win, 6.0–6.5 Mac	—

Keep in Mind

InDesign, being an Adobe product, had support for Photoshop and Illustrator from the get-go, as well as support for the other mainline graphics formats. InDesign CS2 adds support for user-selectable layers in Photoshop, Illustrator, and PDF files. It can also import the Windows EMF format.

InDesign has long supported the ability to choose which page of a multipage PDF file to import, and InDesign CS2 goes further by letting you select multiple pages.

InDesign has also better supported transparency within files which, when combined with native Photoshop and Illustrator support, makes it easier for users to stick with an all-Adobe environment — an Adobe goal.

InDesign Version	Notes	Format
1.0-CS2	Multiple pages supported, layers selectable in vCS2	Acrobat PDF
1.0-CS2	—	EPS
1.0-CS2	—	EPS DCS
1.0-CS2	—	GIF
1.0-CS2	Illustrator v5.5–CS2; layers selectable in vCS2	Illustrator AI
1.0-CS2	—	JPEG
1.0-CS2	—	PCX
not supported	—	Photo CD
1.0-CS2	Photoshop v4–CS2; spot colors supported in InDesign CS–CS2, layers selectable in vCS2	Photoshop PSD
1.0-CS2	—	PICT
1.0-CS2	—	PNG
1.0-CS2	—	Scitex CT
1.0-CS2	—	TIFF
1.0-CS2	—	Windows BMP
2.0-CS2	—	Windows EMF
1.0-CS2	—	Windows WMF

✻Preparing Graphics for Import   ◀ QuarkXPress

In most cases, little prep work is needed for your graphics files before you import them.

Follow These Steps

You may need to do these steps in QuarkXPress:

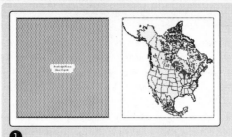

① EPS files from older programs or those that were created on
a different platform may not have a readable preview
header, so all you see in QuarkXPress is a gray box where
the image is. That makes it difficult to position or scale the
image correctly. QuarkXPress for Mac can read PICT, JPEG,
and TIFF preview headers, but QuarkXPress for Windows
can read only TIFF preview headers, so if your illustration
program gives you a choice, always choose TIFF. You can
also open a preview-less EPS file in a program such as
Adobe Illustrator, Macromedia FreeHand, or CorelDraw and
resave the file with a preview, as in the example at right.

② Know what fonts are used. For EPS files, be sure you have
installed the fonts for any text within them, or convert the
text to curves in your illustration program. For PDF files,
either be sure you have the fonts used in them or make
sure that any such fonts are embedded in the PDF file. Otherwise, the text in your graphics may not print correctly.

③ QuarkXPress supports alpha channels and clipping paths in
TIFF files, so if you plan on using text wraps or masking based
on an image's shape, create the appropriate alpha channel
and/or clipping path in Photoshop. This will allow more precise text wrap or masking than you can do by tracing the
shape in QuarkXPress to create a clipping path there.

④ If you use PICT or Photo CD files, you must turn on the
QuarkXPress color management system if you plan to color-
separate these file formats when printing. (In QuarkXPress
6, choose QuarkXPress ➪ Preferences or Option+Shift+⌘+Y
on the Mac or Edit ➪ Preferences or Ctrl+Alt+Shift+Y in
Windows, then go to the Quark CMS pane. In QuarkXPress
4 or 5, choose Edit ➪ Preferences ➪ Color Management.)

⑤ If you have Windows EMF files (created by Microsoft Office
2000 or later applications), you'll need to save them as
Windows WMF files in those programs or convert them
through some other program before you can import them
into QuarkXPress.

⑥ If you have color images that you want to use as grayscale
images in QuarkXPress, you don't have to convert them (or
a copy) to grayscale in Photoshop. Just hold ⌘ or Ctrl when
you click OK when importing the graphic (see page 194).

⑦ Special PDF features — such as buttons, hyperlinks, and
embedded media files— are ignored during import, so you
will have to add them back in QuarkXPress 5 or later.

InDesign

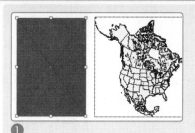

Follow These Steps

InDesign also requires little or no prep in most cases:

① It's possible that EPS files from older programs or those that were created on a different platform may not have a read-able preview header, so all you see in InDesign is a gray box with an *X* through it. This is a rare occurrence, since InDesign can usually create its own preview from the EPS file, but if it can't, it can be a challenge to position or scale a preview-less EPS file correctly. In that case, it's best to open a preview-less EPS file in a program like Adobe Illustrator, Macromedia FreeHand, or CorelDraw and resave it with a preview.

② Know what fonts are used. For EPS files, be sure you have installed the fonts for any text within them, or convert the text to curves in your illustration program. For PDF files, either be sure you have the fonts used in them or make sure any such fonts are embedded in in the PDF file. Other-wise, the text in your graphics may not print correctly.

③ InDesign supports alpha channels and clipping paths in TIFF and Photoshop files, so if you plan on using text wraps or masking based on an image's shape, create the appropriate alpha channel and/or clipping path in Photoshop. This will allow more precise text wrap or masking than you can do by tracing the shape in InDesign to create a clipping path there.

④ InDesign CS or later create swatches for any spot colors used in your Photoshop files. If you use InDesign 2 or ear-lier, be sure to convert them to CMYK in Photoshop before placing them in InDesign.

⑥ If you have color images that you want to use as grayscale images in InDesign, you'll have to convert them (or a copy) to grayscale in Photoshop or similar program. There's no way to import color images as grayscale (something Quark-XPress can do).

⑦ You should not use DCS (the pre-color-separated variant of EPS) in documents that you will output as composite color (such as to an inkjet printer), since InDesign will ignore the information in the CMYK plates and will instead just use the preview plate for output, which can be lower quality. Use EPS instead in this case.

⑧ Special PDF features such as buttons, hyperlinks, and embedded media files are ignored during import, so you will have to add them back in InDesign.

■Importing Vector Graphics

Often, your graphics have components or attributes that you may want to override or take special advantage of. In many cases, you can make those adjustments when importing them.

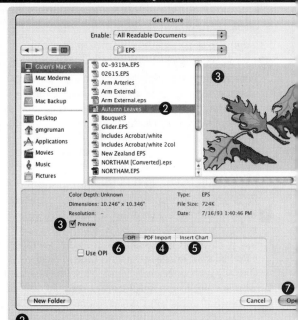

Follow These Steps

Importing vector graphics, such as EPS and PDF, into Quark-XPress starts with a picture box.

1 Select a picture box using either the Content or Item tool, then choose File ➪ Get Picture (⌘+E or Ctrl+E).

2 The Get Picture dialog box will display. Navigate to the folder that contains the desired file.

3 If the Preview checkbox is checked, QuarkXPress will display a preview of the file so you can be sure that it's the one you want.

4 If you've chosen a PDF file and the PDF contains multiple pages, go to the PDF Import pane to choose which page to import. See page 196 for more details.

5 If you've chosen a Microsoft Excel file that has an embedded chart (in QuarkXPress 6.1 or later), go to the Insert Chart pane to select the spreadsheet that has the chart from the chosen Excel workbook.

6 If you are using an Open Prepress Interface workflow, in which high-resolution files are stored elsewhere and designers use lower-resolution surrogates for their layouts, check the Use OPI checkbox in the OPI pane so that Quark-XPress will properly substitute the high-resolution file during output.

7 Click OK to import the graphic.

Note that QuarkXPress has no import options for PICT or Windows WMF vector files.

Cross-Reference: For more on importing PDF files, see pages 196-197.

InDesign

Follow These Steps

Importing vector graphics into InDesign can start with a graphics frame but doesn't have to. You'll also find more import options.

1 If you want, select a frame using either the Selection or Direct Selection tool, then choose File ⇨ Place (⌘+D or Ctrl+D).

2 The Place dialog box will display. Navigate to the folder that contains the desired file. InDesign will show a preview automatically of any supported file you select.

3 If checked, Show Import Options will show you the import options for the selected file; import options are not immediately available in the Place dialog box as they are in the equivalent Get Picture dialog box in QuarkXPress. Replace Selected Item, if checked, will replace the contents of the selected frame with the imported graphic; InDesign assumes that all imported graphics go into their own, new frames unless you select a frame and check this option.

4 Click the Use Adobe Dialog button in InDesign CS2 or the Version Cue button in InDesign CS to switch to Adobe's Version Cue file-management system, which allows shared folders and multiple versions of files in InDesign CS or later (as well as in other Creative Suite applications). Note that the default Version Cue view does not show image previews; be sure to switch to the Thumbnail view to see them. To get the standard dialog boxes, click Use OS Dialog (InDesign CS2) or Local Files (InDesign CS) in the Version Cue interface.

5 If you've chosen an EPS or Illustrator file and Show Import Options is checked, InDesign will display the EPS Import Options dialog box when you click Open. Here, you enable OPI links and Photoshop clipping paths, and choose whether to use the existing preview or generate a new one. Click OK to import the graphic.

6 If you've chosen a PDF file and Show Import Options is checked, InDesign will display the Place PDF dialog box when you click Open. See page 197 for more details.

7 If you are importing Illustrator or PDF files and Show Import Options is checked in InDesign CS2, the dialog box will have a Layers pane that lets you choose which layers should be visible in InDesign and whether these visibility settings should override those in the source file if you later relink the file.

8 If you haven't checked Show Import Options, click Open to import the graphic using default settings. If no frame was selected, click anywhere to import; otherwise, the graphic will go into the selected frame.

Although InDesign can import PICT, Windows EMF, and Windows WMF vector files, it has no import options for them. They'll simply import as is.

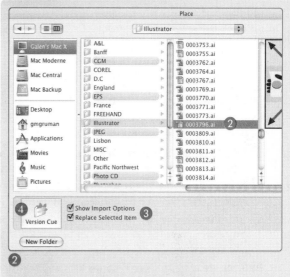

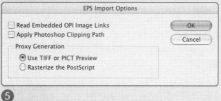

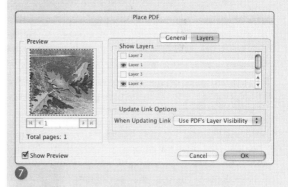

Cross-Reference: InDesign imports Excel charts as part of an Excel spreadsheet, not as separate objects. For details on Excel chart import, see page 95.

✸ Importing Bitmapped Graphics ⟨ **QuarkXPress** ⟩

Your bitmapped graphics may have components or attributes that you want to override or take special advantage of. In many cases, you can make those adjustments when importing them.

Follow These Steps

Importing bitmapped graphics, such as TIFF and Windows BMP files, into QuarkXPress starts with a picture box.

① Select a picture box using either the Content or Item tool, then choose File ➪ Get Picture (⌘+E or Ctrl+E).

② The Get Picture dialog box will display. Navigate to the folder that contains the desired file.

③ If the Preview checkbox is checked, QuarkXPress will display a preview of the file so you can be sure that it's the one you want.

④ If you are using an Open Prepress Interface workflow, in which high-resolution files are stored elsewhere and designers use lower-resolution surrogates for their layouts, check the Use OPI checkbox in the OPI pane so that Quark-XPress will properly substitute the high-resolution file during output.

⑤ If you are using QuarkXPress 6.5 with the free PSD Import XTension installed (from www.quark.com), you can select specific layers to display in your imported file.

⑥ If color management is active, the Color Management pane will also appear in the Get Picture dialog box. Here, you set a color profile for the imported graphic as well as the rendering intent, if desired.

⑦ Click OK to import the graphic. If you want to import a color bitmap as a grayscale bitmap, or a grayscale bitmap as a black-and-white bitmap, hold ⌘ or Ctrl as you click OK.

Note that QuarkXPress has no import options for bitmapped graphics, other than for Photoshop files imported into Quark-XPress 6.5. QuarkXPress 6.5 also lets you apply various effects, such as contrast changes and special-effects filters, to TIFF files after you import them.

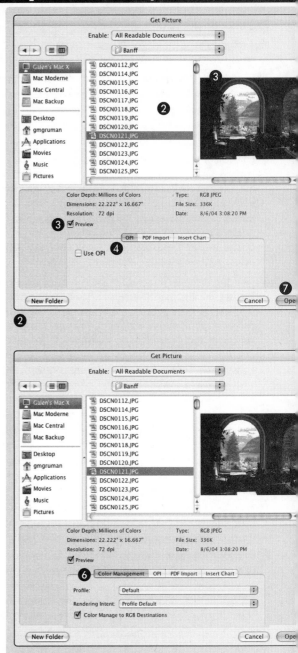

Cross-Reference: See pages 294–297 for more on color management and color profiles.

InDesign

Follow These Steps

Importing bitmapped graphics into InDesign can start with a graphics frame but doesn't have to. You'll also find more import options than QuarkXPress has.

① If you want, select a frame using either the Selection or Direct Selection tool, then choose File ➪ Place (⌘+D or Ctrl+D).

② The Place dialog box will display. Navigate to the folder that contains the desired file. InDesign will show a preview automatically of any supported file you select.

③ You have two checkboxes to consider selecting. Show Import Options will show you the import options for the selected file — import options are not immediately available in the Place dialog box as they are in the equivalent Get Picture dialog box in QuarkXPress. Replace Selected Item, if checked, will replace the contents of the selected frame with the imported graphic.

④ Click Use Adobe Dialog (InDesign CS2) or Version Cue (InDesign CS) to switch to Adobe's Version Cue file-management system, which allows shared folders and multiple versions of files in InDesign CS or later (as well as in other Creative Suite applications). Note that the default Version Cue view does not show image previews; be sure to switch to the Thumbnail view to see them. To get the standard dialog boxes, click Use OS Dialog (InDesign CS2) or Local Files (InDesign CS) in the Version Cue interface.

⑤ If you've chosen a Photoshop, TIFF, JPEG, GIF, PNG, Windows BMP, PCX, or Scitex CT image — and Show Import Options is checked — InDesign will display the Image Import Options dialog box when you click Open. Here, you typically have two panes in InDesign CS or earlier: Image, where you can select any clipping paths or alpha channel, or Color, where you select the color profile. PNG files will have a third pane, PNG Settings, that lets you control transparency and color range (gamma correction).

⑥ InDesign CS2 offers an additional pane for Photoshop files, Layers, that lets you select which layers to make visible for the imported file and whether to use the file's layer visibility options if you relink the file later or to keep the overrides specified here. See step 7 on page 193 for the dialog box.

 Workaround: You cannot import a color bitmap as a grayscale file, or a grayscale bitmap as a black-and-white file, as you can in QuarkXPress. So you'll need to convert the source graphic (or a copy of it) to grayscale before importing. This is key if you are printing color plates and don't want the imported bitmap to print as CMYK color separations. If you are printing as grayscale, then it doesn't matter whether the imported bitmap is grayscale.

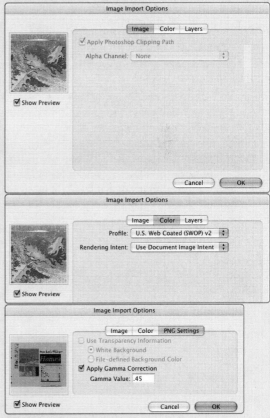

✳Placing PDF Files

PDF files are the most complex type of file that layout programs can import, as they can contain vector graphics, bitmapped graphics, text, fonts, and even multiple pages.

Keep in Mind

QuarkXPress treats PDF files pretty much like any vector graphic when you import them. However, note some additional issues:

1 QuarkXPress 5 or later imports PDF files. You can also import PDF files into QuarkXPress 4.1 if you download and install Quark's free PDF Filter 1.6 XTension from www.quark.com. Note that QuarkXPress will import PDF versions available when that version of QuarkXPress was released. Thus, QuarkXPress 4 and 5 can import PDF 1.3 (Acrobat 4) or earlier files, while QuarkXPress 6 can import PDF 1.4 (Acrobat 5) or earlier files.

2 If the PDF file has multiple pages, you can choose the page to import in the PDF Page field of the PDF Import pane of the Get Picture dialog box (File ➪ Get Picture, or ⌘+E or Ctrl+E) in QuarkXPress 5 or later. QuarkXPress 4.1 has no PDF Import pane; the PDF Page field simply appears in the Get Picture dialog box.

3 If the PDF file has spot colors defined in it, QuarkXPress detects them and adds them to the Colors palette so you can manage them for output and specify whether these colors print on their own plate or are color-separated.

4 QuarkXPress will not detect what fonts are used by the PDF file, so be sure you either embedded the fonts in the PDF file when you created it or that you have those fonts available during output.

InDesign

Keep in Mind

InDesign also treats PDF files pretty much like any vector graphic when you import them. However, InDesign has additional issues and options:

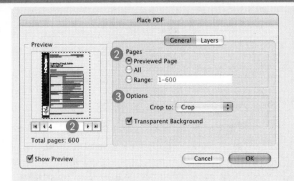

1. InDesign 2 can import PDF 1.4 (Acrobat 5) or earlier files, InDesign CS can import PDF 1.5 (Acrobat 6) or earlier files, and InDesign CS2 can import PDF 1.6 (Acrobat 7) or earlier files.

2. If the PDF file has multiple pages, you can choose the page to import in the Place PDF dialog box, which you get if you checked Show Import Options in the Place dialog box (File ⇨ Place, or ⌘+D or Ctrl+D). Either enter a page in the field below the preview, or use the arrow buttons to navigate through the PDF file. In InDesign CS2, you can choose multiple pages, such as **1-3** for the range of pages 1 through 3, **4, 6, 9** for pages 4, 6, and 9, or **1-3, 5, 9, 20-35** to select pages 1 through 3, 5, 9, and 20 through 35. After you place the first selected page, InDesign will display the Acrobat insertion pointer for the next page, repeating this for each page being imported. This places each page in its own frame.

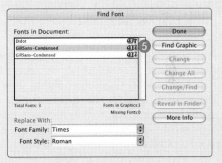

3. The Place PDF dialog box also lets you crop the PDF file and set a transparent background for it. The Crop To pop-up menu's options are Art, Bleed, Bounding Box, Crop, Media (page size), and Trim. The available options will depend on how the PDF file is constructed.

4. If the PDF file has spot colors defined in it, InDesign detects them and adds them to the Swatches pane so you can manage them for output and specify whether these colors print on their own plate or are color-separated.

5. InDesign will detect what fonts are used by the PDF file, and you can see what these fonts are by choosing Type ⇨ Find Font. The Find Font dialog box shows all fonts in use; as you select each font, any that are in graphics will cause the Find First button to become the Find Graphic button, which you use to see what graphic is using that font.

Go Further: InDesign better handles PDF files by recognizing the fonts used in them, by letting you crop the PDF file during import, and in InDesign CS2 by letting you import multiple pages.

Working with Imported Clipping Paths

Clipping paths let you create exact masks (silhouettes) and text wraps.

Follow These Steps

Here is how to work with clipping paths in QuarkXPress:

❶ When you import a TIFF file with an alpha channel or clipping path, QuarkXPress automatically imports the alpha channel and clipping path. (QuarkXPress 5 or later supports multiple clipping paths and alpha channels in a TIFF file; QuarkXPress 4 imports just the first clipping path and alpha channel if there are several.)

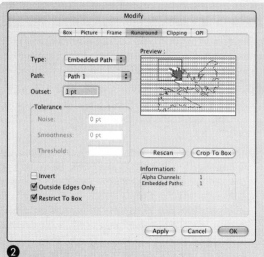

❷ For text runarounds, select the text box containing the TIFF file and choose Item ➪ Runaround (⌘+T or Ctrl+T). Choose Embedded Path or Alpha Channel, as desired, from the Type pop-up menu. If the file has multiple paths or channels, choose the desired one from the Path pop-up menu. Set the text-wrap space in the Outset field, and check Invert, Outside Edges Only, and Restrict to Box as appropriate for your layout. If you chose an alpha channel, you can also specify the Noise, Smoothness, and Threshold settings for the clipping path that QuarkXPress will create from the selected channel.

❸ You can edit a runaround by selecting the picture box with the Content or Item tool and choosing Item ➪ Edit ➪ Runaround (Option+F4 or Ctrl+F10). This displays the runaround path as a Bézier curve that you can edit like any other Bézier curve.

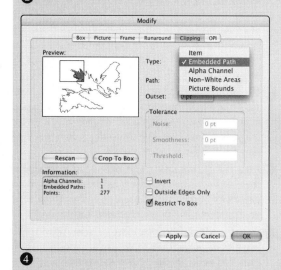

❹ For masking, select the picture box containing the TIFF file and choose Item ➪ Clipping (Option+⌘+T or Ctrl+Alt+T). The options are the same as for text runarounds (see step 2).

❺ You can edit a clipping path by selecting the picture box with the Content or Item tool and choosing Item ➪ Edit ➪ Clipping Path (Option+Shift+F4 or Ctrl+Shift+F10). This displays the clipping path as a Bézier curve that you can edit like any other Bézier curve.

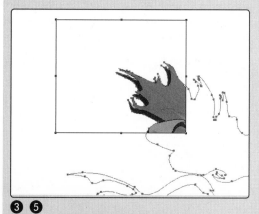

Cross-Reference: For more on text wrap, see pages 112-113. For more on creating and editing Bézier curves and clipping paths, see pages 236-239 and 248-249.

❸ ❺

InDesign

Follow These Steps

InDesign has capabilities similar to those in QuarkXPress for clipping paths, but the tools work a little differently.

① When you import a TIFF or Photoshop file with an alpha channel or clipping path, InDesign gives you the option of importing the alpha channel and clipping path in the Image pane of the Image Import Options dialog box (see page 195).

② For text runarounds, select the text frame containing the TIFF or Photoshop file and open the Text Wrap pane (Window ➪ Text Wrap in InDesign 2 or CS2, or Window ➪ Type & Tables ➪ Text Wrap in InDesign CS, or Option+⌘+W or Ctrl+Alt+W). Choose Photoshop Path, Alpha Channel, or Same as Clipping from the Type pop-up menu. If the file has several paths, choose the desired one via the Path or Alpha pop-up menu.

③ You can edit a runaround by selecting the graphics frame with the Direct Selection tool. This displays the runaround path as a Bézier curve that you can edit like any other Bézier curve. Note that if you later switch the runaround to a different path or channel, and then come back to the path or channel you modified, those modifications will be lost.

④ For masking, select the graphics frame with the TIFF or Photoshop file and apply no fill to it using the Tools palette or the Swatches pane. Choose the clipping path or alpha channel that will act as the mask boundary in the Clipping Path dialog box (Object ➪ Clipping Path, or Option+Shift+⌘+K or Ctrl+Alt+Shift+K). You can also set the threshold, tolerance, inset, and scope (Invert, Include Outside Edges, Restrict to Frame, and Use High Resolution Image) of the clipping path here.

⑤ You can edit a clipping path by selecting the graphics frame with the Direct Selection tool and editing it like any other Bézier curve.

①

②

③ ⑤

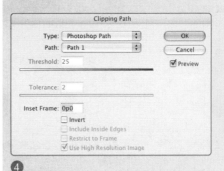

④

✳ Editing Source Graphics

When working in a layout, it's not at all uncommon to realize that you need to make changes to an imported graphic. While you can always edit a source graphic by using the original, or a compatible, program and choosing File ➪ Open (⌘+O or Ctrl+O) from that application, it's more convenient not to have to do so.

Follow These Steps

QuarkXPress lets you open the source graphic directly by opening a compatible editing program for you:

① Select the picture box with the Content tool.

② Double-click the picture. QuarkXPress will open a dialog box that lets you update the graphic or edit it in a compatible application.

③ Click either Update or Edit Original in QuarkXPress 6, or Open Publisher or Get Edition Now as desired in Quark-XPress 5 or earlier.

④ When done editing, save the graphic and return to Quark-XPress. In QuarkXPress 5 or earlier, you will be asked whether to update the graphic in QuarkXPress. In Quark-XPress 6, you must use the Pictures pane in the Usage dialog box (Utilities ➪ Usage) to update the image.

In QuarkXPress 6 for Mac, you must have the free Edit Original XTension installed (downloadable from www.quark.com). QuarkXPress 5 or earlier on the Mac will use Mac OS 9's Publish and Subscribe feature, which works only with Mac OS 9 programs, even if you are running it in Mac OS X. That means, for example, that it won't launch Photoshop CS2 (a Mac OS X–only program) but only an older version of Photoshop if you happen to have one installed.

In Windows, all versions of QuarkXPress use Microsoft's Object Linking and Embedding (OLE) technology to open a program compatible with the graphic, so you don't need to download any XTensions or worry about whether an application was designed for an earlier version of Windows.

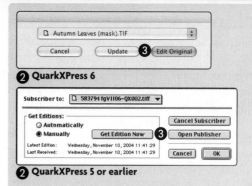

② QuarkXPress 6

② QuarkXPress 5 or earlier

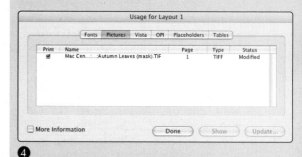

④

Cross-Reference: For details on updating graphics links, see pages 202-203.

Follow These Steps

InDesign lets you easily edit a source graphic:

1 Select the graphics frame with the Selection or Direct Selection tool.

2 Choose Edit ➪ Edit Original. You can also choose Edit Original from the contextual menu. Or you can choose Edit Original from the Links pane (Window ➪ Links, or Shift+⌘+D or Ctrl+Shift+D), as well as choose Relink to update a link.

3 When done editing, save the graphic and return to InDesign. The graphic will be automatically updated with the changes.

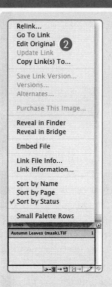

Updating Links to Source Files

Sometimes, source files change. Perhaps you, or someone else, edited them. Either way, your layout needs to deal with changes to the files.

Follow These Steps

QuarkXPress gives you several ways to control how source-file updates are handled:

1 You control QuarkXPress's automatic behavior for changed source files in the General pane of the Preferences dialog box. (In QuarkXPress 6, choose QuarkXPress ⇨ Preferences or Option+Shift+⌘+Y on the Mac or Edit ⇨ Preferences or Ctrl+Alt+Shift+Y in Windows. In QuarkXPress 5, choose Edit ⇨ Preferences ⇨ Preferences, or Option+Shift+⌘+Y or Ctrl+Alt+Shift+Y. In QuarkXPress 4, Edit ⇨ Preferences ⇨ Document, or ⌘+Y or Ctrl+Y.) You have three options in the Auto Picture Import section:

- The On option automatically updates any graphics when you open the QuarkXPress document. Note that any color images imported as grayscale, or grayscale images imported as black-and-white, may lose that formatting and be reimported as color.

- The Verify option (in QuarkXPress 6) or On (Verify) option (in QuarkXPress 5 or earlier) has QuarkXPress check to see if any graphics were updated since the document was last saved and, if so, gives you the chance to update them as you open the file. (You'll need to address missing files using the method in step 2 below.)

- The Off option leaves the graphics unchanged. That means what you see in QuarkXPress may not match what the current graphic actually looks like (and how it will print).

2 You can always update graphics using the Pictures pane of the Usage dialog box (Utilities ⇨ Usage). The pane will show modified and missing graphics. (Any currently selected picture box's graphic will be highlighted.) Select a modified or missing graphic and click Update. QuarkXPress will update the modified graphic. For missing graphics, QuarkXPress will ask you to find the missing graphic and will then offer to update any other missing graphics found in the same folder. In QuarkXPress 5 or later, you can click the Status label and have the Pictures pane sort the graphics for you by status, so all missing ones are listed in one group and all modified ones are listed in another group.

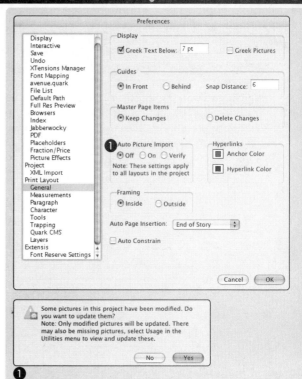

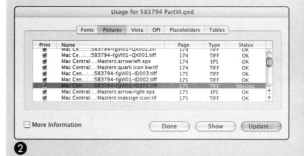

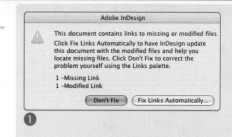

InDesign

Follow These Steps

InDesign also gives you several ways to control how updated source graphics are handled, and puts all the controls in one place:

 InDesign always checks to see if source graphics are modified or missing when you open a document. If the program detects such changes, it displays a dialog box as you open the document to let you ignore the changes or update the links automatically. For missing links, if you click Fix Links Automatically, InDesign will open a dialog box that lets you search for the missing graphics.

❷ You can always update graphics using the Links pane (Window ⇨ Links, or Shift+⌘+D or Ctrl+Shift+D). The pane will show modified and missing graphics using a red circle or yellow triangle, respectively. (Any currently selected graphics frame's graphic will be highlighted.) Select a modified or missing graphic and choose Update Link from the palette menu. InDesign will update the modified graphic. For missing graphics, InDesign will ask you to find the missing graphic.

> **Go Further:** You can use the Links pane to see the status of graphics while still working in your layout. By contrast, the Usage dialog box in QuarkXPress makes it difficult to see the affected graphics because the imposing size of the dialog box means that you can't work in the layout while the box is displayed.
>
> InDesign also lets you embed a graphic into your layout, essentially separating it from the source file; choose Embed File from the Links pane's palette menu.

> **Workaround:** When you are working in the Links pane, InDesign is not smart enough to update all missing graphics that are in the same folder as the one you are currently updating. Instead, you must select them manually in the Links pane (you can select multiple items) and then choose Update Links from the palette menu. But InDesign *is* smart enough to automatically relink all of them when you click Fix Links Automatically when opening a document. If several links need to be updated, it's often easiest to close the InDesign document and reopen it to use the automatic relinking feature.

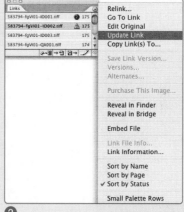

part viii

Creating and Manipulating Graphics

One of InDesign's strengths is its integration with Photoshop and Illustrator. This has many implications for veteran QuarkXPress users as it greatly affects how a designer creates and modifies graphics in InDesign.

Once you get used to the Photoshop/Illustrator interface (with which you may already be familiar from using those programs), you'll find that InDesign is — in most respects — more capable than QuarkXPress when it comes to working with graphics.

Creating Graphics Frames

Graphics frames are essential for holding graphics (called *pictures* by QuarkXPress) that you place in a layout, but QuarkXPress has a more rigid approach to them than does InDesign.

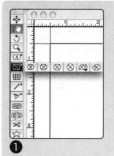

Follow These Steps

To create a picture box in QuarkXPress, you have just one approach:

Drawing Boxes

1. Select one of the picture box tools from the Tools palette.
2. Draw the box to contain the graphic. You'll get a box that has an *X* through it to indicate that it is a picture box.

Converting Boxes

You can also convert a text box or a no-content box to a picture box (the box must be empty for this to work):

1. Select the with the Item tool or Content tool.
2. Choose Item ➪ Content ➪ Picture.

Cross-Reference: For more on placing graphics into frames, see Part VII.

Follow These Steps

InDesign gives you two ways to create graphics frames.

Drawing Frames

QuarkXPress users will typically use this approach, as it mirrors how QuarkXPress works:

1. Select any of the frame or shape tools (rectangle, ellipse, or polygon). It doesn't matter whether you choose a shape or a frame, since InDesign treats all objects as potential containers for text or graphics.

2. Draw the frame or shape. If you chose a frame tool, the frame will have an *X* through it; if you chose a shape tool, the frame will be hollow.

Automatically Creating Frames

1. Import a graphic by choosing File ➪ Place (⌘+D or Ctrl+D).

2. When you get the placement icon, click anywhere in the layout to have InDesign import the graphic and automatically create a frame in which to place it.

Converting Frames

You can also convert a text frame or unassigned frame to a graphics frame (the frame must be empty for this to work) using either of these methods:

1. Select the frame or shape with the Selection tool. Then choose Object ➪ Content ➪ Graphic.

2. Simply place a graphic into an existing frame; an InDesign frame can contain any content and will switch automatically to a graphic or text frame based on what you place in it.

Go Further: InDesign's approach to frames is more flexible than QuarkXPress's approach to boxes, eliminating both the rigid distinction between text and graphics frames and the requirement that a graphics frame exist before you can place a graphic.

Changing Frame Shapes

Sometimes, you are using a graphics frame whose shape is just wrong. Both QuarkXPress and InDesign let you change the shape, although the programs use different methods.

Follow These Steps

Changing a box's shape in QuarkXPress typically requires converting the box from one style to another:

1 Select the box using the Item or Content tool.

2 To change the fundamental shape, such as to go from a rectangle to a polygon, choose Item ➪ Shape and then choose the desired shape from the submenu. To create a polygon or Bézier shape, select the icon that looks like an artist's paint palette (the sixth one in the list). Do not choose the bottom three options, all of which are types of lines; doing so will convert the box into a closed line that cannot hold text or graphics.

3 If you've chosen the Bézier shape, you can now reshape the box with the Content tool, dragging on nodes or sides to move them to new locations. You can add and delete nodes as well to add more sides and curves.

If you want to change just the proportions but not the basic shape (for example, make a rectangle flatter), just select one of the control handles and move it to change the box's proportions.

2

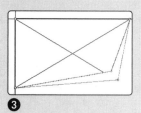

3

Cross-Reference: For more on editing Bézier shapes, see pages 236-237.

InDesign

Follow These Steps

InDesign doesn't require that you convert a frame's shape; all objects in InDesign are Bézier objects that can be edited at any time:

1. Select the frame with the Direct Selection tool.

2. In InDesign CS2, you can change the fundamental shape, such as to go from a rectangle to a polygon. Choose Object ⇨ Convert Shape and then choose the desired shape from the submenu. (InDesign CS or earlier has no equivalent option.) Do not choose the bottom two options, both of which are types of lines; doing so will convert the frame into a closed line that cannot hold text or graphics.

3. No matter the frame's shape, you can always reshape it in any version of InDesign with the Direct Selection tool, dragging on nodes or sides to move them to new locations. You can add and delete nodes, as well add more sides and curves.

If you want to just change the proportions but not the basic shape (for example, make a rectangle flatter), select the Selection tool and then select one of the control handles and move it to change the frame's proportions.

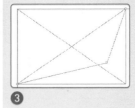

Fitting Graphics into a Frame

When you import a graphic into a frame, both Quark-XPress and InDesign place it at 100% of its size, even if that size is larger or smaller than the frame. Both programs offer similar ways to fit graphics automatically to their frames.

Follow These Steps

To resize a graphic within its box for a better fit, QuarkXPress provides a quick option:

① In QuarkXPress 5 or later, choose Item ➪ Fit Picture to Box (Shift+⌘+F or Ctrl+Shift+F) or Item ➪ Fit Picture to Box (Proportionally) (Option+Shift+⌘+F or Ctrl+Alt+Shift+F). The first option provides an exact fit, distorting the image if necessary; the second option scales the images to fit as well as possible while not distorting the image. (In QuarkXPress 4 or earlier, you'll need to scale the picture as described on page 216.)

② You can also have QuarkXPress 5 or later make the box the same size as the picture by choosing Item ➪ Fit Box to Picture.

③ If you want to center a picture in a box without resizing the picture, choose Item ➪ Center ➪ Center Picture (Shift+⌘+M or Ctrl+Shift+M).

Follow These Steps

InDesign offers nearly identical options:

① Choose Object ⇨ Fitting ⇨ Fit Content to Frame (Shift+⌘+E or Ctrl+Shift+E) or Object ⇨ Fitting ⇨ Fit Content Proportionally (Option+Shift+⌘+E or Ctrl+Alt+Shift+E). The first option provides an exact fit, distorting the image if necessary; the second option scales the images to fit as well as possible while not distorting the image.

② You can also have InDesign make the frame the same size as the graphic by choosing Object ⇨ Fitting ⇨ Fit Frame to Content (Shift+⌘+C or Ctrl+Shift+C). InDesign CS2 also lets you choose Object ⇨ Fitting ⇨ Fit Frame Proportionally (Option+Shift+⌘+C or Ctrl+Alt+Shift+C).

③ If you want to center a graphic in a frame without resizing the graphic, choose Object ⇨ Fitting ⇨ Center Content (Shift+⌘+E or Ctrl+Shift+E).

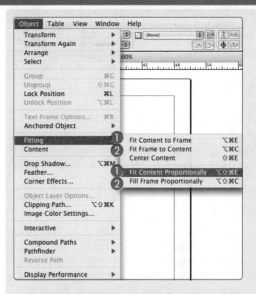

Cropping Graphics

Many times, you don't want the entire graphic visible in its frame. QuarkXPress and InDesign both offer similar approaches to crop graphics to the desired portion.

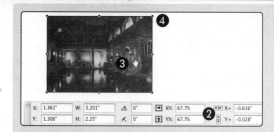

Follow These Steps

1 Select the box with the Content tool.

2 Reposition the picture within the box by adjusting the X+ and/or Y+ values in the Measurements palette or in the Picture pane of the Modify dialog box (Item ⇨ Modify, or ⌘+M or Ctrl+M).

3 You can also simply drag the picture within its box using the mouse.

4 A third option is to resize the box using the Item or Content tool to drag the corner or side points, which lets you crop out undesired positions of the image. You can also change the box's shape, as covered on page 208, to crop out a specific portion, as long as it's permissible for your layout to have a nonrectangular graphic.

Cross-Reference: You can also use clipping paths as a mask to crop a graphic within a shape, as covered on pages 198-199.

InDesign

Follow These Steps

① Select the frame with the Direct Selection tool.

② Reposition the graphic within its frame by adjusting the X+ and/or Y+ values in the Control palette or in the Transform pane (Window ⇨ Objects & Layout ⇨ Transform in InDesign CS2, or Window ⇨ Transform in InDesign CS or earlier, or F9).

③ You can also simply drag the graphic within its frame using the mouse. Note how InDesign displays a separate frame for the graphic itself. (The graphic's frame color varies from the frame's frame color, and each layer has a different set of colors for these two frames. On the default layer, the graphic's frame is brown and the frame's frame is light blue.)

④ A third option is to resize the frame using the Selection or Direct Selection tool to drag the frame's corner or side points to crop out undesired positions of the image. You can also change the frame's shape, as covered on page 209, to crop out a specific portion, as long as it's alright for your layout to have a nonrectangular graphic.

Repositioning Graphics and Points of Origin

Moving graphics is a common task in page layout, and QuarkXPress and InDesign offer similar ways to handle this need. Both use origin points, which set the 0,0 location from which all X and Y coordinates are calculated, but InDesign has an approach to this that is different from QuarkXPress's.

Follow These Steps

QuarkXPress has a very straightforward set of options for repositioning graphics and setting the origin points.

Repositioning Graphics

QuarkXPress offers several ways to reposition a graphic. In all cases, be sure that the Item tool is selected.

❶ Drag the picture box to its new location.

❷ Change the X and Y coordinates in the Measurements palette.

❸ Change the Origin Across and Origin Down coordinates in the Box pane of the Modify dialog box (Item ➪ Modify, or ⌘+M or Ctrl+M).

Working with Origin Points

By default, QuarkXPress sets the upper left corner of the page as the 0,0 origin point for all objects. Also, all X coordinates are applied to the item's left edge while all Y coordinates are applied to the item's top edge. For objects within a box, such as a picture, the position is also based on the box's upper left corner.

You can change the change the 0,0 point as follows:

❶ Drag the zero point from its current position (by default, at the upper left corner where the vertical and horizontal rulers intersect) to a new location in your layout. Wherever you release the mouse sets the new 0,0 location. (To set the 0,0 point back to the default position, double-click the zero point.)

❷ By default, QuarkXPress sets the 0,0 point anew for each page. If you want it to calculate the 0,0 point for a spread, so the righthand page's coordinates are based on the spread's upper left corner rather than the page's upper left corner, choose the Spread radio button in the Item Coordinates section of the Measurements pane of the Preferences dialog box. (In QuarkXPress 6, choose QuarkXPress ➪ Preferences or Option+Shift+⌘+Y on the Mac or Edit ➪ Preferences or Ctrl+Alt+Shift+Y in Windows. In QuarkXPress 5, choose Edit ➪ Preferences ➪ Preferences, or Option+Shift+⌘+Y or Ctrl+Alt+Shift+Y. In QuarkXPress 4, Edit ➪ Preferences ➪ Document, or ⌘+Y or Ctrl+Y.)

❶

❷

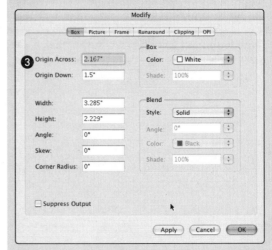

Modify

❸

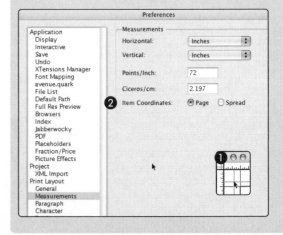

Preferences

❷

InDesign

Follow These Steps

InDesign also has a straightforward set of options for repositioning graphics, but its flexibility in origin points can be confusing.

Repositioning Graphics

InDesign offers several ways to reposition a graphic. In all cases, be sure that the Selection tool is selected.

1. Drag the graphics frame to its new location.

2. Change the X and Y coordinates in the Control palette.

3. Change the X and Y coordinates in the Transform pane (Window ⇨ Objects & Layout ⇨ Transform in InDesign CS2, or Window ⇨ Transform in InDesign CS or earlier, or F9).

1

2

3

Working with Origin Points

By default, InDesign sets the upper left corner of the spread — not the page as in QuarkXPress — as the 0,0 point for all objects. You can change the 0,0 origin point as follows:

1. Drag the zero point to a new location in your layout. Wherever you release the mouse sets the new 0,0 location. (To set the 0,0 location back to the default position, double-click the zero point.)

2. By default, InDesign sets the 0,0 point anew for each spread. If you want it to calculate the 0,0 point for a page, so the righthand page's coordinates are based on the page's upper left corner rather than the spread's upper left corner, choose the Page from the Origin pop-up menu in the Units & Increments pane of the Preferences dialog box (InDesign ⇨ Preferences or ⌘+K on the Mac or Edit ⇨ Preferences or Ctrl+K in Windows). You can also choose Spine to base the coordinates on the spine.

3. Unlike QuarkXPress, InDesign lets you choose how the coordinates for specific objects are determined. It need not be just the upper left corner as in QuarkXPress. Note the nine small squares arranged in a grid on the left side of the Control palette and Transform pane. You can click any point to make it the active point (it will turn black). All coordinates for the selected object are now based on this location.

1

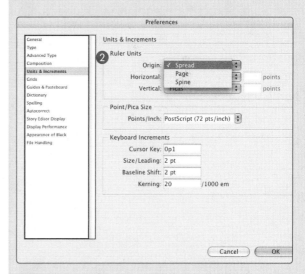

3

Watch Out: Be sure that you're aware of which coordinate location is selected in the Control palette or Transform pane before changing an object's position, so you know that you're entering the correct new position.

Go Further: InDesign lets you set the 0,0 point from a spread's spine, unlike QuarkXPress. Also, by choosing the internal coordinate for objects, you can better position elements against other objects that are not left– or top-aligned.

Resizing Graphics

When you import a graphic into a frame, both Quark-XPress and InDesign place it at 100% of its size, even if that size is larger or smaller than the frame. Both programs offer similar ways to resize graphics manually.

Follow These Steps

To resize a picture manually within its box for a better fit, QuarkXPress provides two options. In both cases, you can select the frame with the Item or Content tool:

1 Use the Measurements palette to change both the X% and Y% scale for the graphic. You'll need to try different settings until you get the right fit.

2 Choose Item ➪ Modify (⌘+M or Ctrl+M) and go to the Picture pane to change both the X% and Y% fields. You'll need to try different settings until you get the right fit.

Cross-Reference: For a quick way to make a graphic fit its frame, see pages 210-211.

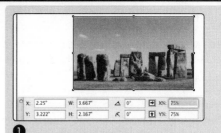

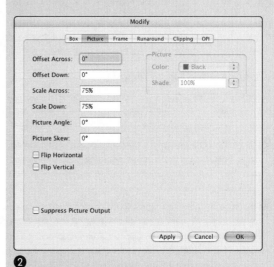

InDesign

Follow These Steps

To resize a graphic manually within its frame for a better fit, InDesign also provides two options. In both cases, first select the frame with the Direct Selection tool:

1. Use the Control palette to change both the Scale X Percentage and Scale Y Percentage settings for the graphic. (If the chain icon shows a solid link, changing one value automatically changes the other; click the icon to switch between having the two values work in concert to having the two values be set independently.) You'll need to try different settings until you get the right fit.

2. Use the Transform pane (Window ➪ Objects & Layout ➪ Transform in InDesign CS2, or Window ➪ Transform in InDesign CS or earlier, or F9) to change both the Scale X Percentage and Scale Y Percentage settings for the graphic. (If the chain icon shows a solid link, changing one value automatically changes the other; click the icon to switch between having the two values work in concert to having the two values be set independently.) You'll need to try different settings until you get the right fit.

Go Further: InDesign offers some small advantages over QuarkXPress for fitting graphics. First, it lets you resize both the width and height simultaneously by entering just one value. Second, it lets you size a frame to the graphic proportionally, not just retaining the frame's existing proportions when resizing it to fit the graphic.

Watch Out: It's important to use the Direct Selection tool when resizing a graphic using the Control palette or Transform pane. Otherwise, you will resize the frame. If the frame has a 0-point stroke, InDesign will also scale the graphic, but if the frame has a larger stroke, the frame will be resized but the graphic will not. Also, when you resize a graphic, you will see its new scale values only if you select the Direct Selection tool; when the Selection tool is in use, the Control palette and Transform pane will display the scale of the frame, not its graphic.

■Working with Image Layers

The most recent versions of QuarkXPress and InDesign let you work with image layers in Adobe Photoshop files, so you can decide which layers in a multilayered image will display and print.

Follow These Steps

In QuarkXPress 6.5 with the free PSD Import XTension installed from Quark's Web site (www.quark.com), you can import Photoshop files and select which layers display as follows:

1 Import the Photoshop file into a picture box by choosing File ⇨ Get Picture (⌘+E or Ctrl+E).

2 Select the image in your layout with the Item or Content tool.

3 Open the PSD Import palette by choosing Window ⇨ Show PSD Import.

4 In the palette, choose the layer(s) to display by clicking the box to their left. If the eye icon is displayed, the layer is visible. You'll see any changes reflected in your image within a few seconds of selecting or deselecting a layer.

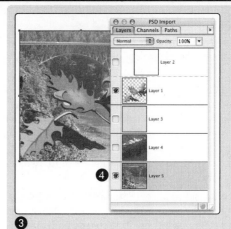

Cross-Reference: You can use the PSD Import palette to work on alpha channels and clipping paths of native Photoshop files, in addition to using the techniques covered on page 198.

The PSD Import palette also lets you apply transparency and color modes to Photoshop files using the pop-up menu and Opacity pop-up menu/field at the top of the palette. These work like InDesign's transparency feature (see page 357), except QuarkXPress offers this only for Photoshop files if you use this free PSD Import XTension; InDesign offers these capabilities for any bitmapped image and has done so for several versions.

InDesign

Follow These Steps

InDesign CS2 lets you manage the visibility of layers in Adobe Photoshop, Illustrator, and Acrobat files.

① When importing a graphic, you can determine which layers to make visible by checking the Show Import Options checkbox in the Place dialog box (File ⇨ Place, or ⌘+D or Ctrl+D).

② After you click Open, the Image Import Options dialog box will appear. In the Layers pane, click the layers you want visible (an eye icon will appear for them). You can also choose whether to retain these layer visibility settings (Keep Layer Visibility Overrides) if you later relink to the source image or to go back to the layer visibility settings in the source image (Use Photoshop's Layer Visibility Options) via the When Updating Link pop-up menu. If layer comps (sets of visible layers) are set in the source file, you can select them in the Layer Comp pop-up menu. Click OK to import the graphic.

③ Whether or not you set layer visibility settings when importing, you can modify them in InDesign at any time. Select the image and choose Object ⇨ Object Layer Options to open the Object Layer Options dialog box. (You can also Control+click or right-click the graphic and choose Graphics ⇨ Object Layer Options to get the dialog box.)

Go Further: InDesign CS2 lets you work with layer visibility in Photoshop, Illustrator, and Acrobat files, not just in Photoshop files as in QuarkXPress 6.5's free PSD Import XTension.

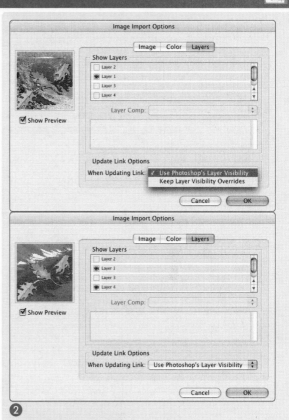

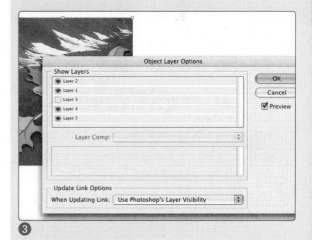

Rotating and Skewing Graphics

Although not used routinely, rotation and skewing (slanting) can be effective graphics techniques in some layouts.

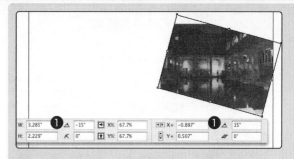

Follow These Steps

Rotating and skewing in QuarkXPress can be a little tricky because some options are available in the Measurements palette and others are not.

Rotating Graphics

Note that negative values rotate to the left and positive values rotate to the right.

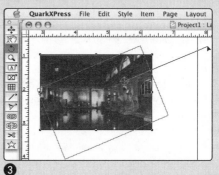

1 Use the two Rotation Angle fields in the Measurements palette to rotate a box (the leftmost Rotation Angle field) and/or its contents (the rightmost Rotation Angle field).

2 Use the Angle field in the Box pane of the Modify dialog box (Item ➪ Modify, or ⌘+M or Ctrl+M) to rotate a box, and/or use the Picture Angle field in the Picture pane of the Modify dialog box to rotate a box's picture. Click OK when done.

3 Select the Rotate tool and then use the mouse to rotate the box. The further away you drag the rotation handle from the box's center, the finer rotation changes you can make. Hold the Shift key when rotating to snap to the nearest 45° increment.

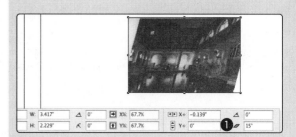

Skewing Graphics

Note that negative values skew to the left and positive values skew to the right.

1 Use the Skew Angle field in the Measurements palette to skew a box's contents.

2 Use the Skew field in the Box pane of the Modify dialog box (Item ➪ Modify, or ⌘+M or Ctrl+M) to skew a box, and/or use the Picture Skew field in the Picture pane of the Modify dialog box to skew a box's picture. Click OK when done.

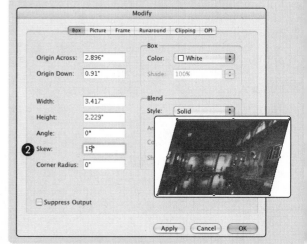

InDesign

Follow These Steps

Rotating and skewing in InDesign is easier in one sense than in QuarkXPress, but trickier in another.

Rotating Graphics

Note that negative values rotate to the left and positive values rotate to the right. Also note that the rotation origin is based on the coordinate selected in the grid of nine squares in the Control palette or Transform pane (Window ➪ Objects & Layout ➪ Transform in InDesign CS2 or Window ➪ Transform in InDesign CS or earlier, or F9). Having the wrong coordinate selected can lead to unintended rotations.

1 To rotate a frame, select it with the Selection tool and enter a value in the Rotation Angle field of the Control palette or Transform pane.

2 To rotate a frame's contents, select it with the Direct Selection tool and enter a value in the Rotation Angle field of the Control palette or Transform pane.

3 Select the Rotate tool and then use the mouse to rotate the box. The further away you drag the rotation handle from the box's center, the finer rotation changes you can make. Hold the Shift key when rotating to snap to the nearest 45° increment.

Shearing Graphics

InDesign can shear objects, not just skew them. The difference is that shearing affects both the X slant and the overall rotation, while skewing affects just the X slant. Note that negative values slant to the left and positive values slant to the right.

1 To skew a frame, select it with the Selection tool and enter a value in the Shear X Angle field of the Control palette or Transform pane. This slants just the horizontal axis.

2 To skew a frame's contents, select it with the Direct Selection tool and enter a value in the Shear X Angle field of the Control palette or Transform pane. This slants just the horizontal axis.

3 To shear a frame and its contents, select it with the Shear tool and then move the mouse to determine the X slant and overall rotation values. Also note that the skew origin is based on the coordinate selected in the grid of nine squares in the Control palette or Transform pane. (To undo a shear, set both the Shear X Angle and Rotation Angle fields to 0°.)

Go Further: InDesign's shearing tool is more powerful than QuarkXPress's skew function because it lets you both slant the X axis and rotate the object, for a more dimensional effect.

The ability choose the rotation or shear coordinate also allows for more precise application of these functions.

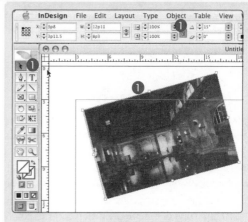

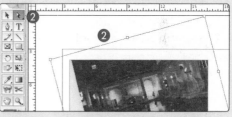

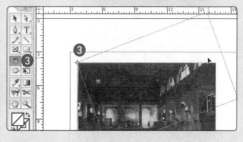

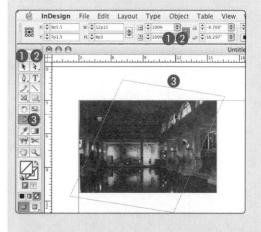

Flipping Graphics

Whether you want to have an image face in the opposite direction for better composition or to flip a graphic horizontally or vertically for a special effect, QuarkXPress and InDesign offer similar capabilities.

Follow These Steps

QuarkXPress offers three ways to flip a picture. Either way, you can select the picture box with the Content or Item tool.

1 Click the Flip Horizontal and/or Flip Vertical buttons in the Measurements palette. The buttons will show the current direction, as well as turn to black if flipping is applied.

2 Check the Flip Vertical and/or Flip Horizontal checkboxes in the Picture pane of the Modify dialog box (Item ➪ Modify, or ⌘+M or Ctrl+M). Click OK when done. The Measurements palette's flip buttons will indicate the current flip status for a selected picture, as described in step 1.

3 Choose Style ➪ Flip Vertical or Style ➪ Flip Horizontal.

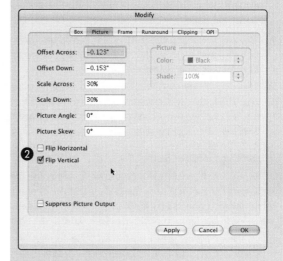

InDesign

Follow These Steps

InDesign offers just one way to flip a graphic. You first select the graphics frame with the Selection or Direct Selection tool.

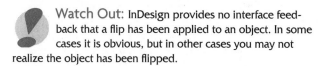 In the Control palette or Transform pane (Window ⇨ Objects & Layout ⇨ Transform in InDesign CS2, or Window ⇨ Transform in InDesign CS or earlier, or F9), choose Flip Vertical, Flip Horizontal, or Flip Both from the palette menu.

 Watch Out: InDesign provides no interface feedback that a flip has been applied to an object. In some cases it is obvious, but in other cases you may not realize the object has been flipped.

Go Further: InDesign lets you flip both axes at the same time, a process that takes two steps in Quark-XPress.

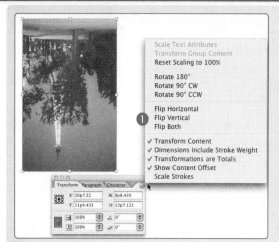

Cutting Graphics with the Scissors Tool

One way to cut out part of an object is to partially mask it with another object, but it's better to change the actual object so — if it is repositioned or resized — the masked portions don't reappear or change. QuarkXPress lets you cut some graphics, while InDesign lets you cut almost any graphic.

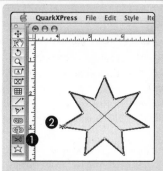

Follow These Steps

QuarkXPress lets you cut shapes created in QuarkXPress, such as boxes, Bézier curves, and polygons. If you try to cut an item that has contents, whether a picture or a fill color, you will lose those contents (QuarkXPress warns you if a picture will be deleted but not that a color fill will be removed). Here's how to cut an object:

1 Select the Scissors tool.

2 Click on the node of the object that you want to cut.

3 Any closed object will be converted into a line, and the node where you had clicked with the Scissors tool now has two nodes: the start node and end node for the line. You can edit or move these nodes with the Item or Content tool.

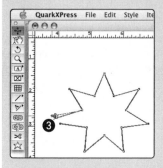

Cross-Reference: For more on modifying shapes and lines, see pages 236-237.

InDesign

Follow These Steps

InDesign lets you cut most objects, but not text frames or text paths. You can cut objects as QuarkXPress does, essentially breaking apart a node, and you can actually cut a segment out of an object. Here's how:

1. Select the Scissors tool.

2. Position the mouse pointer anywhere on the frame edge of an object; the pointer will change to a crosshair. If you click, this becomes the first cut point.

3. If you want to create an open object, you're done. The object will now have two overlapping nodes where you clicked. (If you switch to the Direct Selection tool, you can drag one of the nodes you just created to reshape the that segment.)

4. To cut a whole piece from an object, click a second point on the object's frame. You will now have two frames that you can work with independently. Each will contain whatever fill or graphic portion had been in the area before it was cut.

5. To cut a piece out of an object, cut additional points in the object or on its frame.

Go Further: Because InDesign supports open frames that nonetheless can contain fills and graphics, its Scissors tool provides more options than the QuarkXPress Scissors tool, as the examples here show.

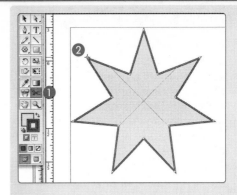

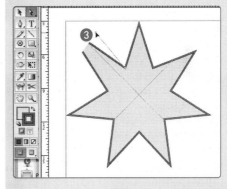

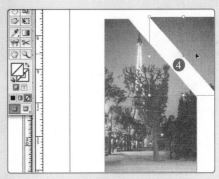

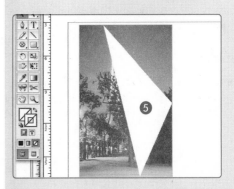

Applying Colors and Shades to Bitmapped Images

Both QuarkXPress and InDesign let you apply colors and tints — but not gradients — to imported black-and-white and grayscale bitmapped graphics. (You can't apply them to color bitmaps or to vector files of any sort, although you can apply colors and shades to their background, so any transparent areas will show the background color.) But in a rare case, InDesign offers less control over the application of colors than does QuarkXPress.

Follow These Steps

In addition to applying colors and shades to the foreground and/or background of monochrome bitmapped images, Quark-XPress also lets you alter the color balance of both color and monochrome images:

❶ To change the background color or shade, open the Colors palette (Window ➪ Colors in QuarkXPress 6, or View ➪ Colors in earlier versions, or F12). Click the Background button (the gray box) and then choose the color and/or enter a shade value in the Colors palette. You can also drag a swatch onto the picture box.

❷ To change the foreground color or shade, open the Colors palette (Window ➪ Colors in QuarkXPress 6, or View ➪ Colors in earlier versions, or F12). Click the Contents button (the box with an *X* through it) and then choose the color and/or enter a shade value in the Colors palette. You can also drag a swatch onto the picture box or choose Style ➪ Colors and/or Style ➪ Shades.

❸ QuarkXPress also lets you change the color balance of bitmapped images. Select the picture box with the Content tool and choose Style ➪ Contrast (Shift+⌘+C or Ctrl+Shift+C) to open the Picture Contrast Specifications box. Here, you can choose from several predefined settings to posterize and invert colors, as well as use the Hand and Pencil tools to draw your own color maps. For color bitmapped images, you can edit the color channels — your choice of hue, saturation, and balance or of cyan, magenta, yellow, and black, chosen through the Model pop-up menu — by selecting the desired channel(s) in the Color section of the dialog box. Another way to produce a negative image without using the Picture Contrast Specification dialog box is by selecting the picture box with the Content tool and then choosing Style ➪ Negative (Shift+⌘+− or Ctrl+Shift+−).

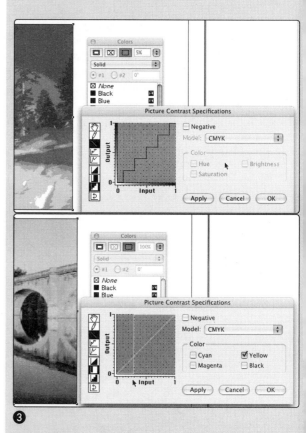

Cross-Reference: For details on applying colors and shades to graphics created in QuarkXPress and InDesign, see pages 246-247.

InDesign

① ②

Follow These Steps

InDesign also offers the ability to apply colors and tints — but not gradients — to monochrome bitmapped images. Quark-XPress users should note that the process in InDesign is different than that in QuarkXPress for applying foreground colors and tints.

① To change the background color or tint, open the Swatches pane (Window ⇨ Swatches or F12). Select the graphics frame with the Selection tool, be sure the Fill button is selected in either the Tools palette or Swatches pane, and then choose the color or tint swatch (or enter a tint value) in the Swatches pane.

② To change the foreground color or tint, open the Swatches pane (Window ⇨ Swatches or F12). Select the graphics frame with the Direct Selection tool, be sure the Fill button is selected in either the Tools palette or Swatches pane, and then choose the color or tint swatch (or enter a tint value) in the Swatches pane. You can also drag a swatch onto the graphics frame, no matter whether the Selection tool or Direct Selection tool is active.

Workaround: To apply color and shade effects like posterization, you'll need to edit the source graphic, or a copy of it, in a program such as Adobe Photoshop and then link to the updated or new source graphic that has the effect applied (see page 201). You cannot apply such effects directly in InDesign.

Working with Lines and Arrows

QuarkXPress

Lines have almost unlimited use in layouts, everything from linking callouts to separating columns of text. QuarkXPress and InDesign provide similar controls for lines and arrows, but they present different interfaces for creating and editing them.

Follow These Steps

1. Select one of the line tools (Line, Orthogonal Line, Bézier Line, or Freehand Line) from the Tools palette and then draw the desired line in your layout. Note that if you hold the Shift key, your lines will be constrained to 45° increments. (The Orthogonal Line is so constrained even if you don't hold the Shift key.)

2. You can change the line's color by choosing a color in the Colors palette (Window ⇨ Colors in QuarkXPress 6, or View ⇨ Colors in earlier versions, or F12). Or you can choose Style ⇨ Color and/or Style ⇨ Shade.

3. You can change a line's thickness by choosing a line thickness from the Measurements palette, by choosing Style ⇨ Width, or by opening the Line pane of the Modify dialog box (Item ⇨ Modify, or Shift+⌘+\ or Ctrl+Shift+\).

4. You can select arrowheads and tailfeathers by choosing an option from the Measurements palette, by choosing Style ⇨ Arrowheads, or by opening the Line pane of the Modify dialog box.

5. You can select a line style by choosing an option from the Measurements palette, by choosing Style ⇨ Line Style, or by opening the Line pane of the Modify dialog box.

6. You can create your own line styles — striped and dashed — by choosing Edit ⇨ Dashes & Stripes. The resulting Dashes & Stripes dialog box works like the Colors and H&J dialog boxes (see pages 56 and 128) in that you create a new element, set up its parameters, and then save it. All changes are reflected in the line styles available in the Measurements palette and Line pane. These line styles can also be applied as frames to boxes.

7. You can move, resize, flip, or rotate a line like any other item. But note that QuarkXPress adds a Mode pop-up menu in the Measurements palette and in the Line pane of the Modify dialog box that lets you select what point(s) on the line (Endpoints, Left Point, Midpoint, and Right Point) are active. This lets you, for example, rotate a line by the right point or move just the left point by entering new coordinates in the Measurements palette or Line pane.

 Cross-Reference: See pages 232-235 for details on drawing Bézier and freeform shapes, including lines.

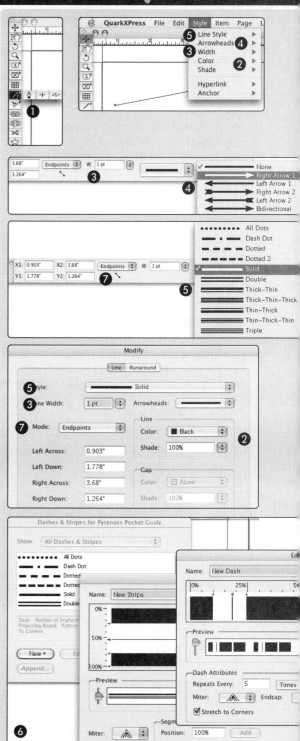

InDesign

Follow These Steps

InDesign offers essentially the same features as QuarkXPress, with a bit more control over the attributes for user-created stroke styles, and a greater selection of arrowheads and tail-feathers.

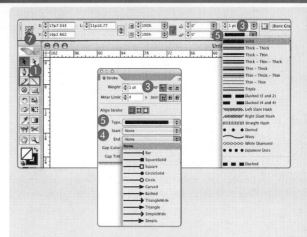

① Select one of the line tools (Line, Pen, or Pencil) from the Tools palette and then draw the desired line in your layout. Note that if you hold the Shift key, your lines will be constrained to 45° increments; there is no equivalent tool to QuarkXPress's Orthogonal Line tool.

② You can change the line's color by choosing a color in the Swatches pane (Window ⇨ Swatches or F5).

③ You can change a line's thickness by choosing a line thickness from the Control palette or from the Stroke pane (Window ⇨ Stroke or F10).

④ You can select arrowheads and tailfeathers by choosing an option from the Start and End pop-up menus in the Stroke pane. Note that you can choose the arrowheads and tailfeathers independently, unlike in QuarkXPress.

⑤ You can select a stroke style by choosing an option from the Control pane or from the Type pop-up menu in the Stroke pane (Window ⇨ Stroke or F10).

⑥ You can create your own stroke styles — including striped, dashed, and dotted — by choosing Stroke Styles from the Stroke pane's palette menu. The resulting Stoke Styles dialog box works like the QuarkXPress Dashes & Stripes dialog box in that you create a new stroke, set up its parameters, and then save it. All changes are reflected in the stroke styles available in the Control palette and Stroke pane. These stroke styles can also be applied to frame edges.

⑦ You can move, resize, flip, or rotate a line like any other item. Use the control points in the left of the Control palette or Transform pane (Window ⇨ Object & Layout ⇨ Transform in InDesign CS2 and Window ⇨ Transform in earlier versions, or F9) to select what point on the line (start, center, or end) is active. (The active point will be indicated by a black square.) This lets you, for example, rotate a line by the start point or move just the end point by entering new coordinates in the Control palette or Transform pane.

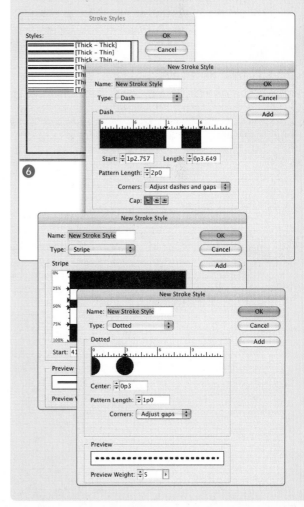

Go Further: InDesign adds a few extras to the line-manipulation features you're used to in QuarkXPress. For example, you'll enjoy a wider choice of arrowheads and tailfeathers, plus you can set them independently. You can also create dotted stroke styles in addition to striped and dashed styles.

Drawing Basic Shapes

Although they are not substitutes for professional illustration tools such as Adobe Illustrator and Macromedia FreeHand, both QuarkXPress and InDesign provide some basic illustration capabilities that you can use for simple graphics.

Follow These Steps

To create basic shapes in QuarkXPress, you'll use both the box and line tools, selecting the appropriate basic shapes — such as rectangles and ellipses — as needed.

1 Choose a box or line tool to create a text or picture box or line in roughly the shape you want. You may need to draw several shapes and overlap them to approximate the desired shape.

2 For star shapes and starbursts, use the Starburst tool. Double-click the tool to set the number of spikes and, for starbursts, the insets for those spike. You can even specify a randomness factor so the spikes have different depths by entering a value for how many of the spikes should have random depths.

3 You can convert these boxes into no-content boxes by selecting them and then choosing Item ➪ Content ➪ None. Note that you will need to apply None to each box individually — the option is not available if you have selected multiple boxes.

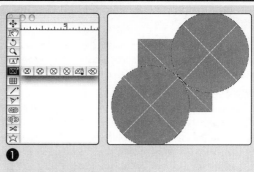

1

2

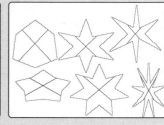

Cross-Reference: Pages 232-235 cover how to create more sophisticated shapes with freeform and Bézier tools. Pages 240-241 cover how to combine items into a single shape. Pages 246-247 cover how to apply colors and gradients to shapes.

InDesign

Follow These Steps

InDesign uses essentially the same techniques to create basic shapes as QuarkXPress, although where you modify outline and color attributes differs from QuarkXPress.

1 Choose a shape or line tool to create a frame in roughly the shape you want. You may need to draw several shapes and overlap them to approximate the desired shape. (You can also use the frame tools, which place an *X* inside the objects they create, to draw shapes and then convert them to contentless frames by choosing Object ⇨ Content ⇨ Unassigned. Unlike in QuarkXPress, you can change multiple frames' content type simultaneously.)

2 For star shapes and starbursts, use the Polygon tool. Double-click the tool to set the number of spikes and, for starbursts, the insets for those spike.

> **Workaround:** Unlike QuarkXPress, InDesign does not let you specify a randomness factor to give a starburst's spikes different depths. For such an effect, you'll need to draw the starburst using the Pen tool, as described on page 235.

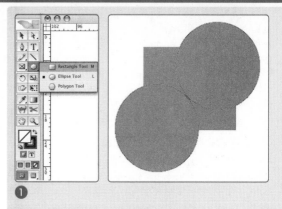

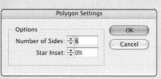

1

2

Drawing Freeform Shapes

Although they are not professional illustration tools, such as Adobe Illustrator and Macromedia FreeHand, both QuarkXPress and InDesign provide a basic freeform drawing tool that you can use for simple graphics. Drawing freeform shapes is easy, provided that you have sufficient hand-eye coordination and perhaps are using a pen stylus rather than a mouse or trackball.

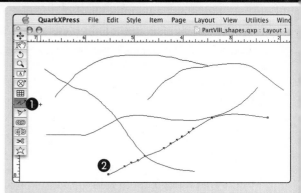

Follow These Steps

QuarkXPress provides two tools for drawing freeform shapes, depending on whether the shape is open (a line) or closed (a box).

1 Select the Freehand Line or the Freehand Picture Box (or Freehand Text Box) tool.

2 Start drawing the desired shape, holding the mouse button until you are done. If you are drawing a closed shape with one of the box tools, the pointer will change to a rounded square when QuarkXPress detects that you've returned to the start point. If you release the mouse before seeing this pointer, QuarkXPress will draw a straight line from where you released the mouse to the start point.

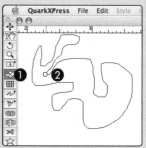

3 If you are drawing closed shapes, you can convert these boxes into no-content boxes by selecting them and then choosing Item ⇨ Content ⇨ None. Note that you have to apply None to each box individually — the option is not available if you have selected multiple boxes.

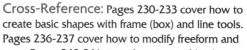

Cross-Reference: Pages 230-233 cover how to create basic shapes with frame (box) and line tools. Pages 236-237 cover how to modify freeform and Bézier shapes. Pages 240-241 cover how to combine items into a single shape. Pages 246-247 cover how to apply colors and gradients to shapes.

InDesign

Follow These Steps

InDesign has just one tool, the Pencil tool, that you use to draw freeform shapes.

1 Select the Pencil tool.

2 Start drawing the desired shape, holding the mouse button until you are done.

3 To end a closed shape, return to the start point before releasing the mouse. To end an open shape, simply hold ⌘ or Ctrl and click anywhere.

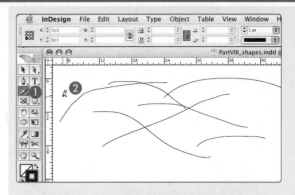

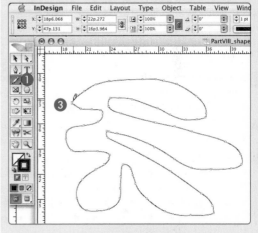

Drawing Bézier Shapes

Named after Pierre Bézier, the French engineer who created the technique in the 1970s, Bézier curves use a system of segments and nodes to create shapes. These nodes have control points that you can move to change the bend of the segments; you can also move the nodes or segments to reshape the object.

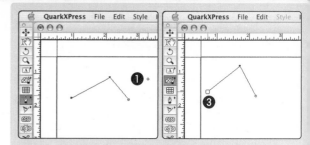

Follow These Steps

Select either the Bézier Line tool or the Bézier Picture Box (or Bézier Text Box tool). Note that if you are drawing closed shapes, you can convert these boxes into no-content boxes by selecting them and then choosing Item ➪ Content ➪ None. Note that you have to apply None to each box individually — the option is not available if you have selected multiple boxes.

Straight Segments

1 Click where you want to create a point. (Make sure you don't drag before you release the mouse button.) This creates a corner point node (indicated by a small, filled-in square).

2 Repeat step 1 for each point; a segment will appear between points.

3 If you are drawing a closed shape with one of the box tools, the pointer will change to a rounded square when QuarkXPress detects you've returned to the start point. Or just release the mouse anywhere; QuarkXPress will draw a straight line from where you released the mouse to the start point.

Curved Segments

1 Click the mouse button at the desired point.

2 Move the mouse button to the next point, and click-and-hold at the desired point.

3 Position the control point by dragging in roughly the same direction as the direction line of the previous point to create a S-shaped curve segment; drag in the opposite direction to create a C-shaped curve.

4 Release the mouse button.

5 Repeat steps 1 through 4 for each segment.

6 If you are drawing a closed shape with one of the box tools, the pointer will change to a rounded square when QuarkXPress detects you've returned to the start point. If you release the mouse elsewhere, QuarkXPress will draw a straight line from where you released the mouse to the start point.

Cross-Reference: Pages 236-239 cover how to modify Bézier and other shapes.

Keep in Mind

Holding down ⌘ or Ctrl while using a Bézier tool lets you edit shapes, on the fly, as you create them. For example, you can reposition points and curve handles, and you can bend curved segments, even though the shape is incomplete. Just make sure you don't keep holding down the key when you're ready to create the next point in the shape.

Pressing Option+⌘+F1 or Ctrl+F1 changes the active point into a corner point. This is handy for connecting curved segments by a corner point rather than a smooth point.

After a Bézier line is created, you can move its points and segments with either the Item or Content tool. To move the entire line without reshaping, switch to the Item tool and choose Item ➪ Edit ➪ Shape (Shift+F4 on the Mac or F10 in Windows) to uncheck the Shape submenu.

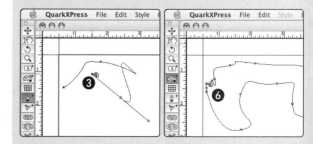

InDesign

Follow These Steps

Select the Pen tool before you start.

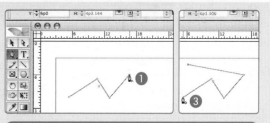

Straight Segments

1 Click where you want to create a point. (Make sure you don't drag before you release the mouse button.) This creates a corner point, indicated by a small, filled-in square.

2 Repeat step 1 for each point; a segment will appear between points.

3 To end a closed shape, return to the start point before releasing the mouse (a hollow oval icon will appear next to the Pen pointer). To end an open shape, simply hold ⌘ or Ctrl and click anywhere.

Curved Segments

1 Click and hold down the mouse button at the desired point.

2 Keep holding the mouse button while you drag the mouse in the direction of the next point. As you drag, the anchor point, its direction line, and the direction line's two handles are displayed.

3 Release the mouse button.

4 Move the Pen pointer to the next anchor point, then drag the mouse. Drag in roughly the same direction as the direction line of the previous point to create a S-shaped curve; drag in the opposite direction to create a C-shaped curve.

5 Release the mouse button.

6 Repeat steps 1 through 5 for each additional smooth point and curved segment.

7 To end a closed shape, return to the start point before releasing the mouse (a hollow oval icon will appear next to the Pen pointer). To end an open shape, simply hold ⌘ or Ctrl and click anywhere.

Keep in Mind

To reposition an anchor point after you click the mouse button but before you release it, hold down the spacebar and drag. As you create a path, you can move any anchor point, direction line handle, or the entire path by holding down ⌘ or Ctrl, then clicking and dragging whatever element you want to move.

To connect curved segments via corner points, move the Pen pointer to where you want to establish the next anchor point — and end the first segment — then press Option or Alt and drag the mouse. As you drag, the anchor point's handle moves and the direction line changes from a straight line to two independent segments. The angle of the direction line segment that you create when you drag the handle determines the slope of the next segment.

Finally, to draw a straight segment after a curved segment, move the Pen pointer over the last anchor point; the Convert Point icon is displayed. Click on the anchor point to convert it from a smooth point to a corner point. Move the Pen pointer to where you want to establish the next anchor point, then click and release the mouse button to complete the straight segment.

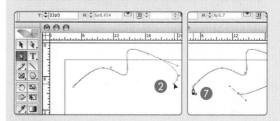

Modifying Freeform and Bézier Shapes

It's rare that a shape you draw can't benefit from some fine-tuning. And at times you might want to reshape an object created through a frame (or box) or line tool. Both QuarkXPress and InDesign offer similar capabilities and approaches to do so.

Follow These Steps

1. To edit an existing Bézier or freeform shape or line, be sure to make it editable by choosing choose Item ➪ Edit ➪ Shape (Shift+F4 on the Mac or F10 in Windows) to check the Shape submenu.

   To edit a straight line or a rectangular, elliptical, or polygonal box as a Bézier shape, convert it to a Bézier shape by choosing the squiggly-line icon (for lines) or artist's-palette icon (for boxes) submenu by choosing Item ➪ Shape.

2. To move a point, select it with the Content tool and drag it.

3. To move a segment, select it with the Content tool and drag it.

4. To change a curve, select its point and then drag and/or move the appropriate control point.

5. To add a point, hold Option or Alt and click at the desired location on a segment.

6. To delete a point, hold Option or Alt and click at the point to deleted.

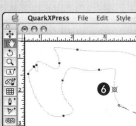

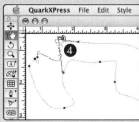

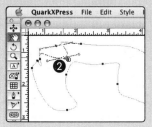

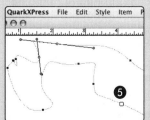

Cross-Reference: Pages 238-239 cover how to modify Bézier points and their control handles.

Follow These Steps

InDesign uses different methods to change curve directions and types, although its method for editing points and segments is similar to QuarkXPress's.

① To edit an existing shape or line — whether or not it was created as a freeform or Bézier object — select the object with the Direct Selection tool.

In InDesign CS2, you can also convert a shape in the familiar QuarkXPress way, by choosing Object ➪ Convert Shape and then selecting the desired shape from the submenu. Also, the Pathfinder pane (Window ➪ Object & Layout ➪ Pathfinder) provides iconic buttons to change shapes.

② To move an object's point, select it with the Direct Selection tool and drag it.

③ To move an object's segment, select it with the Direct Selection tool and drag it.

④ To change a curve, select its point with the Direct Selection tool and then drag and/or move the appropriate control point.

⑤ To add a point, choose the Add Anchor Point tool (hold the Pen tool and choose it from the pop-up menu) and click at the desired location on a segment.

⑥ To delete a point, choose the Delete Anchor Point tool (hold the Pen tool and choose it from the pop-up menu) and click on the point to be deleted.

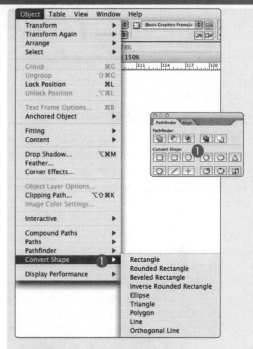

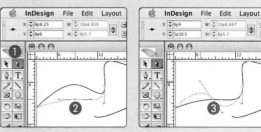

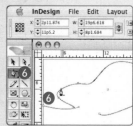

Modifying Bézier Points

The points in Bézier objects do more than link segments; they control the corner types and the curvature (or lack thereof) of segments. QuarkXPress and InDesign ultimately provide the same functionality but use very different techniques.

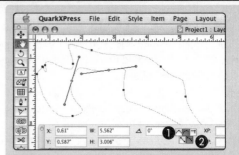

Follow These Steps

QuarkXPress makes it easy to work with points, using buttons to quickly change point and segment types. Start by selecting the Content tool and the desired item.

1 To change a point's type (for example, from smooth to corner), select the point and then click the Symmetrical Point, Smooth Point, or Corner Point button in the Measurements palette.

2 To change a segment from curved to straight or vice versa, select the segment and then click the Straight Segment or Curved Segment button in the Measurements palette.

3 To convert a point's control direction, select its point and then drag and/or move the appropriate control point at least 90°, turning the curve into the opposite direction.

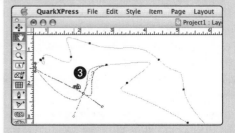

Cross-Reference: Pages 236-237 cover how to modify Bézier and other shapes.

> **InDesign**

Follow These Steps

InDesign's approach to working with points relies solely on manipulating the control points, à la Adobe Illustrator.

Be sure the Direct Selection tool is active and the object has been selected. Depending on the point or segment you want to convert, do one of the following:

1. To convert a corner point to a smooth point, click on the corner point, and then drag (direction lines are created and displayed as you drag).

2. To convert a smooth point to a corner point without direction lines, click and release the mouse on the smooth point.

3. To convert a smooth point to a corner point with independent direction lines, click and drag either of the smooth point's direction handles until the segment flattens.

4. To convert a corner point without direction lines to a corner point with direction lines, click and drag the corner point to create a smooth point, then release the mouse button. Then click and drag either of the direction lines until the segment flattens.

5. To convert a point's control direction, drag the point to the new curve direction.

Workaround: InDesign does not have a feature equivalent to QuarkXPress's Symmetric Point button, which makes both segments adjacent to the point have the same curve. In InDesign, you'll have to move the two control handles manually to create a symmetric curve.

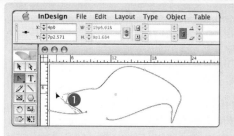

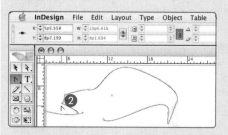

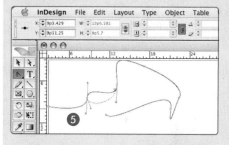

Converting Text to Graphics

While you can do a lot with text in QuarkXPress and InDesign, sometimes you need to treat text as graphics. For example, you might want to place graphics inside letter forms or use the letter forms as masks.

Follow These Steps

QuarkXPress lets you convert text to graphics, but only one line at a time. If you want to convert several lines of text, highlight one line, convert it, then repeat the process for the next line:

1 Select the text with the Content tool.

2 Choose Style ⇨ Text to Box. QuarkXPress will create a new picture box in the shape of the letters. (The original text is left in place.)

3 You can do anything with the new picture box that you could do with an picture box: add a graphic, edit its shape (see page 236), convert it to a text box or no-content box, add a fill color, add a frame, resize it, flip it, and so forth.

InDesign

Follow These Steps

InDesign also lets you convert text to graphics. The process differs slightly from QuarkXPress in two important ways, one of which could be dangerous:

❶ Select the text with the Type tool. Unlike in QuarkXPress, you can select multiple lines of text to convert all at once.

❷ Choose Type ➪ Create Outlines (Shift+⌘+O or Ctrl+Shift+O). InDesign will convert the text into a graphics frame — *replacing* the existing text. That converted text will remain in the same location as the original text but will be in its own frame.

❸ You can do anything with the new graphics frame that you could do with an picture box: add a graphic, edit its shape (see page 237), convert it to a text frame or unassigned frame, add a fill color, add a stroke, resize it, flip it, and so forth.

 Caution: Because InDesign replaces the selected text with a graphics frame, rather than copying it as QuarkXPress does, you can inadvertently lose your editable text. But InDesign provides a workaround to make it work like QuarkXPress: Hold Option or Alt when you choose Type ➪ Create Outlines, or press Option+Shift+⌘+O or Ctrl+Alt+Shift+O.

Go Further: InDesign lets you convert multiple lines of text at once, making it easier to transform, for example, titles in ad copy for use as a graphics frame.

Combining and Separating Shapes ◀ QuarkXPress

In addition to grouping and ungrouping objects, Quark-XPress and InDesign give you ways to combine and separate shapes and lines, letting you merge and separate graphics created within them. InDesign's capabilities in this area have emerged in recent versions, while Quark-XPress has offered them for nearly a decade.

Follow These Steps

QuarkXPress places its object-merging and –separation functions in two places: Item ⇨ Merge and Item ⇨ Split.

Merging Objects

To merge objects, select them with the Item or Content tool, then choose Item ⇨ Merge. Choose the desired option:

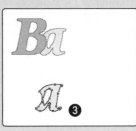
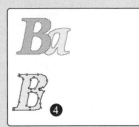

❶ Choosing Item ⇨ Merge ⇨ Union combines all the selected objects into one shape. Space between the objects remains, but the items still behave as if they were one. For example, if two objects had different fill colors and you combined them this way, they would become one object with just one fill color.

❷ Choosing Item ⇨ Merge ⇨ Intersection combines any overlapping portions and deletes the rest.

❸ Choosing Item ⇨ Merge ⇨ Difference removes the top object and any part that overlaps the object below from the object below.

❹ Choosing Item ⇨ Merge ⇨ Reverse Difference removes the bottom object and any part that overlaps the object above from the object above.

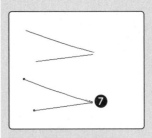

❺ Choosing Item ⇨ Merge ⇨ Exclusive Or removes any overlaps between objects, leaving the rest intact.

❻ Choosing Item ⇨ Merge ⇨ Combine creates one path for all the objects selected. This is similar to Union except that overlapping paths are retained, sometimes creating the same effect as Exclusive Or.

❼ Choosing Item ⇨ Merge ⇨ Join Endpoints will join two lines into one, merging two points into one. These two point must be very close to each other, and this tool is most useful when you are drawing multisegment lines one segment at a time and then want to make them into one seamless line.

Splitting Objects

To split objects, select them with the Item or Content tool:

❶ Choose Item ⇨ Split ⇨ Outside Paths to separate nonoverlapping paths from the others into separate objects.

❷ Choose Item ⇨ Split ⇨ All Paths to separate both nonoverlapping and overlapping paths into separate objects.

InDesign

Follow These Steps

InDesign CS introduced QuarkXPress-like object-merging features with the Pathfinder tool. InDesign 2 offered just the ability to combine and split paths, which InDesign CS or later retains.

Merging Objects

To merge objects, select them with the Selection or Direct Selection tool, then choose the desired option:

1 Object ⇨ Pathfinder ⇨ Add combines all the selected objects into one shape. Space between the objects remains, but the items still behave as if they were one. For example, if two objects had different fill colors and you combined them this way, they would become one object with just one fill color.

2 Object ⇨ Pathfinder ⇨ Intersect combines any overlapping portions and deletes the rest.

3 Object ⇨ Pathfinder ⇨ Subtract removes the top object and any part that overlaps the object below from the object below.

4 Object ⇨ Pathfinder ⇨ Minus Back removes the bottom object and any part that overlaps the object above from the object above.

5 Object ⇨ Pathfinder ⇨ Exclude Overlap removes any overlaps between objects, leaving the rest intact.

6 Object ⇨ Compound Paths ⇨ Make (⌘+8 or Ctrl+8) creates one path for all the objects selected. This is similar to Object ⇨ Pathfinder ⇨ Overlap in that overlapping objects are removed and their borders made part of the compound path. By contrast, choosing Object ⇨ Pathfinder ⇨ Add will merge the overlapping objects into the objects below them.

InDesign CS or later provides the Pathfinder pane (Window ⇨ Object & Layout ⇨ Pathfinder in InDesign CS2 and (Window ⇨ Pathfinder in InDesign CS), shown at right, with the same controls as the menu options decribed above.

Workaround: InDesign combines paths differently that QuarkXPress does. In QuarkXPress, joining endpoints converts multiple lines into one line, if their points are close enough to each other. By contrast, InDesign cannot combine several lines into one line. If you make them into a compound path or choose Object ⇨ Pathfinder ⇨ Add, InDesign makes them become one object composed of multiple lines that remain unjoined and independently editable.

Splitting Objects

To split objects, select them with either selection tool:

1 Choose Object ⇨ Compound Paths ⇨ Release (Option+⌘+8 or Ctrl+Alt+8) to separate paths into their own objects. Unlike QuarkXPress, you can't separate just outside paths.

Applying Strokes

QuarkXPress

Strokes (or frames, in QuarkXPress vernacular), are the edges of objects. QuarkXPress lets you set strokes for frames, while InDesign lets you set strokes for text and shapes.

Follow These Steps

QuarkXPress provides basic controls over frames in the Modify dialog box, as well as more sophisticated controls as part of the definitions of dashes and stripes:

① To modify a frame around a box, select the box and choose Item ➪ Frame (⌘+B or Ctrl+B). Set the frame width and type.

② You can change the color and/or shade in step 1 or later by selecting the box and then clicking the frame button in the Colors palette (Window ➪ Colors in QuarkXPress 6, or View ➪ Colors in earlier versions, or F12), and finally choosing a color.

③ You can adjust the corner and caps for lines and frames in QuarkXPress by editing or creating a stripe or dash (Edit ➪ Dashes & Stripes). The Miter pop-up menu, available for stripes and dashes, lets you set how corners appear, with a choice of Sharp, Rounded, and Beveled. The Endcap pop-up menu, available only for dashes, determines how line endings appear, as Square, Projecting Round, Projecting Square, and Round.

④ You can also set whether frames in your document are placed inside or outside the box's edges by selecting the Inside or Outside radio button for the Framing option of the General pane of the Preferences dialog box. (In QuarkXPress 6, choose QuarkXPress ➪ Preferences or Option+Shift+⌘+Y on the Mac or Edit ➪ Preferences or Ctrl+Alt+Shift+Y. In QuarkXPress 5, choose Edit ➪ Preferences ➪ Preferences, or Option+Shift+⌘+Y or Ctrl+Alt+Shift+Y. In QuarkXPress 4, choose Edit ➪ Preferences ➪ Document, or ⌘+Y or Ctrl+Y.)

Cross-Reference: For more creating lines, see pages 228-229. For more on applying colors, see pages 246-247.

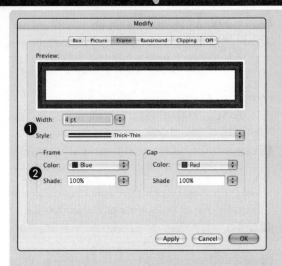

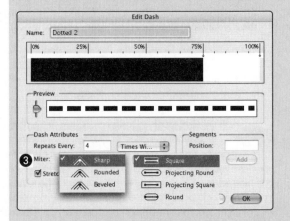

InDesign

Follow These Steps

InDesign lets you apply strokes to shapes (including frames) and text. It also considers lines to be strokes, so you apply stroke settings the same way to lines (see page 229) as you do to other objects. InDesign concentrates its stroke features for easier access than in QuarkXPress, and offers more capabilities in most cases:

❶ To change the stroke width and/or type, use the Stroke pane (Window ⇨ Stroke or F10) after selecting the line, object, or text.

❷ You set the color and/or tint in the Swatches pane (Window ⇨ Swatches or F5). Click the Stroke button in the Swatches pane or the Tools palette, then select a color, gradient, or tint.

❸ You can adjust the corner and caps for lines and frames individually by using the Stroke pane. The Join buttons let you set how corners appear, with a choice of Miter Join, Round Join, and Bevel Join. The Cap buttons determine how line endings appear, as Butt Cap, Round Cap, and Projecting Cap. You can also set the cap for dashed stroke styles (choose Stroke Styles from the Stroke pane's palette menu). Unlike with QuarkXPress's stripes and dashes, you cannot set the cap for stripes, nor can you set the end cap for dashes in InDesign.

❹ In InDesign CS or later, you can also set where the stroke prints relative to the object's edge, using the Center, Inside, and Outside buttons. Unlike in QuarkXPress, you can set this for individual strokes in InDesign.

Go Further: InDesign CS lets you apply strokes to text as well as to lines and frames. Plus those strokes can contain gradients, not just solid colors. Finally, InDesign lets you set the stroke location relative to the frame separately from each object, and it does not require the same settings for the entire document as in QuarkXPress.

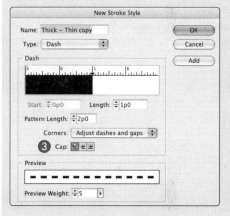

Applying Colors and Gradients

QuarkXPress and InDesign let you apply color and gradients to objects you create in these programs. InDesign uses a different process and provides slightly more capability than QuarkXPress.

Follow These Steps

In QuarkXPress, all objects created in the program are essentially boxes or lines, so you use the box and line tools to apply colors (including shades) and blends.

1 You apply outlines to the boxes by choosing Item ➪ Frame (⌘+B or Ctrl+B) and setting the frame color, type, and weight. You can choose the Frame button in the Colors palette (Window ➪ Colors in QuarkXPress 6, or View ➪ Colors in earlier versions, or F12) and then apply a color. (Note that you can apply frames to multiple boxes at once.)

2 You apply fill colors and shades to boxes and lines, as well as blends to boxes, by selecting the Background button (gray box) in the Colors palette and choosing a color, or you can choose Item ➪ Modify (⌘+M or Ctrl+M) and select a color from the Color menu in the Box or Line pane. (Note that you can apply fills to multiple boxes and lines at once.)

 Cross-Reference: For details on applying colors and shades to monochrome bitmapped images, see pages 226-227.

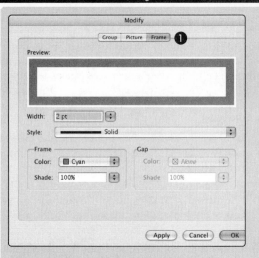

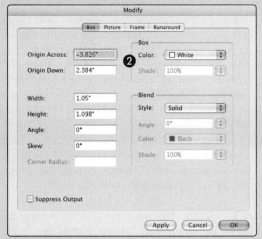

InDesign

Follow These Steps

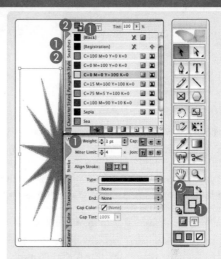

InDesign uses the Swatches and Stroke panes to apply colors, tints, and gradients to frames and shapes created in InDesign:

① You apply outlines to shapes by choosing them with the Selection tool, clicking the Stroke button on the Tools palette or Swatches pane (Window ➪ Swatches or F5), and then choosing a color, tint, or gradient swatch. (Note that you can apply strokes to multiple shapes at once.) Of course, the shapes need to have a stroke weight of more than 0 points for the strokes to be visible; you can set the weight using the Weight field/pop-up menu in either the Control palette or Stroke pane (Window ➪ Stroke or F10).

② You apply fill colors, tints, and gradients to boxes and lines, as well as blends to boxes, by selecting the Fill button on the Tools palette or Swatches pane. (Note that you can apply strokes to multiple shapes at once.)

 Go Further: InDesign lets you apply gradients to strokes, and also lets you simultaneously convert the content of selected frames.

Creating New Clipping Paths

QuarkXPress

Although you can import clipping paths from TIFF and Photoshop files into QuarkXPress and InDesign, you sometimes will want to create your own clipping path inside your layout.

Follow These Steps

QuarkXPress offers two ways to create clipping paths:

1. Select an object and choose Item ⇨ Clipping (Option+⌘+T or Ctrl+Alt+T), then select an option from the Type pop-up menu. Typically, you would choose Item to select the object's boundaries (which may be different than the box's boundaries), Non-White Areas, or Picture Bounds, which essentially resets a clipping path to match the box shape.

2. Draw a new Bézier or other type of picture box, then import the graphic into the new shape (File ⇨ Get Picture, or ⌘+E or Ctrl+E) or, using the Content tool, cut and paste the original graphic into the new box.

 Cross-Reference: For details on working with embedded clipping paths, see pages 198-199.

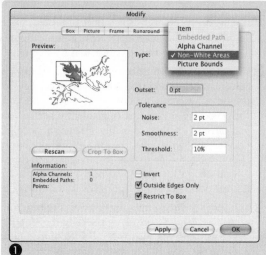

❶

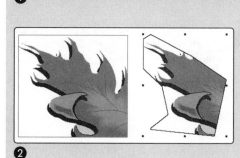

❷

Follow These Steps

InDesign also offers two equivalent ways to create clipping paths:

1 Select an object and choose Object ⇨ Clipping Path (Option+Shift+⌘+K or Ctrl+Alt+Shift+K), then select an option from the Type pop-up menu. Typically, you would choose Detect Edges to try to create a path from the image's internal shape, or you would choose None, which essentially resets a clipping path to match the box shape.

2 Draw a new Bézier or other type of frame, then import the graphic into the new shape (File ⇨ Place, or ⌘+D or Ctrl+D) or paste it into the new shape (Edit ⇨ Paste Into, or Option+⌘+V or Ctrl+Alt+V).

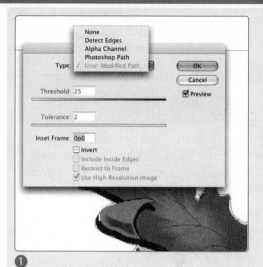

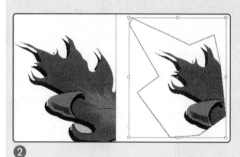

☀Anchoring Graphics in Text   ◀ **QuarkXPress**

Whether it's an icon used essentially as a drop cap, or a special symbol that you use in text (perhaps it's not available in a font), QuarkXPress and InDesign let you embed graphics (as well as text frames) in text. But the latest version of InDesign does much, much more.

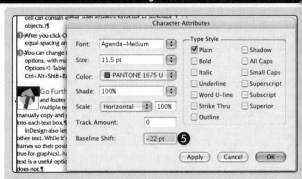

Follow These Steps

In QuarkXPress, the process is simple:

❶ Copy or cut the picture box using the Item tool.

❷ Switch to the Content tool.

❸ Click in the desired location in your text.

❹ Paste the picture box (or other box).

❺ You can move the graphic up or down relative to the text baseline by using the Baseline Shift field in the Character Attributes dialog box (Style ➪ Baseline Shift). You can set text wrap for the anchored graphic (Item ➪ Runaround, or ⌘+T or Ctrl+T), although runaround is limited to the graphic's box (see page 112).

 Cross-Reference: QuarkXPress imports inline graphics from Microsoft Word files (see page 88). InDesign CS2 imports both inline graphics and anchored items from Microsoft Word files (see page 89), while InDesign CS imports just inline graphics. InDesign 2 imports neither.

InDesign

Follow These Steps

InDesign's anchoring varies based on the version you use.

Inline Anchoring

All versions of InDesign can work like QuarkXPress does:

1 Copy or cut the graphic using the Selection tool.

2 Switch to the Type tool.

3 Click in the desired location in your text.

4 Paste the graphics frame (or other frame).

5 Move the graphic up or down relative to the text baseline by using the Baseline Shift field in the Character pane (Type ⇨ Character, or ⌘+T or Ctrl+T). Set text wraps on anchored graphics using the Text Wrap pane (Window ⇨ Text Wrap in InDesign CS2 or 2 and Window ⇨ Type & Tables ⇨ Text Wrap in InDesign CS, or Option+⌘+W or Ctrl+Alt+W), but note that such wraps affect only text that appears on the same line or below the anchored graphic, not text above or text in other frames. Unlike in QuarkXPress, you have full control over types of wraps and can specify no wrap (see page 113).

Inline and External Anchoring

In InDesign CS2, you have more options:

1 Anchor a graphic inside text as described above or choose Object ⇨ Anchored Object ⇨ Insert after you have placed the text-insertion pointer in text. In the Insert Anchored Object dialog box, specify the frame size and its location relative to the text. Set any object and paragraph styles to be applied to this frame. Check Prevent Manual Positioning to keep the anchored frame from being moved with the mouse. Follow step 2 or 3 below, then click OK and import the graphic or text into the anchored frame.

2 Choose Inline or Above Line from the Position pop-up menu to insert an inline frame similar to the basic anchoring described above.

3 Or choose Custom in the Position pop-up menu to create an anchored graphic outside the current text frame, such as a side-bar or pull-quote. Set the anchored point position to indicate where the text frame is on the page and then the reference point to indicate the relative position for the anchored frame.

4 Modify an anchored object by choosing Object ⇨ Anchored Object ⇨ Options. Delete an anchored object by selecting it with the Selection tool and deleting it or by choosing Object ⇨ Anchored Object ⇨ Release.

Go Further: InDesign CS2 lets you anchor objects either inside or outside the text frame (see pages 354-355). QuarkXPress supports only inline frames.

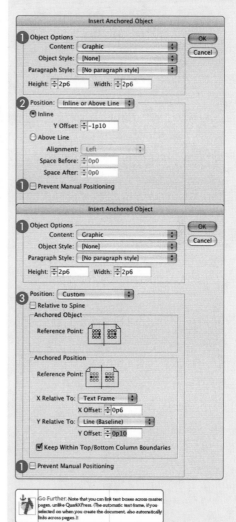

part ix

Working with Objects

You can make many finishing touches to objects, such as changing the corners, skewing them, or adding drop shadows. QuarkXPress and InDesign differ strongly in how they handle such object effects, and this part explains the differences.

In most cases, inDesign offers additional capabilities to what QuarkXPress provides. In many cases, even where the functionality is the same, the InDesign method differs notably from the QuarkXPress method.

Adding Strokes and Fills

QuarkXPress

Both QuarkXPress and InDesign let you fill objects with colors and gradients, as well as apply colors to the outlines of objects. But InDesign offers more capabilities.

Follow These Steps

QuarkXPress provides basic controls over fills (background colors) and frames — its word for outlines — in the Modify dialog box, as well as more sophisticated controls as part of the definitions of dashes and stripes:

1 To modify a frame around a box, select the box and choose Item ➪ Frame (⌘+B or Ctrl+B). Set the frame width and type.

2 You can change the frame's color and/or shade in step 1 or later by selecting the box and then clicking the Frame button in the Colors palette (Window ➪ Colors in QuarkXPress 6, or View ➪ Colors in earlier versions, or F12), and finally choosing a color.

3 You can adjust the corner and caps for lines and frames in QuarkXPress by editing or creating a stripe or dash (Edit ➪ Dashes & Stripes). The Miter pop-up menu, available for stripes and dashes, lets you set how corners appear, with a choice of Sharp, Rounded, and Beveled. The Endcap pop-up menu, available only for dashes, determines how line endings appear, as Square, Projecting Round, Projecting Square, and Round.

4 You can also set whether frames in your document are placed inside or outside the box's edges by selecting the Inside or Outside radio button for the Framing option in the General pane of the Preferences dialog box. (In QuarkXPress 6, choose QuarkXPress ➪ Preferences or Option+Shift+⌘+Y on the Mac or Edit ➪ Preferences or Ctrl+Alt+Shift+Y. In QuarkXPress 5, choose Edit ➪ Preferences ➪ Preferences, or Option+Shift+⌘+Y or Ctrl+Alt+Shift+Y. In QuarkXPress 4, choose Edit ➪ Preferences ➪ Document, or ⌘+Y or Ctrl+Y.)

5 You apply fill colors and shades (tints) to boxes and lines, as well as blends (gradients) to boxes, by selecting the background icon (gray box) in the Colors palette and choosing a color, or you can choose Item ➪ Modify (⌘+M or Ctrl+M) and select a color from the Color menu in the Box or Line pane. (Note that you can apply fills to multiple boxes and lines at once.)

Cross-Reference: For details on applying colors and shades to monochrome bitmapped images, see pages 226-227. For more on applying colors to text, see pages 156-159. For more creating lines, see pages 228-229. See Part III for more on defining colors, tints, and gradients.

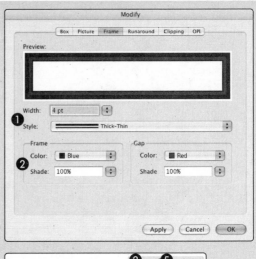

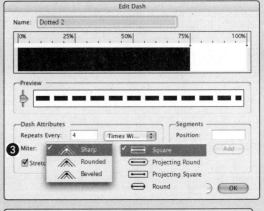

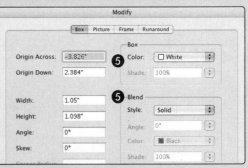

InDesign

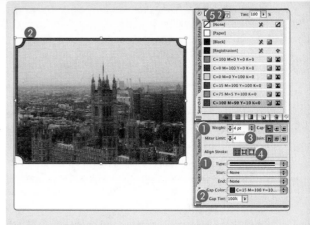

Follow These Steps

InDesign lets you apply fills and strokes to shapes (including frames) and text. It also considers lines to be strokes, so you apply stroke settings the same way to lines (see page 229) as you do to other objects.

① To change the stroke width and/or type, use the Stroke pane (Window ⇨ Stroke or F10) after selecting the line, object, or text.

② You set the color and/or tint in the Swatches pane (Window ⇨ Swatches or F5). Click the Stroke button in the Swatches pane or the Tools palette, then select a color, gradient, or tint.

③ You can adjust the corner and caps for lines and frames individually by using the Stroke pane. The Join buttons let you set how corners appear, with a choice of Miter Join, Round Join, and Bevel Join. The Cap buttons determine how line endings appear, as Butt Cap, Round Cap, or Projecting Cap. You can also set the cap for dashed stroke styles (choose Stroke Styles from the Stroke pane's palette menu). Unlike with QuarkXPress's stripes and dashes, you cannot set the cap for stripes, nor can you set the end cap for dashes, in InDesign.

④ In InDesign CS or later, you can also set where the stroke prints relative to the object's edge, using the Center, Inside, and Outside buttons. Unlike in QuarkXPress, you can set this for individual strokes in InDesign.

⑤ You apply fill colors, tints, and gradients to frames and lines, as well as gradients to frames, by selecting the Fill button on the Tools palette or Swatches pane. (Note that you can apply strokes to multiple shapes at once.)

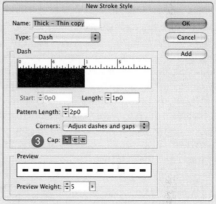

 Go Further: Unlike QuarkXPress, InDesign lets you apply gradients to strokes, and it also lets you simultaneously convert the content of selected frames.

Go Further: InDesign CS or CS2 lets you apply strokes to text as well as to lines and frames. Plus those strokes can contain gradients, not just solid colors. Finally, InDesign lets you set the stroke location relative to the frame separately from each object, not requiring the same settings for the entire document as in QuarkXPress.

New Stroke Style

Name: Thick - Thin copy

Type: Dash

Dash

Start: 0p0   Length: 1p0

Pattern Length: 2p0

Corners: Adjust dashes and gaps

③ Cap:

Preview

Preview Weight: 5

OK
Cancel
Add

Santiago de Compostela

Creating Custom Frame Strokes

Although both QuarkXPress and InDesign come with a set of predefined strokes for lines and frames, both programs let you add your own. Their capabilities are very similar, although InDesign also lets you create dotted lines.

Follow These Steps

QuarkXPress uses the Dashes & Stripes dialog box to let you create, modify, and delete line styles for use in lines and as frames for boxes:

1 Choose Edit ⇨ Dashes & Stripes to open the Dashes & Stripes dialog box. If no document is open, the changes affect all future documents; otherwise, they affect just the current document.

2 Click the New pop-up menu and choose either Dash or Stripe.

3 For a dash, create the dash segment(s) by dragging in the ruler section of the Edit Dash dialog box. You can fine-tune dash segments by clicking on the arrows above them and entering a specific value in the Position field. Set the frequency of the dash by entering a value in the Repeats Every field and by choosing either Times Width or Points to select the repeat size — larger values result in longer segments. The Preview section will show the effects of your settings as you make them. Also, set the corner type using the Miter pop-up menu and the end style (for lines) using the End Caps pop-up menu. Finally, check Stretch to Corners to ensure that the dash covers entire corners; if unchecked, you could get blank segments at corners that make it difficult to discern that they are actually corners. Be sure to give the dash a name in the Name field.

4 To create a stripe, drag in the ruler section of the Edit Stripe dialog box to create the constituent stripe(s). You can fine-tune the stripes by clicking on the arrows to their left and entering a specific value in the Position field. The Preview section will show the effects of your settings as you make them. Also, set the corner type using the Miter pop-up menu. Be sure to give the dash a name in the Name field.

5 Click OK to accept the dash or stripe definition.

6 Create, edit, delete, and/or import (append) other dashes and stripes as desired, then click Save to save all these changes, or Cancel to ignore them.

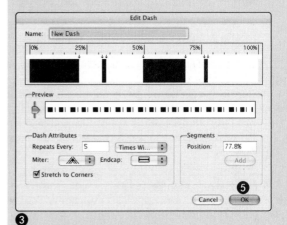

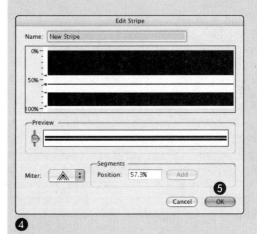

Cross-Reference: See pages 244-245 and 228-229 for more on how to apply strokes to frames and lines, respectively.

InDesign

Follow These Steps

InDesign CS or later uses the Strokes pane to let you create, modify, and delete stroke styles for use in lines and as strokes for frames. (InDesign 2 has no equivalent function.)

1. Go to the Stroke pane (Window ➭ Stroke or F10) and choose Stroke Styles from the palette menu to open the Stroke Styles dialog box. If no document is open, the changes affect all future documents; otherwise, they affect just the current document.

2. Click New to open the New Stroke Style dialog box. Give the style a name in the Name field. The Preview section will show the effects of your settings as you make them.

3. For a dash, choose Dash from the Type menu and create the dash by dragging in the ruler in the Dash section to create the dash segment(s). You can fine-tune the dash segments by clicking on the arrows above them and entering a specific value in the Start and/or Length fields. Set the width of the dash by entering a value in the Pattern Length field. Also, set the end style (for lines) using the Caps buttons. Finally, choose Adjust Dashes and Gaps in the Corners pop-up menu to ensure that the dash covers entire corners; if you choose None, you could get blank segments at corners that make it difficult to tell that they are actually corners.

4. For a stripe, choose Stripe from the Type menu and create the stripe by dragging in the ruler in the Stripe section to create the constituent stripe(s). You can fine-tune stripes by clicking on the arrows to their left and entering a specific value in the Start and/or Width fields. Set the width of the dash by entering a value in the Pattern Length field.

5. For a dotted line, choose Dotted from the Type menu and create the dots by clicking in the ruler in the Dotted section. You can fine-tune their positions by clicking on the arrows above them and entering a specific value in the Center field. Set the width of the dot by entering a value in the Pattern Length field. Finally, choose Adjust Gaps in the Corners pop-up menu to ensure that the dot spacing isn't too much or too little at corners; if you choose None, you could get awkward-appearing corners.

6. Click Add to accept the dash, stripe, or dotted line definition and create another one, or OK to return to the Stroke Styles dialog box.

7. Create, edit, delete, and/or import (load) other dashes and stripes as desired in the Stroke Styles dialog box, then click Save to save all these changes or Cancel to ignore them.

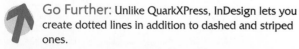

Go Further: Unlike QuarkXPress, InDesign lets you create dotted lines in addition to dashed and striped ones.

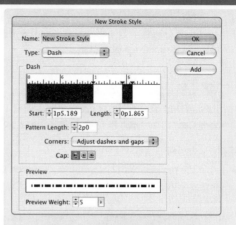

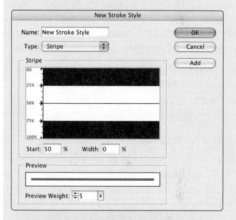

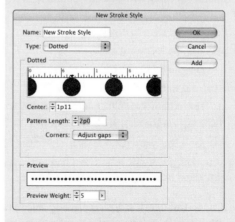

❊ Working with Overlapping Objects ◀ QuarkXPress

Being able to layer objects one over the other can lead to very compelling designs — but it can also make it difficult to work on covered-up objects.

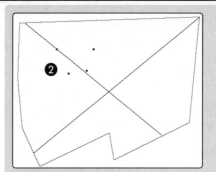

Follow These Steps

In some cases, all you need to do is get to the desired item while, in other cases, you need to change its relative position.

Selecting Covered-Up Items

Assuming that the desired item is completely covered by other items (otherwise, you'd just select the uncovered part of the item you want):

❶ Place the mouse over where you think the desired item is.

❷ Hold Option+Shift+⌘ or Ctrl+Alt+Shift and then click with either the Item tool or Content tool. QuarkXPress will select the item immediately below the one that your mouse is on. Repeat this clicking as necessary to reach the desired item — several times if that item is covered by multiple items.

You can now apply any option from the Modify dialog box (Item ⇨ Modify, or ⌘+M or Ctrl+M), Measurements palette, Colors palette (Window ⇨ Colors in QuarkXPress 6 or View ⇨ Colors in earlier versions, or F12), or any other palette or menu option.

Changing the Position of Items

You may find that it is not enough to select the item, since all QuarkXPress will show you are its sizing handles. But because you can't see what you're doing in any detail, you might want to follow the steps below to move the item to the top and then return it to the desired position. You might also want to change an item's position in the stacking order to change the layout's appearance. Either way, here's how:

❶ Select the desired item as described above.

❷ Choose one of the following options:

- Item ⇨ Bring to Front (F5)
- Item ⇨ Send to Back (Shift+F5)

Or, to move it incrementally, hold Option or Ctrl and choose:

- Item ⇨ Bring Forward (Option+F5 or Ctrl+F5)
- Item ⇨ Send Backward (Option+Shift+F5 or Ctrl+Shift+F5)

❸ Make your changes, if any, to the item and return it to its original position following step 2, if desired.

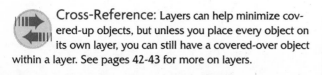

Cross-Reference: Layers can help minimize covered-up objects, but unless you place every object on its own layer, you can still have a covered-over object within a layer. See pages 42-43 for more on layers.

Follow These Steps

In some cases, all you need to do is get to the desired item, while in other cases, you need to change its relative position.

Selecting Covered-Up Objects

Assuming that the desired object is completely covered by other objects (otherwise, you'd just select the uncovered part of the one you want):

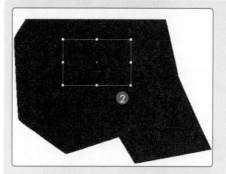

1. Place the mouse over where you think the desired object is.

2. Hold ⌘ or Ctrl and then click with the Selection or Direct Selection tool. Or, in inDesign CS or later, choose Object ➪ Select ➪ Next Object Below (Option+⌘+[or Ctrl+Alt+[). InDesign will select the object immediately below the one that your mouse is on. Repeat this selection as necessary to reach the desired object if it is covered by multiple objects. InDesign also provides these menu options, all via Object ➪ Select:

   - First Object Above (Option+Shift+⌘+] or Ctrl+Alt+Shift+])

   - Next Object Above (Option+⌘+] or Ctrl+Alt+])

   - Last Object Below (Option+Shift+⌘+[or Ctrl+Alt+Shift+[)

You can now apply any option from the Transform pane (Window ➪ Transform or F9), Control palette, Swatches pane (Window ➪ Swatches or F5), or any other pane or menu option.

Changing the Position of Objects

You may find that it is not enough to select the object, since all InDesign will show you are its frame and sizing handles. But since you can't see what you're doing in any detail, you might want to follow these steps to move the object to the top and then return it to the desired position. You might also want to change an item's position in the stacking order to change the layout's appearance, Either way, here's how:

1. Select the desired object as described above.

2. Choose one of the following:

   - Object ➪ Arrange ➪ Bring to Front (⌘+] or Ctrl+])

   - Object ➪ Arrange ➪ Bring Forward (Shift+⌘+] or Ctrl+Shift+])

   - Object ➪ Arrange ➪ Send to Back (⌘+[or Ctrl+[)

   - Object ➪ Arrange ➪ Send Backward (Shift+⌘+[or Ctrl+Shift+[)

3. Make your changes, if any, and return the object to its original position following step 2, if desired.

⬥ Grouping and Ungrouping Objects ⟨ QuarkXPress

Layouts can have dozens, or even hundreds, of items. This complexity can make it a challenge to move, delete, copy, or otherwise work with the right ones. Both Quark-XPress and InDesign let you group objects, so you can act on all of them at once, as well as ungroup them when you need to work on individual items.

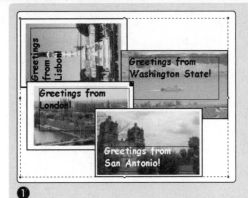

❶

Follow These Steps

QuarkXPress makes it easy to group and ungroup multiple items, as well as to work on individual items in a group:

❶ To group multiple items, select them with the Item tool and choose Item ⇨ Group (⌘+G or Ctrl+G).

❷ To ungroup items, select any item in the group with the Item tool (all will be selected and share a common bounding box), then choose Item ⇨ Ungroup (⌘+U or Ctrl+U).

❸ To work on a specific item in a group, use the Content tool to select it. (See page 258 for details on how to select a covered-up item.) You can make any modification allowed by the Content tool — using the mouse or various palettes and dialog boxes — to just select that item, without affecting other items in the group or removing it from the group. However, functions that work only when an item is selected with the Item tool can't be applied to that one item if it is in a group; functions will apply to all items possible in that group.

Keep in Mind

Note that groups can contain other groups, which can come in very handy. You can group several related items and then group that group with other items, letting you "nest" groups in order of relationship. When you ungroup, these subgroups aren't ungrouped; you'll need to select them individually (after ungrouping them from other objects) and then ungroup the items with the subgroup. For example, in the postcard group in step 1, each postcard is grouped with its "Greetings from" text, and then the four grouped cards are grouped together.

Follow These Steps

InDesign also makes it easy to group and ungroup multiple items, as well as to work on individual items in a group:

① To group multiple items, select them with the Selection tool and choose Object ➪ Group (⌘+G or Ctrl+G).

② To ungroup items, select any item in the group with the Selection tool (all will be selected and share a common bounding box), then choose Object ➪ Ungroup (Shift+⌘+G or Ctrl+Shift+G).

③ To work on a specific object in a group, use the Direct Selection tool to select it. You can make any modification allowed by the Direct Selection tool, using the mouse or various panes and dialog boxes, to just that selected object, without affecting other objects in the group or removing it from the group. However, functions that work only when an item is selected with the Selection tool can't be applied to that one object, if it is in a group; it will apply to all objects possible in that group.

There's no way in InDesign 2 to select a covered-up object in a group without ungrouping it first. (QuarkXPress does let you select covered-up items, whether in a group or not.) To address this, InDesign CS added several menu options to let you select specific items within a group: Object ➪ Select ➪ Previous Object in Group and Object ➪ Select ➪ Next Object in Group. To use these, you must first choose Object ➪ Select ➪ Content. Note that InDesign CS2 adds buttons for all these menu options in the Control palette; the first two display only if you select a group with the Direct Selection tool, and the last two display if you select a group with any selection tool.

①

Select Previous Object in Group ⌐
Select Container ⌐

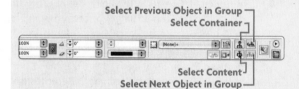

Select Content ⌐
Select Next Object in Group ⌐

Keep in Mind

Note that groups can contain other groups, which can very handy. That way, you can group several related items and then group that group with other items, letting you "nest" groups in order of relationship. When you ungroup, these subgroups aren't ungrouped; you'll need to select them individually (after ungrouping them from other objects) and then ungroup the items with the subgroup. For example, in the postcard group in step 1, each postcard is grouped with its "Greetings from" text, and then the four grouped cards are grouped together.

Constraining and Nesting Objects   QuarkXPress

Sometimes, you want to create objects that cannot be larger than the objects around them — for example, a sidebar's text dimensions should not go beyond that of an enclosing frame used as a border. QuarkXPress and InDesign both offer ways to handle such situations. But their methods and capabilities are quite different.

❸

Follow These Steps

QuarkXPress calls this process "constraining," and its goal is to keep text or picture boxes wholly within other boxes. To constrain boxes in QuarkXPress:

❶ Make sure that the "parent" box wholly encloses the "child" boxes — none of the child boxes can go beyond the edges of the parent box. Likewise, the parent box cannot overlap any other items.

❷ With the Item tool, select all the boxes to be constrained, as well as the parent box, and group them (Item ⇨ Group, or ⌘+G or Ctrl+G).

❸ Choose Item ⇨ Constrain. The boxes are now constrained, so the child boxes can no longer be resized or moved beyond the edges of the parent box.

❹ To automatically have all wholly enclosed child boxes be constrained as you draw them, check the Auto Constrain checkbox in the General pane of the Preferences dialog box. (In QuarkXPress 6, choose QuarkXPress ⇨ Preferences on the Mac or Edit ⇨ Preferences in Windows; in QuarkXPress 5, choose Edit ⇨ Preferences ⇨ Preferences; and in QuarkXPress 4, choose Edit ⇨ Preferences ⇨ Document. QuarkXPress 5 and 6 use the same shortcut, Option+Shift+⌘+Y or Ctrl+Alt+Shift+Y, while QuarkXPress 4 uses ⌘+Y or Ctrl+Y.)

InDesign

Follow These Steps

InDesign has no equivalent to QuarkXPress's size-constraining feature; you must manually ensure that frames stay within the boundaries of others, if that is your design goal.

What InDesign does have is a capability called *nesting*. Nested boxes are really meant for masking graphics; they work like Photoshop's Paste Into function. To nest boxes in InDesign, do the following:

1 Select, then copy or cut all the child objects.

2 Select the parent frame in which the child frame will be nested. Any contents will be overridden.

3 Choose Edit ⇨ Paste Into (Option+⌘+V or Ctrl+Alt+V). The frames are now nested, so the child frame's contents are now masked by the parent frame.

Workaround: To achieve somewhat the same effect as QuarkXPress's constraining capability, you can anchor frames into text, as described on page 251. But this will not work for constraining objects inside a graphics or unassigned frame.

(Conversely, to achieve the masking effect of InDesign's nesting feature in QuarkXPress, use the techniques described on pages 198, 212, and 246.)

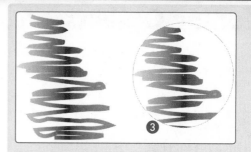

Distributed-Copying and Cloning Objects

In many layouts, you will use the same basic objects repeatedly, so it's handy to have a quick way to copy them. While both QuarkXPress and InDesign offer such options, in this case QuarkXPress offers more sophisticated options than InDesign.

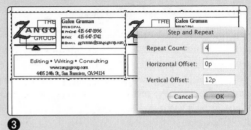

③

Follow These Steps

QuarkXPress has several ways to clone items (boxes and lines), as well as two ways to distribute those copies to specified locations:

① Simply copy and paste the items by choosing Edit ➪ Copy and then Edit ➪ Paste (⌘+C then ⌘+V or Ctrl+C then Ctrl+V). Then move the duplicate to the desired location. (This also works on text selections.)

② Or, more simply, duplicate the items by choosing Item ➪ Duplicate (⌘+D or Ctrl+D). Then move the duplicate to the desired location.

③ A faster option is to choose Item ➪ Step and Repeat (Option+⌘+D or Ctrl+Alt+D) to open the Step and Repeat dialog box. Set the number of copies and the horizontal and/or vertical offset (the distance between copied items), then press OK. QuarkXPress will make the specified number of copies in the specified locations (a distributed copy).

④ For individual items only, QuarkXPress lets you both copy and transform them in one step by choosing Item ➪ Super Step and Repeat to open the Super Step and Repeat dialog box. Here, you set the same options as in the Step and Repeat dialog box plus, if you want, successive rotation, scale, frame or line weight, skew, and shade for each copy, as well as the rotation's start point. Be sure to check the Scale Contents option to apply the transformations to the contents, such as text or pictures. Also be sure any color is already applied so QuarkXPress can apply the shade settings to the items. Click OK to execute the distributed copy and transformation. (In QuarkXPress 4, Super Step and Repeat is available as a free download from www.quark .com; in later versions, Super Step and Repeat is included with the software and automatically installed for you.)

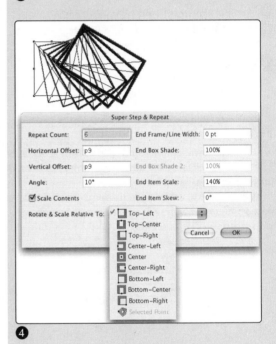

④

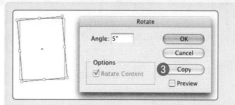

InDesign

Follow These Steps

InDesign provides several ways to clone objects (frames, lines, and in some cases text), but only one way to distribute multiple copies to specified locations:

① Simply copy and paste the objects by choosing Edit ⇨ Copy and then Edit ⇨ Paste (⌘+C then ⌘+V or Ctrl+C then Ctrl+V). Then move the duplicate to the desired location. (This also works on text selections.)

② Or, more simply, duplicate the objects by choosing Edit ⇨ Duplicate (Option+Shift+⌘+D or Ctrl+Alt+Shift+D). Then move the duplicate to the desired location. (This also works on text selections, unlike QuarkXPress's duplicate function.)

③ Another simple way to clone an object (or multiple or grouped objects) is to drag it while holding Option or Alt; this makes a copy. Similarly, applying any transformation (scale, shear, move, or rotate) when holding Option or Alt, or by choosing the Copy button instead of OK in their dialog boxes, will also clone the object, applying the transformation to the clone.

④ A faster option is to choose Edit ⇨ Step and Repeat (Option+⌘+U or Ctrl+Alt+U in InDesign CS2, or Option+⌘+V or Ctrl+Alt+V in previous versions) to open the Step and Repeat dialog box. Set the number of copies and the horizontal and/or vertical offset (the distance between copied items), then press OK. InDesign will make the specified number of copies in the specified locations (a distributed copy). But you cannot apply transformations when using the Step and Repeat dialog box, as you can in QuarkXPress's Super Step and Repeat dialog box.

Go Further: InDesign CS2 adds the ability to repeat transformations such as copying and rotating. Choose Object ⇨ Transform ⇨ Repeat (Option+⌘+3 or Ctrl+Alt+3) to repeat the last transformation applied, or choose Object ⇨ Transform ⇨ Repeat Sequence (Option+⌘+4 or Ctrl+Alt+4) to repeat the last sequence of transformations.

❋Applying Corner Effects

Both QuarkXPress and InDesign let you apply fancy corners to your frames, with a set of predefined corners. For any other effects, you'll need to edit the corners yourself with a Bézier tool.

Follow These Steps

To apply corner effects in QuarkXPress, you have two options to apply the four types of corners (square, rounded, beveled, or concave, as shown at upper right):

❶ Initially, create the box using the desired corner style by choosing the appropriate text box or picture box tool — Rectangular, Rounded Rectangle, Beveled, or Concave Corner — from the Tools palette.

❷ Change an existing box's corners by selecting it with the Item or Content tool and choosing Item ➪ Shape and then selecting the desired shape from the submenu.

❸ To change the corner's size for rounded, beveled, or concave corners, change the Corner Radius amount in the Box pane of the Modify dialog box (Item ➪ Modify, or ⌘+M or Ctrl+M). The larger the number, the larger the corner (the more it cuts into the box).

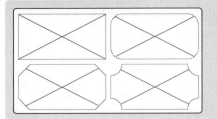

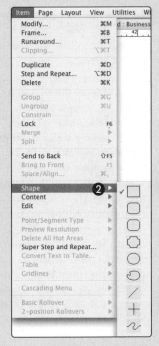

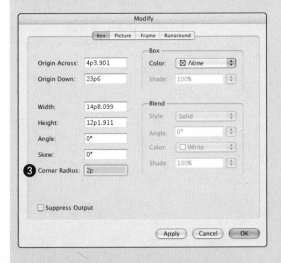

Follow These Steps

In InDesign, you have just one option for applying the six types of corner effects (square, fancy, beveled, inset, inverse rounded, or rounded, as shown at right):

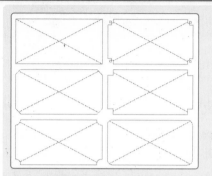

1 Create the shape or frame using the Rectangular Frame, Polygon Frame, Rectangle, Polygon, or Pen tool in the Tools palette, or by placing text or a graphic into your layout.

2 Change the corners of the shape or frame by selecting the shape with the Selection tool and choosing Object ⬄ Corner Effects, and then selecting the desired shape from the Effect menu: None, Fancy, Bevel, Inset, Inverse Rounded, or Rounded.

3 To change the corner's size for all but regular (None) corner effects, change the Size amount in the Corner Effects dialog box. The larger the number, the larger the corner (the more it cuts into the frame).

4 Click OK to apply the corner effect.

Go Further: InDesign lets you apply corner effects to polygon and Bézier frames and shapes, not just rectangular ones.

Changing Frame Shapes

Sometimes you're working on a layout and realize that your objects need to be in a different shape — the rounded frame just doesn't work with the text, or a picture would be better in a triangular frame. QuarkXPress has long had the ability to change box shapes quickly, and InDesign has recently added this ability.

Follow These Steps

1 Select the box with the Item or Content tool.

2 Choose Item ➪ Shape and then select the desired shape from the submenu. If you select the Bézier tool, you can edit the frame's shape to be almost anything you want, such as a polygon or a curved shape. But don't select any of the three line shapes (the bottom three), since doing so will convert your box into a very thin box — not into a line — that will be very difficult to edit.

3 Reshape the box as necessary by dragging its control handles.

 Cross-Reference: For details on editing Bézier shapes, see pages 236-239.

InDesign

Follow These Steps

InDesign CS2 lets you also change a frame's shape, but earlier versions of InDesign do not unless you use the Bézier editing tools. Here's how to quickly change the shape of a frame in InDesign CS2:

❶ Select the frame with the Selection or Direct Selection tool.

❷ Choose Object ➪ Convert Shape and then select the desired shape from the submenu. Select the Polygon or Ellipse option if your goal is to edit the frame's shape into a complex Bézier shape with InDesign's Bézier editing capabilities. Note that if you convert a frame to a line, the contents of the frame will be deleted.

❸ Reshape the frame as necessary by dragging the control handles.

Go Further: InDesign CS2 lets you choose Triangle as a shape option, rather than making you choose Polygon (the equivalent to QuarkXPress's Bézier option) and then editing it into a triangle. Also, InDesign CS2 can convert frames into lines, rather than making them into very thin frames as QuarkXPress does.

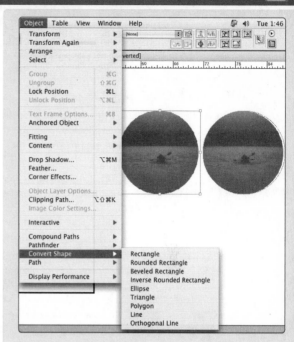

Deleting Objects

QuarkXPress and InDesign provide several ways to delete objects, essentially letting you remove them completely or cut them to the Clipboard for use elsewhere.

Follow These Steps

QuarkXPress offers the following deletion options for items. Use the Item tool to delete the item (box or line); use the Content tool to delete any contents in the box (text or picture) or on a text path:

1. Choose Edit ➪ Cut (⌘+X or Ctrl+X) to delete the item but leave it in the Clipboard, where it will remain available to be pasted until the next time you cut or copy an item. In QuarkXPress 5 or later, you can choose Cut from the contextual menu as well.

2. Choose Edit ➪ Clear (Delete or Backspace) or Item ➪ Delete (⌘+K or Ctrl+K) to remove the item and *not* place it on the Clipboard for later pasting. You can undo a mistaken deletion immediately by choosing Edit ➪ Undo (⌘+Z or Ctrl+Z); QuarkXPress 6 supports multiple levels of undo, so you can repeat the undo command to get to the mistaken deletion.

Follow These Steps

InDesign provides similar deletion option for items. Use the Selection tool to delete the object (frame or line), use the Direct Selection tool to delete any graphics in a graphics frame, or use the Type tool to delete text in a text frame or on a text path:

❶ Choose Edit ➪ Cut (⌘+X or Ctrl+X) to delete the item but leave it in the Clipboard, where it will remain available to be pasted until the next time you cut or copy an item. You can also choose Cut from the contextual menu.

❷ Choose Edit ➪ Clear (Delete or Backspace) to remove the item and not place it on the Clipboard for later pasting. You can undo a mistaken deletion by choosing Edit ➪ Undo (⌘+Z or Ctrl+Z). InDesign supports multiple levels of undo, so you can repeat the undo command to get to the mistaken deletion.

❸ You can drag an item to the Trash Can (Mac) or Recycle Bin (Windows). This has the same effect as choosing Edit ➪ Clear (no copy of the item remains on the Clipboard).

Aligning and Distributing Objects   QuarkXPress

Designers tend to work with the mouse, and this can resulting sloppy placement of objects on a page. Although QuarkXPress and InDesign both let you precisely set objects' size and placement in the Measurements and Control palettes, respectively, as well as use snap-to grids to enable more precise mouse-based sizing and placement, most layouts still have many variances among objects. Although it's no substitute for these precise options, both programs let you align objects, so at least their relative positions are correct. Coupled with other precision tools, these techniques make your layouts extremely precise, yielding optimal results.

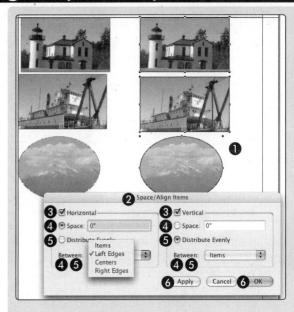

Follow These Steps

After you've created the objects to align:

1 Select the objects with the Item or Content tool.

2 Choose Item ➪ Space/Align (⌘+, or Ctrl+,) to open the Space/Align Items dialog box.

3 Choose the axes along which to align or distribute by checking (or unchecking) the Horizontal and/or Vertical checkboxes.

4 To align objects, select the Space radio button and then choose the appropriate option from the Between pop-up menu.

5 To distribute objects evenly, select the Distribute Evenly button and then choose the appropriate option from the Between pop-up menu.

6 Click Apply to preview the settings. Click OK when done.

InDesign

Follow These Steps

After you've created the objects to align:

1. Select the objects with the Selection or Direct Selection tool. (If you use the Direct Selection tool, InDesign will use the content's rather than the frame's boundaries for its alignment and distribution calculations.)

2. Open the Align pane (Window ⇨ Object & Layout ⇨ Align in InDesign CS2 or Window ⇨ Align in earlier versions; or Shift+F7 in InDesign CS or later, or F8 in InDesign 2).

3. Choose the alignment settings by clicking the appropriate button in the Align Objects section; the icons show the alignment. (These buttons are also available in the InDesign CS2 Control palette.)

4. To distribute objects evenly, select an amount of space from one object's center or specified edge to another's in the Use Spacing field (be sure it is checked) of the Distribute Objects section and click the appropriate button; the button icons show the distribution. These buttons work more like the QuarkXPress Step and Repeat dialog box (see page 264) than like the QuarkXPress Space/Align dialog box. To set spacing more like how QuarkXPress does it, select an amount of space between objects' edges in the Use Spacing field (be sure it is checked) in the Distribute Spacing section and click the appropriate button; again, the icons show the distribution.

Locking Objects

It's easy to inadvertently move or resize an object when you work with the mouse, which is why locking is such a nice feature. Both QuarkXPress and InDesign let you lock objects, but they do so differently.

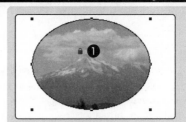

Follow These Steps

To lock items in QuarkXPress:

1 Select the item(s) with the Item or Content tool and choose Item ⇨ Lock (F6). A lock icon will appear on the item when you move the mouse over it.

2 To unlock items, select them and choose Item ⇨ Unlock (F6).

You can still adjust a locked item, but you can't do so with the mouse. To change its settings, select the item and use the Measurements palette, Modify dialog box (Item ⇨ Modify, or ⌘+M or Ctrl+M), or other dialog boxes and palettes. To lock an item so it cannot be changed at all, place it on a locked layer.

Cross-Reference: For more on layers (including how to lock them), see pages 42-43.

Follow These Steps

To lock objects in InDesign:

1. Select the object(s) with the Selection tool and choose Object ➪ Position (⌘+L or Ctrl+L). A lock icon will appear on the object when you try to resize or move it. Also, panes and dialog boxes will have size, position, and related options grayed out.

2. To unlock objects, select them and choose Object ➪ Unlock Position (Option+⌘+L or Ctrl+Alt+L).

Unlike in QuarkXPress, you cannot adjust a locked object's position or size. You'll need to unlock it first. That's because InDesign's Lock Position feature is meant to keep an object from being changed, while QuarkXPress's Lock feature is meant to prevent accidental changes via the mouse.

To prevent any changes to an object, not just those related to size and location, you should place the object on a locked layer.

Making Objects Nonprinting

Layouts often have items not designed to be printed. These could be layout specs, dummy elements, or elements used as grid points. Both QuarkXPress and InDesign let you make objects nonprinting, although their methods and override capabilities differ.

Follow These Steps

To make an item nonprinting in QuarkXPress:

1 Select the item(s) with the Item or Content tool.

2 Go to the Box or Line pane of the Modify dialog box (Item ⇨ Modify, or ⌘+M or Ctrl+M).

3 Check Suppress Output (in QuarkXPress 6) or Suppress Printout (in earlier versions) to keep the box or line from printing.

4 To have QuarkXPress not print pictures but print any frames or backgrounds for the picture box, uncheck Suppress Output (in QuarkXPress 6) or Suppress Printout (in earlier versions) in the Box pane and, instead, check Suppress Picture Output (in QuarkXPress 6) or Suppress Picture Printout (in earlier versions) in the Picture pane.

5 Click OK.

You can also suppress printing for entire layers in QuarkXPress 5 or later. In QuarkXPress 6, you can override layer print suppression in the Print dialog box's Layers pane by checking the Print checkbox for each layer you want to print. This lets you suppress printing but easily override it without having to change your layer settings.

However, you cannot override the individual print suppression set in the Modify dialog box when you print.

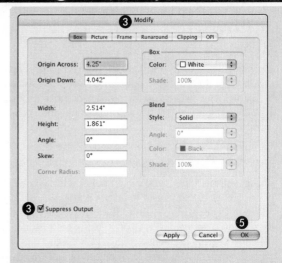

Cross-Reference: For more on layers (including how to make them nonprinting), see pages 42-43.

InDesign

Follow These Steps

To make an object nonprinting in InDesign:

1 Select the object(s) with the Selection or Direct Selection tool. Using the Selection tool will control printing over the frame and its contents, while using the Direct Selection tool will affect just the contents (this is the same as Quark-XPress's Suppress Picture Output or Suppress Picture Print-out options).

2 Open the Attributes pane (Window ⇨ Attributes).

3 Check Nonprinting.

InDesign lets you override objects' nonprinting settings when you print; check Print Non-Printing Objects in the General pane of the Print dialog box to print all objects marked as nonprinting.

InDesign also lets you keep layers from printing by hiding them. Note that there's no way to override hidden layers when you print, as there is in QuarkXPress.

☀ Applying Drop Shadows to Graphics ⟨ **QuarkXPress**

Drop shadows are an elegant way to give objects dimension in your layout. QuarkXPress doesn't offer drop-shadow capabilities, although some third-party XTensions add it, so most QuarkXPress users end up simulating drop shadows. InDesign, by contrast, offers sophisticated drop shadowing.

Follow These Steps

To make a primitive drop shadow in QuarkXPress:

1 Duplicate the item behind which you want to have a drop shadow. Use the Step and Repeat dialog box (see page 264) to quickly and easily place the duplicate item at an appropriate offset distance.

2 Change the background color of the item that will serve as the drop shadow. (If it's a box, remove any pictures by selecting the box with the Content tool and pressing Delete or Backspace; this will keep the file size manageable and will not bog down printing by having the printer work on the obscured picture.)

1

2

 Cross-Reference: See pages 154-155 for details on drop shadows for text.

Keep in Mind

QuarkXPress lets you apply a predefined drop shadow to text (top example below). A quick-and-dirty way to create a custom text drop shadow in QuarkXPress is to duplicate your text frame, change the color of the text (usually to a lighter tint), and position the copy below the original text frame, offset slightly to achieve a drop-shadow effect, as shown in the bottom example below. (This is the same technique suggested above for box drop shadows in QuarkXPress.)

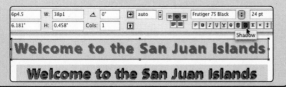

InDesign

Follow These Steps

InDesign offers real drop-shadow capabilities, so its process —
and the results you can achieve — are quite different from what
you get with QuarkXPress:

1. Select the object(s) to apply the drop shadow to.

2. Choose Object ➪ Drop Shadow (Option+⌘+M or
   Ctrl+Alt+M) to open the Drop Shadow dialog box.

3. Check Drop Shadow to enable drop shadows. Check Preview
   to see the effects of your settings before finalizing them.

4. Set the drop shadow's location by entering values in the X
   Offset and Y Offset fields; these coordinates move the drop
   shadow left and down, respectively; negative values move
   in the opposite directions.

5. In the Mode pop-up menu, set the drop shadow's mode
   using one of the 16 lighting effects (called *blend modes*).
   Also, choose the Opacity (transparency) using the Opacity
   field.

6. Set the degree of blur for the drop shadow in the Blur field.
   This sets the change in darkness as the drop shadow extends
   away from the object, simulating a real shadow. Larger values increase the fade distance (lightening the shadow).

7. In InDesign CS2, you can also set the spread and noise
   using the Spread and Noise fields. A higher spread value
   increases the shadow's darkness, essentially counteracting
   the blur. A higher noise value pixelates the drop shadow,
   making it increasingly blotchy.

8. Choose the drop shadow's color by picking a color model in
   the Color pop-up menu and then setting the color using the
   sliders or swatches (determined by the chosen color model).

9. Click OK to apply the settings.

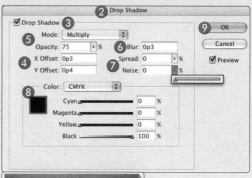

Keep in Mind

If you apply a drop shadow to a text frame, InDesign
will apply the shadow to the text if the frame has no fill
color (see the top example below). If the frame has a fill
color, InDesign will instead apply the shadow to the
frame (see the bottom example below). There is no way
to override this behavior.

Welcome to San Juans Islands

Welcome to San Juans Islands

Go Further: InDesign's drop-shadow
capabilities far surpass QuarkXPress's,
matching the capabilities even of third-party
XTensions for QuarkXPress.

part

X

Working with Output

The ultimate goal of publishing is to create a printed or electronic version for distribution to the audience. This part shows you how to output your documents in InDesign, translating the techniques from QuarkXPress to their InDesign equivalents.

In many ways, the two programs handle output similarly, with some notable differences in the management of color calibration, traps, separations, and inks and plates, as well as significant differences in the output methods for PDF files.

Managing Printer Settings

QuarkXPress

Different printers naturally have different settings, including many settings that you may need to tweak if you use more than one printer and switch among them. Both QuarkXPress and InDesign let you save printer settings — similar to style sheets for text or swatches for colors — for easy reuse.

Follow These Steps

In QuarkXPress, it's critical that you define print styles *before* you need them — you can't change settings in the Print dialog box and then decide to save them for use again later.

Defining Print Styles

1. Choose Edit ⇨ Print Styles to open the Print Styles dialog box.
2. Click New to create a new print style.
3. In the Edit Print Style dialog box, give the style a name, and go through each pane to set up your preferred options for that printer.
4. Click OK when done.
5. You can now define (or edit or delete) another print style by clicking the appropriate buttons in the Print Styles dialog box. You can also export print styles to files for other users to import, as well as import print styles created by other users.
6. Click Save to save any new and changed print styles.

Using Print Styles

1. To use print styles, select them in the Print Style pop-up menu in the Print dialog box (File ⇨ Print, or ⌘+P or Ctrl+P). Note that a bullet (·) will appear in front of the print style name if you change any of its settings in the Print dialog box.

Cross-Reference: The rest of Part X covers most of the settings available for print styles.

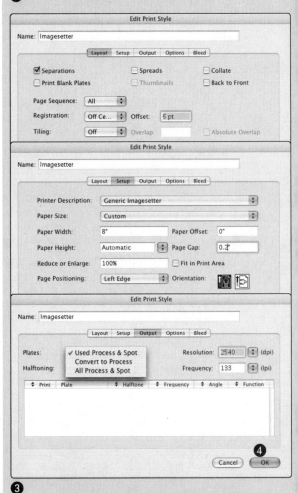

InDesign

Follow These Steps

InDesign lets you create printer presets before you print or while you are printing.

Defining Presets before You Print

To create printer presets in InDesign before you print:

1. Choose File ➪ Print Presets ➪ New to open the Print Presets dialog box. (Note that InDesign 2 uses the phrase "printer style" or "style" in its menus and dialog boxes rather than "print preset" or "preset.")

2. Click New to create a new print preset.

3. In the New Print Preset dialog box, give the preset a name, and go through each pane to set up your preferred options for that printer.

4. Click OK when done.

5. You can now define (or edit or delete) another print preset by clicking the appropriate buttons in the Print Presets dialog box. You can also save (export) print presets to files for other users to import, as well as load (import) print presets created by other users.

6. Click OK to save any new and changed print presets.

Defining Presets While Printing

To create print presets when in the Print dialog box (File ➪ Print, or ⌘+P or Ctrl+P):

1. Set the output settings as needed.

2. Click Save Preset.

3. Give the print preset a name and click OK to save it.

Using Printer Presets

No matter if you define printer presets before or during printing, here's how you apply them:

1. Select the desired preset in the Print Style pop-up menu in the Print dialog box (File ➪ Print, or ⌘+P or Ctrl+P). Note that the print preset name will change to [Custom] if you change any of its settings in the Print dialog box.

Go Further: InDesign is more flexible than Quark-XPress in defining printer presets — you define them ahead of time or you can save them after making changes in the Print dialog box.

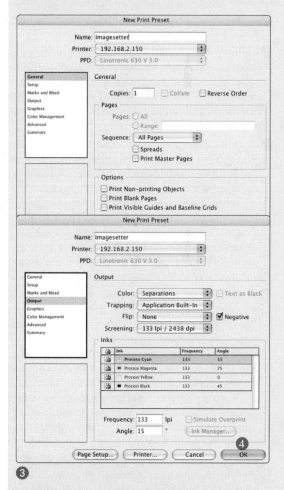

❋ Setting Bleeds and Crops

When you print to an imagesetter, you need to account for important aspects of your document. In addition to the printed portion of the page that the reader sees, the page size needs to be large enough to accommodate bleeds and crop marks. QuarkXPress and InDesign differ in how they handle bleeds, but they are similar in how they handle crop marks.

Follow These Steps

QuarkXPress handles both bleed and crop-mark settings in its Print dialog box:

❶ Choose File ➪ Print (⌘+P or Ctrl+P) to open the Print dialog box.

❷ Go to the Layout pane in QuarkXPress 6, or to the Document pane in earlier versions, to enable crop marks. In that pane, choose Centered or Off Center from the Registration pop-up menu. If you choose Off Center, in the Offset field specify the distance between the crop marks and the page edge.

❸ Go to the Bleed pane to set up bleed settings. In Quark-XPress 5 and later, choose Asymmetric or Symmetric from the Bleed Type pop-up menu. If you choose Symmetric, set the bleed size in the Amount field; if you choose Asymmetric, set the bleed sizes for each side separately in the Top, Left, Right, and Bottom fields. (In QuarkXPress 4, choose Custom from the Bleed Type pop-up menu and set the bleed amount for each side.) Check Clip to Bleed Limits to prevent output of anything beyond the bleed area (this will slightly speed up printing).

❹ In the Setup pane, make sure that the paper size is large enough to accommodate the crop marks and bleed area. You may have to choose a custom page size or a larger paper size to fit everything: Either choose a larger paper size from the Paper Size pop-up menu or, for imagesetters and similar devices, by entering the Paper Width and Paper Height values. You may also need to set the Page Gap to place space between pages on an imagesetter and perhaps rotate the page or change the Page Positioning pop-up menu's settings, as directed by your service bureau or production manager. (Be sure that your output device can handle the paper size and related settings that you've chosen.)

❺ Preview the output in the Preview pane; it will show whether the bleed and crop marks will fit within the current page size.

❻ When all print settings have been made, click Print to print.

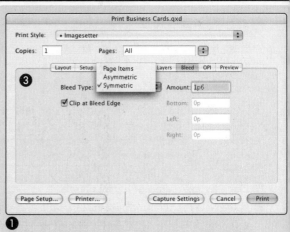

InDesign

Follow These Steps

InDesign sets the bleed area as part of the document setup, while also letting you change it and the crop marks in the Print dialog box. You can also set the slug area (where the crop marks and similar information is placed). Note that slug controls are available only in InDesign CS and later.

❶ When you create a new document, you can set the bleed and slug settings in the New Document dialog box (File ➪ New ➪ Document, or ⌘+N or Ctrl+N), or you can do so later in the Document Setup dialog box (File ➪ Document Setup, or Option+⌘+P or Ctrl+Alt+P). You may need to click the More Options button to see these settings.

❷ You can also set document bleed settings, overriding any set in your document, in the Marks and Bleed pane of the Print dialog box (File ➪ Print, or ⌘+P or Ctrl+P). (In InDesign 2, you set the bleed settings in the Marks & Bleed pane of the Print dialog box; you cannot set the bleed when you create a new document or via the Document Setup dialog box.) You also determine whether to include the slug area defined in the New Document or Document Setup dialog box by checking the Include Slug Area checkbox.

❸ To set crop marks, go to the Marks and Bleed pane of the Print dialog box. Check the marks you want output; check All Printer's Marks to have all of them print. You can also set the weight and offset amounts for the crop marks. (The Type pop-up menu has only one option — Default — so you may ignore this setting.)

❹ In the Setup pane, make sure that the paper size is large enough to accommodate the crop marks and bleed area. InDesign offers several custom sizes, such as Letter.Extra and Letter.Extra.Transverse to help you do so. You may have to define your own page size by choosing Custom from the Paper Size pop-up menu and entering values in the Width and Height fields. You may also need to set the Gap to place space between pages on an imagesetter and perhaps rotate the page (check Transverse) or change the Page Positioning pop-up menu's settings, as directed by your service bureau or production manager. (Be sure that your output device can handle the paper size and related settings that you've chosen.)

❺ Preview the output in the lower left of any pane in the Print dialog box to make sure that everything will fit.

❻ When all print settings have been made, click Print to print.

 Go Further: InDesign is more flexible than Quark-XPress in defining bleeds and slugs — you can define them ahead of time or you set them when printing.

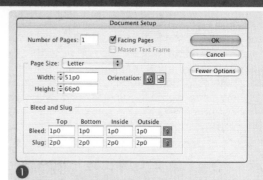
❶

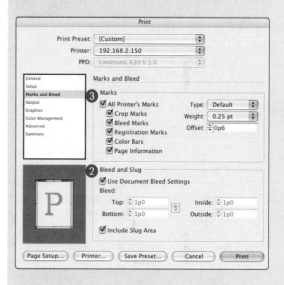

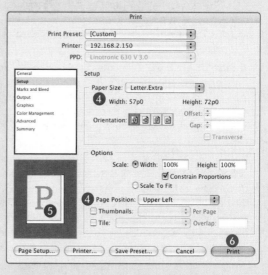

Controlling Color Screens

When printing color plates, you normally use the default screen angles for the four process (CMYK) colors — the screen angles are offset from each other so that each color's dots are visible, letting them then combine in the reader's eye as natural colors. However, if you are working with multiple spot colors, you may need to change these CMYK-optimized defaults. (Be sure to consult with your service bureau or production manager first.)

Follow These Steps

QuarkXPress lets you change the screen angle for individual color plates — including the standard process colors (cyan, magenta, yellow, and black) — as follows:

① For spot colors, choose what **CMYK** color plate screening angle QuarkXPress uses when you define the color (Edit ➪ Colors or Shift+F12). Select the plate in the Halftone pop-up menu. If you are printing spot colors that by and large don't overlap other colors, the plate angle doesn't matter. If there will be repeated overlap, select a color that the spot color is unlikely to overlap.

② For both spot and process colors, you override the default screening angle in the Output pane of the Print dialog box (File ➪ Print, or ⌘+P or Ctrl+P). Select the desired color, then click the pop-up menu at the top of the Angle column. Choose Custom from the pop-up menu and enter a new angle in the resulting dialog box.

③ You can change the screening frequency — higher numbers make for finer dots and thus more natural-looking images — for all plates by entering a new value in the Frequency field. You can also specify separate frequencies for individual colors by selecting the desired plate in the Output pane and then clicking the the pop-up menu at the top of the Frequency column.

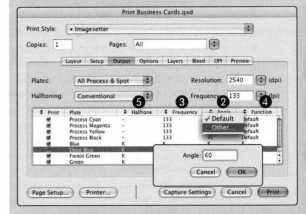

④ You can change the element (function) that makes up the dots in photographs the same way: select the color and then choose the pop-up menu at the top of the Function column to select from Dot, Line, Square, Ellipse, and Tridot. You can also choose Default to use the printer's default element (usually a dot).

⑤ Finally, you can set a spot color to take on the settings of one of the process colors, including any overrides applied to that process color, by selecting the color and then choosing the pop-up menu at the top of the Halftone column to select a different plate (cyan, magenta, or yellow; the default is black). You can still modify the Angle, Frequency, and/or Function settings after choosing a different Halftone setting.

InDesign

Follow These Steps

InDesign also lets you change the screen angle for individual color plates — including the standard process colors (cyan, magenta, yellow, and black) — as follows:

❶ For both spot and process colors, you override the default screening angle in the Output pane of the Print dialog box (File ⇨ Print, or ⌘+P or Ctrl+P). To change the screen angle, select the desired color in the Inks section and then enter a new value in the Angle field.

❷ You can also change the screening frequency — higher numbers make for finer dots and thus more natural-looking images — for all plates by choosing a new value in the Screening pop-up menu field. You can also specify separate frequencies for individual colors by selecting the desired plate in the Inks section pane and then entering a new value in the Frequency field.

❸ Finally, you can set a spot color to take on the settings of one of the process colors, including any overrides applied to that process color. When defining or editing colors (choose New Color Swatch or Swatch Options from the palette menu of the Swatches pane [Window ⇨ Swatches or F5]) or when printing (in the Output pane of the Print dialog box), select the color and then choose the process color to use as the default for its settings from the Ink Alias pop-up menu.

Workaround: By default, all spot colors are set to 45°, the standard setting for black ink. Unlike in QuarkXPress, in InDesign you cannot specify a default screen angle for spot colors when you define them. Instead, you'll need to override them when you print. There is no way to adjust the halftone or element (function) settings in InDesign as there is in QuarkXPress.

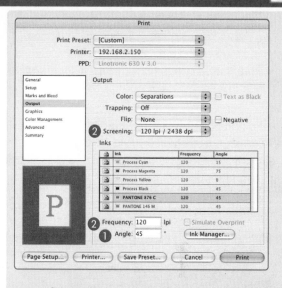

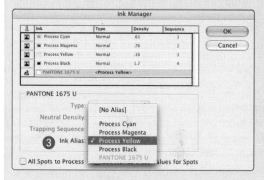

☀ Managing Color Separations

Color separations can be frustrating to output correctly. For example, colors may be defined as spot colors even though they need to be color-separated. QuarkXPress and InDesign provide similar controls to set separation options, both when creating and printing colors.

Follow These Steps

To manage color separations in QuarkXPress:

① When you create or edit colors (Edit ⇨ Colors or Shift+F12), you can set them as spot colors or as process colors. By default they are process colors; check Spot Color to make them spot colors, which means that each color prints on its own plate if you output the document as color separations.

② You decide which plates to print in the Output pane of the Print dialog box (File ⇨ Print, or ⌘+P or Ctrl+P). Uncheck any plates that you do not want to print.

③ You can also have QuarkXPress convert all spot colors to process colors by choosing Convert to Process from the Plates pop-up menu. In QuarkXPress 5 and later, you can also choose Used Process & Spot to output plates only for spot colors actually used in the document, as well as the four process colors, thus eliminating the output of blank plates for each unused spot color.

Remember that the Separations checkbox must be checked in the Layout pane (in QuarkXPress 6) or Document pane (in earlier versions) of the Print dialog box to enable these controls over color separation.

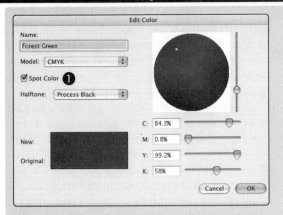

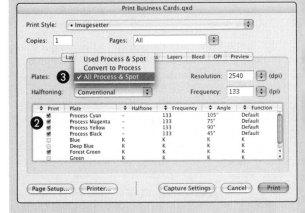

![InDesign]

Follow These Steps

To manage color separations in InDesign:

❶ When you create or edit colors (choose New Color Swatch or Swatch Options from the palette menu of the Swatches pane [Window ➪ Swatches or F5]), you can set them as spot colors or as process colors. By default they are process colors; choose Process or Spot as appropriate in the Color Type pop-up menu. (Note that InDesign will default to whatever type was chosen for the previously defined color.)

❷ You decide which plates to print in the Output pane of the Print dialog box (File ➪ Print, or ⌘+P or Ctrl+P). Uncheck any plates that you do not want to print; the printer icon will disappear.

❸ You can also have InDesign convert all spot colors to process colors by clicking Ink Manager to open the Ink Manager dialog box. Then check All Spots to Process. You can also convert individual spot colors to process (or change them back) by clicking the icon to the left of the color name; a circle-in-square icon indicates a spot color, while the four-triangle icon indicates a process color.

Remember that the Color pop-up menu must be set to Separations or In-RIP Separations in the Output pane of the Print dialog box to enable these controls over color separation.

Watch Out: InDesign has no equivalent to QuarkXPress's Used Process & Spot option to output plates only for spot colors actually used, as well as the four process colors. So be careful that all unused spot-color plates are unchecked when you output separations. Otherwise, you will output blank negatives or plates for each unused spot color — an expensive proposition for longer documents.

Go Further: InDesign's Ink Manager's aliasing feature lets you control the ink density when printing, which lets you accommodate the peculiarities of your printing press and inks. See page 363 for details.

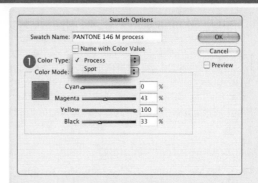

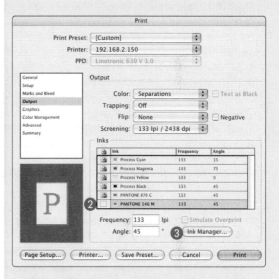

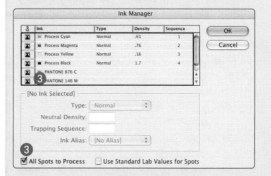

Defining Color Traps

Color traps — the management of overlap of colored objects to account for the slight shifting of color plates during printing that can otherwise lead to white gaps where colors should abut — can be tricky to manage, which is why, in most cases, you should stick with the defaults in QuarkXPress and InDesign. But if you need to change color traps, both programs offer basic trapping capabilities.

Follow These Steps

You set up the trap settings as documentwide preferences:

① Open the Trapping pane of the Preferences dialog box. (In QuarkXPress 6, choose QuarkXPress ▷ Preferences on the Mac or Edit ▷ Preferences in Windows; in QuarkXPress 5, choose Edit ▷ Preferences ▷ Preferences; and in Quark-XPress 4, choose Edit ▷ Preferences ▷ Document. Quark-XPress 5 and 6 use the same shortcut, Option+Shift+⌘+Y or Ctrl+Alt+Shift+Y, while QuarkXPress 4 uses ⌘+Y or Ctrl+Y.)

② Choose a trapping method: Absolute, Proportional, or Knockout All. Absolute uses the values specified in the pane, while Proportional modifies those values on a case-by-case basis in which more saturated colors get more trapping overlap and lighter colors get less. The Knockout All setting essentially disables trapping.

③ Determine which colors are trapped by checking or unchecking Process Trapping (which applies trapping to the four process colors) and Ignore White (which doesn't bother to trap to white since there is no danger of gaps due to misregistration).

④ Set the trap values in the Auto Amount and Indeterminate fields. Auto Amount controls the trapping overlap for solid colors, while Indeterminate controls the trap for multicolor objects, such as gradients and photographs.

⑤ Set boundaries in trapping by entering values in the Knockout Limit and Overprint Limit fields. The former determines whether light colors are knocked out (a value higher than 0) or just actual whites (a value of 0); the latter determines how dark a color is before it simply overprints rather than being trapped (95% is the default).

⑥ You can set the trap values for individual colors as well. In the Colors dialog box (Edit ▷ Colors or F12), select a color and then click Edit Trap. In the resulting Trap Specifications dialog box, you can set the trap settings from the current color to another color. Click that other color in the list, then choose the trap type in the Trap pop-up menu at the top of the column. Use the Reverse column to set traps from that other color to the current color. Normally, the same trap settings are used in both directions, but you can set them to be different by choosing Independent Traps (↵⌐↑) in the Trap Direction (↵?↑) pop-up menu.

①

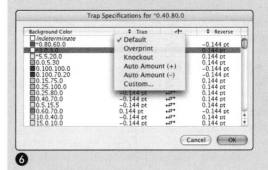

⑥

Follow These Steps

InDesign sets its trap settings through a different approach than QuarkXPress, specifying traps for ranges of pages rather than across the document. The capabilities also differ.

① Create a trap preset by choosing Window ➪ Output ➪ Trap Presets in InDesign CS2, Window ➪ Trap Presets in InDesign CS, or Window ➪ Trap Styles in InDesign 2 to open the Trap Presets pane, then click New Preset in the palette menu. This opens the New Trap Preset dialog box.

② Text and vector graphics are always trapped, but InDesign lets you choose the trap approach for bitmapped images by checking (or unchecking) Trap Objects to Images, Trap Images to Images, Trap Images Internally (avoid this option, since it can muddy photographs by trapping individual pixels throughout the image), and Trap 1-Bit Images (monochrome images). You also set the trap's placement, using the Trap Placement pop-up menu. This determines how the trap is placed relative to the image's edge; selecting Choke could cause the abutting object to intrude too much into the image, while the other three options (Center, Spread, and Neutral Density) reduce that possibility.

③ Set the trap appearance by choosing options from the Join Style and End Style pop-up menus in the Trap Appearance section. Your choices are Miter, Round, and Bevel, which work just like stroke corners (see page 245) and handle traps at corners of abutting objects.

④ Set the trap values in the Default and Black fields. InDesign provides by default a bigger trapping overlap for black than it does for other colors, which could be problematic if you have lots of very thin lines or strokes.

⑤ Set boundaries in trapping by entering values in the Trap Thresholds section. Black Color works like QuarkXPress's Overprint Limit field, except it's just for black ink; Black Density acts like Overprint Limit for other colors. Step determines how different the color saturation should be before trapping is engaged, while Sliding Trap acts like QuarkXPress's Proportional trapping method and lets you specify at what saturation difference to start adjusting the trapping overlap. Trap Color Reduction limits the saturation level for overlapping colors; to prevent bleedthrough, choose a lower value if most of your objects are dark colors.

⑥ You can set the trap values for individual colors as well. In the Swatches pane (Window ➪ Swatches or F5), select a color and then click Ink Manager from the palette menu. In the resulting Ink Manager dialog box, you can set the trap order for each color and also the trap type (Normal traps the color, Transparent overprints it, Opaque traps only the edges, and Opaque Ignore traps nothing).

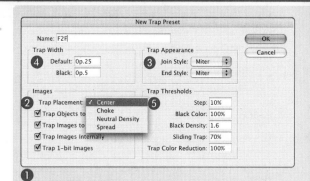

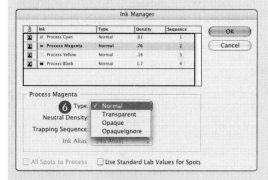

☀️Working with Color Traps

With color traps defined, QuarkXPress lets you apply the traps to specific objects, while InDesign lets you apply traps to specific pages.

Follow These Steps

You can override traps for selected objects in QuarkXPress as follows:

1️⃣ Select the object using the Item tool or Content tool as appropriate (for example, select a box with the Item tool to adjust the trap for its frame and background, but select a box or text with the Content tool to adjust the trap for the contents).

2️⃣ Open the Trap Information palette by choosing Window ⇨ Show Trap Information in QuarkXPress 6 or View ⇨ Show Trap Information in earlier versions, or press Option+F12 or Ctrl+F12.

3️⃣ The adjustable items will be in black, while other options will be grayed out. Initially, the items will be set at Default, and the settings will be displayed at their left. If desired, click the 🛈 button in QuarkXPress 5 or later, or the **?** button in QuarkXPress 4, to get a more detailed explanation of the current trap settings.

4️⃣ Select the trap options from the available pop-up menus. your choices are Default, Overprint, Knockout, Auto Amount (+), Auto Amount (–), and Custom (where you enter a value in the field at right).

Cross-Reference: See pages 290-291 for details on how to set up traps and what the various settings mean.

Follow These Steps

You can override traps for selected objects in InDesign in two ways: by forcing strokes and/or fills for specific objects to over-print and by applying trap presets to a range of pages.

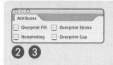

① Select the object using the Selection or Direct Selection tool; select text with the Type tool.

② Open the Attributes palette by choosing Window ⇨ Attrib-utes.

③ The adjustable items will be in black, while other options will be grayed out. Check Overprint Fill, Overprint Stroke, and/or Overprint Gap (available in InDesign CS or later) to overprint those elements rather than trap them.

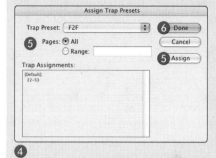

④ To apply a trap preset to one or more pages, open the Trap Presets dialog box (Window ⇨ Output ⇨ Trap Presets in InDesign CS2, Window ⇨ Trap Presets in InDesign CS, or Window ⇨ Trap Styles in InDesign 2) to open the Trap Pre-sets pane, then click Assign Trap Preset in the palette menu. This opens the Assign Trap Presets dialog box.

⑤ Select the desired preset from the Trap Preset pop-up menu, then enter a range of pages in the Range field or select the All radio button to apply the preset to all pages. Click Assign. You can apply a different preset to other pages by repeating this step.

⑥ Click Done when finished assigning trap presets.

Setting Color Calibration Rules

QuarkXPress

Color calibration is a tricky area in which software tries to automatically adjust objects' colors to help them print accurately despite the differences between the physics and chemistry of the output device and the original creation device. The more tools through which images pass, the greater the chance that such calibration will misjudge the original intent, which is why both QuarkXPress and InDesign give you control over some of those calibration assumptions.

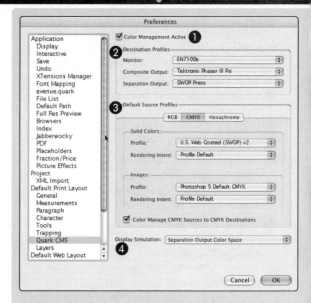

Follow These Steps

Note that QuarkXPress 4, 5, and 6 vary in their dialog boxes and some options for color management, although the fundamentals are the same:

① Turn color management on by checking Color Management Active in the Quark CMS pane (in QuarkXPress 6) or Color Management Preferences pane (in earlier versions). In QuarkXPress 6, choose QuarkXPress ⇨ Preferences on the Mac or Edit ⇨ Preferences in Windows, or press Option+Shift+⌘+Y or Ctrl+Alt+Shift+Y, then go to the Quark CMS pane. In QuarkXPress 4 or 5, choose Edit ⇨ Preferences ⇨ Color Management.

② Choose the destination profiles (what the calibration should be targeting) for the monitor, proofing printer (composite output), and separations printer (imagesetter output) in the Destination Profiles section. This will minimize differences between what you see onscreen and what you print to both your proof printer and your imagesetter.

③ Choose the source profiles (what most objects were created in, so QuarkXPress knows what color issues to take into account based on the specifics of those devices) in the Default Source Profile section. You'll see a separate subpane each for RGB, CMYK, and Hexachrome; click on the tabs to switch among them. There are also two subsections for these subpanes: Solid Colors (for objects created in Quark-XPress, Adobe Illustrator, and other illustration software) and Images (for photographs and other bitmapped images from scanners, digital cameras, and software such as Adobe Photoshop). QuarkXPress 5 or later lets you set both the profile and the rendering intent, which controls the color saturation: Perceptual is typically used for photographs, while the others are used for charts and other objects composed mainly of solid colors.

④ If you want, have QuarkXPress change the monitor appearance to simulate either the composite or separation color space (monitors can display a greater range of colors than most printers).

InDesign

Follow These Steps

InDesign provides similar options to those in QuarkXPress for setting up color calibration, although InDesign offers a few additional options:

1 Color management is always on in InDesign CS2; in earlier versions, turn color management on by checking Enable Color Management in the Color Settings dialog box (Edit ⇨ Color Settings). In all versions, use this dialog box to set color calibration defaults.

2 You can pick a predefined set of calibration settings by choosing an option from the Settings pop-up menu. Or you can choose the settings individually, as described in steps 3 through 5.

3 Set up the working spaces (the equivalent to QuarkXPress's destination profiles) using the RGB and CMYK pop-up menus. This tells InDesign how to manage output to both printers and monitors (you do not enable or disable these individually as in QuarkXPress).

4 In InDesign, you do not choose default source profiles as you do in QuarkXPress. Instead, you use the RGB and CMYK pop-up menus in the Color Management Policies section to have InDesign use the graphics' embedded profiles, to override them to match your Working Spaces settings, or to turn off color management for the selected color type. In InDesign CS2, you have the additional option in the CMYK pop-up menu of simply passing through the CMYK values, which ignores any embedded profiles but lets inDesign color-manage the colors based on the CMYK values.

5 If Advanced Mode is checked, you will see the Conversion Options section. Here, you choose the color-calibration engine (the choices will vary between Mac and Windows) and the rendering intent for objects whose colors are converted to the working spaces. You can also check Black Point Compensation, which helps make dark grays and blacks print more accurately.

Go Further: Compared to QuarkXPress, InDesign offers several extra functions, including black-point compensation and the ability to control whether color profiles are checked during import.

InDesign CS2 also lets you apply the same color calibration settings to all your Adobe Creative Suite 2 applications, so graphics are color-managed consistently. Open the Adobe Bridge application and choose Edit ⇨ Creative Suite Color Settings. Then choose one of the color-calibration sets (these match the options in the Settings pop-up menu of InDesign CS2's Color Settings dialog box) to apply the set to all installed CS2 programs.

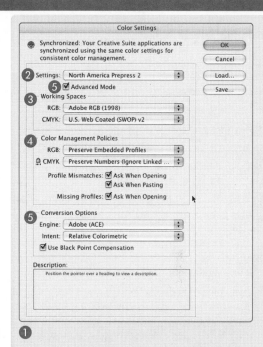

Applying Color Calibration to Objects

WIth color management enabled and the defaults set, both QuarkXPress and InDesign let you apply specific color profiles to objects on an object-by-object basis.

Follow These Steps

If color management is active, you can control the application of color profiles to specific pictures, both when you import them and after they are imported:

1 When you import pictures (File ➪ Get Picture, or ⌘+E or Ctrl+E), select a profile and/or rendering intent to override whatever profile is embedded in the picture by using the Profile and Rendering Intent pop-up menus in the Color Management subpane. (Note that QuarkXPress 4 does not let you set the rendering intent.)

2 After a picture has been imported, you can change its profile and/or rendering intent by selecting it and new settings from the Profile and Rendering Intent pop-up menus in the Profile Information palette (Window ➪ Show Profile Information in QuarkXPress 6, or View ➪ Show Profile Information in earlier versions). You can also disable color management for that picture by unchecking Color Manage. (Note that QuarkXPress 4 does not let you set the rendering intent.)

3 When printing, you can change the target for color calibration in the Profiles pane of the print dialog box (File ➪ Print, or ⌘+P or Ctrl+P). Choose a different target from the Separation and/or Composite pop-up menus. This doesn't change the profiles for specific graphics but does change how the objects are printed based on comparing those profiles to the output device's new profile.

 Cross-Reference: For details on enabling color management and setting default options, see pages 294-295.

1

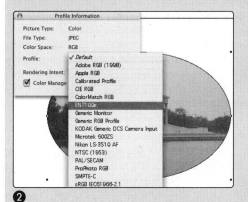

2

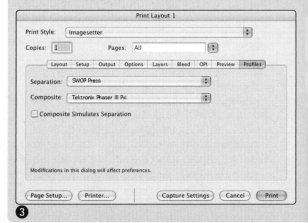

3

InDesign

Follow These Steps

InDesign also lets you set color calibration profiles both during and after import:

❶ When you import graphics (File ⇨ Place, or ⌘+D or Ctrl+D), check Show Import Options in the Place dialog box. Choose the graphic to import and click OK. You will see the Import Options dialog box (or a variation of it) that includes the Color pane. Go to that pane to select a profile and/or rendering intent to override whatever profile is embedded in the picture by using the Profile and Rendering Intent pop-up menus.

❷ After a graphic has been imported, you can change its profile and/or rendering intent by selecting it and new settings from the Profile and Rendering Intent pop-up menus in the Image Color Settings dialog box (Object ⇨ Image Color Settings).

❸ When printing, you can change the target for color calibration in the Color Management pane of the print dialog box (File ⇨ Print, or ⌘+P or Ctrl+P). Choose a different target from the Printer Profile pop-up menu. This doesn't change the profiles for specific graphics but does change how the objects are printed based on comparing those profiles to the output device's new profile.

Go Further: Unlike QuarkXPress, InDesign will check to see if graphics have modified or missing color profiles each time you open a document unless you disable this automatic check, as described on page 295.

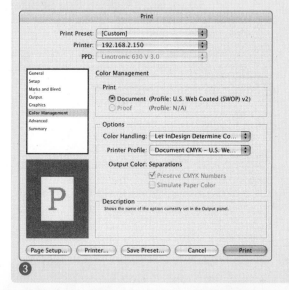

■Packaging Documents for Service Bureaus

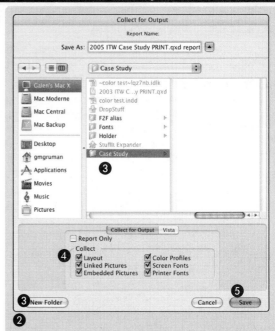

When you're finished with a document, you may need to provide it to a service bureau, production department, or perhaps another layout artist. Copying the layout file is insufficient since graphics, fonts, and other elements are typically needed for output or further work. Both Quark-XPress and InDesign provide similar tools for gathering all these required elements into one location.

Follow These Steps

To gather all the needed files into one place in QuarkXPress:

① Save your document (File ➪ Save, or ⌘+S or Ctrl+S).

② Choose File ➪ Collect for Output to open the Collect for Output dialog box. (If QuarkXPress detects any missing or modified elements, it will notify you and give you the option of canceling.)

③ Navigate to the folder where you want to place the files. You can also click New Folder to create a new folder in which to place them.

④ Decide what elements you want collected by checking the appropriate checkboxes. If you want only a report of the layout's font, picture, profile, and XTension usage, check Report Only. The other options will vary based on the version of QuarkXPress you are using:

- Version 6.5: Layout, Linked Pictures, Embedded Pictures (this creates files for each of them), Color Profiles, Screen Fonts, Printer Fonts, and, in the Vista subpane, Render Picture Alterations.

- Versions 5.0, 6.0, and 6.1: Layout, Linked Pictures, Embedded Pictures (this creates files for each of them), Color Profiles, Screen Fonts, and Printer Fonts.

- Versions 4.0 and 4.1: These versions offer no options; the layout, linked pictures, and color profiles are collected.

⑤ Click Save to begin the collection process.

InDesign

Follow These Steps

To gather all the needed files into one place in InDesign:

1 Save your document (File ⇨ Save, or ⌘+S or Ctrl+S).

2 Choose File ⇨ Package (Option+Shift+⌘+P or Ctrl+Alt+Shift+P) to open the Package dialog box. (If InDesign detects any missing or modified elements, it will notify you and give you the option of canceling.) You may then see a dialog box similar to that in step **4** the first time you package a document.

3 You will then see the Instructions dialog box, in which you can enter instructions for the service bureau if desired. Whether or not you enter instructions, click Continue.

4 Navigate to the folder where you want to place the files. You can also click New Folder to create a new folder in which to place them.

5 Decide which elements you want collected and check the appropriate checkboxes. The options are Copy Fonts (Except CJK) in InDesign CS2 and Copy Fonts (Roman Only) in earlier versions, Copy Linked Graphics, Update Graphic Links in Package, Use Document Hyphenation Exceptions Only, Include Fonts and Links from Hidden Document Layers, and View Report. The Copy Fonts (Except CJK)/Copy Fonts (Roman Only) option prevents the copying of Chinese, Japanese, and Korean (CJK) fonts, which tend to be very expensive. The View Report option displays a report of fonts, pictures, profiles, plug-ins, and other elements used in the document; the report is packaged with the other files whether or not you view it.

6 Click Save, and InDesign will begin gathering all the needed files.

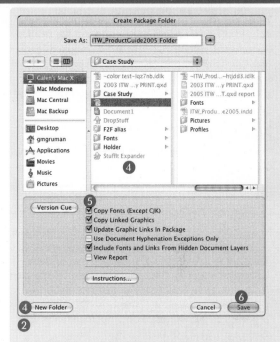

☀ Exporting PDF Files

Whether you post them on the Web or intranet site or deliver them to service bureaus to use for printing your documents, Adobe PDF files are a standard form of output. QuarkXPress and InDesign both provide PDF export options, although InDesign's PDF output is better integrated with Adobe Acrobat and other PDF tools.

Follow These Steps

The process for PDF exports differs based on the version of QuarkXPress you use.

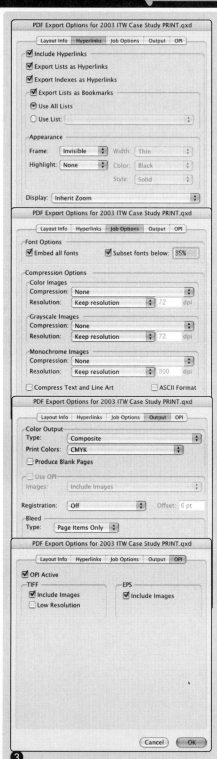

Exporting PDFs from QuarkXPress 5 or 6

To create PDF files from your documents in QuarkXPress 5 or 6:

① In QuarkXPress 6, make sure that the desired layout in a multilayout project is displayed onscreen and then choose Export ⇨ Layout as PDF. In QuarkXPress 5, choose Export ⇨ Document as PDF. This opens the Export as PDF dialog box. Note that you must have Adobe Acrobat Distiller installed to be able to export documents to PDF format in Quark-XPress 5; QuarkXPress 6 does not require Distiller.

② Navigate to the folder where you want to place the files. You can also click New Folder to create a new folder in which to place them.

③ Click Options to set up your PDF export settings in the various panes. The first, Layout Info in QuarkXPress 6 and Document Info in QuarkXPress 5, is where you enter comments, title, and author information. The other four panes are shown at right (QuarkXPress 5 does not have the OPI pane). Click OK when done.

④ If you want spreads output as single pages, rather than as separate pages, check Spreads. In the Pages field, enter the pages you want to export (type **All** for all pages).

⑤ Click Save to create the PDF file.

Exporting PDFs from QuarkXPress 4

To create PDF files in QuarkXPress 4, first install the free PDF Filter XTension from www.quark.com. Then follow these steps:

① Choose File ⇨ Print (⌘+P or Ctrl+P).

② On the Mac, click the Printer button, then choose File in the Destination pop-up menu. Now choose Save as File from the unnamed pop-up menu below the Printer pop-up menu, and set the output options that appear. Click Save to create the PDF file.

In Windows, choose Adobe PDF or PDF-XChange 2.5 DE from the Printer pop-up menu. Click Properties to set the PDF export options and click OK. Click Print to create the PDF file.

③

InDesign

Follow These Steps

To create PDF files from your documents in InDesign (no matter the version):

1. Choose File ⇨ Export (⌘+E or Ctrl+E), then select Adobe PDF in the Format pop-up menu.

2. Navigate to the folder where you want to place the files. You can also click New Folder to create a new folder in which to place them.

3. Click Save, which opens the Export Adobe PDF dialog box.

4. Choose a PDF/X standard, if desired, from the Standard pop-up menu, as well as the Acrobat version in the Compatibility pop-up menu that you want the file saved as. You can also open a predefined set of PDF export options via the Adobe PDF Preset pop-up menu in InDesign CS2, the Preset pop-up menu in InDesign CS, or the Style pop-up menu in InDesign 2.

5. Set up your PDF export settings in the various panes. InDesign CS2 has one more pane than InDesign CS and earlier: Output, which handles color conversion and PDF/X options.

6. You can save these settings to use later by clicking Save Preset in InDesign CS and later and Save Style in InDesign 2.

7. Click Export to create the PDF file.

Go Further: InDesign lets you save PDF export options as preset files, making it easy to generate consistent PDF files for all sorts of documents. The only way to accomplish this in QuarkXPress is to print a PostScript file and then use Adobe Acrobat Distiller to convert it to a PDF file, choosing a job options file to regulate the PDF export. (QuarkXPress's PDF Filter XTension will save some PDF export settings, but it does not provide the complete customization that Distiller's job-option files provide.)

InDesign also lets you set security settings for your PDF documents, plus specify the Acrobat version to create the file in and, in InDesign CS and later, the type of PDF/X compatibility desired for the file (useful for print production).

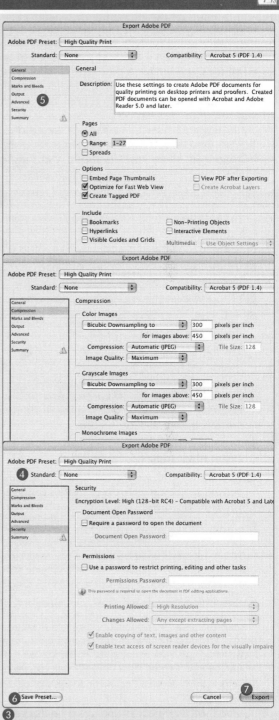

❊Using Documents on the Web

Publishers increasingly are repurposing print content for the Web, treating content as a resource for multiple media. QuarkXPress 5 and 6 let you create and save HTML files, and version 6 even lets you convert a print layout to a Web one. QuarkXPress's Web capabilities are weak but can be the first step in print-to-Web conversion. InDesign 2 can export print layouts to HTML format, but InDesign CS and CS2 limit you to exporting only to Adobe's GoLive Web authoring tool. QuarkXPress and InDesign both let you save layouts as XML files for use in sophisticated content-management systems, but this usually requires a complex production process.

Follow These Steps

To create an HTML file from a print layout in QuarkXPress 6:

❶ Choose Layout ➪ Layout Properties to open the Layout Properties dialog box.

❷ Choose Web from the Layout Type pop-up menu.

❸ Change the page width and link colors if desired. You can also set a background image. Click OK when done.

❹ The Web Tools palette will appear to let you create buttons, menus, and rollovers. You can also create hyperlinks using the Hyperlinks palette (Window ➪ Hyperlinks) in both print and Web layouts (for use in PDF and HTML files) and set up cascading style sheets by choosing Edit ➪ CSS Font Families. Modify your layout as needed.

❺ To create an HTML file, choose Export ➪ HTML to open the Export HTML dialog box.

❻ Navigate to the folder where you want to place the files. You can also click New Folder to create a new folder in which to place them.

❼ Choose HTML, XHTML 1.1, or XSLT 1.0 in the Export As pop-up menu. You can also choose which pages to output in the Pages field and have QuarkXPress create a cascading style sheet (CSS) file, rather than embed these styles in the HTML file, by checking the External CSS File checkbox.

❽ Click Export to create the HTML (or XHTML or XSLT) file.

In QuarkXPress 5, you determine whether a document is a print or Web document when you create it by choosing File ➪ New ➪ Document (⌘+N or Ctrl+N) or File ➪ New ➪ Web Document (Option+Shift+⌘+N or Ctrl+Alt+Shift+N). (Note that the settings in the New Web Document dialog box are the same as those in QuarkXPress 6's Layout Properties dialog box.) Once the document is created, its type cannot be changed.

Follow steps 4 through 8 above to create the HTML file. Note that you cannot choose a format for export in QuarkXPress 5, which supports only HTML.

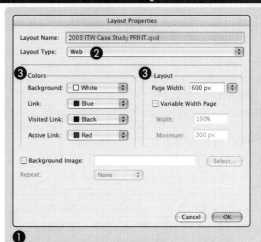

InDesign

Follow These Steps

Because InDesign stopped supporting HTML export after version 2, InDesign CS and later present many fewer options for using InDesign files on the Web than those in QuarkXPress 5 or later — unless you use Adobe's GoLive Web-authoring tool.

Exporting for the Web in InDesign CS and CS2

Follow these steps to create files that can be edited in GoLive:

1. Save your document (File ⇨ Save, or ⌘+S or Ctrl+S).

2. Choose File ⇨ Package for GoLive to open the Package Publication for the GoLive dialog box.

3. Navigate to the folder where you want to place the files. You can also click New Folder to create a new folder in which to place them.

4. Click Save. You will then see the Package for GoLive dialog box, in which you specify the pages to export, the encoding (important for non-Latin-alphabet documents), and which items are copied to the destination folder.

5. Click Package to export the document for use in GoLive.

6. In GoLive, choose File ⇨ Import ⇨ From InDesign ⇨ Browse and choose the folder that you chose in InDesign's Package Publication for GoLive dialog box (in step 3). Click Choose.

7. GoLive will create a preview window of the file with panes for the InDesign layout, the assets (linked graphics and other elements), and HTML preview.

8. To create an HTML file from the InDesign file, choose File ⇨ Export ⇨ As HTML. The Export as HTML dialog box will appear to let you select the pages to export and the base page's name, plus a template if desired. Click OK. You'll then be asked to choose a folder for the file; do so and click Save. Finally, you'll be asked to find the accessories for the file. (Accessories are located in a subfolder whose name includes "Accessories" inside the folder where you first exported the InDesign file.) Select the folder and click Choose. GoLive will now create the HTML file.

Exporting for the Web in InDesign 2

Follow these steps to create HTML files editable in any Web-authoring program or used directly on the Web:

1. Choose File ⇨ Export (⌘+E or Ctrl+E).

2. Choose HTML from the Formats pop-up menu, then click Save.

3. In the Export HTML dialog box, set the various export options in the four panes, then click Export to save the HTML file.

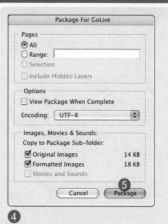

④

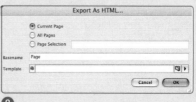

⑦

⑧

part XI

Specialty Issues

This is the odds-'n'-ends part, covering a variety of QuarkXPress functions and their InDesign equivalents. Topics include managing fonts, working with multichapter documents, creating indexes and TOCs, sharing files, and working cross-platform.

QuarkXPress and InDesign share core approaches to many of these areas, such as multichapter projects and indexing, but differ in specific functions and features, with InDesign generally offering greater capabilities than QuarkXPress.

✳ Managing Fonts

QuarkXPress

Fonts are typically managed by your operating system or with software such as Extensis Suitcase. But in a collaborative business such as publishing, you're bound to deal with documents that use fonts you don't have. Both QuarkXPress and InDesign help you deal with this issues.

Follow These Steps

QuarkXPress lets you deal with missing fonts when you open a document or handle it later.

When You Open a Document

❶ QuarkXPress displays an alert when you open a document, informing you that some fonts are not available. Click Continue to ignore this warning and open the document, leaving the fonts unchanged. Click List Fonts to see what fonts aren't available and, optionally, replace them with other fonts. (In QuarkXPress 6.5, you can click Buy Missing Fonts to purchase them online from Linotype, although this option appears even if missing fonts aren't available from Linotype.)

❷ If you clicked List Fonts, the Missing Fonts dialog box lists them and lets you choose replacement fonts. Select the missing font and then click Replace to get a list of available fonts. When done, click OK to continue opening the document.

❸ In QuarkXPress 6.5, you can have QuarkXPress automatically replace missing fonts. In the Font Mapping pane of the Preferences dialog box (QuarkXPress ➪ Preferences or ⌘+K on the Mac and Edit ➪ Preferences or Ctrl+K in Windows), check Specify Default Replacement Font and then choose a font from the pop-up menu below. This can be dangerous — it permanently changes the fonts used in the document, not giving you the chance to change them on a case-by-case basis or, more simply, make the missing fonts available. Also in QuarkXPress 6.5, if you clicked Save as Rule in the Missing Fonts dialog box in step 2, you can change this setting by choosing Utilities ➪ Font Mapping and editing the substitution. You can also export this rule for use by others and import others' rules.

After You Open a Document

You can replace fonts in a document — whether they are missing or not — any time using the Usage dialog box:

❶ Choose Utilities ➪ Usage to open the Usage dialog box. Go to the Fonts pane.

❷ Missing fonts will have their names enclosed in braces: { and }. Available fonts will be listed normally. Select a font and click Replace to get a list of available fonts, selecting the new desired font and clicking OK. Repeat for as many fonts as you want, then click Done.

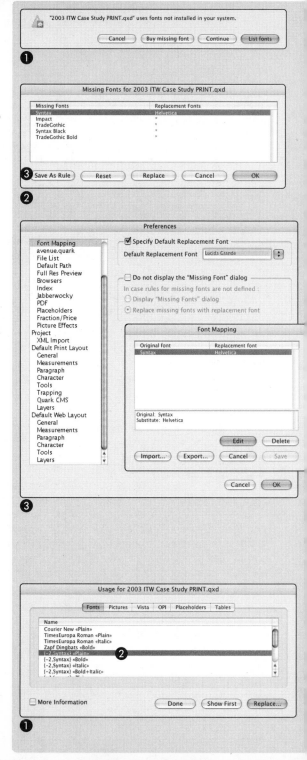

InDesign

Follow These Steps

InDesign also lets you handle missing fonts, both when you open a document and later on.

When You Open a Document

1. InDesign opens the Missing Fonts dialog box automatically if it detects fonts in the document that are not available on your system. The missing fonts are displayed in this dialog box. Click OK to continue opening the document as is, or click Find Font to replace any or all of these fonts.

2. If you clicked Find Fonts, InDesign will open the Find Font dialog box in which missing fonts are indicated with a warning icon (an exclamation mark in a yellow triangle). Select a font to replace it, choose a new font using the Font Family and Font Style pop-up menus, and click Change All. Repeat for every font you want to replace. Click Done to continue opening the document.

3. To see what fonts are missing in your document, you can tell InDesign to highlight the missing fonts by placing a pink background behind any text using them. InDesign does this by default, but if this option has become disabled, re-enable it by going to the Composition pane in Preferences dialog box (InDesign ⇨ Preferences or ⌘+K on the Mac and Edit ⇨ Preferences or Ctrl+K in Windows) and check the Substituted Fonts checkbox.

After You Open a Document

1. You can also replace missing fonts, as well as those that aren't missing, any time after you open a document. Choose Type ⇨ Find Fonts to open the Find Font dialog box (see step 2 above). Missing fonts are indicated with a warning icon (an exclamation mark in a yellow triangle). Other fonts will show an icon indicating their format (PostScript Type 1, TrueType, or OpenType). Select a font to replace it, choose a new font using the Font Family and Font Style pop-up menus, and click Change All. Repeat for every font you want to replace. Click Done when finished.

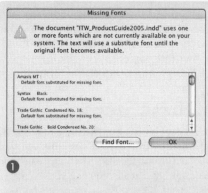

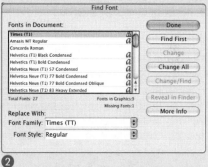

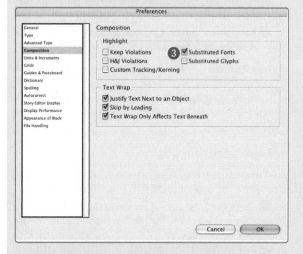

■Working with Multiple Page Types ⟨ **QuarkXPress**

Most publications use the same size paper for all pages, but occasionally you may want a page with a different size, perhaps for a foldout or a wider tabbed divider. Support for multiple page sizes is weak in both QuarkXPress and InDesign, and is weakest in InDesign.

Follow These Steps

QuarkXPress 6 allows project files that have multiple layouts, each of which can use different page sizes. But you cannot mix page sizes within a layout. QuarkXPress 5 and earlier do not allow multiple page sizes at all, requiring you to create multipage spreads instead. (QuarkXPress 6 supports both multilayout files and the use of multipage spreads.)

Multilayout Projects

In QuarkXPress 6, you create multilayout projects as follows, giving each layout the page size desired:

1 Create a new project by choosing File ➪ New ➪ Project (⌘+N or Ctrl+N). Specify the page size and related attributes in the New Project dialog box for the initial layout. It's best to give the layout a name so you can easily identify it. Click OK.

2 Create a new, additional layout by choosing Layout ➪ New. Specify the new layout's page size and related attributes. Click OK. Repeat for each layout desired for the project.

3 You switch between layouts using the tabs at the bottom of the document window.

Note that colors, style sheets, and so forth defined in one layout are available to all layouts, but hyphenation exceptions and spell-checking apply only to the current layout. Also, you cannot use QuarkXPress's book feature (see page 310) with multilayout projects.

Multipage Spreads

Multipage spreads let you create wider pages, but only in multiples of the current page size. The process is simple:

1 Open the Page Layout palette in QuarkXPress 6 (Window ➪ Page Layout or F10) or the Document Layout in QuarkXPress 5 or earlier (View ➪ Show Document Layout or F10).

2 Choose the master page to use as the basis for the foldout pages, then drag the master page onto the bottom part of the pane, creating document pages based on the master page. For the pages that fold out, drag an additional master page next to an existing page to create the folded-out portion.

3 If your document is two-sided, be sure to have the same number of pages on the opposite side of the next spread.

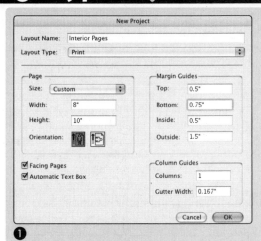

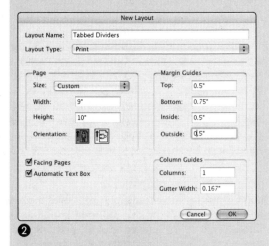

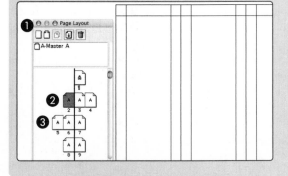

InDesign

Follow These Steps

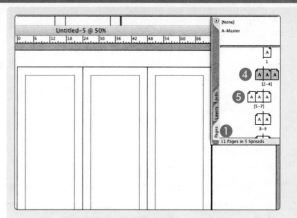

InDesign lets you create multipage spreads like QuarkXPress does but it has no equivalent to QuarkXPress 6's multilayout projects:

1 Open the Pages pane (Window ⇨ Pages or F12).

2 Choose the appropriate master page to use as the basis for your foldout pages, then drag it onto the bottom part of the pane, creating document pages based on the master page.

3 Select the document spreads (or single document pages if you're working in a single-sided document) that will have the foldouts) and then choose Keep Spread Together from the Pages pane's palette menu. Brackets will appear around the page numbers for the selected pages in the Pages pane.

4 For the pages that fold out, you can now drag one or more additional master pages next to an existing page to create the folded-out portion. (If you do not do step 3, a step not required by QuarkXPress, InDesign will not let the foldout pages dock themselves next to existing pages.)

5 If your document is two-sided, be sure to have the same number of pages on the opposite side of the next spread.

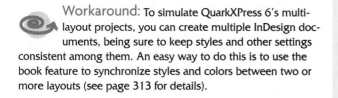

Workaround: To simulate QuarkXPress 6's multi-layout projects, you can create multiple InDesign documents, being sure to keep styles and other settings consistent among them. An easy way to do this is to use the book feature to synchronize styles and colors between two or more layouts (see page 313 for details).

Setting Up Multichapter Projects   **QuarkXPress**

Many layouts are parts of a bigger publication — individual articles in a magazine's issue or chapters in a book — and thus share common elements such as styles, indexes, and page numbering. In both QuarkXPress and InDesign, you can create books, which collect multiple layouts and let you standardize elements and handle page numbering across them.

Follow These Steps

To create a book and bring individual layouts into it:

1 Choose File ⇨ New ⇨ Book to open the New Book dialog box.

2 Navigate to the folder where you want to store the book file, give it a name, and click Save.

3 A palette will appear titled with the name of the book.

4 Add documents to the book by clicking the Add Chapter button and then choosing a document in the resulting dialog box.

5 QuarkXPress will number the chapters in the order they appear in the book palette. Initially, they will be listed alphabetically, but you can rearrange them by dragging a chapter to a new location within the palette or by selecting it and using the up and down arrow buttons to move it.

6 Chapters whose page numbers are specified via section starts in their documents (see page 34) will not be renumbered; they are indicated by asterisks after their page numbers. You must use the section start within your documents rather than the book palette's automated page numbering if your layouts start on lefthand (verso) pages. (The only way to have a facing-pages document start on a left page is to give it a section start whose page number is even, such as 2 or 34.) You might also use a section start to force a page number, such as for a chapter that follows a supplied insert that the printer will insert later in the publication.

7 Click Print Chapters to print the selected chapter(s) or, if no chapters are selected, to print all of them.

8 Click Remove Chapters to delete the selected chapter(s).

Cross-Reference: Pages 312-313 cover how to keep elements such as colors and styles consistent across documents in a book. Pages 314-315 cover printing.

InDesign

Follow These Steps

To create a book and bring individual layouts into it:

1 Choose File ⇨ New ⇨ Book to open the New Book dialog box.

2 Navigate to the folder where you want to store the book file, give it a name, and click Save.

3 A pane will appear titled with the name of the book.

4 Add documents to the book by clicking the Add Document button, or choosing Add Document from the palette menu, and then choosing a document in the resulting dialog box. You can also drag InDesign files from the desktop directly into the pane to add them to the book.

5 InDesign will number the documents in the order they appear in the book pane. Initially, they will be listed alphabetically, but you can rearrange them by dragging a document to a new location within the pane.

6 Chapters whose page numbers are specified via section starts in their documents (see page 35) will not be renumbered; unlike QuarkXPress, InDesign provides no visual indication for chapters numbered via section starts.

7 But InDesign does give you control over the book's overall page numbering (choose Book Page Numbering Options from the palette menu) and over individual documents' page-numbering options (select a document then choose Document Page Numbering Options from the palette menu). Repagination in InDesign is slow, so you may want to turn it off in the Book Page Numbering Options dialog box and manually repaginate periodically by choosing Repaginate from the palette menu.

8 Click Print Selected Documents, or choose Print Documents from the palette menu, to print the selected document(s) or, if none are selected, to print all of them.

9 Click Remove Documents, or choose Remove Documents from the palette menu, to delete the selected document(s).

10 Save book changes by clicking Save Book or choosing Save Book from the palette menu. (QuarkXPress automatically saves book changes, so it has no Save Book feature.)

Go Further: Compared with QuarkXPress, InDesign provides several enhancements to its book feature. A key enhancement is the ability to manage page-numbering settings from the book pane's palette menu.

Workaround: InDesign does not indicate documents whose page numbering is fixed. Your only clue will be that its page numbers don't change as page numbers of other documents in the book do.

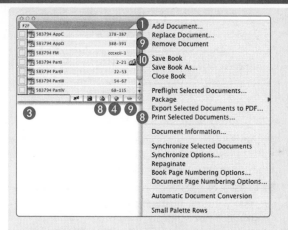

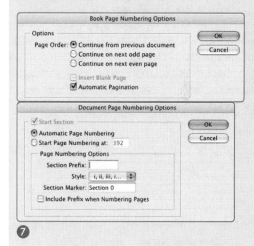

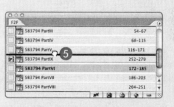

❋ Synchronizing Multichapter Projects ◀ QuarkXPress

A key benefit to books is the ability to standardize — synchronize — style and color settings across layouts. While the books feature won't guarantee that you're using the correct styles and colors, it will ensure that all chapters share those styles and colors.

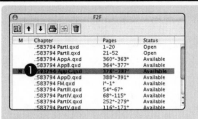

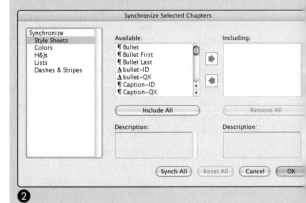

Follow These Steps

The key to synchronizing styles and colors is choosing a document to serve as the master, from which all other documents in the book will get their style and color settings:

① In the book palette, click in the M column next to the chapter you want to be the master. The letter M will move to that chapter's row to indicate it is the new master. (The first document you import is, by default, the master.)

② Select the documents whose styles and colors you want synchronized and then click Synchronize to have QuarkXPress update the other documents to match the master's style and color settings. The Synchronize Selected Chapters dialog box lets you decide which elements to copy to the other documents. (It acts like QuarkXPress's Append feature [File ⇨ Append, or Option+⌘+A or Ctrl+Alt+A].) Go through the various panes and decide what to synchronize by clicking the arrow buttons or the Include All button, then click OK to perform the synchronization. Note that any unique styles or colors in the target chapters are not deleted by synchronizing.

③ Go through the documents to see if the style changes have caused text reflow or repagination that affects your layout, and make adjustments as needed.

Cross-Reference: See pages 310-311 for details on setting up books and pages 314-315 for details on printing them.

Follow These Steps

In InDesign, the key to synchronizing styles and colors is also choosing a document to serve as the style source from which all other documents in the book will get their style and color settings:

1 In the book pane, check the box to the left of the document you want to be the style source. The style-source icon will appear to indicate that this document is the new style source. (The first document you import is, by default, the style source).

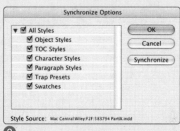

2 Set the synchronization options by choosing Synchronize Options from the palette menu. The resulting dialog box will let you choose what to synchronize. By default, everything is synchronized. You can synchronize now, or just click OK to update the settings.

3 Select the documents whose styles and colors you want synchronized and then click Synchronize, or choose Synchronize Selected Documents from the palette menu, to have InDesign update the other documents to match the style source's style and color settings. If no documents are selected, all documents will be synchronized. Note that InDesign does not let you choose individual styles and color to synchronize, as QuarkXPress does, and it also requires you to choose which types of elements to synchronize (in step 2) before you click Synchronize. Also note that any unique styles or colors in the target documents are not deleted by synchronizing.

4 Go through the documents to see if the style changes have caused text reflow or repagination that affects your layout, and make adjustments as needed.

Printing Multichapter Projects

With a book's chapters properly paginated and synchronized, you're ready to print.

Follow These Steps

Printing book chapters is straightforward in QuarkXPress:

1 Select the chapter(s) you want to print.

2 Click the Print Chapters button.

3 In the resulting Print dialog box, set your output settings and click Print.

 Cross-Reference: See Part X for more details on printing and exporting to PDF files. See pages 310-313 for more on setting up multichapter projects.

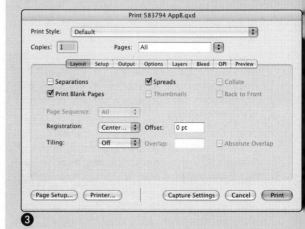

InDesign

Follow These Steps

Printing book chapters is straightforward in InDesign, which lets you both export to PDF and package book documents:

① Select the document(s) you want to print.

② To print selected documents, choose Print Selected Documents from the palette menu. To print all documents, you can just click Print the Book; otherwise, make sure that no documents are selected and choose Print Book from the palette menu.

③ In the resulting Print dialog box, set your output settings and click Print.

Go Further: InDesign lets you export documents to PDF, as well as package them for delivery to a service bureau, using the palette menu options in both cases. In QuarkXPress, you can print a book to PDF only by choosing the Acrobat PDF virtual printer or by exporting each chapter individually. Also, QuarkXPress makes you package each chapter individually.

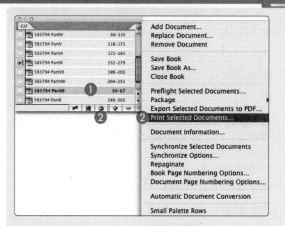

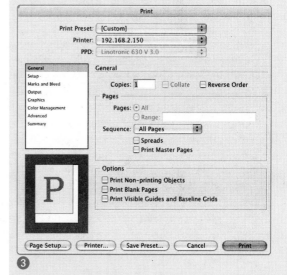

✳ Creating TOCs and Lists

Constructing lists, such as tables of contents, by hand is a time-consuming and error-prone process. Fortunately, QuarkXPress and InDesign help automate the process.

Follow These Steps

In QuarkXPress, you can have the tables of contents (TOCs) and other lists created automatically through the use of style sheets. All items to be included must use the same style sheet (and no other text should use that style sheet). With your text properly tagged:

1 Choose Edit ➪ Lists to open the Lists dialog box.

2 Click New to create a new list.

3 In the resulting Edit List dialog box, give the list a name.

4 Then select the style sheet(s) to be used to build the list. You can use more than one style sheet. Note that Quark-XPress lets you build lists from both paragraph and character style sheets, so you could use character style sheets to capture words that, for example, would appear in a list of people, companies, or products mentioned in a story.

5 You can set the level associated with each style sheet to create sublists using the pop-up menu in the Level column. (A TOC typically has just one level.)

6 You can also set the formatting for the page number from the pop-up menu in the Numbering column; your choices are Text Only (no page number will be generated), Text ... Page #, and Page ... Text.

7 Choose the style to be applied to the list's text in the For-mat As column's pop-up menu. (If you hadn't yet created these style sheets, you can come back to this dialog box later by choosing New from the Lists dialog box and select-ing the style sheets then.)

8 Check Alphabetical to have QuarkXPress generate the list in alphabetical order rather than in the default order of appear-ance. You would check Alphabetical, for example, when creating a list of people, companies, or products in a story, while you would not check it for a TOC or list of figures.

9 Click OK to complete the definition of the list. This returns you to the Lists dialog box where you can create, edit, and/or delete other lists in the Lists dialog box. When done, click Save. You can generate a current list any time after you have defined the list rules.

 Cross-Reference: For more on how to actually generate list once it's been defined, see pages 318-319.

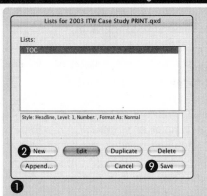

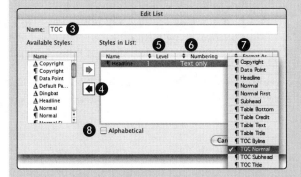

InDesign

Follow These Steps

InDesign offers richer features for creating TOCs but is less flexible for other types of lists. (Although labeled *Table of Contents*, InDesign's TOC feature can create almost any kind of list.) As with QuarkXPress, all items to be included must use the same style (and no other text should use that sheet). Unlike in QuarkXPress, you can only use text tagged with paragraph styles, limiting your ability to create lists of such things as people, companies, or products mentioned in a story.

Also unlike QuarkXPress, defining a list and generating it are essentially the same action in InDesign, although you can define list rules (called list styles) and later generate a list similar to how QuarkXPress works, as done here.

With your text properly tagged:

① Define any styles to be used in your TOC (or list), such as for the TOC title, TOC text, and TOC page numbers.

② Choose Layout ➪ Table of Contents Styles to open the Table of Contents Styles dialog box. Click New to define a new TOC style.

③ Enter title in the Title field. This text will appear above your TOC when you generate it. Choose a style for that title from the Style pop-up menu.

④ Select style(s) from the Other Styles window and click «Add to move them to the Include Paragraph Style menu. Any paragraphs using these added styles will be added to the list.

⑤ Set the formatting for the TOC entries generated from a specific added style by clicking the style name in the Include Paragraph Styles list and then selecting the paragraph style to apply in the Entry Style pop-up menu.

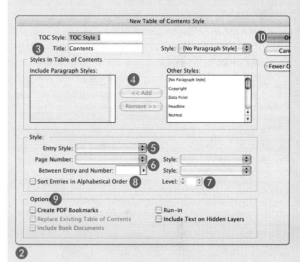

⑥ You can set the position of the page number using the Page Number pop-up menu and the character style applied to the page number. You can also select the character to insert between the entry and its page number using the Between Entry and Number pop-up menu, as well as a character style for it using the Style pop-up menu.

⑦ You can also set the level, such as for sublists, by choosing a value in the Level pop-up menu.

⑧ Check Sort Entries in Alphabetical Order to have InDesign generate the list in alphabetical order rather than in the default order of appearance.

⑨ In the Options section (click More Options to see this), you have several other self-explanatory choices.

⑩ Click OK to complete the TOC style, which returns you to the Table of Contents Styles dialog box. There, you can create, edit, delete, import, or export TOC styles, and click OK when done to save the changes.

❋Generating TOCs and Lists

In QuarkXPress, you need to define a list in one step and then generate it in a second step. In InDesign, you can also work that way, or you can combine the definition and creation in one step.

Follow These Steps

Any time after you have defined your list:

1 Create or select a text box in which to flow the list.

2 Open the Lists palette (Window ➪ Show Lists in Quark-XPress 6 or View ➪ Show Lists in earlier versions, or Option+F11 or Ctrl+F11).

3 With the text-insertion pointer placed in a text box, choose the list to be generated from the List palette's List Name pop-up menu, then click Build. (Click Update to update a list already in place at the text-insertion point.)

4 You can edit and format the list just as you can any other text, although any changes made will be wiped out if you later update the list.

Note that if you are working in a book project, the list must be defined in the master chapter and then be synchronized to all chapters for QuarkXPress to create the list based on all the book's chapters.

Cross-Reference: For details on defining list rules used to generate TOCs and other lists, see pages 316-317. For details on books, see pages 310-315.

Follow These Steps

In InDesign, you can define a TOC style and later use it to generate a TOC or other list, or you can define and generate the list in one step:

1 Whether or not you have defined a TOC style, choose Layout ⇨ Table of Contents to open the Table of Contents dialog box.

2 If you have previously defined a TOC style, choose it from the TOC Style pop-up menu.

3 Using steps 3 through 9 on page 317, edit the existing TOC style (if desired) or create new settings (if no TOC style exists for this specific list). If you are creating a new TOC style, click Save Style to save it for future use.

4 Click OK to generate the list.

5 InDesign will display the loaded-text icon. Click anywhere to have InDesign create a text frame with the list text.

6 You can edit and format the list just as you can any other text, although any changes made will be wiped out if you later update the list.

7 To update an existing list, click anywhere in it and choose Layout ⇨ Update Table of Contents.

Note that if you are working in a book project, the list must be defined in the master document and then be synchronized to all chapters for InDesign to create the list based on all the book's chapters.

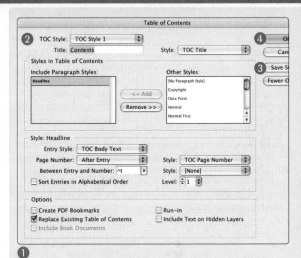

CONTENTS

✹ Creating Indexes

Typically used by book publishers, indexes are lists based on individual words and phrases that help readers find specific topics in text. QuarkXPress and InDesign provide similar tools for generating indexes.

Follow These Steps

To add index entries in QuarkXPress:

1 Open the Index palette by choosing Window ⇨ Show Index in QuarkXPress 6, or View ⇨ Show Index in earlier versions.

2 Select the text you want indexed.

3 Click either Add or Add All from the Index palette. Index All will find all occurrences of the word or phrase and add them to the index. That can be good or bad: good if all the uses are meaningful and deserving of being called out in the index; bad if some are just incidental and thus a waste of a reader's time when using the index. Note that if you add all occurrences, you must apply the same settings to all of them, while if you add them individually, you can set different settings for each.

4 Set the index entry's options in the palette:

- Enter text in the Sort As field if you want to sort the text based on something else (for example, enter **IEEE 802.11b** to have the *802.11b* entry listed as *IEEE 802.11b* in the index).

- Choose the level for the entry in the Level pop-up menu. The default is First Level, which makes the entry its own item in the index list. Choose another level to make the entry subordinate to another entry; click that entry in the window at the bottom of the palette.

- Choose a character style sheet for the index entry in the Style pop-up menu.

- Determine the scope of the index entry using the Scope pop-up menu. The default is to index the entry based on the page number on which it starts. Other options will let you specify a range, such as to a specified number of paragraphs, so the entry indicates all relevant pages. You can also choose to suppress the page number or to make the reference a cross-reference, such as making *802.11b* a cross-references to *IEEE 802.11b*.

5 Index entries are indicated by red brackets in the text.

6 A quick way to add an index entry is to highlight the text and press Option+Shift+⌘+I or Ctrl+Alt+Shift+I. This uses the settings last specified in the Index palette.

 Cross-Reference: See pages 322-325 for details on formatting and generating indexes.

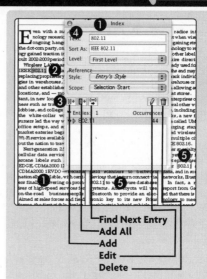

Find Next Entry
Add All
Add
Edit
Delete

InDesign

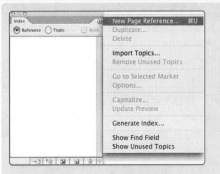

Follow These Steps

To add index entries in InDesign:

1 Open the Index pane by choosing Window ⇨ Type & Tables ⇨ Index in InDesign CS or later, or Window ⇨ Index in InDesign 2. The shortcut is the same for all versions: Shift+F8.

2 Select the text you want indexed.

3 Choose New Page Reference from the Index pane's palette menu or press ⌘+U or Ctrl+U to add the entry. The New Page Reference dialog box will appear. Click Add to add the selected text or Add All to find all occurrences of the word or phrase and add them to the index. That can be good or bad: good if all the uses are meaningful and deserving of being called out in the index; bad if some are just incidental and thus a waste of a reader's time when using the index. If you add all occurrences, you can later apply different settings to each of them — unlike in QuarkXPress.

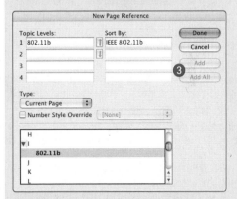

4 Set the index entry's options in the pane:

- Enter text in the Sort By field if you want to sort the text based on something else (for example, enter **IEEE 802.11b** to have the *802.11b* entry sorted as if it were *IEEE 802.11b*).

- By default, entries are added to the Top Level 1 field, which makes the entry its own item in the index list. But you can demote an entry to make it a subentry to another entry. For example, to make *80211.b* a subentry to *IEEE*, first add *IEEE* to the index, then add *802.11b*. With the *802.11b* entry displayed in the New Page Reference dialog box, select *IEEE* from the pane at the bottom of the screen, then click the ↓ button to demote the *802.11b* entry to Level 2, making it a subentry of *IEEE*.

- There is no option for overriding the index entry's character style; that's handled later, as covered on page 323.

- Determine the scope of the index entry using the Type pop-up menu. The default is to index the entry based on the number of the page on which it starts. Other options will let you specify a range, such as a specified number of paragraphs, so the entry indicates all relevant pages. You can also choose to suppress the page number or to make the reference a cross-reference.

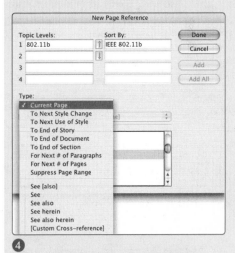

5 Index entries are indicated by carets in the text.

6 A quick way to add an index entry is to highlight the text and press Option+Shift+⌘+[or Ctrl+Alt+Shift+[in InDesign CS2 and Option+⌘+U or Ctrl+Alt+U in earlier versions. This uses the settings last specified in the Index palette. To quickly insert a reversed index entry (such as *Gruman, Galen* for the text *Galen Gruman*), press Option+Shift+⌘+] or Ctrl+Alt+Shift+] in InDesign CS2, or Shift+⌘+F8 or Ctrl+Shift+F8 in earlier versions.

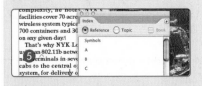

❀ Setting Up Index Formatting

QuarkXPress

With your index entries made, you still need to determine the index's formatting. In both QuarkXPress and InDesign, you do part of this work when you add index entries and the rest later on.

Follow These Steps

When adding index entries in QuarkXPress, you specify much of the formatting related to the entry's presentation. The rest is handled as a document setting.

① When adding index entries, you specify the entry's level, any special sort (such as overrides on how entries are alphabetized in the index itself), the scope (the page[s] that will be reported in the index), and the special character style sheet for the index entry, as described in step 4 on page 320.

② You can change formatting for index entries by double-clicking them in the Index palette and changing the options, again as described in step 4 on page 320.

③ For the index itself, you specify the settings globally for your document in the Index pane of the Preferences dialog box. (In QuarkXPress 6, choose QuarkXPress ➪ Preferences on the Mac or Edit ➪ Preferences in Windows, or press Option+Shift+⌘+Y or Ctrl+Alt+Shift+Y; in QuarkXPress 4 or 5, choose Edit ➪ Preferences ➪ Index.) In addition to changing the onscreen color of the brackets that indicate an index entry, you also set the spacing and punctuation for the entries and their page numbers, as well as the character style sheet used for cross-reference entries.

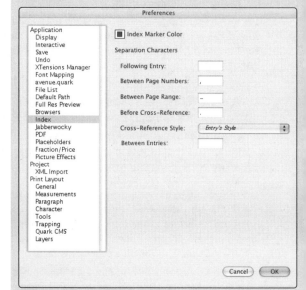

Cross-Reference: See pages 320-322 for details on adding index entries and pages 324-325 for details on generating indexes.

InDesign

Follow These Steps

When adding index entries in InDesign, you likewise specify much of the formatting related to the entry's presentation. The rest is handled as a setting.

 When adding index entries, you specify the entry's level, any special sort (such as overrides on how entries are alphabetized in the index itself), the scope (the page number[s] that will be reported in the index), and the special character style sheet for the index entry, as described in step 4 on page 321.

② You can change formatting for index entries by double-clicking them in the Index pane and changing the options, again as described in step 4 on page 321.

③ For the index itself, you specify the settings for the index in the Generate Index dialog box (choose Generate Index in the Index pane's palette menu). Click More Options to see all the settings. Here, you set the spacing and punctuation for the entries and their page numbers, as well as the character style sheet used for both index entries and cross-reference entries. (In QuarkXPress, you set the entry style sheets when you generate the index.)

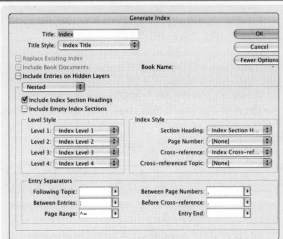

☀ Generating Indexes

With the index entries in place and your formatting set up, you can now generate the index.

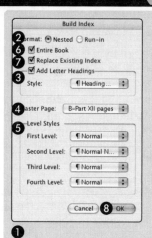

Follow These Steps

In QuarkXPress, do the following:

1 Choose Utilities ➪ Build Index to open the Build Index dialog box.

2 Choose whether the index is nested or run-in. A nested index puts each subentry on its own line beneath the main entry, indented a bit. A run-in list puts all the subentries on the same line as the main entry, separating them with whatever you chose in the Index pane of the Preferences dialog box (see page 322).

3 Check Add Letter Headings to have QuarkXPress create subheads in the index for each letter of the alphabet for which there are index entries. Select a style for those subheads from the Style pop-up menu.

4 Choose a master page from which to create the index. QuarkXPress will place the index at the end of the current document, on new pages.

5 Select the style sheets for each level of index entry.

6 If you are working on a book, check Entire Book. Note that you need first to have created index entries in each of the book's chapters in order for QuarkXPress to be able to include them now.

7 Check Replace Existing Index to replace any previously generated index.

8 Click OK to generate the index.

Cross-Reference: See pages 320-323 for details on adding and formatting index entries. See pages 310-315 for more on books.

InDesign

Follow These Steps

In InDesign, you generate the index at the same time you format it:

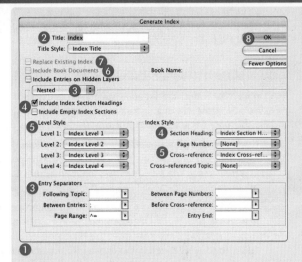

❶ Open the Generate Index dialog box (choose Generate Index in the Index pane's palette menu). Click More Options to see all the settings.

❷ You can give the index a title by entering text in the Title field. You specify the paragraph style for that title in the Title Style pop-up menu.

❸ Choose whether the index is nested or run-in using the unnamed pop-up menu. A nested index puts each subentry on its own line beneath the main entry, indented a bit. A run-in list puts all the subentries on the same line as the main entry, separating them with characters chosen at the bottom of the dialog box.

❹ Check Index Section Headings to have InDesign create subheads in the index for each letter of the alphabet for which there are index entries. Select a paragraph style for those subheads from the Section Heading pop-up menu.

❺ Select the paragraph styles for each level of index entry, as well as the character styles for the page numbers and cross-references.

❻ If you are working on a book, check Include Book Documents. (If a book is open, its name will appear after Book Name; if several books are open, choose the book in the Book Name pop-up menu that will appear.) Note that you need first to have created index entries in each of the book's chapters for InDesign to be able to include them now.

❼ Check Replace Existing Index to replace any previously generated index.

❽ Click OK to generate the index.

❾ InDesign will then present the loaded-text icon. Click anywhere to create a frame with the index text, or click an existing text frame to place the index text within it.

✳ Adding Hyperlinks

Although fairly useless in print documents, Web hyperlinks can be handy to include in PDF documents.

Follow These Steps

QuarkXPress 5 and later let you create Web documents, as well as include hyperlinks in any document. Those hyperlinks are clickable only if you export to PDF or HTML formats.

① Open the Hyperlinks palette by choosing Window ➪ Show Hyperlinks in QuarkXPress 6, or View ➪ Show Hyperlinks in QuarkXPress 5. The palette differs in QuarkXPress 5 and 6, although the basic capabilities are the same.

② In QuarkXPress 6, create a hyperlink by clicking New Hyperlink. In the New Hyperlink dialog box, enter a name for the hyperlink, choose the type from the Type pop-up menu (URL, Anchor, or Page). If you chose URL, enter the URL below; otherwise, choose the anchor (destination point previously defined somewhere in the document) or page from the pop-up menu below. Click OK when done. In Quark-XPress 5, you can enter only a URL and then click OK.

③ Select the text or other object to which to apply the hyperlink and then click that hyperlink in the Hyperlink palette to associate it. (Any text or object selected when you create a hyperlink has the hyperlink automatically applied to it.) In QuarkXPress 6, that text will be highlighted with a blue underline onscreen, while in QuarkXPress 5 you must click the Show Text Hyperlink button in the Hyperlinks palette to see this visual indication. You can see what text is associated with a specific hyperlink in the Hyperlinks palette by clicking the arrow to the hyperlink's left.

④ Note that if you export to PDF, any hyperlinks set won't be formatted with the typical underlined blue formatting familiar in Web browsers. You will need to add any such formatting in QuarkXPress. You might want to create a Hyperlink Text character style sheet to do so, so you can easily add this formatting to all text in a document destined for PDF export and then remove the formatting for the print version by changing the character style sheet's settings. (If you export to HTML, you set any hyperlink formatting in the Preferences dialog box or else rely on the browser settings of the document's users.)

⑤ To define an anchor point, click New Anchor and enter an anchor name in the resulting dialog box. Click OK, then select the text or object you want to be the anchor point and click the anchor name in the Hyperlinks palette.

 Cross-Reference: For more on exporting to the Web, see pages 302-303.

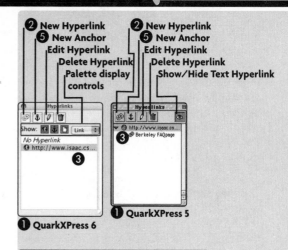

② New Hyperlink
⑤ New Anchor
　Edit Hyperlink
　　Delete Hyperlink
　　　Palette display controls

② New Hyperlink
⑤ New Anchor
　Edit Hyperlink
　　Delete Hyperlink
　　　Show/Hide Text Hyperlink

① QuarkXPress 6　　　① QuarkXPress 5

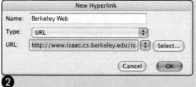

New Hyperlink

Name: Berkeley Web
Type: URL
URL: http://www.isaac.cs.berkeley.edu/is.　Select...

Cancel　　OK

②

InDesign

Follow These Steps

InDesign's process for creating hyperlinks is similar to the process in QuarkXPress. Note that InDesign doesn't let you create Web pages in InDesign CS or later, unless you are also using Adobe GoLive CS or later. Still, you may want hyperlinks for use in PDF documents exported from InDesign.

InDesign uses the concepts of *hyperlink* and *hyperlink destinations*, which can be confusing. A hyperlink destination is essentially a saved location (page, anchor point, or URL) that you can use when you apply a hyperlink to text or an object. A hyperlink is the connection between the selection and the destination, although you can create a hyperlink directly without having to have previously specified a destination for it — InDesign lets you specify the destination as part of creating that hyperlink. Thus, some users will do step 5 after step 1 below, while others will use the order presented here; both are valid.

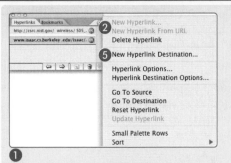

1️⃣ Open the Hyperlinks pane (Window ➪ Interactive ➪ Hyperlinks in InDesign CS or later, or Window ➪ Hyperlinks in InDesign 2; InDesign 2 also offers the shortcut Shift+F7).

2️⃣ If you have URL text selected in your document, you can quickly create a hyperlink from it by choosing New Hyperlink from URL in the Hyperlinks pane's palette menu. Otherwise, select text or another object and choose New Hyperlink to open the New Hyperlink dialog box.

3️⃣ In the Destination section of the New Hyperlink dialog box, choose the hyperlink type (URL, Page, or Anchor) in the Type pop-up menu. The Name pop-up menu will let you choose the destination page, previously defined URL (see step 5), or anchor, while the Document pop-up menu will let you choose a different InDesign document in which the desired page or anchor resides. If you are entering a URL, do so in the URL field. Be sure to give the hyperlink a name in the Name field.

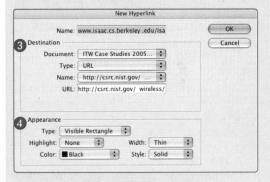

4️⃣ Set the appearance for the hyperlink in the Appearance section of the Hyperlinks pane. This affects how the link will appear in a PDF file as well as within InDesign, but it will not affect print output. Note that the appearance options are the same as provided in Adobe Acrobat, but by specifying them in InDesign as part of the hyperlink, you will save the manual effort of applying them in Acrobat.

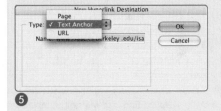

5️⃣ To create an anchor point or other type of destination, select the text or object and then choose New Hyperlink Destination from the Hyperlinks pane's palette menu. In the resulting New Hyperlink Destination dialog box, choose the destination type (URL, Anchor, or Page). The rest of the dialog box will change to let you enter the appropriate information for the destination type chosen. Click OK when done. You can now select this destination when you create other hyperlinks in steps 2 through 4.

Sharing Files

Publishing is almost always a cooperative endeavor, and both QuarkXPress and InDesign make it easy to share files with other users.

Keep in Mind

The biggest issues you'll encounter when sharing QuarkXPress files with other users fall into two categories: software versions and subsidiary files.

Software Versions

QuarkXPress can read files in its version as well as files from any previous version. But QuarkXPress can save only in its own version and in the previous version, so you could have significant problems if one person uses QuarkXPress 6 and another person uses QuarkXPress 4. The QuarkXPress 6 user can open the version 4 files, but can save the files only as version 5 or 6. To address this issue, you may need to keep interim versions of QuarkXPress available to make intermediate copies (for example, save a file in QuarkXPress 6 to version 5, then open it in QuarkXPress 5 to save it to version 4 for the QuarkXPress 4 user).

Note that any formatting that is not supported by the previous version is removed from the document when you save to an earlier version.

Subsidiary Files

Layouts typically use fonts and graphics, both of which reside in other files. If you give someone a QuarkXPress file, they may have trouble using it if they don't have the same fonts or access to the source graphics.

For missing fonts, QuarkXPress will use whatever is available to display the affected text but will not change the internal font information, so when the original user reopens the file, the original fonts will be used. However, the person who worked on the file who didn't have the right fonts may have made some inappropriate layout adjustments because of what appeared onscreen, so check the document carefully.

For missing source graphics, QuarkXPress will retain a preview copy in the layout, so another person can work on the document. That person won't be able to do any accurate fine adjustments to the images or text wraps around them, but otherwise will be OK.

Optimally, you would send the graphics (and fonts) to the document's other users, or have the graphics stored on a central server, but that's often not possible.

Cross-Reference: See pages 306-307 for how to manage missing fonts, pages 298-299 for how to gather all related files for delivery to other users, and pages 330-333 for how to share preferences and other elements.

InDesign

Keep in Mind

InDesign works very similarly to QuarkXPress when it comes to sharing files, although only InDesign CS2 provides any backward compatibility with earlier versions. However, unlike QuarkXPress, InDesign offers a network-aware file-sharing mechanism.

Software Versions

InDesign can read files in its version as well as files from any previous version (as well as QuarkXPress 3 and 4 files). But InDesign CS or earlier can save only in their own versions and offer no way for, for example, for an InDesign CS user to save a file in InDesign 2 format. InDesign CS2 corrected this incredible deficiency by letting you export InDesign CS2 files to the InDesign Interchange format (choose File ⇨ Export, or press ⌘+E or Ctrl+E, then choose InDesign Interchange from the Format pop-up menu), which inDesign CS can open. Practically speaking, this means that you need to ensure that everyone you work with has at least version CS.

Note that any formatting in InDesign CS2 not supported by InDesign CS is removed from the document or converted to the most similar format when you save to the earlier version.

Subsidiary Files

InDesign handles missing fonts and graphics files essentially the same way as QuarkXPress, so you can manage these issues as you are used to doing.

But InDesign CS or later also provides a mechanism called Version Cue that lets you save your documents to a special folder available to other Creative Suite users and programs. Enable Version Cue in your control panels (in InDesign CS) and in the File Handling pane of the Preferences dialog box (in InDesign CS2; choose Adobe InDesign ⇨ Preferences or press ⌘+K on the Mac and choose Edit ⇨ Preferences or press Ctrl+K in Windows).

When saving, be sure that you are working in the Version Cue workspace (to do so, click the Version Cue button if it is visible). This saves the files in the network-available Version Cue workspaces.

Version Cue tracks the status of documents, such as which are in use and which have been changed locally but have not been updated to the Version Cue directory. It also lets you save multiple versions of your documents so you can go back to a previous version if you don't like or want to review the recent changes you — or someone else — made.

 Go Further: Version Cue provides a consistent version-management environment for Creative Suite applications. QuarkXPress has no equivalent function.

InDesign CS2 without Version Cue

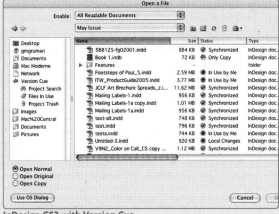

InDesign CS2 with Version Cue

✳ Sharing Common Elements

Layout files have many internal elements that you may want use as standards, such as a selection of color swatches or paragraph styles. Both QuarkXPress and InDesign let you share many of these elements across documents.

Follow These Steps

QuarkXPress lets you transfer many common elements in one convenient dialog box, as well as through individual dialog boxes:

❶ Choose File ➪ Append (Option+⌘+A or Ctrl+Alt+A) to open the Append dialog box, in which you choose another Quark-XPress document from which to import common elements. After selecting the file to open, click Append. At left is a list of the elements you can import. Go to each pane in turn and choose the elements to import from the Available list, clicking the ▶ button to move them to the Including pane (or click Include All). Click OK when done. (QuarkXPress 4 will not display Web-oriented items, as it doesn't support them, while QuarkXPress 5 will display them only if you have opened a Web document.)

❷ You import or export print styles by choosing Edit ➪ Print Styles to open the Print Styles dialog box. (This is the only style that cannot be imported from the Append dialog box.)

You can also import common elements individually from the dialog boxes in which you create and edit them:

❸ Choose Edit ➪ Style Sheets (Shift+F11) to import character and paragraph style sheets.

❹ Choose Edit ➪ Colors (F12) to import colors.

❺ Choose Edit ➪ H&Js (Option+⌘+H or Ctrl+Shift+F11 in QuarkXPress 5 and earlier, or Option+⌘+J or Ctrl+Shift+F11in QuarkXPress 6) to import H&J sets.

❻ Choose Edit ➪ Lists to import tables of contents and other lists.

❼ Choose Edit ➪ Dashes & Stripes to import dashes and stripes.

❽ Choose Utilities ➪ Auxiliary Dictionary to attach a different exception dictionary to the current layout (in QuarkXPress 6) or document (in earlier versions).

❾ Choose Utilities ➪ Kerning Table Edit and click Edit to import or export kerning tables. Similarly, choose Utilities ➪ Tracking Edit and then click Edit to import or export tracking tables.

❿ In QuarkXPress 5 and later, choose the appropriate options from the Edit menu to import various Web– and XML-oriented elements: Tagging Rules, Hyperlinks, Menus, Meta Tags, Font Families, and Cascading Menus.

Cross-Reference: A simple way to share common elements is to create a template using them, as explained on pages 32-33.

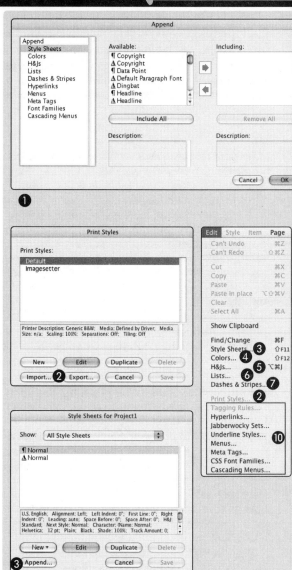

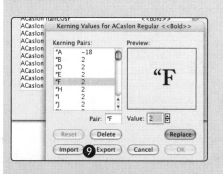

InDesign

Follow These Steps

Like QuarkXPress, InDesign lets you import and export many types of common elements across documents. Unlike Quark-XPress, InDesign has no central facility to do this. But you can import and export elements through their individual dialog boxes and panes using the Load and Save commands:

1 Import and export color definitions through the Swatches pane's palette menu (Window ➪ Swatches or F5). You can also just drag swatches from one document's Swatches pane to another layout's document window.

2 Import character, paragraph, and (in InDesign CS2) object styles through their respective panes' palette menus: Window ➪ Type & Tables ➪ Character Styles or Shift+F11, Window ➪ Type & Tables ➪ Paragraph Styles or F11, or Window ➪ Object Styles, or ⌘+F7 or Ctrl+F7. Note that the Type & Tables submenu is called Type in InDesign 2. Also note that paragraph styles include the equivalent of QuarkXPress's H&J sets.

3 In InDesign CS and later, import stroke styles in the Stroke Styles dialog box, accessed by choosing Stroke Styles in the palette menu of the Stroke pane (Window ➪ Stroke or F10).

4 Import transparency presets in the Transparency Flattener Presets dialog box, accessed by choosing Edit ➪ Transparency Flattener Presets.

5 Import trap presets via the palette menu of the Trap Presets pane (Trap Styles in InDesign 2): Window ➪ Output ➪ Trap Presets in InDesign CS2, Window ➪ Trap Presets in InDesign CS, or Window ➪ Trap Styles in InDesign 2.

6 In InDesign CS2, import or export PDF presets by choosing File ➪ Adobe PDF Presets ➪ Define to open the Adobe PDF Presets dialog box.

7 In InDesign CS and later, import or export document presets by choosing File ➪ Document Presets ➪ Define to open the Document Presets dialog box. You can also save them in the New Document dialog box (File ➪ New ➪ Document, or ⌘+N or Ctrl+N).

8 Import or export printer presets by choosing File ➪ Printer Presets ➪ Define to open the Printer Presets dialog box (Printer Presets are labeled Printer Styles in InDesign 2.) You can also save them in the Print dialog box (File ➪ Print, or ⌘+P or Ctrl+P).

9 Import or export color settings by choosing Edit ➪ Color Settings to open the Color Settings dialog box.

10 In InDesign CS2, import or export dictionary exceptions by choosing Edit ➪ Spelling ➪ Dictionary.

11 Import Table of Contents Styles by choosing Layout ➪ Table of Contents Styles to open the Table of Contents Styles dialog box.

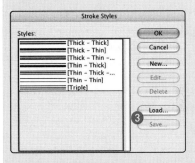

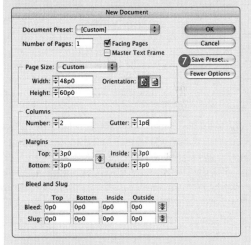

❋Sharing Preferences

In a workgroup environment, it's important that everyone work with consistent settings, so that documents don't reflow from user to user and to prevent final documents from looking like a hodgepodge. QuarkXPress and InDesign let you share basic program preferences across users if you're willing to dive into the various folders (some hidden in Windows) that contain them.

Keep in Mind

QuarkXPress lets you share many preferences among users:

❶ The XPress Preferences.prf file (called just XPress Preferences in QuarkXPress 4) contains many settings, including those chosen in the Application panes of the Preferences dialog box, any settings made when no document is open, and any changes to the default kerning tables, tracking tables, hyphenation exceptions, and default auxiliary dictionary. It resides in `Users\user name\Library\Preferences\Quark\QuarkXPress 6.0` for QuarkXPress 6 and in the Preferences folder of the folder containing the QuarkXPress application for earlier versions on the Mac, and in `Program Files\QuarkXPress x.0\Preferences` in Windows. You can store a master copy of the XPress Preferences.prf file on a server. All users will need to drag a copy to their Preferences folders in their QuarkXPress folder (the file cannot be aliased). If you're working in a multiplatform environment, you'll need to maintain a Mac and Windows version of the XPress Preferences.prf file, because it isn't cross-platform.

❷ If you keep the XPress Preferences.prf file current with all your preferences, you can apply these preferences to all previously created projects. To do this, open each project and click the Use XPress Preferences button in the Non-matching Preferences dialog box. (Newly created projects always use the current XPress Preferences settings.)

❸ On the Mac, color profiles are stored in `Library\ColorSync\Profiles` in QuarkXPress 6 or in `System Folder\Preferences\ColorSync Profiles` in earlier versions. In Windows, the profiles are stored in the `System32\Color` directory in the directory that contains the Windows operating system. Note that color profiles on Mac and Windows are also not interchangeable. You can also store color profiles in a second folder of your choice, which you select via the Auxiliary Profile Folder option in the Profile Manager dialog box (Utilities ➪ Profile Manager).

 Cross-Reference: See pages 330-331 for how to share common elements, including color profiles in InDesign and hyphenation dictionaries in QuarkXPress.

InDesign

Keep in Mind

InDesign offers similar preference-sharing capabilities:

❶ The InDesign preferences file, called InDesign Defaults, saves preferences you set when working in InDesign through the Preferences dialog box and through various panes and dialog boxes. This file is stored in `Users\` `user name\Library\Preferences\Adobe` `InDesign\Version x.0.` on the Mac and `Documents` `and Settings\user name\Application Data\` `Adobe\InDesign\Version x.0` in Windows. You can use the Mac's alias feature or the Windows shortcut feature to use an InDesign Defaults file stored in a folder other than the one in which InDesign resides. On a network, being able to use this technique means that everyone can share the same InDesign Defaults file. (You can also set keyboard shortcuts sets, spelling and hyphenation dictionaries, libraries, and swatch libraries to be shared this way.) Note that if you're sharing these across platform, you'll need to create a Windows shortcut from Windows to these files as well as a Mac alias from the Mac. The InDesign Defaults file cannot be shared across platforms, so if you want to have a master copy on a network server, you'll need to maintain two masters — one for Macintosh and one for Windows. Because the files have the same name on both platforms (this file in Windows has no filename extension), you'll need to store them in separate directories or add something to the name such as "Mac" and "Windows." If you do change the name, note that the alias and shortcut on each user's system must simply be named InDesign Defaults.

❷ The Presets folder in the InDesign application folder contains these folders for preference-related elements: InDesign Shortcut Sets, InDesign Workspaces, Scripts, and Swatch Libraries. The Presets folder also includes any document preset files. You can move these files to other users' computers in the same locations.

❸ The spelling and hyphenation exception dictionaries that come with InDesign are stored in the `Plug-ins\` `Dictionaries\Proximity` folder inside the InDesign application folder. But the exception dictionaries you create when adding words and hyphenation breakpoints in InDesign's spell checker and dictionary tools are stored elsewhere: `Users\user name\Library\` `Preferences\Adobe InDesign\Version` `x.0\Dictionaries\Proximity` on the Mac and `Documents and Settings\user name\` `Application Data\Adobe\InDesign\Version` `x.0\Dictionaries\Proximity` in Windows.

Working Cross-Platform

Both QuarkXPress and InDesign have removed most barriers to working on both Windows and Macintosh platforms, letting you easily share files and their common elements, and sometimes even some application preferences.

Keep in Mind

Note just a few issues in QuarkXPress when working cross-platform:

1. Always include the Windows filename extension: .qxp for QuarkXPress 6 projects or .qxd for earlier-version documents, .qpt for QuarkXPress 6 templates or .qdt for earlier-version templates, .qwd for QuarkXPress 5 Web documents, .qxt for QuarkXPress 5 Web templates, .xtg for XPress Tags text files, .qdt for auxiliary dictionaries, .qpj for printer styles, and .krn for kerning tables. To open filenames without extensions, change the Files of Type pop-up menu in the Open dialog box to Display All Files (*.*).

2. QuarkXPress libraries on Macs and Windows are not compatible, so you'll need to maintain two sets of libraries if you work in a cross-platform environment.

3. Although color profile files cannot be exchanged across the two platforms, both Mac and Windows QuarkXPress retain color-profile information from the other platform's files. If a color profile is not available on the new platform, you can apply a new profile or ignore the issue. If you print with a missing profile, QuarkXPress will substitute the default profile based on the type of color model used.

4. XTensions must be present on both platforms if you're moving documents that use specific XTensions. You'll need versions specific to each platform, because XTensions are essentially miniprograms that must be written to work on the Mac or Windows; these files are not interchangeable.

5. PostScript font files can't be moved across platforms, so be sure to buy copies in both formats. Some TrueType fonts *can* be used across platforms, so check first.

6. AppleScripts in the Mac version cannot be used in Windows QuarkXPress, which has no scripting functionality.

7. Windows QuarkXPress does not support ligatures, so ligatures in Mac files are converted to regular characters in Windows, and converted back when reopened on the Mac. Be aware that this could cause text reflow.

8. In QuarkXPress 5 and earlier, auxiliary dictionaries are not cross-platform. But in QuarkXPress 6, they are.

Cross-Reference: See pages 330-331 on how to share common elements and 332-333 on how to share preferences among users.

Keep in Mind

InDesign also has few requirements for cross-platform work:

1. Be sure to use Windows filename extensions on all your files, so Windows programs know how to open them. Use .indd for documents, .indl for libraries, .indt for templates, .not for hyphenation additions, .udc for spelling additions, and, in InDesign CS2, .inx for InDesign Interchange files. (If the filename extension is missing, be sure to choose All Documents from the Show pop-up menu [Macintosh] or Files of Type pop-up menu [Windows] in the Open a File dialog box.)

2. Although color profile files cannot be exchanged across the two platforms, both the Mac and Windows InDesign versions retain color-profile information from the other platform's files. And if both platforms have color profiles for the same device (monitor, scanner, printer, and so on), InDesign will apply the correct color profiles. If a color profile is not available on the new platform, you can apply a new profile or ignore the issue. (If you ignore this issue, the correct profile will be in place when you bring the document back to the original platform.) If you print with a missing profile, InDesign will substitute the default profile based on the type of color model used (RGB or CMYK).

3. Plug-ins must be present on both platforms if you're moving documents that use specific plug-ins' features. You'll need versions specific to each platform, because these are essentially miniprograms that must be written to work on the Mac or Windows; these files are not interchangeable across platforms.

4. PostScript font files can't be moved across platforms, so be sure to buy copies in both formats. Some TrueType fonts *can* be used across platforms, so check first.

5. The following elements cannot be moved across platforms:

   - Shortcut sets
   - The InDesign preferences file
   - Scripts other than those using JavaScript

Working with Scripts

Scripts are a great way to automate complex actions that you do repeatedly, and can save you time. But scripting requires a solid understanding of the underlying programming language, so it's not something that most individual designers tackle. However, if you or your company has the resources to develop your own scripts or can hire a scripter, take advantage of this powerful feature.

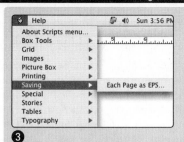

Follow These Steps

QuarkXPress supports scripts in just one language — Apple-Script — on just the Macintosh platform.

1. Make sure that scripting is enabled. The Scripts XTension should be active, which you can verify by choosing Utilities ⇨ XTensions Manager

2. Place any AppleScripts in the Script folder inside the folder that contains the QuarkXPress application. You can place folders containing scripts inside the Scripts folder; each folder will appear as a submenu when you select scripts in QuarkXPress. Note that any scripts you place in the Scripts folder while QuarkXPress is running will be unavailable until you exit and relaunch QuarkXPress.

3. To run a script, choose it from the Script menu.

Follow These Steps

InDesign supports scripts in several languages — AppleScript on the Mac and VBScript in Windows, plus, beginning with InDesign CS, JavaScript on both platforms.

❶ Scripting is enabled by default in InDesign.

❷ The easiest way to work with scripts is to place them in the Scripts folder inside the folder that contains the InDesign application. Scripts don't have to be in the Scripts folder — they can be anywhere on your computer — but to use a script outside this folder means you have to double-click the script from your desktop rather than access it in InDesign.

❸ To run a script from the Scripts folder, double-click it or choose Run Script from the palette menu in the Scripts pane (Window ➪ Automation ➪ Scripts in InDesign CS2, Window ➪ Scripting ➪ Scripts in InDesign CS, or Window ➪ Scripts in InDesign 2). To use a script stored outside this folder means you have to double-click the script from your desktop rather than access it in InDesign.

❹ You might be wondering what the Script Labels pane is for in InDesign CS and later. It lets you apply a name to a selected object in your layout to which you can then have a script refer. For example, you could name a text frame containing a title *Title*, and then have the script operate on Title.

Go Further: InDesign's support of JavaScript lets you create scripts that work on both Macintosh and Windows, although you may need to do some customization of these scripts to account for platform differences, such as naming conventions for folders.

InDesign also lets you edit scripts by choosing Edit Script from the Scripts pane. Choosing this option will open the script editing program appropriate for the script; if your system has no such editor, InDesign will open a text editor such as TextEdit or WordPad.

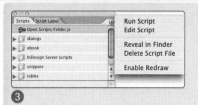

❸

■ Working with Plug-Ins

When QuarkXPress 2 was released in the late 1980s, it revolutionized desktop publishing with theretofore unimaginable controls over typography. But it also brought a second revolution: the use of plug-ins (called XTensions by Quark) to let other vendors add capabilities to a program. This let Quark focus on developing main-stream functionality while letting other companies address specialty needs, all while giving users a common publishing tool. Today, plug-ins are widely used, especially by Quark rival Adobe. Both programs make it pretty easy to manage any plug-ins that you may have.

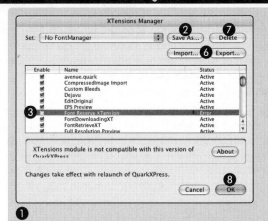

Follow These Steps

QuarkXPress lets you create sets of plug-ins, so you can activate and deactivate them easily. It's always a good idea to make sure your current settings are saved in a set before installing new XTensions.

① Choose Utilities ⇨ XTensions Manager to activate and deactivate XTensions, as well as to create sets. The XTensions Manager dialog box will appear.

② Save the current set of XTensions by clicking Save As, then entering a name such as Default XTensions in the dialog box that appears, and clicking Save. This way, you can easily revert to the current status if any XTensions you install cause problems.

③ Activate and deactivate XTensions by checking or unchecking the box to the left of each XTension's name. Note that any changes in available XTensions won't take effect until you quit and relaunch QuarkXPress. Deactivated XTensions are not deleted from your computer but are moved from the XTensions folder inside the folder that contains the QuarkXPress application to a folder named Disabled XTensions.

④ After deactivating or activating XTensions, create any sets desired by saving a new set after making such changes. For example, you might have a set for print-only publishing, which would let you streamline the interface for users who don't work on Web documents. (You would choose your default XTensions set to re-enable the Web features.)

⑤ After you install new XTensions (follow the directions that come with the CD or download), consider either saving the new configuration as your default set, replacing the one created in step 2, or saving the configuration as a new set.

⑥ Click Delete to remove the current XTensions set.

⑦ Click Import to import XTensions sets from other users, and click Export to create XTension sets for use by other users.

⑧ Click OK to save your changes.

InDesign

Follow These Steps

InDesign likewise lets you create sets of plug-ins, so you can activate and deactivate them easily. Note that the process differs from QuarkXPress, so be sure not to follow the QuarkXPress sequence for creating sets when working in InDesign.

1 Choose InDesign ⇨ Configure Plug-Ins on the Mac and Help ⇨ Configure Plug-ins in Windows to activate and deactivate plug-ns, as well as to create sets. The Configure Plug-Ins dialog box will appear.

2 Save the current set of plug-ins by clicking Duplicate, then entering a name such as Default Plug-ins in the dialog box that appears, and clicking Save. This way, you can easily revert to the current status if any plug-ins you install cause problems.

3 Activate and deactivate plug-ins by checking or unchecking to the left of each plug-in's name. Note that a lock icon indicates a required plug-in that InDesign must have to function properly. Also note that any changes in available plug-ins won't take effect until you quit and relaunch InDesign. Finally, note that InDesign does not move disabled plug-ins to a different folder as QuarkXPress does.

4 Because InDesign uses so many plug-ins itself, you can help streamline the choices for activation and deactivation by checking or unchecking the various options in the Display section.

5 *Before* deactivating or activating plug-ins — and before installing new plug-ins (following the directions that come on the CD or download) — create a new set by clicking Duplicate. Then make your changes, which will be saved automatically to whatever set is currently in use. (If you make changes to one of the sets that comes preconfigured in InDesign, you will be asked to create a new set.) This creation of a new set to reflect changes will let you more easily revert to a previous state, which is important because many InDesign plug-in programs actually install several plug-in files, making it difficult to know which files to deactivate.

6 Click Delete to remove the current plug-in set.

7 Click Import to import plug-ins sets from other users, and click Export to create plug-in sets for use by other users.

8 Click OK to save your changes.

part XII

What Only InDesign Can Do

This part differs from the preceding 11 parts in that it doesn't compare QuarkXPress procedures to their InDesign equivalents. That's because it can't — the pages in this part highlight features unique to InDesign, providing a visual guide to using those most intriguing and powerful.

While there are a few things that QuarkXPress does that InDesign cannot do — create Web pages, synchronize text boxes that contain the same text, adjust halftones, build fractions, and use Hexachrome colors — that list has gotten awfully short, while the list of what only InDesign can do continues to grow.

Setting Up a Custom Workspace   InDesign

Follow These Steps

InDesign has tons and tons of palettes and panes — 41 in InDesign CS2 — which can be overwhelming. While Adobe adds even more panes and palettes to each version of InDesign, it also added a tool to help manage them in InDesign CS: workspaces.

Essentially, a workspace is a preset that stores the panes and palettes you want to have open when you launch InDesign, as well as their locations onscreen.

1 Arrange the panes and palettes as you prefer — move them, combine them, separate them, and/or dock them.

2 Choose Window ➪ Workspace ➪ Save Workspace. You'll be prompted to give the workspace a name.

3 Switch from one workspace to another by choosing a workspace from the Workspace menu. In addition to the workspaces you define, the menu will always have [Default], which is the workspace that InDesign uses when you first launch it.

4 Delete unwanted workspaces by choosing Window ➪ Workspace ➪ Delete Workspace.

Follow These Steps

While InDesign comes with a variety of standard page sizes based on those common in the U.S. and Europe, most publications use other sizes. For example, magazines often uses pages sized at 8⅛" by 10⅞". That means you need to create a custom page each time you start a new document or template, which could lead to incorrect page sizes if someone enters the wrong information when creating the document.

InDesign lets you create your own custom page sizes that will then appear in the list of page sizes in the New Document dialog box (File ⇨ New ⇨ Document, or ⌘+N or Ctrl+N). InDesign CS or later gives you two ways to do this:

1 InDesign has a file called New Doc Sizes.txt in the Presets folder inside the folder that contains the InDesign application. You add new page sizes to that file by opening it in a text editor, such as the Mac's TextEdit or Windows' WordPad, or by using a word processor. Each line contains the page type's name, page width, and page height, all separated by tabs. For example, `Magazine → 8.125" → 10.875"` (→ indicates a tab) would create a new page type in the New Document dialog box's Page Size pop-up menu.

2 InDesign CS or later also lets you define document presets, which save the settings in the New Document dialog box so you can use them over and over by choosing them in the Document Preset pop-up menu. You create a document preset by setting the New Document dialog box's options as desired and clicking Save Preset, then giving the preset a name in the dialog box that appears.

You'll likely end up using both techniques. A document preset saves much more than the page size so you might consider using it for documents that share common settings, such as the number of columns and pager margins, while you'll add new page sizes to the New Doc Sizes.txt so they can be used in multiple types of documents (and document presets).

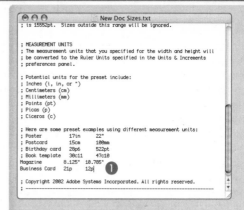

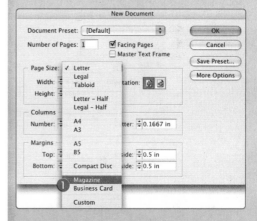

Using Child Master Pages

Follow These Steps

Master pages are a powerful feature to automate page formatting. Once a QuarkXPress strength, InDesign has taken the master-page concept further by letting you base one master page on another. Just as is true for text style sheets, having a parent/child capability lets you be more efficient, because changing an attribute in the parent master page changes the same attributes in all children master pages as well.

This book is a good example of the concept: This part uses a different color scheme from the preceding ones that compare QuarkXPress to InDesign. Some of the graphics differ as well, but many elements, such as the text frames and folios, are the same. In InDesign, all you need to do is use a child master page, so changes in common elements, such as text frames and folios, are changed in all children master pages. In Quark-XPress, these elements would need to be manually updated in each similar master page.

1. Create a master page the regular way: Choose New Master Page from the palette menu of the Pages pane (Window ➪ Pages or F10).

2. In the resulting New Master dialog box, fill in the Prefix, Name, and Number of Pages as you normally would. But in the Based on Master pop-up menu, choose a parent master page.

3. You will now see that the new master page indicates the parent master in the Pages pane.

4. Adjust your new master pages as desired. Anything that you change that was derived from the parent master won't be affected by any changes in the parent — only items that are identical in both will be changed in the child when they are changed in the parent.

Cross-Reference: For more on master pages, see pages 26-31.

Follow These Steps

When you do extensive editing in text, it can be difficult to work in the layout view since you often have to scroll up and down columns, around objects, and from page to page. While you might be tempted to work in a word processor and re-import the text, you'll lose any touch-up formatting applied in InDesign.

That's why InDesign CS and later offer the Story Editor, a mini-word processor in which you can edit entire stories in one window, without having to maneuver through your layout.

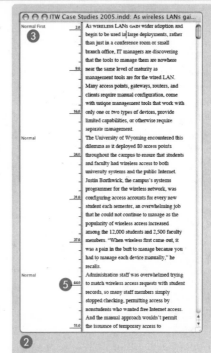

1 Select the story you want to edit by clicking anywhere in it with the Type tool.

2 Choose Edit ➪ Edit in Story Editor (⌘+Y or Ctrl+Y) to open the Story Editor window.

3 You can edit the text as needed, as well as see what styles might be applied (from the left side of the window) and what local formatting is applied (the text will show attributes such as italics, boldface, and small caps).

4 You apply styles and other text attributes using the standard InDesign mechanisms, such as the Paragraph Styles and Character Styles panes and the Type menu.

5 InDesign CS2 also shows you the line depth for your text and will highlight overset text (text that does not fit in the text frames) by placing the code *OV* to the text's left and placing a light pink frame around the overset text.

6 You can switch back to the layout by clicking in the layout. The Story Editor window will disappear, but you can get it back by choosing it from bottom of the Window menu, in the list of open documents.

7 You can also close or minimize the Story Editor window using the standard Mac and Windows window-control buttons, as well as resize it by dragging its edges or corners.

8 You can change Story Editor display settings, such as the font used and type of cursor displayed, by going to the Story Editor Display pane of the Preferences dialog box (InDesign ➪ Preferences or ⌘+K on the Mac and Edit ➪ Preferences or Ctrl+K in Windows).

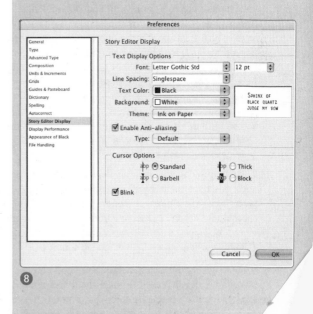

Using Automated Bullets and Numbering

Follow These Steps

Word processors have long provided automated bullets and numbering, so as you edit your text, bullets are added automatically, and numbers are automatically added and reordered. Finally, a layout program — InDesign CS2 — now does the same:

1 When you create paragraph styles (Window ➪ Type & Tables ➪ Paragraph Styles or F11), one of the panes is Bullets and Numbering. Go there to set automated bullets or numbering.

2 If you are creating a bulleted list, choose Bullets from the List Type pop-up menu to set your bullet character. Choose from one of the bullet characters displayed, or click Add to get a dialog box in which you add other ones to the available bullet characters. (Choose the bullet's font using the Font Family and Font Style pop-up menus.) Choose the bullet size and color using the Size pop-up menu/field and Color pop-up menu. Click OK when done. Set the tabs, indent, and so forth using the other panes in the New Paragraph Style dialog box (when creating a style) or in the Paragraph Style Options dialog box (when editing a style).

3 If you are creating a numbered list, choose Numbers from the List Type pop-up menu to set your numbering settings. Choose the numbering style from the Style pop-up menu; your choices are 1, 2, 3, 4, …, I, II, III, IV, …, i, ii, iii, iv, …, A, B, C, D, …, and a, b, c, d, …. Choose the separator character (which appears after the number) from the Separator pop-up menu/field. Enter the start number in the Start At field. Choose the number's font using the Font Family and Font Style pop-up menus. Choose the size and color of the numerals by using the Size pop-up menu/field and Color pop-up menu. Click OK when done. Set the tabs, indents, and so forth using the other panes in the New Paragraph Style dialog box (when creating a style) or in the Paragraph Style Options dialog box (when editing a style).

4 If you are working with text that doesn't have paragraph styles applied, set automatic bullets and numbering in the Paragraph pane (Type ➪ Paragraph, or Option+⌘+T or Ctrl+Alt+T) by choosing Bullets and Numbering from the pane's palette menu. You'll get the same options as in steps 2 and 3, except that you also specify any indent and tab settings.

When InDesign imports automated bulleted and numbered lists from Word files, it will retain the bullet characters and the numbers, but they will no longer be automatic. If you use automated numbered and bulleted lists in Word, remove the numbers and bullets in Word and apply a unique style such as Num List or Bullet. In InDesign CS2, edit the Num List and Bullet styles imported from Word to use InDesign's automatic numbers and bullets.

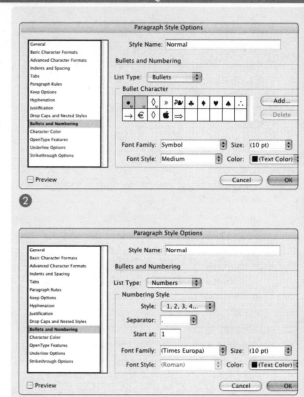

2

3

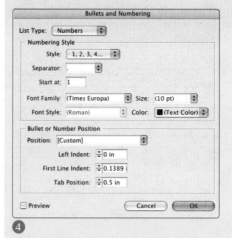

4

InDesign ⟩ AutoCorrecting Text

Follow These Steps

The more text entry you do in a layout program, the more you realize how dependent you've become on your word processor's built-in spelling checker and autocorrection features. InDesign CS2 brings that same crutch to page layout, with the ability to automatically correct text as you type it, as well as to highlight possible misspellings.

You can use the autocorrect feature for more than fixing common spelling errors: It's a great tool for having InDesign convert two consecutive hyphens (--) to an em dash (—) or replace short codes with the actual text. Or use it to add trademark symbols (® and ™) after product names automatically, ensuring that the correct symbol is used.

① Go to the Autocorrect pane of the Preferences dialog box (InDesign ⟹ Preferences or ⌘+K on the Mac and Edit ⟹ Preferences or Ctrl+K in Windows).

② To turn on autocorrection, check Enable Autocorrect. If you want InDesign to fix capitalization errors as well, check AutoCorrect Capitalization Errors. From the language menu, choose the dictionary that InDesign will consult to identify and fix spelling errors.

③ Click Add to enter your own corrections and/or codes. In the Add to Autocorrect List dialog box, enter the misspelled word or code in the Misspelled Word field and the corrected or expanded text in the Correction field. Press OK to add it.

④ InDesign CS2 can also check spelling as you type (as well as for text already imported), alerting you to suspect words that it can't find in the current dictionary. Go to the Spelling pane and check Enable Dynamic Spelling. Optionally, choose different colors in the Underline Color section to highlight the different kinds of errors listed. In your document, InDesign CS2 will underline the suspect words so you can easily find them.

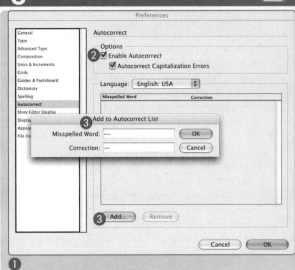

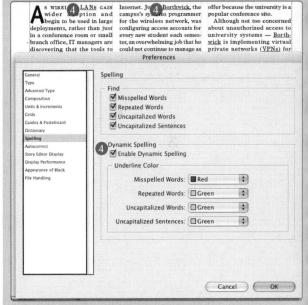

Aligning Text to the Spine

Follow These Steps

Some documents alter the text alignment depending on what page the text is on. For example, text on the right page would be left-aligned, while text on the left page would be right-aligned. An example is pull-quotes.

Implementing such a layout requires having two styles — one for each alignment — and ensuring that you apply the correct one to text based on where it falls. But InDesign CS2 has removed that manual work, providing a new alignment option that automatically applies the correct alignment based on what kind of page the text falls on.

Two new alignments are available in InDesign CS2: Towards Spine and Away from Spine. Towards Spine aligns the side closest to the spine, while Away from Spine aligns the margin furthest from the spine. These two alignments are available in the same places where the other alignments are available:

1. In the Control palette (Window ➪ Control, or Option+⌘+6 or Ctrl+Alt+6; be sure the ¶ button is selected).

2. In the Paragraph pane (Type ➪ Paragraph, or Option+⌘+T or Ctrl+Alt+T).

3. When creating or editing new paragraph styles in the Paragraph Styles pane (Window ➪ Type & Tables ➪ Paragraph Styles or F11); go to the Indents and Spacing pane in the New Paragraph Style dialog box or Paragraph Style Options dialog box.

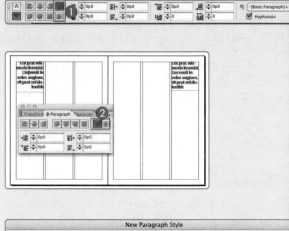

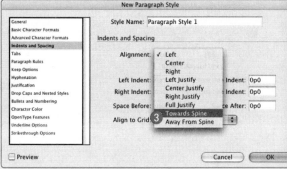

InDesign ▸ **Working with Footnotes**

Follow These Steps

Books, journals, and other documents use footnotes, but layout programs have not handled these well. Both QuarkXPress and InDesign retain the footnote characters and place the footnoted text at the end of the story, but they don't permit the end-of-column or end-of-page footnotes more commonly used, nor do they permit the automated numbering and renumbering as footnotes are added and deleted. InDesign CS2 changed that, and provides more standard footnote capabilities.

① When you import Word files with footnotes, you can tell InDesign to retain them. In the Place dialog box (File ⇨ Place, or ⌘+D or Ctrl+D), check Show Import Options before selecting the text file and clicking Open. In the Import Options dialog box, make sure that Footnotes and Endnotes are checked.

② Set InDesign CS2's footnote controls by choosing Type ⇨ Document Footnote Options. In the Numbering and Formatting pane, choose the options for the footnotes themselves: the characters (in the Style pop-up menu), the numbering, and any prefixes or suffixes for the numbers (such as the current chapter number in a book). You also set the formatting for the footnote character in text and for the footnoted text entry.

③ In the Layout pane, set the appearance of the footnoted text, including spacing, position relative to the baseline, placement of endnotes, and specifications for the ruling line above the footnoted text.

④ To enter a footnote in InDesign CS2, choose Type ⇨ Insert Footnote. InDesign will automatically number the footnote and let you enter the footnoted text.

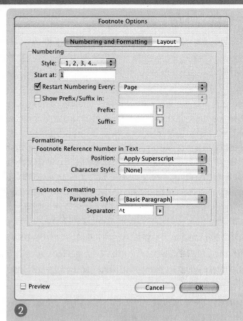

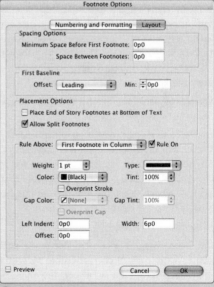

Merging Data

InDesign

Follow These Steps

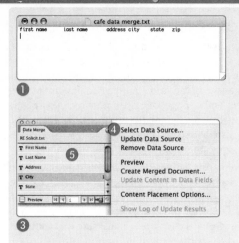

Mail merge lets you create form letters easily in word-processor files. InDesign CS2's Data Merge capability brings that concept to layouts, letting you create form letters, catalogs, and other types of documents.

① Create a text file with the various source data separated either by tabs or commas (use just one as your separator in the file, rather than mix the two). Start a new record by pressing Enter or Return (a new paragraph). The first row should contain the names of the fields. To import graphics as inline graphics, precede the field name with @, such as *@photo*. The record fields will then need to provide the complete path to the graphic file, which must be in a supported format. For example, MacintoshHD:Images:myphoto.tiff on the Mac or C:\Images\myphoto.tif in Windows.

② With the source file ready, create or go to the text frame in which you want to flow your data, selecting the insertion point with the Type tool.

③ Open the Data Merge pane by choosing Window ➪ Automation ➪ Data Merge.

④ Choose Select Data Source from the Data Merge pane's palette menu, and navigate to the desired file using the resulting dialog box. Click Open. (If your data file changes, you can import the most current version by choosing Update Data Source from the Data Merge pane's palette menu. Choose Remove Data Source to remove a data file from the pane.)

⑤ The Data Merge pane will now list the data file and the fields it contains.

⑥ Drag the fields to the appropriate spots in your layout. Or double-click a field name to insert it at the current text-insertion point. The field names will be enclosed in French quotation marks («»). You can use a field more than once in the layout. The pane will show which page numbers each field is used in (to the right of the field name).

⑦ Format the fields as desired.

⑧ Click the Create Merged Document icon at the bottom right of the Data Merge pane or choose Create Merged Document from the palette menu to import the entire data file's contents into your layout. The Create Merged Document dialog box will open with the Records pane. In the Records to Merge section, choose which record(s) to import. You can choose all, a specific record, or a range. In the Records per Document Page pop-up menu, choose Single Record if you want a new page output per record (such as in a form letter) or Multiple Records if you want to print multiple copies of the same record on a page (such as for business cards).

InDesign

9. If you choose Multiple Records, you'll set up the placement of these records in the Multiple Record Layout pane. Note that InDesign CS2 will copy the entire text frame containing the data fields when you choose Multiple Records. If you are creating multiple records on a page, be sure that you've left blank the space where the labels' fields will be copied to — the Data Merge tool won't work around objects in the layout. Instead, it blindly follows the specs in the Multiple Record Layout pane, repeating fields until the page is full or until it runs out of fields. Also don't copy the frames containing the Data Merge text in your layout to fill out your page — the Data Merge tool will do that for you. Instead, there should just be one occurrence of your repeating record in your layout, placed at its upmost and leftmost position.

10. Go to the Options pane and verify that the import options work for your document. In the Image Placement section, choose how to fit any imported graphics by choosing an option in the Fitting pop-up menu. You'll typically pick the default, Fit Images Proportionally. You can also check the Center in Frame checkbox to center the imported graphics and the Link Images checkbox to link to the source graphics files rather than embed the graphic into the InDesign layout. In the lower section of the pane, you can have InDesign remove blank lines created by empty fields by checking the Remove Blank Lines for Empty Fields checkbox. This is handy, for example, if your layout permits two address lines per recipient; anyone with a single address line will have no space between that address and their city if this box is checked. You can also limit the number of pages in the merged document by checking Page Limit per Document and entering a value in its field.

11. Click OK. InDesign will create a new document based on the original layout and merged data. The merged text is now editable and is no longer linked to its source data, so to update the document, you'll need to regenerate it from the document that contains the Data Merge records. (That's why InDesign creates a new document for the resulting data rather than replace the source file.) One key exception: If you place the records on a master page, Data Merge will create document pages based on the imported data within the current document, rather than create an entirely new document. If you place the records on a master page, you can later update the records via the Data Merge pane and have the document pages updated as well.

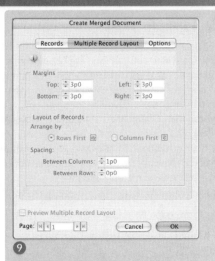

9

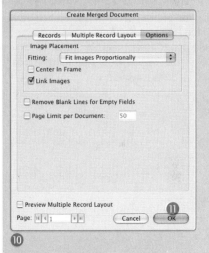

10

11

⚓ Modifying Text Strokes

Follow These Steps

While both QuarkXPress and InDesign let you convert text to graphics frames to which you can then apply outlines, that makes the text uneditable and removes it from its text frame. QuarkXPress also lets you use the Outline style to apply a black outline to text, making the text white (see pages 156-157), but although you can then change the outline color by apply a new color to the text, you can't change the fill or the outline's thickness, so this is a limited option. InDesign gives you another way to style text outlines without having to make a drastic conversion or limit your formatting options.

1 Select the text with the Type tool.

2 Open the Stroke pane (Window ➪ Stroke or F10).

3 Establish a stroke thickness by entering a value in the Width pop-up menu/field.

4 Open the Swatches pane (Window ➪ Swatches or F5).

5 Be sure that the Stroke button is selected in the Swatches pane or in the Tools palette. Apply a color, gradient, or tint to the stroke by clicking a swatch in the pane. (To change the color of the fill, select the Fill button in the Swatches pane or Tools palette instead.)

InDesign ▶ Using Object Styles

Follow These Steps

Paragraph and character styles are great ways to save time and ensure consistency in formatting text. With object styles, InDesign CS2 extends that concept to objects such as lines and frames. Object styles work very much like the familiar character and text styles:

❶ Open the Object Styles pane (Window ➪ Object Styles, or ⌘+F7 or Ctrl+F7).

❷ If you have an object formatted that you want to use as the basis of the new object style, select it with the Selection tool.

❸ Choose New Object Style from the Object Style pane's palette menu. In the New Object Style dialog box, modify the various panes' settings as desired. You can base an object style on an existing object style using the Based On pop-up menu, give the style a keyboard shortcut via the Shortcut pane, and see the style's settings in the General pane by clicking the arrows next to each pane in the Style Settings section.

❹ Uncheck a style pane's name to apply none of that pane's settings to the object. This is sort of a No Style option for individual panes. For example, if you choose Clear Attributes Not Defined by Style in the pane's pop-up menu, any formatting that would otherwise be defined in unchecked panes will be left untouched in the selected object(s), while all other formatting will be removed. Likewise, if you choose Clear Overrides, any formatting in the checked panes will be reapplied to the object(s) but any formatting that would have been specified in the unchecked panes will be retained in the object(s).

❺ Click OK when done.

❻ You apply object styles by selecting the desired object(s) and clicking a style in the Object Style pane. Hold Option or Alt when clicking to override all formatting applied to the object; otherwise, that local formatting will be retained.

❼ In the Object Styles pane's palette menu, you have menu options to edit, delete, and apply styles.

❽ In the palette menu, note two options unique to the Object Styles pane: Default Text Frame Style and Default Graphics Frame Style. In their submenus, you choose the default style for new text frames and graphics frames, respectively — a handy way to have new objects have the desired specifications automatically (similar to QuarkXPress's Tool preferences, which let you set the basic attributes for each of the box and line tools).

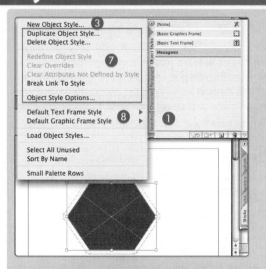

Anchoring Objects to Text

Follow These Steps

While QuarkXPress and InDesign both let you copy a graphic into text as an inline graphic (see pages 250-251), only InDesign CS2 lets you anchor frames to text so that the frame is outside the text but follows the text as the text reflows. Here are the steps to creating such anchored objects:

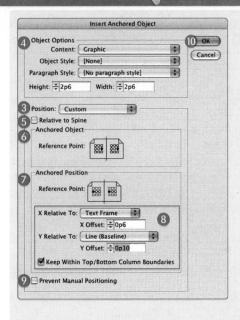

1. Select the Type tool, then click within a text frame to establish the insertion point.

2. Choose Object ➪ Anchored Object ➪ Insert.

3. Choose Custom from the Position pop-up menu; this displays the Insert Anchored Object dialog box.

4. In the Object Options section, specify the anchored frame's settings. Choose the type of frame (text, graphics, or unassigned) in the Content pop-up menu, apply an object style using the Object Style pop-up menu, apply a paragraph style for the frame's text contents if desired using the Paragraph Style pop-up menu, and set the inline frame's dimensions using the Height and Width fields.

5. Decide whether to check Relative to Spine. If unchecked, the anchored frame will be placed on the same side of the text frame on all pages, whether left-facing or right-facing. If checked, InDesign will place the text frame on the outside of both pages or inside of both pages, depending on how the anchored position is set.

6. In the Anchored Object section of the dialog box, click one of the positioning squares to set up the text frame's relative position. For example, if you want the anchored frame to appear to the right of the text reference, click one of the right-hand squares. (Remember that the Relative to Spine checkbox can override this, making the righthand pages' positions mirror that of the lefthand pages, not be identical to them.) If you choose the topmost righthand square, the anchored frame will be placed to the right of the text reference and vertically appear at or below that text reference. You'll need to experiment with your layout to see what works best.

7. In the Anchored Position section of the dialog box, click one of the positioning squares to set up the text reference's relative position. Although there are nine squares shown, only three matter: those in the middle row. Typically, you'd have the text reference be on the opposite side of the anchored frame — if you want the anchored frame to be to the left, you thus would indicate that the text reference is to the right. (If you set the text reference to be on the same side as the anchored frame, InDesign will place the anchored frame over the text.) The three squares (left, middle, and right) accommodate layouts where you'd want some anchored frames to appear to the left of the text and

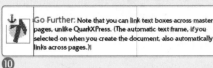

Go Further: Note that you can link text boxes across master pages, unlike QuarkXPress. (The automatic text frame, if you selected on when you create the document, also automatically links across pages.)

10.

some to the right; in that case, you'd choose the middle position here and select the righthand or lefthand position in the Anchored Object section as appropriate to that object.

8 Three options in the Anchored Position section give InDesign more precise instructions on how to place the anchored frames: The X Relative To pop-up menu tells InDesign from where the horizontal location is calculated, using the following options: Anchor Marker, Column Edge, Text Frame, Page Margin, and Page Edge. The correct option will depend both on where you want the anchored frames placed and whether you have multicolumn text boxes (in which case Text Frame and Column Edge result in different placement, while in a single-column text frame they do not). You can also specify a specific amount of space to place between the chosen X Relative To point and the anchored frame by entering a value in the X Offset field. Similarly, the Y Relative To pop-up menu tells InDesign from where the horizontal location is calculated, using the following options: Line (Baseline), Line (Cap-height), Line (Top of Leading), Column Edge, Text Frame, Page Margin, and Page Edge. As you would expect, you can also specify a precise amount of space to place between the chosen Y Relative To point and the anchored frame by entering a value in the Y Offset field.

9 No matter which position settings you apply, you can check the Prevent Manual Positioning checkbox to ensure that individual frames' positions can't be adjusted using InDesign's other frame-positioning controls (such as the Control palette's or Transform pane's X and Y fields). This forces users to use this dialog box to change the anchored frame's position.

10 Click OK to insert the anchored frame.

11 To converting existing frames to anchored frames, follow the steps on page 251 to create an inline frame and then choose Object ➪ Anchored Object ➪ Options to display the Anchored Object Options dialog box. Using the Position pop-up menu, choose Custom. This converts the frame from an inline frame to an anchored frame. Adjust the position for the newly minted anchored frame as described in steps 5 through 8 above. Click OK when done.

12 If you no longer want an anchored frame to be anchored to a text location, you can release the anchor. To do so, select the anchored frame with the Selection or Direct Selection tool and then choose Object ➪ Anchored Object ➪ Release.

13 To delete an anchored frame, select it with the Selection or Direct Selection tool and then choose Edit ➪ Clear or press Delete or Backspace. If you want to remove the object but keep it in the Clipboard for pasting elsewhere, choose Edit ➪ Cut, or press ⌘+X or Ctrl+X.

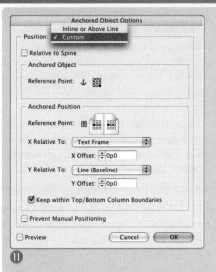

11

Go Further: InDesign's approach to frames is more flexible than QuarkXPress's approach to boxes, eliminating both the rigid distinction between the two and not requiring that a graphic frame exist before you can place a graphic.¶

11

⬛Placing Images in Open Shapes

Follow These Steps

QuarkXPress containers must be wholly closed, such as rectangles or ellipses. That's not true in InDesign, which lets you place a graphic even in open shapes. When doing so, InDesign will use the shape's contours to determine an area in which to place the shape.

1 Create the open shape by drawing it with the Pen or Pencil tool, or open a closed shape using the Erase or Scissors tool or, in InDesign CS2, by splitting a Bézier point by choosing Object ➪ Paths ➪ Open Path.

2 Select the shape with the Selection or Direct Selection tool.

3 Choose File ➪ Place (⌘+D or Ctrl+D) to import a graphic.

4 The graphic will be placed in the selected open shape when you click Open in the Place dialog box.

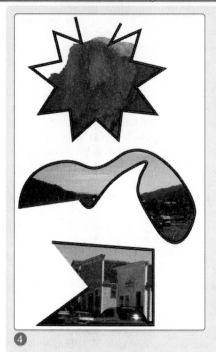

4

Follow These Steps

In traditional publishing, objects are either fully there or not there at all, but digital media permit in-between states using transparency that in the pre-digital era required photographic tricks in the darkroom. InDesign is more modern than that, letting you apply transparency to objects to let them fade away, fade into each other, and otherwise have different degrees of solidity.

① Open the Transparency pane (Window ⇨ Transparency or Shift+F10).

② Select the object(s) for which to apply transparency effects. (Transparency applies to frames and their complete contents, so you cannot apply transparency just to some letters in a text frame, for example.)

③ Choose one of the 16 effects from the Blend Effects pop-up menu.

④ Choose a level of opacity (70% opaque equals 30% transparent) in the Opacity pop-up menu/field. This will have different effects based on the blend effect chosen. In the images at right:

- The top image applies the Screen blending mode to a graphic frame and an Opacity of 80% to lighten the image portion under the text. (That image portion is in its own frame overprinting the full picture.)

- The second image keeps the Blend Mode at Normal with an Opacity of 60% to lighten it.

- The third image is the same as the second image except that the text frame has a Blend Mode of Luminosity and Opacity of 70%.

- The bottom image shows a second photo overlaying the FDR photo, both with Opacity settings of 70%, which lets the images blend together.

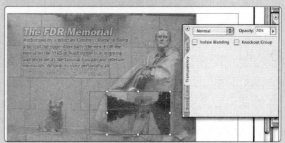

⑤ InDesign also lets you control how transparency is handled during output through flattener presets. (Be sure to check the settings with your service bureau.) You can set them in the Flattener pane (Window ⇨ Output ⇨ Flattener in InDesign CS2, Window ⇨ Output Preview ⇨ Flattener in InDesign CS, or Edit ⇨ Transparency Flattener Styles in InDesign 2). Choose Flattener Presets from the palette menu, which opens a dialog box where you can edit or create flattener presets.

⑥ You can apply flattener presets to specific pages by choosing Spread Flattening in the palette menu of the Pages pane (Window ⇨ Pages or F12).

⑦ You can also apply different transparency flattener settings when printing in the Advanced pane of the Print dialog box (File ⇨ Print, or ⌘+P or Ctrl+P) by choosing an option in the Transparency Flattener section.

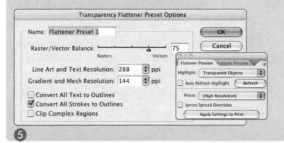

⑤

Working with Drop Shadows and Feathering

Follow These Steps

Drop shadows are a time-honored effect that layout programs have long ignored. Sure, you can simulate a drop shadow by placing an object behind the current one and offsetting it slightly, but that's a poor substitute (see pages 278-279). InDesign offers real drop-shadow capabilities, as well as related function called *feathering*.

Applying Drop Shadows

1 Using the Selection or Direct Selection tool, select the frame(s) to which you want to apply drop shadows.

2 Open the Drop Shadow dialog box by choosing Object ➪ Drop Shadow (Option+⌘+M or Ctrl+Alt+M).

3 Check the Drop Shadow checkbox to enable the drop shadow.

4 Set the blend style in the Mode pop-up menu; these 16 blends will produce different effects, so experiment with them by checking the Preview checkbox to see what they do.

5 Set the drop shadow's other attributes: the color, opacity, degree of blur, size (via the X Offset and Y Offset fields), and, in InDesign CS2, the Spread and Noise percentages, which affect the blur appearance.

6 Click OK to apply the drop shadow.

7 Change a drop shadow by repeating steps 1, 2, and 4-6.

8 Delete a drop shadow by repeating steps 1 and 2, and unchecking the Drop Shadow checkbox and clicking OK.

If you apply a drop shadow to a text frame, InDesign will apply the shadow to the text only if the frame has no fill color. Otherwise, InDesign will apply the shadow to the frame.

Applying Feathering

Feathering is similar to drop shadows, except that it applies the blur to all four sides. You can use feathering with drop shadows (as in the image at right) or by itself.

1 Using the Selection or Direct Selection tool, select the frame(s) to which you want to apply feathering.

2 Open the Feather dialog box by choosing Object ➪Feather.

3 Check the Feather checkbox to enable the feathering.

4 Set the feathering width and corner shape. In InDesign CS2, you can also select the noise level (which affects the blur).

5 Click OK to apply the feathering.

7 Change feathering by repeating steps 1, 2, 4, and 5.

8 Delete feathering by repeating steps 1 and 2, and unchecking the Feather checkbox and clicking OK.

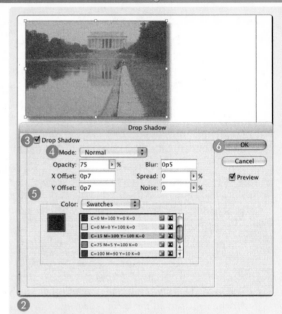

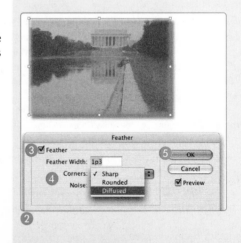

Follow These Steps

Often, you want a paragraph style that's more sophisticated than applying attributes to everything in the paragraph. Nested styles, introduced in InDesign CS, let you specify a sequence of rules and attributes so you can perform more sophisticated formatting.

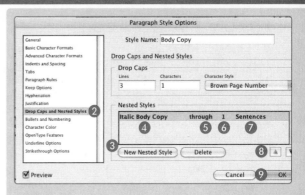

1 Define any character styles that you'll apply to text via a nested style. The Nested Styles feature cannot apply any attributes other than those in character styles.

2 Go to the Paragraph Styles dialog box (Window ➪ Type & Tables ➪ Paragraph Styles in InDesign CS or later, or Window ➪ Type ➪ Paragraph Styles in InDesign 2, or F11) and select Drop Caps & Nested Styles.

3 Click the New Nested Style button. An entry will appear under the Nested Styles label.

4 The first column is where you choose from existing character styles. This is what will be applied to text.

5 The second column determines the scope end point: Through or Up To. For example, if you choose Through for a nested style that is set for four words, all four words will get the nested style. If you choose Up To, the first three words will get the style and the fourth will not.

6 The third column is where you specify how many items you want InDesign to count in determining the scope's end point. For example, if you want the first seven characters to have the style applied, choose 7. If you want to have the style applied up to the first tab, choose 1.

7 The fourth column is where you specify the scope of text to which you're applying the nested style. The options break into three groups: a number of items (characters, words, and so on), a specific character (tab, em space, and so on), and a specific marker character (inline graphic marker, auto page number, and section marker).

8 Whatever you choose needs to be consistent in all your text, since InDesign will follow these rules slavishly. InDesign applies styles in the order in which they appear in the dialog box, and each starts where the other ends. Use the ▲ and ▼ buttons to change the order of nested styles.

9 Click OK when you're done.

About the only thing missing from the Nested Styles feature is, unfortunately, an effect favored by many designers: applying a format to the first line in a paragraph, such as small caps, then switching to normal capitalization for the rest of the paragraph. But in InDesign, the best you can do is highlight this text manually and apply the small caps attribute yourself, or you can use the Nested Styles feature and manually insert the End Nested Style Character at the end of each line (choose Type ➪ Insert Special Character ➪ End Nested Style).

Working with OpenType

Follow These Steps

The OpenType font format permits multiple variations of characters and can also include a broad set of special symbols in the font that used to be placed in separate fonts (such as expert collections that included small caps, old-style numerals, and fractions). InDesign fully supports OpenType, giving you access to all the font's characters and even letting you have specify variations applied automatically through styles.

① In the Character pane (Type ➪ Character, or ⌘+T or Ctrl+T) or in the Character pane (the A icon) of the Control palette, apply OpenType attributes to selected text by choosing in the palette menu the OpenType option and then the desired option from the submenu.

② For a character style, open the Character Styles pane by choosing Window ➪ Type & Tables ➪ Character Styles in InDesign CS or later, or Window ➪ Type ➪ Character Styles in InDesign 2, or Shift+F11). Then choose New Character Style to create a style, or choose Character Style Options to edit one. Go to the OpenType Features pane and select the desired options. In the various checkboxes, a checkmark means to apply the attribute, a – (dash) means to leave the text unchanged, and an empty box means to remove the attribute. You apply two kinds of OpenType attributes — figure styles and stylistic sets — via pop-up menus.

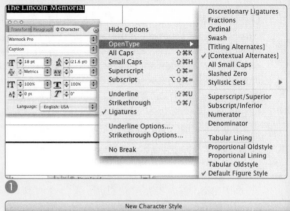

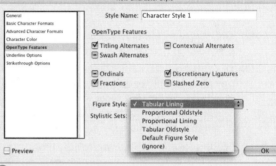

Keep in Mind

OpenType has several types of attributes. Among those not obvious by their name are:

① Ordinal, which raises the *st*, *nd*, and *th* portions of ordinal numbers such as *1st*, *22nd*, and *345th*.

② Swash, which adds embellishments in front of the first character or at the end of the last letter of a word.

③ Titling Alternates, which uses variants of a font for use in titles that are usually a little clearer than the body-text version in the larger size of titles and with the usually greater white space around titles.

④ Contextual Alternates, which uses variants for specific characters to improve legibility in some contexts. For example, a contextual alternate for *t* might drop the left side bar in the *t* so it doesn't bump against an adjacent letter.

⑤ Discretionary Ligatures, which uses other ligatures than the standard fi, fl, ffi, and ffl.

⑥ Slashed Zero, which adds a slash over a 0 character (Ø) for fonts that support it. The slashed zero is often used in European writing to differentiate from the letter *O*.

⑦ Stylistic Sets, which let you choose which sets of variants within a font to use (for fonts that have them).

⑧ Various types of numerals; lining numerals are modern ones while oldstyle numerals have ascenders and descenders. Tabular varieties line up when typed, since each numeral has the same width, while proportional numerals vary in width for better appearance outside of tables.

MARTHA & BROS.

3868 24th St⑧415) 641-4433; 1551 Church St Cortland St. (Bernal Heights), (415) 642-758 St. (Pacific Heights), (415) 931-2281. Family-o Martha's is the neighborhood ⑤ffee ②int, w weekends. Th⑤sta.ff knows its customers, se favorites before they even reach the counter lar, and the folks at ②artha's even remembe

Follow These Steps

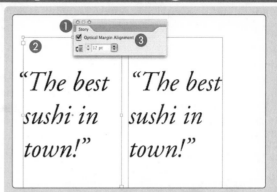

A very nice way that InDesign offers to provide more visually pleasing text alignment is called *optical margins*. Normally, a layout program aligns text to the margin so that the outer edge of the character abuts the margin. That's fine for most body text, but in larger text such as headlines, you can get awkward white space from having some characters like *T* or open quotes that tend to appear to be indented slightly. Optical margins adjusts the characters' positions along the margins so visually they seem more aligned, even though in fact they are not.

1. Open the Story pane (Window ⇨ Type & Tables ⇨ Story in InDesign CS or later, or Window ⇨ Type ⇨ Story in InDesign 2).

2. Select the text frame on which to use optical margin alignment, using the Selection tool or Direct Selection tool.

3. Check the Optical Margin Alignment checkbox to enable alignment. If desired, choose a new value for the alignment depth in the Align Based on Size pop-up menu/field below; the larger the number, the deeper that InDesign will look to balance text alignment; smaller numbers tend to produce better results because they let InDesign optimize more lines of text independently.

Working with Multiple Document Views

Follow These Steps

Sometimes when working on a document, you want to have multiple windows open so you can, for example, switch among pages easily. QuarkXPress lets you open multiple documents at once, but not multiple windows of the same document. However, InDesign can.

1. To open a new window, choose Window ➪ Arrange ➪ New Window in InDesign CS or later, or Window ➪ New Window in InDesign 2.

2. Resize, move, minimize, or apply window controls (such as tiling and stacking) just as you would if you had multiple documents open. (You apply tiling and stacking via the Window menu.)

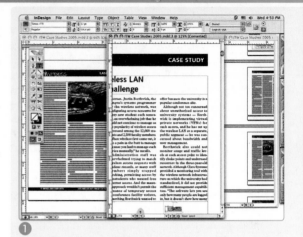

Follow These Steps

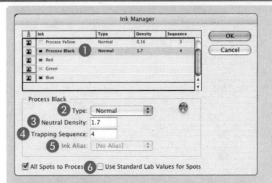

When you trap colors (see pages 290-293), InDesign must account for the different densities of each color, so light colors like yellow don't get overwhelmed by dark ones like black. InDesign lets you handle such issues with the Ink Manager dialog box, which you can use to set a specific color swatch by choosing Ink Manager in the Swatches pane (Window ➪ Swatches or F5) or for a specific print job by clicking Ink Manager in the Output pane of the Print dialog box (File ➪ Print, or ⌘+P or Ctrl+P). Be sure to coordinate these settings with your service bureau.

① Select an ink from the list.

② You can change the ink type in the Type pop-up menu. Most inks should be left at Normal. Use Transparent for varnishes and other finishes that let color through — you don't want InDesign to trap to such "colors"; if they did, no color would print under the finish. Use Opaque for metallics, pastels, and other such colors; this setting trap adjacent colors to the edge of opaque objects but it prevent trapping of underlying colors (since they will be totally covered over). Use Opaque-Ignore for inks that don't trap well with any other color.

③ You can change the neutral density, which tells InDesign how to handle the trapping of differently saturated inks. For example, a dark color (highly saturated) will need to be trapped more conservatively against a light color to prevent excess intrusion. Higher numbers tell InDesign that the color is more saturated (denser).

④ Some commercial printers let you arrange the order in which color negatives print. This affects the trapping, because InDesign presumes that the colors are printed in the standard order — cyan, then magenta, then yellow, then black, then any spot colors — and factors that into its trapping adjustments. In some cases, changing the printing order can improve a publication's color balance. For example, if there's a lot of black in the background, you might want to print black first, so other colors overprint it, giving it a warmer feel than if black were printed on top of the other colors as is normal. To change the order of output, select a color, and change its number in the Trapping Sequence field; all other colors' sequences will be automatically adjusted.

⑤ Use the Ink Alias pop-up menu to apply a process color's settings to a spot color, a handy way to control spot colors' appearance in some cases. It's also a very handy way to essentially assign multiple colors — such as those imported from EPS files — to the same plate, so that differently named colors (such as PMS 123 and Pantone 123) will use the same plate.

⑥ In InDesign CS2, use the Use CMYK Alternates for PMS/HKS checkbox to force InDesign to substitute the basic CMYK process colors for the similar Pantone and HKS colors.

appendix a

n its very first version, Adobe made sure that InDesign could open QuarkXPress files, recognizing the preeminence of QuarkXPress in the publishing world. Since then, Quark modified the QuarkXPress file format (starting in version 5) to prevent InDesign from opening its files, but since most QuarkXPress users have stayed with version 4, the InDesign ability to open QuarkXPress files remains valuable.

Opening QuarkXPress Documents

The Open command (File ⇨ Open, or ⌘+O or Ctrl+O) lets you select and open documents and templates saved in QuarkXPress versions 3.3 through 4.11 on Macintosh or Windows. InDesign CS2 also opens QuarkXPress Passport files for the same versions. (You can't open libraries or books, though, nor version 5 or 6 files.) All the text, graphics, items, master pages, style sheets, and more in the QuarkXPress document are converted to their InDesign equivalents. If the document contains items, content, or formatting that can't be converted, an alert notifies you of the issues. When converted to InDesign, the document displays as a new, untitled document.

Once you open a QuarkXPress file in InDesign, you can only save it as an InDesign file. InDesign will automatically append the .indd filename extension to the QuarkXPress filename, so unless you explicitly change the filename extension when saving, there's no chance of accidentally overwriting that original QuarkXPress file.

Conversion Issues

Now that you know what InDesign is supposed to do, take a look at how well it actually performs. Yes, you can open QuarkXPress documents, save them as InDesign documents, and continue working with them. But the documents don't convert perfectly: You're likely to lose some formatting because InDesign doesn't have equivalent formatting, or because its options work differently. In general, you can expect to use a QuarkXPress document as a starting point for a design — usually with a little repair work — but you should not expect to simply open a QuarkXPress document in InDesign and have it still look and print exactly the same way.

Tip: After realizing which QuarkXPress features are not supported or do not convert well, and considering how your own QuarkXPress documents are created, you can decide on a document-by-document basis whether conversion is worth the effort. In some cases, it might be easier to simply reconstruct a document, while in other cases you might be able to start working on the converted document almost immediately.

When you convert QuarkXPress documents to InDesign, you can expect the following:

- Master pages are converted, including all items, content, and guides.
- All line and frame styles are converted to dashed or plain strokes.

- Text boxes are converted to text frames; picture boxes are converted to graphics frames.

- Baseline adjustments often don't carry over, especially when applied to inline boxes.

- Text paths are converted.

- All paragraph and character style sheets are converted to InDesign styles.

- Incremental auto leading (such as **+4**, which adds 4 points to the largest font size on the line) is converted to InDesign's standard auto leading.

- Next Column (keypad Enter) or Next Box (Shift+keypad Enter) characters (which you use to bump text to the next column or next text box rather than resizing the box) are retained.

- Bold and Italic type styles are converted to the appropriate typeface (if available), and Underline, Strike Thru, Superscript, Subscript, All Caps, and Small Caps are converted. Superior, Word Underline, Outline, and Shadow revert to plain text.

- Index tags are not maintained, and you may have difficulty opening chapters of a book.

- If a picture is missing or modified in QuarkXPress, it won't display in the InDesign document. If you want to retain the picture, you'll need to update the links in QuarkXPress (Utilities ⇨ Usage ⇨ Pictures) before converting.

- Pictures that are pasted (embedded), imported using OLE or Publish and Subscribe, or created with third-party XTensions will not convert.

- Rotated graphics in QuarkXPress may not remain rotated when imported into InDesign.

- Color graphics imported into QuarkXPress as grayscale will appear as color in InDesign. Likewise, grayscale graphics in QuarkXPress imported as black-and-white will appear as grayscale in InDesign.

- The customizable dashes in QuarkXPress are converted to solid and dashed lines — note that stripes do convert properly.

- Clipping paths created in QuarkXPress or imported with an image into QuarkXPress are not converted, so the image's display will change.

- The Same as Clipping Runaround feature in QuarkXPress leaves a runaround shape based on the clipping path in InDesign — but if you've resized the image in QuarkXPress, the runaround path stays at 100 percent in InDesign.

- Items for which Suppress Printout is checked are placed on a separate layer called "Nonprinting layer." To view these objects in InDesign, view the layer.

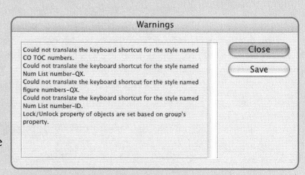

Figure A-1. The warning dialog box that InDesign presents when it cannot convert an element in a QuarkXPress file.

- If a group contains an item for which Suppress Printout is checked, all the items are ungrouped and the suppressed items are placed on the nonprinting layer.
- ICC-compliant color profiles (used in QuarkXPress 4.0 and greater) are retained; other profiles (the EfiColor profiles used in QuarkXPress 3.3x) are not retained.
- Colors in QuarkXPress 3.3x documents are converted to InDesign swatches according to their CMYK values (except for HSB colors, which are converted to RGB swatches).
- Colors in QuarkXPress 4.x documents are converted to InDesign swatches according to their RGB values (except for HSB and LAB colors, which are converted to RGB swatches). Hexachrome colors are not converted.
- Blends are converted to linear or circular blends.

Tip: When converting QuarkXPress files to InDesign format, not everything will translate smoothly. You can minimize issues by first setting your non-style-sheet typographic preferences in InDesign to match your QuarkXPress preferences (for example, for small caps, superscripts, and subscripts). Also, you will likely find that your converted paragraph and character styles are no longer in alphabetical order and that some clipping paths around graphics are incorrect. For the style-sheet issue, delete one style and add it back — doing so usually forces the names to be correctly reordered. For the clipping-path issue, turn off the clipping path and then turn it back on for the affected graphics to correct the display.

As you open a QuarkXPress document, InDesign will highlight any conversion issues, as Figure A-1 shows. You can save the warning's text to a text file by clicking the Save button; doing so will give you a reference to the issues to refer to later.

Tip: After converting a QuarkXPress file to InDesign, you can use a semitransparent PDF file of the original QuarkXPress document to locate the differences between the original and the converted XPress file. In the converted InDesign document, create a new layer with the Layers pane (Window ⇨ Layers or F7). In that layer, place the PDF by choosing File ⇨ Place (⌘+D or Ctrl+D) and checking the Show Import Options checkbox in the Place dialog box. Select the PDF file and click Open. In the Import Options dialog box, select the page of the PDF to import and choose Crop from the Crop To pop-up menu so the imported PDF file will match the exact page dimensions. Click OK to place the PDF page and be sure that the frame containing the PDF page is placed exactly at the top and left edge of the page (with X and Y coordinates of 0). In the Transparency pane (Window ⇨ Transparency or Shift+F10), set Opacity for the frame containing the PDF page to 60% or 70%. This will let you see through the PDF to the layer below. Lock the layer in the Layers pane. Adjust the InDesign objects and type on the other layer(s) until they are aligned with the objects displayed in the semitransparent layer. Toggling the PDF layer off and on again lets you locate differences, too. Repeat these steps for each page.

appendix D

Differences in a Nutshell

Learning to use new software, or even learning to use an upgrade of a familiar application, can be so intimidating that many users resist passionately. Even if an application is woefully out of date and lacking in functionality, you cling to it knowing you can accomplish your mission — often with workarounds — with less frustration than with an untried, but powerful, new application. Users are particularly passionate about their choice of page-layout software — which is usually QuarkXPress — probably because they're working with it for up to 12 hours a day. (A QuarkXPress user once said he spent more time with Quark-XPress than with his wife, so you can see the level of dedication.)

But times, circumstances, and jobs change. Eventually, your old software won't run on your zippy new machine, or you switch jobs, or you simply prefer another vendor. No matter what circumstances lead you to choosing InDesign, this appendix is designed to help you let go and move forward, summarizing you the differences between your old layout application and InDesign, and pointing out a few benefits of InDesign as well. InDesign lets you open documents created in both QuarkXPress and PageMaker so you can continue working with existing designs, and you can apply much of your page-layout knowledge to InDesign.

Understanding Tool Differences

For the QuarkXPress veteran, the toughest thing about switching to InDesign is adjusting to the set of tools. In your world, you've been using the Item tool (which you might call the pointer) and the Content tool (the little hand) for almost everything. Not only did you use them all the time, but the Item tool or Content tool was selected automatically for you most of the time (since object-creation tools snap back to the last-used selection tool). Over time, the two tools have evolved almost into one, so you might have been using the Content tool all the time, pressing ⌘ or Ctrl when you needed to manipulate an entire item.

You need to forget about this way of working entirely. In InDesign, you'll be switching tools constantly. (There is a workaround when working on text frames: hold ⌘ or Ctrl to switch temporarily to the Selection tool. Also, as in QuarkXPress, you can hold Option or Alt to switch temporarily to the Hand tool.) When you create an object, its tool remains selected so you can't move or resize the objects immediately after creation — unless you hold ⌘ or Ctrl.

More dramatically, the Selection tool only lets you move and resize objects, while the Direct Selection tool lets you reshape objects and work with graphics. The difference between InDesign's Selection tool and Direct Selection tool takes some getting used to for QuarkXPress users. In terms of working with content, the Direct Selection tool is much like the QuarkXPress Content tool, but it also lets you edit the frame as if it were a Bézier object. For example, if the Direct Selection tool is selected and you drag a point on the frame, you'll move that point and thus change the shape of the object — a rectangle will be converted into a polygon, since the lines immediately adjacent to the moved point will move with the point, while the rest of the frame will not be affected. In QuarkXPress, if the Content tool is selected and you drag a point on the frame, you'll resize the frame (perhaps nonproportionally) but the entire side(s) adjacent to the point will move with the point, so a rectangle would still be a rectangle. To change a frame in InDesign way you would in QuarkXPress with both the Content and Item tools, use the Selection tool in InDesign.

Think of the Type tool as a combination of the Rectangle Text Box tool and the Content tool for text. You must have the Type tool to work with text, but there's no moving or resizing of text frames while you're using it — unless you hold ⌘ or Ctrl.

This will seem restrictive to you at first — but the key for some users is to embrace InDesign's single-letter shortcuts for selecting tools. Others will prefer QuarkXPress-like keyboard commands, such as ⌘ or Ctrl and Option or Alt, for temporarily activating tools.

As long as the Type tool isn't selected, you can activate any tool by pressing the letter displayed next to it in the tool's Tool Tip. In particular, you'll want to memorize the following:

- Press V for the Selection tool.
- Press A for the Direct Selection tool.
- Press T for the Type tool.
- Press H for the Hand tool (you can also press the spacebar; when editing text, you can press Option or Alt).
- Press Z for the Zoom tool (you can also press ⌘+spacebar or Ctrl+spacebar then click the mouse to zoom in, and Option+⌘+spacebar or Ctrl+Alt+spacebar then click the mouse to zoom out).

If you're also a Photoshop user, the single-letter shortcuts might be familiar to you, but these shortcuts are an odd concept for a QuarkXPress-only user. Once you get the hang of it, however, you'll appreciate how fast and easy it is to switch tools with these single letters.

A few overall interface differences between QuarkXPress and InDesign might hang you up initially. Keep in mind that many menu commands simply display a pane (which may already be open) rather than showing a dialog box. Get used to deciphering icons or using Tool Tips on the panes because a few dialog boxes contain named fields as you're used to in the QuarkXPress Character Attributes, Paragraph Attributes, and Modify dialog boxes. Contextual menus are implemented on a much broader scale than in QuarkXPress, so you can Control+click or right+click on objects, rulers, and more to make changes quickly.

InDesign CS and CS2 also offer docking panes, whose tabs can be aligned to the screen edges so they're not in the way, as well as docked to the top of the screen like Microsoft

Word's formatting palettes. You can drag these docked panes to your document to make them floating panes à la QuarkXPress. Note that InDesign's panes can be rearranged and combined into multipane palettes by dragging them on top of each other — QuarkXPress's palettes are fixed and cannot be combined. QuarkXPress also lets the widely used Tools and Measurements palettes float anywhere, so they often get covered up by other interface elements. InDesign can work that way, but InDesign CS or later are smarter about the equivalent Tools and Control palettes, placing them by default away from the window so they stay available.

Because InDesign has so many panes, it needs a way to manage them. Unlike QuarkXPress, InDesign lets you save these interface settings using its Workspaces feature (Window ⇨ Workspace, whose submenu lets you select, create, and delete these workspaces).

InDesign uses all of the measurement abbreviations of QuarkXPress, as well as its own. For example, InDesign (in version CS or later) accepts QuarkXPress's use of " to indicate inches, as well as InDesign's own standard of **in** and **inch**. Likewise, it accepts QuarkXPress's **mm** for millimeter, as well as InDesign's own standard of **m**.

Tip: InDesign offers a set of keyboard commands similar to those in QuarkXPress (Edit ⇨ Keyboard Shortcuts). I recommend that you avoid this set and learn the commands in InDesign. This will help you in communicating about InDesign and working with other Adobe software.

Converting Keyboard Shortcuts

If you're switching from QuarkXPress and committed to learning InDesign's keyboard shortcuts, skim Table B-1 to see the primary differences.

Document Differences

By and large, documents in InDesign and QuarkXPress are the same. You have master pages, layers (available in QuarkXPress 5 or later), and pages. You can also set bleeds for objects that go beyond the page boundary. But note some differences:

* InDesign lets you specify a slug area, which reserves space during printing for the printer's marks.

* QuarkXPress 6 permits several layouts in one document file, called a *project*, so you can mix layouts with different page sizes. InDesign does not permit that.

* The InDesign master text frame is not the same as QuarkXPress's automatic text box on a master page. You cannot flow text into a QuarkXPress automatic text box while you're working on a master page — instead, an empty text box is placed on each of your layout pages for you automatically. Although you can have QuarkXPress flow text into automatic text boxes across pages as you add pages to your layout, you can also place text in these boxes individually, without them being linked. An InDesign master text

Table B-1:
Keyboard Shortcuts Translated from QuarkXPress to InDesign

Action	QuarkXPress Shortcut	InDesign Equivalent
Zoom in	Control *or* Ctrl	⌘+= *or* Ctrl+=
Zoom out	Control+Option *or* Ctrl+Alt	⌘+− *or* Ctrl+−
Page grabber hand	Option *or* Alt	H, *or* spacebar, *or* Option *or* Alt *(in text)*
Preferences	Option+Shift+⌘+Y *or* Ctrl+Alt+Shift+Y	⌘+K *or* Ctrl+K
Get Text/Picture	⌘+E *or* Ctrl+E	⌘+D *or* Ctrl+D *for Place*
Paragraph formats	⌘+Shift+F *or* Ctrl+Shift+F	Option+⌘+T *or* Ctrl+Alt+T
Character formats	Shift+⌘+D *or* Ctrl+Shift+D	⌘+T *or* Ctrl+T
Style Sheets palette	F11	F11 *(Character Styles),* Shift+F11 *(Paragraph Styles)*
Spelling (word)	⌘+L *or* Ctrl+W	⌘+I *or* Ctrl+I
Modify dialog box	⌘+M *or* Ctrl+M	*no equivalent*
Delete selection	⌘+K *or* Ctrl+K	Delete
Duplicate	⌘+D *or* Ctrl+D	Option+Shift+⌘+D *or* Ctrl+Alt+Shift+D
Step and Repeat	Option+⌘+D *or* Ctrl+Alt+D	Shift+⌘+V *or* Ctrl+Shift+V
Lock/Unlock	F6	⌘+L *or* Ctrl+L *(lock),* Option+⌘+L *or* Ctrl+Alt+L *(unlock)*
Ungroup	⌘+U *or* Ctrl+U	Shift+⌘+G *or* Ctrl+Shift+G
Space Align	⌘+, *or* Ctrl+,	F8
Send to Back	Shift+F5	Shift+⌘+[*or* Ctrl+Shift+[
Send Backward	Option+Shift+F5 *or* Ctrl+Shift+F5	⌘+[*or* Ctrl+[
Bring to Front	F5	Shift+⌘+] *or* Ctrl+Shift+]
Bring Forward	Option+F5 *or* Ctrl+F5	⌘+] *or* Ctrl+]

frame is linked automatically from page to page and is not meant for holding text that does not flow from page to page.

- QuarkXPress 5 and 6 support Web documents, which InDesign does not. InDesign CS and CS2 also cannot export print layouts to the Web's HTML format.

- InDesign can generate TOCs only based on paragraph style sheets, not on character style sheets. This means that you can't create other kinds of lists, such as a list of companies in a magazine article or research report, based on the use of character style sheets. InDesign doesn't have a flexible Lists feature as QuarkXPress does, just the Table of Contents feature that is essentially a subset of QuarkXPress's Lists feature. However, you can use the InDesign Table of Contents feature to create some lists other than TOCs. Also, the level of formatting you can achieve over TOC entries in InDesign is greater than in QuarkXPress.

- The InDesign index features are similar to those in QuarkXPress, although the InDesign

Index pane and QuarkXPress Index palette have very different interfaces.

- The corner-style feature in InDesign (Object ⇨ Corner Effects) is similar to the text-box and picture-box variants in QuarkXPress, which offer the same selection of corners except for the Fancy option. In QuarkXPress, you create, or convert, a box to a variant that has one of these corner effects, while in InDesign, you apply the corner effect to a frame.

- InDesign's nested frames are similar to QuarkXPress's constrained boxes — the biggest difference is that, to nest a frame in InDesign, you paste a frame into another (Edit ⇨ Paste Into, or Option+⌘+V or Ctrl+Alt+V). In QuarkXPress, you choose Item ⇨ Constrain.

Working with Objects Rather Than Items

In QuarkXPress, you're used to items such as text boxes, picture boxes, lines, and maybe text paths. In InDesign, you have paths and frames, with the only difference being that frames contain graphics or text. You can, therefore, make a one-to-one relationship between text boxes and text frames, and picture boxes and graphic frames. Just keep in mind that, with InDesign, you're not restricted to using boxes for content — you can fill any path, even an open one, with text or graphics and have it become a frame. And if you don't make a box (or the right kind of box) up front, you can still import graphics and text in InDesign (unlike in QuarkXPress, which requires you to change the box type first).

While selecting and manipulating objects with tools, remember the following:

- Use the Selection tool to move objects or resize frames. It's somewhat similar to the QuarkXPress Item tool.

- Use the Direct Selection tool to reshape objects, work with graphics, and change the endpoints of lines (it's a bit like QuarkXPress's Content tool).

- When reshaping objects, you can use the Pen tool, Add Anchor Point tool, and Delete Anchor Point tool in addition to the Direct Selection tool.

- You can't just click on master-page objects to select them on the document pages: Instead, select them using Shift+⌘+click or Ctrl+Shift+click.

When modifying objects, remember the following:

- InDesign CS and CS2 add a more-capable clone of QuarkXPress's Measurements palette, called the Control palette in InDesign (Window ⇨ Control, or Option+⌘+6 or Ctrl+Alt+6). You can also use the Transform pane in InDesign (Window ⇨ Transform in InDesign 2 and CS, Window ⇨ Object & Layout ⇨ Transform in InDesign CS2, or F9). Use these tools for the equivalent of the QuarkXPress Modify dialog box's Box and Line panes.

- To specify runaround, choose Window ⇨ Types & Tables ⇨ Text Wrap in InDesign 2 and

CS or Window ⇨ Text Wrap in InDesign CS2, or press Option+⌘+W or Ctrl+Alt+W, to open the Text Wrap pane.

- To specify attributes of text frames, choose Object ⇨ Text Frame Options, or press ⌘+B or Ctrl+B, to open the Text Frame Options dialog box. This is roughly equivalent to the Text pane in QuarkXPress's Modify dialog box.

- In InDesign CS2, you can create object styles that let you apply consistent formatting — and update that formatting easily — across multiple objects. This is the same concept as style sheets for text.

- The InDesign Shear tool is not the same as the QuarkXPress Skew tool — Shear both slants and rotates an object, while Skew just slants it. To simulate the QuarkXPress Skew tool, hold the Shift key while you move the mouse horizontally when using the InDesign Shear tool — this ensures that there is no rotation. You can also use the Shear fields in the Control palette or Transform pane to only slant an object.

Working with Text

InDesign works with text very differently than QuarkXPress in many cases, even though the fundamental capabilities are the same in both programs. Veteran QuarkXPress users will be frustrated initially with InDesign's more-laborious approach to text flow and formatting, but will eventually appreciate some of InDesign's more powerful capabilities, such as stroke formatting and nested styles.

Flowing text

Once you learn how to flow text in InDesign, you'll find it's easier and more flexible than in QuarkXPress. It's easy to revert to habit and to restrict yourself to QuarkXPress techniques. To prevent that, keep these differences in mind:

- To import a text file, use File ⇨ Place, or ⌘+D or Ctrl+D. You can also drag files and text from the desktop or any application that supports drag and drop.

- InDesign CS2 gives you much more control over import options for Word and RTF files, plus it lets you save those options as presets so you and others can use them repeatedly.

- You do not need to create or select a text frame before you import text; you'll be able to create or select a text frame after choosing the file to import.

- InDesign does not have linking tools. To link text from frame to frame, use a selection tool to click the out ports and in ports on text frames. (Choose View ⇨ Show Text Threads if text frames are not visible so you can see the in and out ports.)

- To flow text and add pages automatically, check Master Text Frame in the New Document dialog box (File ⇨ New ⇨ Document, or ⌘+N or Ctrl+N). Then, you'll need to Shift+⌘+click or Ctrl+Shift+click the master text frame on a document page. Finally,

Option+click or Alt+click the loaded-text icon.

Editing text

A few minor differences exist when it comes to editing and selecting text:

- InDesign 2 and CS don't support "smart spaces" the way QuarkXPress 4.0 and later does, so when you double-click to select, then cut and paste a word, you won't also select the trailing space. (InDesign CS2 supports "smart spaces.")

- To type special characters — such as ñ, •, or ¶ — you can use Type ⇨ Glyphs rather than system utilities or key combinations.

- The control for showing invisible characters, such as spaces, tabs, and paragraph returns, is Type ⇨ Show Hidden Characters, or press Option+⌘+I or Ctrl+Alt+I.

- InDesign lets you select from various Western European languages for spell checking and hyphenation — you first apply a Language to text selections via the Character or Character Styles panes. The Passport edition of QuarkXPress has a similar feature to specify the hyphenation and spelling language, but not the standard version of Quark-XPress. InDesign CS2 expands this capability to allow multiple user exception dictionaries per language.

Formatting text

In general, formatting text in InDesign will feel comfortable to QuarkXPress users. You'll miss those nice, big Character and Paragraph Attributes dialog boxes (featuring real words, not icons!), but you'll have most of the same power. Review these differences, and keep them in mind while formatting text:

- Use the Control palette (Window ⇨ Control, or Option+⌘+6 or Ctrl+Alt+6) to format highlighted characters and paragraphs in a way that is almost identical to how the familiar QuarkXPress Measurement palette works.

- For more options, use the Character pane (Type ⇨ Character, or ⌘+T or Ctrl+T) to format highlighted characters. You'll notice that there are no type style buttons — InDesign requires you to choose the appropriate version of a typeface rather than attributes such as bold and italic, while other type styles are listed in the Character pane's palette menu.

- Leading is a character-level format in InDesign, therefore the controls are in the Character pane rather than the Paragraph pane as you might expect. Fortunately, you can change the leading behavior by selecting the Text pane of the Preferences dialog box (the Type pane in InDesign CS2) and checking Apply Leading to Entire Paragraphs. Checking this box will make InDesign match the behavior of leading in QuarkXPress. Leading is always measured from baseline to baseline in InDesign.

- Unlike QuarkXPress, InDesign can stroke and fill characters.

- Use the Paragraph pane (Type ⇨ Paragraph, or Option+⌘+T or Ctrl+Alt+T) to format selected paragraphs; the palette menu includes additional commands for adding rules and controlling hyphenation.

- InDesign lets you apply OpenType settings to OpenType fonts, using the palette menu of the Character pane or Control palette or, in InDesign CS2, using the OpenType Features pane of the Character Styles pane. QuarkXPress can use OpenType fonts but applies only standard formatting to them.

- InDesign does not have H&J sets, so set up your hyphenation using the Paragraph pane and save your settings in paragraph style sheets.

- Use the Tabs pane (Type ⇨ Tabs, or Shift+⌘+T or Ctrl+Shift+T) to set tabs for selected paragraphs.

- To create style sheets, use the New commands in the palette menus on the Character Styles pane (Type ⇨ Character Styles or Shift+F11) and the Paragraph Styles pane (Type ⇨ Paragraph Styles or F11). To share style sheets with other documents, use the Load commands in the same menus to import them.

- Applying style sheets to text with local formatting has the opposite effect as it has in QuarkXPress. Style sheets always wipe out local formatting when first applied — unless you hold the Option or Alt key when applying the style sheet. If you add local formatting later and want to revert the text to the style sheet's formats, click the style sheet twice. (Note that applying [No Style] in InDesign 2 and CS or choosing Break Link to Style option in the palette menu in InDesign CS2 and then applying the desired style sheet does not work, as it does in QuarkXPress.)

- InDesign 2 and CS import all style sheets when you use one of the Load commands. They do not let you select specific style sheets for import, as QuarkXPress does. This difference can add a lot of irrelevant style sheets to your InDesign document, unfortunately. (InDesign CS2 lets you select specific styles sheets for import.)

- Unlike Windows QuarkXPress, InDesign for Windows supports automatic ligatures in the Windows fonts that include them.

- Unlike QuarkXPress, InDesign CS2 supports footnotes and lets you control their placement and formatting.

- InDesign has no equivalent to QuarkXPress's fraction-building tool, but if you use OpenType fonts, you can use the fraction glyphs in those font to build your own by choosing the numerator, virgule, and denominator characters and kerning them to fit.

- InDesign has no equivalent to QuarkXPress's Underline Styles. Instead, specify custom underlines and strikethroughs as part of a character style sheet. To add stripes and dashed lines, open the Strokes pane (Window ⇨ Stroke or F10) and select the Stroke Styles option from the palette menu.

- You may be surprised at the seemingly large kerning and tracking values produced by all of the program's kerning and tracking methods. Keep in mind that InDesign lets you adjust space in 0.001-em units (¹/₁,₀₀₀th of an em). In QuarkXPress, for example, the kerning unit is 0.005 em (¹/₂₀₀th of an em). So if you're a QuarkXPress user, you should not be surprised to see kerning and tracking values that are 10 to 20 times greater than you're used to — in InDesign, you're working with multiples of finer increments. However, QuarkXPress lets you enter kerning and tracking values in increments of 0.1, while InDesign allows only whole numbers, so QuarkXPress provides finer overall control.

Working with Tables

Recent editions of QuarkXPress and InDesign have added significant table formatting capabilities. Among the differences:

- InDesign does a good job of importing Word tables and Excel spreadsheets as tables, unlike QuarkXPress, which except for version 6.1 or later does not support tables during import without extra-cost add-on software.

- InDesign tables and QuarkXPress tables have several differences. Although both treat tables as collections of cells, InDesign offers more formatting options for cell strokes than QuarkXPress does. InDesign has more controls for text and row placement than QuarkXPress offers. InDesign also imports Word, Excel, and RTF tables, while QuarkXPress does not. But QuarkXPress offers more control over the flow of text among cells in a table — InDesign doesn't let you flow text from one cell to another, for example, much less control the order of that flow.

- In one way, InDesign is more savvy about text-to-table conversion than QuarkXPress is, since InDesign lets you choose any string as the column or row separator during conversion (just enter that string in the appropriate field). But in another way, InDesign is less savvy: QuarkXPress lets you "pivot" data during conversion, so you can swap columns and rows for a better fit.

- InDesign treats tables as elements inserted into text, so they can flow with other text in a text frame or be in their own frame, as you prefer. QuarkXPress keeps tables in separate boxes. Also, InDesign lets you insert tables into table cells, so you can nest them; QuarkXPress does not.

Working with Graphics

Importing and manipulating graphics in InDesign is very similar to the process in Quark-XPress. As long as you remember to use the Direct Selection tool to select a graphic rather than its frame, you and the InDesign graphics features will get along fine. Differences between the programs include the following:

- To import a graphics file in InDesign, use File ⇨ Place, or ⌘+D or Ctrl+D. You can also drag files in from the desktop or other programs if InDesign supports their file formats.

- InDesign cannot convert imported color bitmap images to grayscale (while retaining the original file's colors) as QuarkXPress can. Thus, in InDesign, you'll need to convert the files in Photoshop or print in grayscale.

- You do not need to create or select a graphics frame before you import a graphic; you'll be able to create or select a graphics frame after choosing the file to import.

- Use the Control palette (Window ➪ Control, or Option+⌘+6 or Ctrl+Alt+6) or the Transform pane (Window ➪ Transform in InDesign 2 and CS or Window ➪ Object & Layout ➪ Transform in InDesign CS2, or F9) to rotate, scale, and skew graphics. You can create clipping paths by choosing Object ➪ Clipping Paths or pressing Option+Shift+⌘+K or Ctrl+Alt+Shift+K.

- To automatically scale a graphic to fit within its frame — proportionally or not — use the Fitting commands in the Object menu, or their keyboard equivalents. As a bonus, you get a Fit Frame to Picture command, a task you have to perform manually in Quark-XPress.

- When you resize graphics in InDesign, note that you will see the new scale in the Control palette and Transform pane if you have selected the graphic with the Direct Selection tool. If you select the graphic with the Selection tool, chances are that the scale will still read as 100%, since the Selection tool reports on the frame stroke's scale, not the graphic's. Also note that InDesign lets you change both the H and W scale at the same time, by ensuring the chain icon is unbroken — QuarkXPress forces you to change both every time.

- The InDesign Stroke Styles feature (accessed via the Strokes pane's palette menu) looks and works very much like the QuarkXPress Dashes & Stripes feature. The major difference is that InDesign has a separate option for dotted lines.

- Although InDesign doesn't have background, frame, and contents icons in its Swatches pane to let you select where color is applied, as QuarkXPress does, InDesign lets you determine what component of the image gets the color based on how you apply the color. Drag a color swatch onto an object to change the foreground color. Click a graphics frame and then the Fill or Stroke button in the Tools palette, then select a color from the Swatches pane to change the background or frame color, respectively. Furthermore, you can use the Control palette's Select Container and Select Contents buttons to choose whether the image background or contents, respectively, are colored when you click a swatch.

- InDesign offers a customizable drop-shadow tool (Object ➪ Drop Shadow, or Option+⌘+M or Ctrl+Alt+M) that lets you determine the shadow angle, distance, and lighting effects. Although InDesign's drop shadow can be applied to any object, not just a text frame, it cannot be applied to selected text. By contrast, QuarkXPress's fixed drop shadow can be applied only to selected text as a character attribute.

- InDesign lets you feather the edges of objects, to create soft outlines and other lighting-oriented effects, by choosing Object ⇨ Feather. QuarkXPress has no equivalent.

- QuarkXPress has no equivalent to InDesign's transparency settings, which let you make objects transparent or semitransparent, allowing a wide variety of special effects. Quark-XPress users instead must rely on such settings in Adobe Photoshop and Illustrator for imported pictures and do without them for objects created in QuarkXPress. InDesign also provides controls for how overlapping transparent objects are output, since they can sometimes interfere with printing.

- To track the location of graphics files, use the Links pane (File ⇨ Links, or Shift+⌘+D or Ctrl+Shift+D).

- InDesign's relink function is not as smart as QuarkXPress's equivalent Picture Usage. If you have multiple broken links to the same file in an InDesign document, you must relink each one manually from the Links pane. QuarkXPress will automatically fix all links to the same file as soon as you correct any link to it. That's another reason to use InDesign's automatic fix when you open a document and InDesign identifies that links are broken or out of date.

- QuarkXPress uses a very different approach to changing direction points from smooth to corner: It has iconic buttons in its Measurements palette that let you easily convert segment and corner types. The InDesign approach is more efficient in that it uses one tool and relies on a mouse-based tool (since you're likely using the mouse when you edit a shape), but it does require a bit more getting used to initially.

- The InDesign Pathfinder options to connect paths are similar to the QuarkXPress Merge options for paths. And InDesign CS2 adds a menu item (Object ⇨ Convert Shape) to convert one shape to another, similar to QuarkXPress's Item ⇨ Shape.

Manipulating Pages

You'll find the controls for working with document pages and master pages to be quite similar to those in QuarkXPress — if not slightly better. Once you realize the differences and start working, you can take advantage of InDesign's improvements. The differences mostly relate to guides and using the InDesign Pages pane rather than the QuarkXPress 4 and 5 Document Layout palette or QuarkXPress 6 Page Layout palette:

- InDesign provides three methods for creating guides: Drag them off the ruler as you do in QuarkXPress, double-click the ruler where you want a guide, or choose Layout ⇨ Create Guides. InDesign CS2 also provides column guides that can be managed separately from other ruler guides.

- To delete guides, you need to select them and click Delete. (To select all guides on a page, press Option+⌘+G or Ctrl+Alt+G.)

- Use the Pages pane (Window ⇨ Pages, or F12) as you would the QuarkXPress Document Layout palette (called the Page Layout palette in QuarkXPress 6). To place more than two pages side-by-side, you'll need to use the Keep Spreads Together command in the pane's palette menu.

- If you're missing the QuarkXPress Page menu, look for your favorite commands in the InDesign Layout menu and in the Pages pane's palette menu. You'll find a bonus in the Type ⇨ Insert Special Characters submenu: an Insert Page Number command (Option+Shift+⌘+N or Ctrl+Alt+Shift+N) so you don't have to remember that odd ⌘+3 or Ctrl+3 that QuarkXPress requires.

- You can base one master page on another, the same way you can base a style sheet on another. QuarkXPress does not offer this capability.

- To share master pages among documents, you can drag a master page (or document page) icon into another document window. In QuarkXPress, you cannot do this.

Working with Color

Not to intimidate you, but color will confound you (although Photoshop users will have an easier transition). Basically, try to forget everything you know about creating and applying colors in QuarkXPress. Here's what you need to know to work with colors in InDesign:

- Most of your work with colors happens through the Swatches pane (Window ⇨ Swatches or F5) — not through the Color pane as QuarkXPress users might think.

- To create colors, use the New Swatches command in the Swatches pane's palette menu. (You cannot create Hexachrome colors in InDesign.) You can create color, gradient, and tint swatches in InDesign — QuarkXPress can create only color swatches.

- To apply colors, first click the Stroke or Fill button on the Tools palette to specify where the color goes on the selected object. Then click a color in the Swatches pane.

- Use the Tint field in the Swatches pane (Window ⇨ Swatches or F5) to specify a shade (tint) of a color to just the currently selected object(s).

- InDesign's Paper color is equal to the QuarkXPress White color. Both programs use the color None for transparency, but InDesign provides None in both the Swatches pane and as a button on the Tools palette.

- To share colors among documents, drag a colored object into another document window.

Printing and Output

InDesign and QuarkXPress offer many of the same output capabilities — such as print styles (called print presets in InDesign), PDF export, color calibration, and color separation support. But pay attention to the notable differences beyond the different organization of their Print dialog boxes:

- You cannot print hidden layers in InDesign as you can in QuarkXPress 6. You must make them visible before printing.

- To suppress printout of individual objects, use the Attributes pane (Window ➪ Attributes) and choose Nonprinting. You can also hide layers using the Layers pane (Window ➪ Layers or F7), which works pretty much like QuarkXPress's Layers feature.

- InDesign's Thumbnails option is more flexible than QuarkXPress's, letting you choose the number of thumbnails per page.

- Note that InDesign does not have any options to change image contrast or line-screen element for grayscale and black-and-white images, as QuarkXPress does. You'll need to apply such effects in an image editor.

- InDesign and QuarkXPress offer similar levels of color output controls, but InDesign has several options QuarkXPress does not. One is setting ink density, another is automatic calculation of screen angles for spot colors. A third is the ability to more accurately preview documents with overprinting colors. A fourth is the ability to color-separate inks with different names onto the same plate, which solves the problem of having an imported color using one name for an ink and your document using another. (In Quark-XPress, you'd have to change the ink name in your document to avoid printing two plates.) InDesign also can apply black-point compensation as part of its color calibration during output. And InDesign lets you save your color-management preferences for use in other documents.

appendix C

Shortcuts Cheat Sheet

Shortcuts are essential to making the most of InDesign. Sure, you can access everything from a menu or pane, but shortcuts make the work much faster. This appendix covers InDesign's keyboard shortcuts. It also shows how to work with contextual menus, which let you use the mouse to find out what options are available for specific objects.

Because InDesign has so many keyboard shortcuts, the following table has them broken into functional areas to help you find them more easily.

Action or command	Macintosh	Windows
Opening/closing/saving		
New document	⌘+N	Ctrl+N
New default document	Option+⌘+N	Ctrl+Alt+N
Open document	⌘+O	Ctrl+O
Open library	Option+Shift+⌘+L	Ctrl+Alt+Shift+L
Close document	⌘+W	Ctrl+W *or* Ctrl+F4
Close all documents	Option+Shift+⌘+W	Ctrl+Alt+Shift+W
Quit program	⌘+Q	Ctrl+Q *or* Alt+F4
Save document	⌘+S	Ctrl+S
Save document as	Shift+⌘+S	Ctrl+Shift+S
Save copy of document	Option+⌘+S	Ctrl+Alt+D
Export document to PDF or EPS	⌘+E	Ctrl+E
Place text and graphics	⌘+D	Ctrl+D
Viewing		
Hide/show panes	Tab	Tab
Hide/show all panes but Tools palette	Shift+Tab	Shift+Tab
Zoom in	⌘+=	Ctrl+=
Zoom out	⌘+− (hyphen)	Ctrl+− (hyphen)
Fit page/spread in window	⌘+0	Ctrl+Alt+=
Fit spread in window	Shift+⌘+0	Ctrl+Alt+0
Fit entire pasteboard in window	Option+Shift+⌘+0	Ctrl+Alt+Shift+0
Display actual size	⌘+1	Ctrl+1
Display at 50%	⌘+5	Ctrl+5
Display at 200%	⌘+2	Ctrl+2
Display at 400%	⌘+4	Ctrl+4
Overprint preview	Option+Shift+⌘+Y	Ctrl+Alt+Shift+Y
Switch between current and previous view	Option+⌘+2	Ctrl+Alt+2
Set magnification	Option+⌘+5	Ctrl+Alt+5
Set all pages to same view	⌘+*percent in view field*	Ctrl+*percent in view field*
Switch to previous document window	Shift+⌘+F6	Ctrl+Shift+F6
Switch to next document window	⌘+Y	Ctrl+F6

Action or command	Macintosh	Windows
Show/hide text threads	Option+⌘+Y	Ctrl+Alt+Y
Show/hide frame edges	⌘+H	Ctrl+H
Show/hide rulers	⌘+R	Ctrl+R
Show hidden characters	Option+⌘+I	Ctrl+Alt+I
Preference/setup		
Preferences dialog box	⌘+K	Ctrl+K
Document setup	Option+⌘+P	Ctrl+Alt+P
Tools		
Selection tool	V	V
Direct Selection tool	A	A
Type tool	T	T
Text Path tool	Shift+T	Shift+T
Pen tool	P	P
Ellipse tool	L	L
Rectangle tool	M	M
Rectangle Frame tool	F	F
Rotate tool	R	R
Scale tool	S	S
Shear tool	O	O
Scissors tool	C	C
Hand tool	H	H
Temporary Hand tool	Shift+space	Shift+space
Zoom tool	Z	Z
Temporary zoom-in tool	⌘+space	Ctrl+space
Temporary zoom-out tool	Option+⌘+space	Ctrl+Alt+space
Gradient tool	G	G
Fill button	X	X
Stroke button	X	X
Swap Fill/Stroke button	Shift+X	Shift+X
Default Fill/Stroke button	D	D
Apply Color button	, (comma)	, (comma)
Apply Gradient button	. (period)	. (period)
Apply None button	/	/
Panes		
Apply value in field	Option+Enter	Shift+Return
Show Control palette	Option+⌘+6	Ctrl+Alt+6
Show Links pane	Shift+⌘+D	Ctrl+Shift+D

Action or command	Macintosh	Windows
Show Layers pane	F7	F7
Show Pages pane	F12	F12
Show Swatches pane	F5	F5
Show Color pane	F6	F6
Show Transform pane	F9	F9
Show Character pane	⌘+T	Ctrl+T
Show Paragraph pane	Option+⌘+T	Ctrl+Alt+T
Show Character Styles pane	Shift+F11	Shift+F11
Show Paragraph Styles pane	F11	F11
Show Object Styles pane (InDesign CS2)	⌘+F7	Ctrl+F7
Show Quick Apply palette (InDesign CS2)	⌘+Return	Ctrl+Enter
Show Text Wrap pane	Option+⌘+W	Ctrl+Alt+W
Open Text Frame Options dialog box	⌘+B	Ctrl+B
Show Index pane	Shift+F8	Shift+F8
Show Table pane	Shift+F9	Shift+F9
Show Tabs pane	Shift+⌘+T	Ctrl+Shift+T
Show Align pane	Shift+F7	Shift+F7
Show Stroke pane	F10	F10
Show Transparency pane	Shift+F10	Shift+F10
Show Info pane	F8	F8
Guides		
Show/hide guides	⌘+; (semicolon)	Ctrl+; (semicolon)
Lock/unlock guides	Option+⌘+; (semicolon)	Ctrl+Alt+; (semicolon)
Snap to guides on/off	Shift+⌘+; (semicolon)	Ctrl+Shift+; (semicolon)
Show/hide baseline grid	Option+⌘+"	Ctrl+Alt+"
Show/hide document grid	⌘+"	Ctrl+"
Snap to document grid on/off	Shift+⌘+"	Ctrl+Shift+"
Select all guides	Option+⌘+G	Ctrl+Alt+G
Create zero-point guidelines	⌘+*click zero point when dragging guides*	Ctrl+*click zero point when dragging guides*
Adding and navigating pages		
Add new page	Shift+⌘+P	Ctrl+Shift+P
Go to first page	Shift+⌘+PgUp	Ctrl+Shift+Page Up
Go back one page	Shift+PgUp	Shift+Page Up
Go forward one page	Shift+PgDn *or* ⌘+PgDn	Shift+Page Down *or* Ctrl+PgDn
Go to last page	Shift+⌘+PgDn	Ctrl+Shift+Page Down
Go to last page viewed	⌘+PgUp	Ctrl+PgUp
Go forward one spread	Option+PgUp	Alt+Page Up

Action or command	Macintosh	Windows
Go back one spread	Option+PgDn	Alt+Page Down
Object selection		
Select master page	Shift+⌘+click	Ctrl+Shift+click
Select topmost object	Option+Shift+⌘+]	Ctrl+Alt+Shift+]
Select object above current object	Option+⌘+]	Ctrl+Alt+]
Select bottommost object	Option+Shift+⌘+[	Ctrl+Alt+Shift+[
Select object below current object	Option+⌘+[	Ctrl+Alt+[
Go to last frame in thread	Option+Shift+⌘+PgDn	Ctrl+Alt+Shift+Page Down
Go to next frame in thread	Option+⌘+PgDn	Ctrl+Alt+Page Down
Go to first frame in thread	Option+Shift+⌘+PgUp	Ctrl+Alt+Shift+Page Up
Go to previous frame in thread	Option+⌘+PgUp	Ctrl+Alt+Page Up
Moving objects		
Move selection 1 point	left, right, up, and down cursors	left, right, up, and down cursors
Move selection 10 points	Shift+left, right, up, and down cursors	Shift+left, right, up, and down cursors
Bring object to front	Shift+⌘+]	Ctrl+Shift+]
Bring object forward	⌘+]	Ctrl+]
Send object to back	Shift+⌘+[	Ctrl+Shift+[
Send object backward	⌘+[	Ctrl+[
Object commands		
Cut	⌘+X	Ctrl+X
Copy	⌘+V	Ctrl+V
Paste	⌘+P	Ctrl+P
Paste into	Option+⌘+V	Ctrl+Alt+V
Paste in place	Option+Shift+⌘+V	Ctrl+Alt+Shift+V
Paste without formatting (InDesign CS2)	Shift+⌘+V	Ctrl+Shift+V
Clear	Backspace	Backspace *or* Del
Duplicate object	Option+⌘+D	Ctrl+Alt+D
Step and repeat (InDesign CS2)	Shift+⌘+U	Ctrl+Shift+U
Step and repeat (InDesign 2 and CS)	Shift+⌘+V	Ctrl+Shift+V
Resize proportionately	Shift+drag	Shift+drag
Resize frame and content	⌘+drag	Ctrl+drag
Center content	Shift+⌘+E	Ctrl+Shift+E
Fill frame proportionally (InDesign CS2)	Option+Shift+⌘+C	Ctrl+Alt+Shift+C
Fit content proportionally	Option+Shift+⌘+E	Ctrl+Alt+Shift+E
Fit content to frame	Option+⌘+E	Ctrl+Alt+E
Fit frame to content	Option+⌘+C	Ctrl+Alt+C

Action or command	Macintosh	Windows
Decrease size/scale by 1%	⌘+, (comma)	Ctrl+, (comma)
Decrease size/scale by 5%	Option+⌘+, (comma)	Ctrl+Alt+, (comma)
Increase size/scale by 5%	Option+⌘+. (period)	Ctrl+Alt+. (period)
Duplicate	Option+Shift+⌘+D *or* Option+drag, *or* Option+ left, right, up, and down cursors	Ctrl+Alt+Shift+D *or* Alt+drag, *or* Alt+ left, right, up, and down cursors
Group	⌘+G	Ctrl+G
Ungroup	Shift+⌘+G	Ctrl+Shift+G
Lock	⌘+L	Ctrl+L
Unlock	Option+⌘+L	Ctrl+Alt+L
Drop shadow	Option+⌘+M	Ctrl+Alt+M
Transform again (InDesign CS2)	Option+⌘+3	Ctrl+Alt+3
Transform sequence again (InDesign CS2)	Option+⌘+4	Ctrl+Alt+4

Graphics handling

Convert text to outlines	Shift+⌘+O	Ctrl+Alt+O
Create outlines without deleting text	Option+Shift+⌘+O	Ctrl+Alt+Shift+O
Image color settings	Option+Shift+⌘+D	Ctrl+Alt+Shift+D
Make clipping path	Option+Shift+⌘+K	Ctrl+Alt+Shift+K
Make compound path	⌘+8	Ctrl+8
Release compound path	Option+⌘+8	Ctrl+Alt+8

Text selection

Select all	⌘+A	Ctrl+A
Deselect all	Shift+⌘+A	Ctrl+Shift+A
Select word	double-click	double-click
Select one word to left	Shift+⌘+left cursor	Ctrl+Shift+left cursor
Select one word to right	Shift+⌘+right cursor	Ctrl+Shift+right cursor
Select range	Shift+left, right, up, and down cursors	Shift+left, right, up, and down cursors
Select line	triple-click	triple-click
Select paragraph	quadruple-click	quadruple-click
Select one paragraph before	Shift+⌘+up cursor	Ctrl+Shift+up cursor
Select one paragraph after	Shift+⌘+down cursor	Ctrl+Shift+down cursor
Select to start of story	Shift+⌘+Home	Ctrl+Shift+Home
Select to end of story	Shift+⌘+End	Ctrl+Shift+End
Select whole story	quintuple-click	quintuple-click

Moving within text

Move left one word	⌘+left cursor	Ctrl+left cursor
Move right one word	⌘+right cursor	Ctrl+right cursor

Action or command	Macintosh	Windows
Move to start of line	Home	Home
Move to end of line	End	End
Move to previous paragraph	⌘+up cursor	Ctrl+up cursor
Move to next paragraph	⌘+down cursor	Ctrl+down cursor
Move to start of story	⌘+Home	Ctrl+Home
Move to end of story	⌘+End	Ctrl+End
Text/paragraph formats		
Bold	Shift+⌘+B	Ctrl+Shift+B
Italic	Shift+⌘+I	Ctrl+Shift+I
Normal	Shift+⌘+Y	Ctrl+Shift+Y
Underline	Shift+⌘+U	Ctrl+Shift+U
Strikethrough	Shift+⌘+/	Ctrl+Shift+/
All caps on/off	Shift+⌘+K	Ctrl+Shift+K
Small caps	Shift+⌘+H	Ctrl+Shift+H
Superscript	Shift+⌘+=	Ctrl+Shift+=
Subscript	Option+Shift+⌘+=	Ctrl+Alt+Shift+=
Update character style based on selection	Option+Shift+⌘+C	Ctrl+Alt+Shift+C
Update paragraph style based on selection	Option+Shift+⌘+R	Ctrl+Alt+Shift+R
Drop caps and nested styles	Option+⌘+R	Ctrl+Alt+R
Paragraph rules	Option+⌘+J	Ctrl+Alt+J
Set horizontal scale to 100%	Shift+⌘+X	Ctrl+Shift+X
Set vertical scale to 100%	Option+Shift+⌘+X	Ctrl+Alt+Shift+X
Increase point size by 1 point	Shift+⌘+›	Ctrl+Shift+›
Increase point size by 10 points	Option+Shift+⌘+›	Ctrl+Alt+Shift+›
Decrease point size by 1 point	Shift+⌘+‹	Ctrl+Shift+‹
Decrease point size by 10 points	Option+Shift+⌘+‹	Ctrl+Alt+Shift+‹
Text alignment and spacing		
Align left	Shift+⌘+L	Ctrl+Shift+L
Align right	Shift+⌘+R	Ctrl+Shift+R
Align center	Shift+⌘+C	Ctrl+Shift+C
Justify full	Shift+⌘+F	Ctrl+Shift+F
Justify left	Shift+⌘+J	Ctrl+Shift+J
Justify right	Option+Shift+⌘+R	Ctrl+Alt+Shift+R
Justify center	Option+Shift+⌘+C	Ctrl+Alt+Shift+C
Autohyphenation on/off	Option+Shift+⌘+H	Ctrl+Alt+Shift+H
Hyphenation on/off (selected text)	Option+⌘+H	Ctrl+Alt+H
Set spacing and justification	Option+Shift+⌘+J	Ctrl+Alt+Shift+J

Action or command	Macintosh	Windows
Set keep options	Option+⌘+K	Ctrl+Alt+K
Increase leading by 2 points*	Option+up cursor	Alt+up cursor
Decrease leading by 2 points*	Option+down cursor	Alt+down cursor
Increase leading by 10 points*	Option+⌘+up cursor	Ctrl+Alt+up cursor
Decrease leading by 10 points*	Option+⌘+down cursor	Ctrl+Alt+down cursor
Use autoleading	Option+Shift+⌘+A	Ctrl+Alt+Shift+A
Increase kerning/tracking by 20 units*	Option+right cursor	Alt+right cursor
Increase kerning/tracking by 100 units*	Option+⌘+right cursor	Ctrl+Alt+right cursor
Decrease kerning/tracking by 20 units*	Option+left cursor	Alt+left cursor
Decrease kerning/tracking by 100 units*	Option+⌘+left cursor	Ctrl+Alt+left cursor
Clear all kerning/tracking (set to 0)	Shift+⌘+Q	Ctrl+Shift+Q
Increase baseline shift by 2 points*	Option+Shift+up arrow	Alt+Shift+up arrow
Increase baseline shift by 10 points*	Option+Shift+⌘+up arrow	Ctrl+Alt+Shift+up arrow
Decrease baseline shift by 2 points*	Option+Shift+down arrow	Alt+Shift+down arrow
Decrease baseline shift by 10 points*	Option+Shift+⌘+down arrow	Ctrl+Alt+Shift+down arrow
Align to grid on/off	Option+Shift+⌘+G	Ctrl+Alt+Shift+G
Table editing		
Insert table	Option+Shift+⌘+T	Ctrl+Alt+Shift+T
Insert column	Option+⌘+9	Ctrl+Alt+9
Insert row	⌘+9	Ctrl+9
Select table	Option+⌘+A	Ctrl+Alt+A
Select column	Option+⌘+3	Ctrl+Alt+3
Select row	⌘+3	Ctrl+3
Select cell	⌘+/	Ctrl+/
Delete column	Shift+Delete	Shift+Backspace
Delete row	⌘+Delete	Ctrl+Backspace
Table setup	Option+Shift+⌘+B	Ctrl+Alt+Shift+B
Set cell text options	Option+⌘+B	Ctrl+Alt+B
Find/change text, spelling, and indexing		
Edit in Story Editor	⌘+Y	Ctrl+Y
Find/change	⌘+F	Ctrl+F
Find next	Option+⌘+F	Ctrl+Alt+F
Search for selected text	Shift+F1	Shift+F1
Add selected text to Find What field	⌘+F1	Ctrl+F1
Add selected text to Change To field	⌘+F2	Ctrl+F2

*These increments can be changed in the Units & Increments pane of the Preferences dialog box (InDesign ⇨ Preferences or ⌘+K on the Mac and Edit ⇨ Preferences or Ctrl+K in Windows).

Action or command	Macintosh	Windows
Change current selection	⌘+F3	Ctrl+F3
Change current selection and search forward	Shift+⌘+F3	Ctrl+Shift+F3
Check spelling	⌘+I	Ctrl+I
Add new index entry (InDesign CS2)	Option+Shift+⌘+]	Ctrl+Alt+Shift+]
Add new index entry (InDesign 2 or CS)	Option+⌘+U	Ctrl+Alt+U
Add new index entry (reversed) (InDesign CS2)	Option+Shift+⌘+[	Ctrl+Alt+Shift+[
Add new index entry (reversed) (InDesign 2 or CS)	Shift+⌘+F8	Ctrl+Shift+F8
New index/open index entry dialog box	⌘+U	Ctrl+U
Special characters		
Bullet (•)	Option+8	Alt+8
Ellipsis (…)	Option+; (semicolon)	Alt+; (semicolon)
Copyright (©)	Option+G	Alt+G
Registered trademark (®)	Option+R	Alt+R
Trademark (™)	Option+2	Alt+2
Paragraph (¶)	Option+7	Alt+7
Section (§)	Option+6	Alt+6
Switch between keyboard and typographic quotes	Option+Shift+⌘+"	Ctrl+Alt+Shift+"
Em dash (—)	Option+Shift+— (hyphen)	Alt+Shift+— (hyphen)
En dash (–)	Option+— (hyphen)	Alt+— (hyphen)
Nonbreaking hyphen (-)	Option+⌘+— (hyphen)	Ctrl+Alt+— (hyphen)
Discretionary hyphen (-)	Shift+⌘+— (hyphen)	Ctrl+Shift+— (hyphen)
Em space ( )	Shift+⌘+M	Ctrl+Shift+M
En space ( )	Shift+⌘+N	Ctrl+Shift+N
Thin space ( )	Option+Shift+⌘+M	Ctrl+Alt+Shift+M
Hair space ()	Option+Shift+⌘+I	Ctrl+Alt+Shift+I
Nonbreaking space	Option+⌘+X	Ctrl+Alt+X
Soft return	Shift+Enter	Shift+Return
Column break	keypad Enter	keypad Enter
Frame break	Shift+keypad Enter	Shift+keypad Enter
Page break	⌘+keypad Enter	Ctrl+keypad Enter
Indent to here	⌘+\	Ctrl+\
Right-indent tab	Shift+Tab	Shift+Tab
Insert current page number	Option+Shift+⌘+N	Ctrl+Alt+Shift+N
Insert next page number	Option+Shift+⌘+]	Ctrl+Alt+Shift+]
Insert previous page number	Option+Shift+⌘+[	Ctrl+Alt+Shift+[

Action or command	Macintosh	Windows
Printing and output		
Print document	⌘+P	Ctrl+P
Preflight document	Option+Shift+⌘+F	Ctrl+Alt+Shift+F
Package document	Option+Shift+⌘+P	Ctrl+Alt+Shift+P
Miscellaneous		
Help	Help	F1
Undo	⌘+Z	Ctrl+Z
Redo	Shift+⌘+Z	Ctrl+Shift+Z

appendix d

More Resources

Technology doesn't stand still, especially not in an area as dynamic as publishing, where multiple products work together. That's why I've created two independent Web sites that help both InDesign and QuarkXPress users stay current on tools and techniques. Both www.InDesignCentral.com and www.QuarkXPressCentral.com provide the following resources:

- Tools: Links to plug-ins and XTensions, scripts, utilities, and Adobe and Quark downloads
- Tips: My favorite tips, as well as reader tips
- Resources: Print publishing links, Web publishing links, Mac OS X links, and Windows 2000/XP links
- *Adobe InDesign Bible* series, *InDesign CS2 For Dummies, QuarkXPress Bible* series, and *QuarkXPress For Dummies* series: Excerpts from the books, including color versions of the screenshots from the chapters that cover color, as well as updates from after the books' release

Figure D-1 shows the sites' home pages.

Wiley Publishing (www.wiley.com), the publisher of this

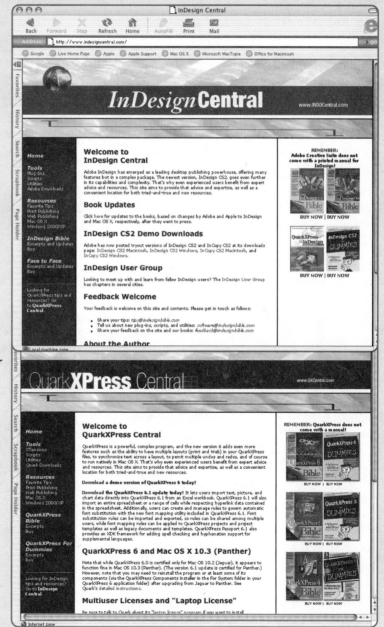

Figure D-1: The home pages for the InDesign Central and QuarkXPress Central Web sites.

book, also offers a wide range of books to help layout artists and publication designers exploit the publishing tools to the fullest:

- *Adobe InDesign CS2 Bible* and *Adobe InDesign CS Bible* by Galen Gruman give you extensive insight and tips on using the newest versions of InDesign in professional publishing environments.

- *Adobe InDesign CS2 For Dummies* by Barbara Assadi and Galen Gruman is a great way to quickly get up to speed on the newest version of InDesign.

- *Photoshop CS2 Bible* and *Photoshop CS Bible* by Deke McClelland provide an in-depth look at how to make the most of Photoshop's extensive image-editing capabilities.

- *Photoshop CS2 Bible, Professional Edition* and *Photoshop CS Bible, Professional Edition* by Deke McClelland go even further, adding new and expanded coverage of high-end topics, such as creating and optimizing Web graphics, using filters, working with convolution kernels and displacement maps, harnessing actions and batch processing, and adjusting color.

- *Photoshop CS2: Top 100 Simplified Tips & Tricks* by Dave Huss and *Photoshop CS: Top 100 Simplified Tips & Tricks* by Denis Graham provide clear, illustrated instructions for 100 tasks that reveal cool secrets, teach time-saving tricks, and explain great tips to make you a better Photoshop user.

- *Photoshop CS2 For Dummies* by Peter Bauer and *Photoshop CS For Dummies* by Deke McClelland and Phyllis Davis are a great way to quickly get up to speed on the newest

Figure D-2: The covers for related Wiley Publishing books for layout artists and publication designers.

version of Photoshop.

- *Illustrator CS2 Bible* by Ted Alspach and Brian Underdahl and *Illustrator CS Bible* by Ted Alspach and Jennifer Alspach include in-depth coverage on using Illustrator for print and Web graphics, as well as show how to integrate Illustrator with Photoshop.

- *Illustrator CS2 For Dummies* and *Illustrator CS For Dummies* by Ted Alspach are a great way to quickly get up to speed on the newest version of Illustrator.

- *Adobe Acrobat 7 PDF Bible* and *Adobe Acrobat 6 PDF Bible* by Ted Padova feature complete coverage of using Acrobat and PDF for print prepress, the Internet, CD-ROMs, and all the new media.

- *Adobe Creative Suite 2 Bible* and *Adobe Creative Suite Bible* by Ted Padova, Kelly L. Murdock, and Wendy Halderman provide an all-in-one resource for users of Adobe's cornerstone tools (Photoshop, Illustrator, Acrobat Professional, and InDesign).

- *QuarkXPress 4 Bible*, *QuarkXPress 5 Bible*, and *QuarkXPress 6 Bible* by Galen Gruman and Barbara Assadi provide deep advice on using QuarkXPress for a variety of publications.

- *QuarkXPress 4 For Dummies*, *QuarkXPress 5 For Dummies*, and *QuarkXPress 6 For Dummies* by Barbara Assadi and Galen Gruman provide a quick look at key QuarkXPress features, a handy way for experienced users of previous versions to quickly get up to speed.

- *Digital Photography: Top 100 Simplified Tips & Tricks* by Gregory Georges provides clear, illustrated instructions for 100 tasks that reveal cool secrets, teach time-saving tricks, and explain great tips to make you a better digital photographer.

- *Total Digital Photography: The Shoot to Print Workflow Handbook* by Serge Timacheff and David Karlins offers complete, end-to-end workflow advice from shoot to print in a full-color presentation.

Figure D-2 shows some of the books' covers.

index

Index